Invisible Women

What's Wrong With Women's Prisons?

Angela Devlin is a writer and broadcaster, and—since the success of her first book *Criminal Classes* (Waterside Press, 1995)—is in regular demand as a speaker on criminal justice matters. While researching *Invisible Women* she spent five years visiting 12 of the 16 prisons taking women, interviewing staff and prisoners. With her husband Tim she led the campaign which in 1997 brought about the release, retrial and subsequent acquittal of Sheila Bowler, wrongfully convicted of murder. She has written about the case in *Anybody's Nightmare: The Sheila Bowler Story* (Taverner Publications, 1998). Angela Devlin is also the author of *Prison Patter* (Waterside Press, 1996), a unique dictionary of prison slang and jargon.

Invisible Women
What's Wrong With Women's Prisons?

Published 1998 by
WATERSIDE PRESS
Domum Road
Winchester SO23 9NN
Telephone or Fax 01962 855567
INTERNET:106025.1020@compuserve.com

ISBN Paperback 1 872 870 59 7

Cataloguing-in-Publication Data A catalogue record for this book can be obtained from the British Library

Printing and binding Antony Rowe Ltd, Chippenham

Cover John Good Holbrook Ltd, Coventry. Front cover design by Sebastian Devlin.

Invisible Women

What's Wrong With Women's Prisons?

Angela Devlin

WATERSIDE PRESS
WINCHESTER

Acknowledgments

I am most grateful to Sir David Ramsbotham, HM Chief Inspector of Prisons, and Colin Allen, Deputy Chief Inspector, for their encouragement in this project.

I would particularly like to thank the prison governors who allowed me to carry out my research, and prison staff and other professionals outside prison who were prepared to spare me so much of their time.

Finally, I want to thank all the women prisoners—serving and released—who trusted me enough to speak to me.

This book is for them.

Angela Devlin

June 1998

Royalties

All royalties from this book go to the Female Prisoners' Welfare Project and its sister organization Hibiscus.

Invisible Women

What's Wrong With Women's Prisons?

CONTENTS

INTRODUCTION

Why a Book About Women's Prisons? And Why Now?

Many more women are now being sent to prison. In 1965 the then home secretary said that by the year 2000 there would be hardly any women in prison at all. But on the thirtieth anniversary of that remark there were 2,000 women in jails in England and Wales. As this book goes to press there are 3,064 female prisoners, a doubling of the number over the last five years, according to the Prison Reform Trust, which says 'Both the total numbers and the rate of increase have been without precedent in the modern era.'[1] This figure puts the female prison population at its highest since 1905. If we take the number of *convicted* women, the increase is even greater. According to the National Association of Probation Officers (NAPO), these figures show an increase of 76 per cent in the four years since summer 1993, more than twice the increase for men.[2] The figures refer to the number of women *held* on a particular day, but it has to be remembered that the number of women *going through* the prison system is far greater: in just one prison, Risley, between 4,000 and 5,000 women are received into custody each year, though the women's unit has only 150 places.

It seems we are going the way of the USA, where the war on drugs and mandatory minimum sentencing policies have meant that there are now more than five times as many American women in prison than in 1980.[3] Media coverage of the case of Louise Woodward in 1997 drew British attention to conditions in American women's prisons: overcrowding has reached crisis proportions, and some jails are operating at 150 per cent capacity, according to a report published in July 1997 by the United States Justice Department.

Although Britain puts more of its people behind bars than almost any other country in Western Europe,[4] female prisoners still make up only a tiny percentage—around five per cent—of the total prison population of 65,000 (and currently rising at a rate of ten per cent a year).

The title of this book, *Invisible Women*, stems from a 1996 research study[5] on women's prisons. The author, Stephanie Hayman, wrote 'The smallness of the female prison population has contributed to their invisibility'. Women become 'invisible' as soon as they pass through the prison gates because they are subsumed into a world that is predominantly masculine and insensitive to their very different needs.

Methodology: (i) Aims of two research periods

My research was carried out over two separate periods. The first period was part of the work I undertook between 1992 and 1995 for my earlier book *Criminal Classes: Offenders at School*[6] which examined the links between educational failure and later criminal offending. With Home Office permission I surveyed 250 prisoners (138 men and 112 women) in twelve prisons—six women's and six men's. I followed up responses to an initial written questionnaire with interviews, spending at least one hour with each of 52 men and 48 women. Although I was interviewing prisoners about their educational background, inevitably during these lengthy in-depth interviews we discussed the nature of the establishments and those who work there, the way sentences were proceeding and what rehabilitative work was going on in prison to address the reasons for offending and to reduce the likelihood of recidivism. Because of the nature of that project I confined myself to interviewing education staff, though I also spoke to some disciplinary staff and governor grades. In fact, the motivation for a book specifically about women's prisons arose from the striking contrasts I perceived in the provision of educational facilities for male prisoners and those for women.

In the second research period, from June 1996 to April 1998, I looked specifically at the provision of custody for women, considering as many aspects as possible.

Methodology: (ii) Establishments

Thanks to the helpful contacts I had made during the first project, I was able to approach prison governors directly and was permitted to revisit some of the six female prisons I had previously surveyed. This time I spent three-day periods of concentrated research in each prison, and also interviewed staff at Holloway.[7]

I felt it important to carry out the research in as many different kinds of prison as possible. Women prisoners are not categorised in the same way as men, except for a few category A female prisoners. The rest are simply deemed suitable for open or closed conditions and allocated accordingly, whatever their age: there are no female young offender institutions and I found a number of girls aged 15 in adult prisons—though while I was completing the research the High Court ruled (in August 1997) that it was unlawful to hold a girl of 16 alongside adult female offenders.

Women remanded in custody are first sent to a remand centre like Risley or Holloway where, if they are given a very short custodial sentence, they may stay until release. Those serving longer sentences are sent either to open or closed conditions in one of the other prisons that take women: there are currently 16 prisons that do so. The only further categorisation is for longer term prisoners who begin their sentence at a 'first stage' closed establishment like HMP Bullwood Hall and then move on to a 'second stage' prison like Cookham Wood and so on until the final portion of the sentence, which most will serve in an open prison like Drake Hall or Askham Grange (though like male prisoners they can be returned to closed conditions for security reasons). The twelve women's prisons I visited during the two research projects are listed in the *Appendix*, although I should mention that my knowledge of HMP Foston Hall is confined only to social visiting: events overtook me and I was unable to apply to visit this prison for a longer period of research.

Methodology: (iii) Interviewees

During both research periods I used the self-referral method to access prisoners' views. In the first project all the interviewees had responded to a formal questionnaire distributed by prison staff. The second research was carried out less formally: at the start of each visit I would introduce myself to staff and prisoners and as I became recognised going round the establishment, those prepared to speak to me would volunteer to do so. I worked from a set list of questions, but allowed interviewees the flexibility to develop some points at the expense of others. Interviews generally lasted between 40 minutes and one-and-a-half hours. By the end of both research projects, I had spoken to 150 women (48 in the first project and 102 in the second) and 112 prison staff and visiting professionals.

Each prison visit consisted of a three-day session, with each day of interviews lasting usually from 9 a.m. to 5 p.m., though in the two open prisons I stayed much later into the evening speaking to officers on late shifts and women alone in their cells or in small groups in dormitories and recreation areas.

I also became a volunteer helper on a minibus service that escorted children to see their parents in prison: I felt strongly that by meeting the families of women prisoners I would have a fuller picture of what being in prison means to a woman whose children are left at home. I maintained contact by telephone and letter with a number of women after their release. Quite coincidentally I had become involved in a campaign to release a life-sentenced prisoner, Sheila Bowler, who was indeed proved to be the victim of a miscarriage of justice. In February 1998 an Old Bailey jury unanimously found her not guilty of murder. Over a four year period my almost daily telephone conversations with her, and my visits through the normal visiting system of HMP

Holloway and HMP Bullwood Hall, gave me yet another insight into the reality of prison life.

I felt it was important too to consult those who work professionally in women's prisons. Although most research has concentrated on seeking the views of women prisoners—the 'clients' of the Prison Service who are therefore best placed to comment on the provision of custody—criminologists have long recognised the importance of seeking the views of prison staff. As Frances Heidensohn[8] has said: 'Women prison officers have been a remarkably silent group. There have been no modern personal accounts by them.' Rebecca and Russell Dobash, in their comprehensive history[9] of women's imprisonment, called for more research on the role of female staff. Prison officers suffer just as much from stereotyping as the prisoners they supervise.

I therefore sought to interview both female and male officers from governor grades to new recruits. When I requested interviews with disciplinary staff I was often greeted with surprise and some enthusiasm. This is a group of professionals who have rarely been consulted, perhaps because of the constraints of the Official Secrets Act which they have had to sign.

Once I had given written assurances of anonymity[10] and of the fact that anything said would be non-attributable, and once my presence had been authorised by the governing governor, most staff in all the prisons I visited were only too happy to speak to me openly and at length. As one woman officer put it: 'Nobody ever asks us for our side of the story'.

The official response of the Prison Service to its higher public profile in recent years has been a *perceived* greater openness. As one governor explained:

> The Prison Service has undergone a bit of a re-think. Every officer still has to sign the Official Secrets Act but the decision has been made to be much more open to the public—because we are accountable to the public. So we are all getting used to being under public scrutiny.

Perhaps this is also a predictable public relations response to media criticism: Derek Lewis, the former Director General of the Prison Service, has shown no reluctance in speaking to journalists, especially in the days after his departure from office. There has been no shortage of disaffected ex-governors prepared to speak out in media interviews, thanks to clashes with Michael Howard and resentment of his decision to freeze recruitment and cut expenditure while expecting staff to cope with a thousand more prisoners every month. Following his electoral defeat the media revelled in his public clash with former prisons minister Ann Widdecombe.

Yet prisons themselves still remain very secret places. For all the PR-speak of public accountability, prisoners certainly do not feel that officers regard themselves as accountable for what happens once the gates are closed, nor do they think that officers all act in accordance with the Prison Service's own mission statement.[11]

I interviewed other people working in prisons or visiting them professionally. I spoke to civilian training officers—staff for instance in charge of the prison works and maintenance departments, gardens and laundries: some of these are non-uniformed staff who come into daily contact with prisoners and see them from a different perspective. I spoke to prison-based probation officers, education staff, health-care staff, chaplains and visiting counsellors and members of prison Boards of Visitors. I tried always to interview as wide a range of professionals as possible in terms of gender, ethnicity, age and experience. Outside the prisons I interviewed officials at Prison Service Headquarters, criminologists and other academics, and spokespeople for prisoners' support groups.

As I was about to embark on writing up this research, I found it reassuring to read a paragraph in a short essay by Mitch Egan, the woman governor of HMP Leicester, a men's prison, quoted in a training pack produced for the Prison Service about the special needs of young women in prison.[12]

> There are few safe conclusions from things that are currently known, but every reason in the world to go on asking questions—both of practitioners who work on a daily basis with incarcerated women, and of researchers in the field—and to ensure the answers shape policy. Only a greater understanding of why there are manifest and perceived differences between men and women in custody will allow us to create viable policy to deal with the offending behaviour, custody, throughcare and release of women.

I hope that by speaking to women in prison, disciplinary staff at all levels, and a wide range of other penal professionals, I have been able to present as broad and accurate a picture as possible of the women's prisons as a series of diverse and complex total institutions in need of radical reform to meet the needs of women prisoners. With proper management and a change of ethos this ought to be possible. To quote Sir David Ramsbotham, HM Chief Inspector of Prisons: 'The women's estate is a manageable entity with the potential to achieve best practice in every establishment'.[13]

Above all I hope this book will help readers—especially those who have never set foot inside a prison—to 'see' the invisible women behind the bars.

Endnotes

1. News release from Prison Reform Trust, 23 February 1998.
2. National Association of Probation Officers (NAPO): *Women and Crime*, July 1997. The figures quoted were as follows: in 1993 there were 1,560 women in prison, including 395 on remand. In May 1997 there were 2,600 women in prison, including 550 on remand. The 76 per cent increase was calculated using the figures for *convicted* women. The Prison Reform Trust calculated a similar increase of 68 per cent between 1992 and 1996.
3. See *The Female Offender: Girls, Women and Crime*, Meda Chesney-Lind, Sage Publications, 1997. She quotes a figure of 12,000 women in US prisons in 1980, compared with nearly 65,000 a decade and a half later. Barbara Bloom, another American criminologist, says the figure in New York State is even higher (six times the 1980 figure). Chesney-Lind also comments on women prisoners' invisibility: 'The least visible of these [petty offenders in US jails] are the women we are now jailing'. The figures for October 1997 are even higher: in that month there were 74,730 women in US state and federal prisons—about 6 per cent of all prisoners.
4. *The Prison Population: Britain, The Rest of Europe and the World*, Prison Reform Trust, July 1997.
5. *Community Prisons for Women*, Stephanie Hayman, Prison Reform Trust, 1996.
6. *Criminal Classes: Offenders at School*, Angela Devlin, Waterside Press, 1995.
7. Although I am in close touch with a number of individual prisoners and some staff at Holloway, I deliberately avoided too great an involvement with women there as that prison is so frequently targeted by researchers.
8. *Women and Crime*, Frances Heidensohn, Macmillan, first published 1985; 9th (revised) edition 1996.
9. *The Imprisonment of Women*, Dobash R, Dobash R and Gutteridge S, Basil Blackwell, 1986.
10. To preserve their anonymity, names of all interviewees (officers, other staff and prisoners) have been changed and every effort has been made to omit any information that might link them to a particular prison and allow them to be identified. The only exceptions are those officials (serving and retired) whose permission to quote them has been requested and granted. Two released prisoners were happy for me to give their names in full. These are Sheila Bowler and Sara Thornton, both released after retrials.
11. The following statement may be seen displayed at the entrance to every prison: 'Her Majesty's Prison Service serves the public by keeping in custody those committed by the Courts. Our duty is to look after them with humanity and to help them lead law-abiding lives in custody and after release'.
12. *Understanding and Working with Young Women in Custody*, Juliet Lyon and John Coleman, Trust for the Study of Adolescence/HM Prison Service, 1996.
13. *Women in Prison: A Review*, HM Inspectorate of Prisons, Home Office, 1997.

CHAPTER ONE

Who Goes to Prison?

It is 7.45 on a sunny morning in mid-June. The tall prison gates swing open and in roll the sweatboxes, great sealed white vans with a row of small square blacked-out windows on either side, rattling noisily through the arched gateway one after another. Each has a uniformed male driver and a woman officer in the front passenger seat. They stare straight ahead like Lego people. Voices bawl over the din: 'Seventeen females picking up!' Shades of tumbrils, cattle trucks, concentration camps. There are two blackboards side by side on the wall, one with chalked white figures, the other with large printed words:

STATE OF ALERT

BLACK SPECIAL

Males	588
Females	151
Total	739

Inside the prison, the gateway echoes with shouted numbers: 'Mornin'—181 please!' Behind their glass screen in a booth like a station ticket office the gate officers are plucking bunches of keys off a board of hooks with lightning speed, slinging them under the barrier in return for numbered brass tally disks. There is chaffing morning banter as 50 or so officers in spotless black uniforms and crisp white shirts jostle in the queue with civilian workers in overalls. Numbers, noise and numbers.

Inside, on the wings, more numbers. 'We're waiting for the numbers', says the duty governor. 'That's the order to unlock—it's given out once all the inmates are accounted for.' Soon the order comes over the central tannoy system, echoing through the squat blocks to the high fence, over the razor wire[1] to the fields and the motorway beyond. 'I unlocked 156 this morning', says the governor of the women's side. I had 13 new numbers and I've filled the wings and the hospital. And I've only got six away to court this morning.' Numbers, noise and numbers.

'NEXT!' It's now 8.15 and the gravelly voice of prison officer Doris Briggs, a four foot eleven grey-haired chainsmoker, bellows through the reception area. A few women prisoners in a little huddle are shuffling about, some looking nervously over their shoulders. At Doris's

13

command one of them, a lanky woman in torn pink shirt and baggy striped shorts, breaks reluctantly away from the group and follows the officer towards the grandly named Allocation and Transfer Board. The door opens into a small office where the board, in the person of principal officer Jim Davies, sits waiting behind a desk. I follow Doris too. The governor has given me permission to sit in as an observer.

The woman edges onto the chair in front of Mr Davies. She is desperately thin and her long hair clings to her temples. Her eyes are red-rimmed, her cheeks hollow, her teeth discoloured. Mr Davies launches into his routine: 'My name is Mr Davies and I'm a principal officer. It's my job to roughly allocate you to another prison so I need to find out your details. But I have no control over what happens to you over the move. I've just got to ask you a few questions.'

The woman's name is Michelle. She is 30 years of age and she says she was done for theft. 'Did you breach bail, love?' asks Mr Davies. Michelle looks blank. 'Did you go to court, Michelle, or did they 'ave to send the bobbies round to yer?' prompts Doris. The questions continue: Mr Davies works his way through the Transfer Board Assessment Form with Michelle looking more and more spaced out. 'Got any children, love?' 'One girl, three—she's with me sister'. 'Are you on any drugs or are you withdrawing?' 'No, I'm not takin' nothin'.

Doris snorts loudly, 'Look at 'er! She's withdrawing for sure!' Principal officer Davies sighs: 'Well, off you go now, love. Mrs Briggs'll give you your EDR [earliest date of release] some time today. We'll try and get you somewhere nearer home—it depends where the vacancies are so we can't promise. But you'll be out shortly anyway.'

After Michelle, the other women are summoned in one by one. A black woman called Mary, 34, has been given four months for TWC (taking a vehicle without consent). She is a crack addict, her skin covered with sores. She is homeless and has had a previous sentence for loitering. Mr Davies scribbles 'NFA' (no fixed abode) on her form and tells her she'll be going to a closed prison because she breached her bail. The name of this prison galvanises Mary and her face becomes contorted with terror: 'I can't go there, there's people there that's out to get me!' Mr Davies looks irritated: 'You'll go where we send you. You'll have to suffer for your own actions because you breached your bail. We can't trust you now. Next one!'

In comes another black woman, tall and elegant. Her hair is gathered back in a smooth French pleat, she wears a pale lilac sweater. She says she's been remanded till next week for handling stolen goods. Her children are aged five and seven. 'Why did you spit at a police officer?' demands officer Davies. 'Because he twisted my arm and there was no need. He could have asked me and I'd have walked for him.'

14

Lesley is next and it takes only a few seconds for Mr Davies to recognise her as an old-stager. They set up an almost instant rapport based on shared knowledge of insider jargon which comes as naturally to Lesley as to her interrogator.

Lesley hardly waits for the first question before launching confidently into her details without drawing breath:

Lesley with an "E" and a "Y". I'm 31 next birthday. I got 28 days from Manchester Crown for perverting the course of justice. I bought a car last year and I had my cousin's name and address on it. It was only for my own use, not to re-sell or anything. I got put on CS [community service order] for that and I was then in breach with a warrant out for no bail. I did 15 months in here back in '89 for drugs offences. Last year I was done for intimidation of witnesses and I was up at Manchester maj [magistrates' court] for committal.

Mr Davies nods and scribbles everything down. 'We may have to keep you here, Lesley. Normally I'd send you to open but they won't want to take you and produce you[2] in that short time.'

The next two women are jointly accused of fraud and deception. They are younger—in their early twenties—well dressed, quietly spoken and articulate. Mr Davies straightens his tie and asks Sophie to take a seat. She wears a smart checked shirt, jeans with pressed creases and gold-rimmed glasses. Her fair hair is neatly brushed to one side. Mr Davies clears his throat:

'How old are you, dear? 21—right, ever taken drugs?'
'Well—only Es when I go out dancing—and amphetamines.'
'When was that?'
'Last Saturday.'
'Well, don't you go taking drugs in here or we'll slap your wrists for you! Now, we'll look to send you to an open prison. With your background that should be possible. But if you walk away from there— and you might well be tempted because there are no big walls—and if the police catch you—and they *will* catch you, have no fear—the courts will impose a further term of imprisonment upon you. So behave yourself and do your time like a good girl. OK, young lady. Thank you very much, off you go now.'

Sophie's co-accused, Sally, is 22. She has long dark hair and wistful brown eyes. She is wearing a long patterned skirt, immaculate white Indian cotton shirt and smart white shoes with straps. She reveals that she is 14 weeks pregnant. Mr Davies shakes his head gloomily and runs through the same routine.

15

A woman and her young stepdaughter follow, jointly convicted of possession of drugs and given long sentences. All they want is to be kept together. Mr Davies says he'll see what he can do. Then there is a very thin girl who looks about 10 years old. She is 20 with a two-year-old son and has been given a sentence of one month on four charges of shoplifting by a court in Blackburn. Doris guffaws: 'We don't like little shoplifters in Blackburn, do we love!'

There is a delay before the next prisoner arrives, hobbling with a walking-stick and wearing a large white surgical collar. May is a qualified engineer in her forties, convicted of deception and given four months. She shattered her spine six years ago when some scaffolding at work collapsed. Her main concern now is to get someone to move her car: she'd gone to court yesterday expecting to be released[3] and left the car with its disabled sticker on a yellow line outside the courtroom. It's now been there more than 24 hours. Mr Davies is sympathetic and promises her a phone call to deal with the car. He warns May to be careful not to let the other women manipulate her into getting drugs brought into the prison. May looks pale. He promises to put her on the privileged wing for the time being, then he'll try his best to get her into an open prison with no stairs.

The last woman this morning is Diane, given 28 days for drink-driving. She is a comfortably plump woman of 32. She has six children, aged three to 18. Principal officer Davies is glad of a little light relief and says with a chuckle, 'Found out what causes it yet, love?' Diane looks confused. 'Oh never mind,' says Mr Davies laying down his pen with a sigh. 'This is what we call primitive allocation',[4] he tells me as this last woman leaves. 'There's only beds for 150 women in here so they tell us we're not important. But the throughput is far, far bigger. We'll have had about 2,500 through here in the first six months of this year alone. It's getting much worse now with all the drugs girls we've got coming in. All we can do is get them bedded down and then get them out again. They're often the same people—some girls will be in and out of here ten times. We're now into the second generation of addicts. I counted five women out of the 150 in the prison today whose mothers were remanded out of here to give birth to them in one of our neighbouring prisons which had the facilities.'

Now it's time for the Governor's Induction—when the governor briefly meets the new prisoners coming in that day and explains initial prison procedures. Again I sit next to Doris beside another desk in the reception area—a narrow little room with a stained carpet covered in litter, two rows of battered easy chairs facing each other and scores of official notices, each headed 'INFORMATION FOR NEW INMATES', pinned up on the walls. One of them is a faded hand-printed notice saying 'DRUGS: your friendly advisors are listed below. Come and see us anytime'. Someone has scrawled in pencil underneath 'GET TO FUCK'. A large TV is fixed high on the wall. The eleven women look more relaxed now as they sit staring up at the breakfast show. Richard and Judy chatter away as cheerfully to prisoners as to early risers all over the country. 'It's not too bad today', says the governor, 'but we get women in here straight off the streets withdrawing and they can be rolling round the floor. Reception can be quite stressful and that's why we have the Richard and Judy breakfast show on'.

I feel relieved that Michelle, fortified with a mug of coffee, now looks much better. The governor tells her that her EDR is a week next Thursday—but she will still have to go off to a closed prison.

'Can't I go to open?'
' I don't think so: let's see, theft, shoplifting—and it says here you only left Holloway in March this year—now that's not very good, is it Michelle?'
'I was just nicking things for me 'ouse.'
'What did you take?' asks Doris.
'Ten swimming cozzies.'

Doris is convulsed: 'Oh, *lovely* furniture, swimming costumes! I got 20 in me bedroom, draped all round the room!'
Michelle brightens up at the joke: 'They had bugs[5] in the crutch an' all, Miss!'[6]

The rest of the women join in, enjoying the joke: 'Didn't yer foil[5] the fuckers Mitch?' yells Mary. 'Language!' says the governor, 'We don't have language like that in here!' 'Get yer feet off that table!' bellows Doris. It is now 10.45 a.m. and I have been in the prison for three hours.

• • •

This tiny slice of prison life contains in microcosm the reality of women's prisons today with all their problems of overcrowding, understaffing and drug control. Prisons reflect life on the outside and all society's ills are here writ large: poverty and need, homelessness and greed, racism, escapism and violence, destitution and loss—the list could go on and on.

In this first brief encounter with women prisoners we find the bizarre conjunction of comedy and tragedy that makes TV series like *Prisoner Cell Block H, Within These Walls, Porridge, The Governor* and *Insiders* such compelling viewing. But any visit to a real prison exposes the selectivity of media images. Film and TV can only offer a crude

17

impression of complex prison realities: the loss of identity; indignity; confusion and pain; shame and fear; humour and camaraderie; patronising and stereotyping; use and abuse of language, power and control.

The eleven women I saw passing through these reception interviews provide a snapshot of the women's prison population as we approach the end of this century. What is typical about this group of women is their very *atypicality*—they defy any form of classification. Women prisoners themselves resent being thought of as 'typical' prisoners. Lisa Roland-Shrubb, a Foston Hall prisoner, wrote an angry letter to the local newspaper[7] in January 1998 in response to an article it had printed, giving the governor's views about Christmas in the prison.

Many of the women felt distraught and upset. We felt that the governor's stereotypical image of women prisoners being portrayed as homeless, living in care, sexually abused by their family members, and drug addicts was an abominable misrepresentation. There are women here who have experienced these problems but there are also other professional working women such as a public relations manager, a computer supervisor, a civil engineer and an insurance adviser. Often these women have just made silly mistakes or have been unable to make ends meet and pay their bills.

Some staff do try to challenge the stereotype. A young male officer said he meets it constantly:

The public perception of women in prison is all wrong because people only know the myths. When people hear that I work in a women's prison they will ask me, "What are they really like?"and I will say, "They could be you, or your daughter, or your sister." The public only hear about notorious prisoners like Myra Hindley and they think women prisoners are all like that.

Home Office statistics give the figures, and the women in my sample reflect the current trends. Only 26 per cent of women receive a custodial sentence after spending an average of 41 days in prison on remand; three-quarters of them are remanded into custody for non-violent property crimes;[8] two-thirds are under 30;[9] two-thirds have few or no previous convictions;[10] 40 per cent are first time offenders and 71 per cent have not served a prison sentence before; and more than half have dependent children at home.[11] One third were in local authority care as children.[12] Two thirds were unemployed when sent to prison.[13]

Prison, as my 'fly on the wall' experience shows, is all about numbers, and numbers can certainly identify patterns in the backgrounds of incarcerated people. But what the numbers cannot tell you is anything that even begins to approach the whole picture. They cannot tell you that each woman is an *individual* with her own story, her own friends and family—or lack of them—and her own tragedy. They cannot tell you anything about the unique set of circumstances that put her into the sweatbox driving through those prison gates. Nor can they tell you anything about the way she is treated in custody.

Endnotes

1. Although the wire with jagged razor-like barbs used along the top of prison walls is commonly called razor wire, it is in fact a different type. In response to a query in the prison newspaper *Inside Time* (Spring 1997), a Prison Service spokesperson responded: 'Razor wire is an American product and it is not used by the Prison Service. The wire that is used has a different technical specification and is in fact called 'S-wire'.

2. As the woman's sentence was so short, an open prison would not want the trouble of sending an escort to collect her from the remand prison, or a further escort to produce her at the court for her trial.

3. A report on women prisoners commissioned in 1995 by the Home Office found that more than half had not expected a prison sentence: *Managing the Needs of Female Prisoners*, Allison Morris *et al*.

4 HM Inspectorate's 1997 report *Women in Prison: A Review* complained (5.17) that 'no clear criteria were used in decisions about allocations'. The inspectors recommended that allocation criteria should be drawn up.

5. The security devices ('bugs') on goods in department stores are covered with silver foil by shoplifters to deactivate them.

6. Women staff and visitors to both male and female prisons are commonly called 'Miss', men are called 'Boss' or 'Sir'.

7. 'Inmates Had No Reason to Party', *Derby Evening Telegraph,* 16 January 1998.

8. The figure was 72 per cent in my sample.

9. The average age of my sample was 31: 53 per cent were 30 or under.

10. Women prisoners are almost twice as likely as men to have few or no previous convictions. The latest published breakdown of prisoners' previous convictions is for 30 June 1994 (*Prison Statistics 1994*, Home Office, 1996). Sixty per cent of the women had two or fewer previous convictions, including 20 per cent with none. For the male prisoners the comparative figures were 33 per cent and 16 per cent respectively. In my own sample, 66 per cent were in prison for the first time.

11. In my sample the figure was 51 per cent.

12. Thirty per cent in my sample.

13. Sixty-six per cent in my sample.

CHAPTER TWO

Sweatboxes

One summer morning I find myself stuck in the area of a prison where women prisoners are being checked out into waiting security vans, ready to be moved to another prison. I have been brought this far from the gate by a passing officer but there is nobody free to escort me to my next appointment, so I have to wait. It's plain I am being a nuisance. A young woman officer glares at me through her rimless glasses: 'You can't stay here, I'm afraid—you're in the way.' I find a seat in an empty office and watch through the open door. Other officers herd the women through at breakneck speed, checking their possessions and stuffing these into huge transparent plastic sacks stamped in royal blue with a large crown and the letters 'HM PRISON SERVICE'. The tension is heightened by the revving of the security vans on the sweltering forecourt.

Some of the women have already had to face long journeys from court in these monsters. Euphemistically referred to by officers as 'cellular vehicles' or 'personnel carriers', they are more accurately described by prisoners as 'sweatboxes' or 'meat wagons'. Inside there is a central corridor with tiny individual cells on either side, each with its own window with one-way glass to foil the prying public. The prisoner sits on a hard bench seat with a solid panel directly in front of her. Her knees may touch the panel and there are similar panels behind her and beside her. In wet weather the roof may leak and she will have to try and find some way of mopping up a pool of water before she sits down. There are no seat belts and women on their way to prison mother-and-baby units will have to hold on to their small children as best they can as the van hurtles along motorways and rattles over bumpy country roads towards the prison. (Nursing staff told me of their disgust that women seven months pregnant could be sent to court in these vehicles and a female governor said 'I believe EC regulations cover conditions for livestock transportation, but contain nothing about transport of these women'). The escort may decide there is no time to stop for the toilet, and a woman locked in her tiny cubicle will have no means of communication with the escorting officers.[1] Prisoners tell of travelling from Holloway to Durham—a six hour journey—without a stop.

• • •

Few prisoners—whether new arrivals or transfers—can be fully prepared for what they will find at the end of their miserable journey to a new prison. Women coming straight from the courts will go to one of six[2] prisons, regarded for this purpose as 'local' prisons, though in fact they are most unlikely to be local to a woman's own area. Holloway is the only establishment specially built to house female prisoners. Now Western Europe's largest women's prison, completed in 1985, it was controversially designed on the model of a psychiatric hospital. The female prison 'estate' is spectacularly centralised: in 1996 Holloway received 3,500 of the 7,300 women processed through the prison system. At any one time, over 500 women are held there and they can be of any age, race, offence, length of sentence and security category.

The rest of the buildings that comprise the 16 prisons[3] in the women's estate have been acquired over the years in *ad hoc* fashion more out of pragmatism than with any regard for suitability of purpose. Indeed, the support group Women in Prison has called for an audit of existing buildings so that the cost of running such unsuitable establishments can be assessed. Women's prisons follow in the tradition begun in the mid-nineteenth century when the Brixton House of Correction was hurriedly converted into the first prison solely for women. This was itself a pragmatic decision made to meet the crisis caused by the end of convict transportation.[4]

A convicted prisoner sent to HMP Styal, a closed prison in Cheshire with a mother and baby unit, will find herself in one of the bleak houseblocks of a former Victorian orphanage. Then there are the sprawling stately mansions of two of the open prisons, HMP Askham Grange in Yorkshire and HMP East Sutton Park in Kent, with their mullioned windows, converted ballrooms, manicured lawns and oak panelling. (Chris Tchaikovsky, Director of Women in Prison, called East Sutton Park a 'tinderbox'). Another open prison, Drake Hall in Staffordshire, was once a hostel housing World War II munitions workers. The closed prison Bullwood Hall, set in lovely Essex farmland, gets its name from the once elegant mansion still there in its grounds, but the prison itself is an ugly barracks-like red brick building—a former girls' borstal—surrounded by tarmac and a vomit coloured fence.[5] With ingenuous irony that pays little regard to those caged inside, its blocks until 1997 bore the names of free-flying birds: Eagle, Falcon, Jay, Kestrel and Condor. They are now being replaced with letters and numbers (except for Nightingale, the medical wing, where the name has more appropriate connotations). Foston Hall, a relatively new addition to the women's estate, is a brick mansion in the middle of the Derbyshire countryside. Like most women's prisons it has been recycled—it used to be the lifers' wing of HMP Sudbury, the male prison two miles down the road.

Most intimidating of all is Durham Prison's H Wing, the tall narrow block where between 40 and 50 women considered to be a very high security risk serve their long sentences in the midst of the 844 male prisoners in this, the city's local prison. The windows of the top landing cells look out over some of the finest architecture in Europe, but women incarcerated there describe the claustrophobia of living in this prison within a prison. Twelve of the 16 prisons are entirely separate women-only establishments; the other four are on sites shared with male prisons, though the women's wings are physically separate and have their own staff.[6]

Prisoners fall into three groups: unconvicted remand prisoners, innocent unless proved guilty; convicted prisoners who have not yet been sentenced (sometimes called 'JRs'—judges' remands); and sentenced prisoners. These groups are not kept separate, nor are they categorised in the same way that male prisoners are, i.e. categories A to D. They are simply treated as suitable for open or closed conditions, apart from a very few women classed as a high security risk who *are* category A prisoners.[7]

The criminal justice process is a mass of bizarre contradictions. One of its oddest aspects is the extraordinary management of time: there is such variation in the pace of events. Many of the women I interviewed reported waiting long months for their cases to be brought to trial—yet their barristers had not found time to meet them until a few hours—sometimes only minutes—before they stood in the dock. For many the trial seems to be over so quickly, proceeding at such a pace (and in such obscure and unfamiliar language) that they feel dazed and powerless, mere observers as their fate is sealed. Women arriving from the courts at a busy remand prison can be stampeded through the reception process, allocated to a wing there, or shipped out to their next prison with scarcely a pause for breath.

Then time stands still. For the prisoner spending that first night in her first prison there is suddenly all the time in the world. Time stretches ahead, a terrifying void, whether it is a week, a month, a year, a lifetime—because it is time out, time away from everything she knows and understands. And time back at home will never be the same again. As 'doing time' becomes a reality, every minute is prescribed in the aching daily routine of bang-up, inactivity, rushed mealtimes, association and often purposeless work—until one morning at six o'clock the cell door is flung open, a screw yells 'Gerrup, you're on the ghost train!'[8] and the whole process starts all over again.

When a prisoner arrives at her allocated establishment, what help will she be given to settle in? A senior official I interviewed at Prison Service Headquarters emphasised the importance of the period when a woman first comes into prison: 'Far more women than men are first offenders and this means there is a need for lots of reception input and far more time spent in the induction process. There are also far more likely to be difficulties at home for a woman—she may have been sent to jail when she didn't expect it[9] and her children may still be at school. So you have to be very quick to deal with these things for her.'

The chief inspector, in his major thematic review[1] of women's prisons, considered this initial period to be so important that he devoted the longest chapter to recommendations for needs-based reception and induction. He recommended that the reception period should be a time when the seeking of information needed by the establishment is combined with dealing with urgent personal matters for the prisoner. The induction period, flowing smoothly on from the reception period, should have a three-fold purpose: the imparting of information, the assessment of medium and long term needs, and the giving of appropriate assistance. Inspectors were disturbed to find that reception and induction processes in most prisons make no distinction as to whether or not women are in prison for the first time. Prison staff complain that they are told very little about the women's personal histories and—as *Chapter 1* indicated—reception interviews are cursory to say the least. Healthcare staff may be given no information at all about a prisoner's medical background, and unless a woman chooses to tell them, will not know what drugs—prescribed or illegal—she is using, making it impossible to maintain her on any coherent programme. Few prisoners I interviewed recalled being offered any opportunity to talk privately to staff in depth about their life histories, or having any real involvement in what happened to them in custody.

Women in every one of the 12 prisons in my research project complained of lack of information about the prison itself, and minimal access to any means of solving outside problems. The resulting feelings of confusion, frustration and disempowerment were for many the worst aspect of coming into prison. First-time prisoners described their experiences of the reception process at Holloway and at Risley:

Cathy
Cathy told me about her reception into Holloway. A laboratory assistant in her thirties, she is a single parent with a son of 13. She was given eight months for fraud, her first ever offence, and taken straight from a London Crown Court to Holloway:

I'd had no idea at all that I'd be sent to prison. I arrived from court at 3.30 in the afternoon. My reception into Holloway was the most frightening thing in my life. They call out your surname and send you into a big room called Reception where you see a lot of officers. They take all your possessions like jewellery and put it in a safe then you wait hours till you hear your name called again. I knew nobody but a lot of the women knew each other. I saw drugs being passed and the officers didn't seem very interested. Then you are strip-searched, which I found very degrading, and sent to the reception wing. It was 8.45 p.m. by this time and I had not eaten all day. They'd brought me lunch at the court but it was chicken tandoori and I'm a vegetarian so I couldn't eat it. I was put in a big dormitory but there was only one other girl in there and she kept watching me, trying to suss me out. I couldn't sleep a wink — I think I was in shock. I should have had a reception phone call to my son but I didn't get it till ten days later when I was sent here.[10]

Candida

Candida was also sent first to Holloway. A heroin addict for seven years (between the ages of 18 and 25) she was judged to have failed a programme in a rehabilitation unit after a trial period of just one month, and was jailed when her baby—her first child—was six months old:

I went back to Marylebone Court to face five outstanding shoplifting charges. It's a Dickensian place with ancient wooden benches and you expect Scrooge to come out at any minute and write with a feather pen. The judge said "You have a terrible record and I'm going to protect the public from you. I'm giving you eight months." I was carted down to the cells then driven off to Holloway.

Holloway's a very intense place. Even walking past people in the corridor for the first time is an ordeal. Everyone follows you with their eyes, sizing you up, wondering what you're into. If you look directly at anyone they'll say "Who d'you think you're looking at then?" You can't look anywhere — you might as well look up in the air, but then they think you're a loony. A lot of women there were in prison for their first offence, like not paying their poll tax. But some had been there for a long time. Soon after I got there I said to one woman "I'd go mad if I was in here for long!" and she said "You get used to it." She'd been inside for 17 years. But at first I didn't talk to anyone. I was still in shock. I didn't know what was going on at all. I didn't understand the prison culture so I didn't know how to do anything, even simple things like sending a letter. Nobody tells you what's going on or where you're going next.

Alison

Alison missed the Holloway experience: 'I was supposed to go to Holloway but it was full, so I was sent to Risley for five days to start

24

with.' Alison is a 43-year-old grandmother who had never been in trouble with the law until she became involved in a relationship with a lifer in a high security men's prison. She was caught trying to smuggle a small amount of cannabis into the prison for him and jailed for three months:

> He couldn't understand why on earth I did it. He said he could get any drug he wanted in there. But I wanted to give him a present. I'd crutched[11] it in a condom because the girl I got it from told me that's how you do it. I didn't even know the resin form of cannabis came in a lump—that's how innocent I was about drugs. I was lucky I suppose because I could have got a much longer sentence. But when I heard they were sending me to prison I was in shock and I was crying because I knew my family were out there wanting to know, and all I could think of was—three months in prison. They let my family come in and see me in a room in the court, and they had my granddaughter with them which I found even more tear-jerking. Then I was driven off hundreds of miles away to a prison up north, shut in a dull cold cell and put on Basic[12] on the Ones.

Alison was unusual in being placed in a single cell. Almost all women are initially put in a dormitory on the reception wing or—if they have been given a long sentence—in the prison hospital, because they are assumed to be at risk of harming themselves. If they are lifers, they will usually be given priority for a single room, though this move may take some days or weeks. Alison had been given a relatively short sentence, but her shame and fear were nevertheless very great:

> The cell had no curtains, only bars, and I tell you, if I'd had a knife I'd have ended it all then. I thought, here I am, 43, a grandmother for God's sake, dressed up smart for court. They know I'm not a hardened criminal. That first night I was shaking all night because the wing I was in was opposite another block and the girls were yelling all night and flicking wet toilet paper across the yard at each other. I know now that it was just kids being stupid but I was terrified and thinking I'd have to share the blame. I don't think I slept at all.

> At 7.30 next morning the officers unlocked my door—but they didn't say I could come out and get a drink or anything, so I just sat there. They'd given me a plastic mug and toothbrush and washing stuff but there was no water in my cell. What I didn't know was that at the end of every wing there's a hot water geyser you're allowed to go to. You see all these people walking past the door and to me they all looked like crackheads so I was afraid to go out—and anyway I hadn't been told by an officer I was allowed to. One girl finally said to me "Are you coming to breakfast?" But I soon discovered she just wanted to use me to her own advantage. She was soon asking if I'd got

25

any units[13] and crying and saying she couldn't ring her family. She was only young and at first I fell for it and before I knew it she'd used up four units. When I'd got my card back from her I found she soon drifted away from me and I was on my own again.

So I soon learned to keep myself to myself and I picked things up just by watching. I had no idea at first how to post a letter or what you are allowed to have in prison with you. Even by the time I was moved from that prison after five days I'd still not been told. I asked the wing officer what I should be doing all day and he said there was no chance of me getting a job or going to education — at least he put me up to Standard regime.[12] But still I had no idea what I could spend so when it was canteen[14] I spent £12 of the £15 I'd brought in with me. Only then I realised I was only allowed one private spend[15] a month.

Sara
Sara, 20, was given two years for growing cannabis plants and also sent to Risley:

I went in on a Friday night. I went to the toilet but there was no paper and nobody told me you had to ask for it. I felt utterly trapped, utterly useless. I felt like ending it all. I was banged up all Friday, Saturday and Sunday. They bang you up all the time there. I would not wish that place on anybody. If you asked the screws anything they spoke to you like a piece of shit. They are utter bastards. On the Monday I was let out of the cell for three hours to make my reception phone call[16] but the other women are all queuing up behind you and you can't hear a word.

Foston Hall has been criticised in the press for the 'luxury' of its provision. Women there agree that the rooms are of a much higher standard than any other prison they have seen. 'The rooms here are really pleasant', said one. 'They've got in-cell shower units and no bars on the windows'. But ironically prisoners only move to these rooms when they move on to a Standard or Enhanced regime.[12] All women when they first arrive are put on Basic regime. A prisoner moved there from Brockhill was shocked, especially as she had heard of the reputed comfort:

The Basic regime accommodation is in the old building and is horrible, with no in-cell sanitation. Women can get out to the toilet at 10 pm and after that there isn't even a chamber pot in the cell. You have to wait till the morning however desperate you are. You spend your week or two reception/induction period in this basic unit and the only induction programme you get is to watch videos about AIDS. They may have spent a lot on refurbishing the rooms, but there's only one probation officer to deal with all the women's needs.

Most prisoners perceived the induction period as traumatic. Small deprivations like the ban on bringing in any toiletries sometimes hurt most: some women described being issued with antiquated green tooth-cleaning powder in a paper bag instead of toothpaste. Destitute women who had come straight off the streets, out of care homes or from overseas described having to wear the same dirty clothes for up to a week after their arrival: without relatives or friends to bring them a change of clothes they had to wait till 'the WVS cupboard' was opened and they could be issued with clean clothing, usually old-fashioned and ugly.

Whether by design or default by staff dealing with them, these women's experiences during their reception periods were the beginning of the process known to sociologists as 'role dispossession'. Erving Goffman in *Asylums*[17] described admission procedures into institutions (particularly prisons) as deliberately designed to reinforce the barriers between new inmates and the world outside. These include the replacement of a name with a number, the removal of personal possessions and their replacement with prison issue, the indignities of the strip search and the lack of privacy.

There is evidence[18] that those prisoners who take their own lives tend to do so early in their period of custody. Both Alison and Sara were by their own admission at real risk that first night in prison, and Alison was also deeply depressed after the move to her second prison. In 1997 suicides in prison reached record levels. Most of the 70 victims were remand prisoners, innocent until proved guilty. Women are particularly at risk because many of them are in jail for the first time, and most of them[9] will not have expected to be given a custodial sentence. Without warning they find themselves in a new and terrifying world. The Prison Service's own internal document *Caring for the Suicidal in Custody*[19] acknowledges the dangers of this period. For all 'first receptions' it recommends that staff should aim to:

- offer reassurance to prisoners by explaining procedures, identifying their immediate needs and giving information about what help is available
- encourage prisoners to disclose their concerns to staff.

The extent to which prison staff are able to implement these recommendations is discussed in more detail in *Chapter 12*. Many women said that in any case they would prefer to talk to other prisoners. The listeners scheme, whereby the Samaritans train volunteer prisoners for six weeks, can be an enormous support.

Listeners should be available to all new prisoners on reception. A listener at Brockhill prison explained:

> Women coming in on remand are specially insecure and frightened. Their crime is very recent, maybe committed just the day before, and they are very raw. They've come with preconceived ideas and they're terrified, so just to see a smiling face makes all the difference. It's easier to come to us than to an officer. They want to know how we coped ourselves. They ask "Does time pass?"

But at Holloway a befriender—the Holloway equivalent of a listener—described the constraints under which she works:

> We are not allowed to give advice. We have to use a stupid formula and ask women "if they have heard of" certain helpful pieces of information. And we can't offer to lend things to them either.[20] I have tried to comfort women in floods of tears because they are wearing filthy clothes, and I can't even lend them a clean shirt. You feel so helpless.

The Inspectorate review[21] recommended that listeners should be involved in the reception process and that additional support should come from trained 'prisoner assistants'.

Annette
Annette is a tough, likeable Geordie. She killed her abusive common-law husband ten years ago and during her life sentence has done the rounds of most of the women's prisons. To her the traumas of newly-imprisoned women are all too familiar. She suggests that prisons should arrange some form of mentor or 'buddy' system to match new prisoners with established inmates and help them through those first few days—a role she often takes upon herself:

> The dining room is the worst part of going to jail, whether you're in your first prison or just moving to a new one. People have already got their seats with their friends and you don't know where to sit. You might sit down and somebody'll come up and say "That's my place!" Then you're in trouble. I've seen young girls come in on their own and they're terrified. It can be very hard.

The Inspectorate also recommended that after women's immediate needs had been dealt with, all prisons should provide a core induction programme, with additional information about that particular establishment. Most of the women I spoke to complained of a lack of information, of not knowing what was going on, and of being fobbed off, rather than reassured, by officers. All prisoners are supposed to be given a copy of the admirable *Prisoners' Information Book*, produced jointly by the Prison Service and Prison Reform Trust and updated annually. It is generally known as 'The Yellow Book' (though the 1997 edition has a blue cover.) It is an accessible, user-friendly document that would be helpful to any new prisoner (as long as he or she is literate), and is now available in 16 languages. I have been in prisons where no prisoner has received one, yet in one prison the designated induction officer gave me a free copy from a filing cabinet full of them. Women often said they felt such information was deliberately withheld from them, because if they knew their rights they were more likely to cause trouble. Others felt that official documents bear little relation to the reality of prison life: 'That Yellow Book's useless, man—it's got the rules but they don't uphold their own rules in this place.'

The problems of overcrowded prisons have been well-publicised. Richard Tilt, director general of the Prison Service, spoke in a *Panorama* interview[22] in January 1997 of prisoners having to be moved round the system 'looking for a bed'. At a remand centre like Risley women's prison any information given to prisoners has to be readily accessible as there may be very little time to assimilate it. The prison produces a 'First night information sheet for new prisoners', though according to prisoners like Alison it is not always given to newcomers. It is a desktop-published double-sided A4 sheet with boxes containing notes answering likely questions. It is quite user-friendly: the first box, headed 'What happens tomorrow?', contains a simple timetable:

0730 Get up — Breakfast
0800 If sentenced you will be allocated to prison where you will serve your sentence
0900 Canteen; fingerprints; photographs

and so on throughout the day. Another box, reassuringly headed 'Walkman/Radio' advises: 'Have one sent in or buy cheap one in canteen so you will not be bored in cell. Earphones must be used.' Other boxes on the sheet contain advice and information about visits, letters, money, clothing, the chaplaincy ('all religions catered for'), medical problems and so on. Interspersed between the nuggets of practical advice are clear messages about the dangers of prison life: 'Bullying: Do not give, lend or let any inmate bully or frighten you. Always *tell the Staff*. Write a letter to the governor. Do not let the bullies win'. 'Telephone: buy telephone cards, £2 each. Never, never *lend* or *borrow.'* 'On visits: *No* food. *No* toiletries, *no* cosmetics. Buy these in canteen.'

But written information like this will inevitably be of limited use to many women coming into prison straight from the courts: they are often in shock at the severity of their sentence, or at getting a prison sentence at all.[9] Almost 50 per cent of imprisoned women are primary carers:[23] they may have left children at home with friends or neighbours, or there may be elderly relatives waiting by the phone. Many will be withdrawing from drugs. Many have literacy problems and other special needs. As the inspectors' report recognised, they need informed professional help to meet their immediate concerns.

Jane, a probation officer at a busy women's remand prison, confirms that most women are in crisis at the beginning of a sentence:

> If a woman comes in here we have to offer her what we can. We don't know how long we'll have her because she may be moved to another prison at any time. But we can at least get to women immediately and listen to them. We get involved with people on a murder charge the very day after they may have killed someone. We would make a beeline for them and see what we can do. Many women come in withdrawing from drugs — the effects are terrible. Women will be vomiting, sleepless for weeks and they get into a panic at being banged up in their cells and not being able to sleep.

Dr Mary James (not her real name), is a woman psychologist based at the same prison. She also described crisis management:

> What you have to realise is that in here we are meeting women first when they are in a state of crisis. It might be the day after a woman killed her husband. So all you can give them is basic support and crisis management. I do a lot of bereavement counselling. A woman may be a killer but we mustn't forget that she is suffering a bereavement as well. So often we are seeing the result of an accumulation of traumas which culminated in the offence. A woman will come into prison with a range of emotions: there will be all the trauma before she came in, and on top of that, the trauma of separation from family and children.
>
> For some women this will be the first time they have been removed from violence for years. For them, prison may seem like a haven. After the initial crisis intervention, a woman may need time and space to stand back and evaluate what has gone on in her life — dangerous things she has got sucked into. All I can do is to initiate a few things that may facilitate change, and be with them through the tangled mess of their lives. I listen to them and together we look at who they were before they came in, who they are now, who they would like to be.

There is a lot of overlap with Jane. Probation is practically based and Jane assesses their problems and does the best she can with a transient population. As a service we are becoming much more reactive because that's all we can do without the resources to plan ahead.

Hilary

Hilary is just one woman with good reason to be grateful to Dr James and Jane: without them she is not sure whether she would have survived. She was in three abusive relationships before she killed Robert, her fourth partner, with a kitchen knife:

> At the police station I kept saying over and over again "I had a white dress on". I remember the floor of the police cell had coloured squares and I thought they were coming up towards me. I was charged with murder at the magistrates' court then sent here. I came in here and I was in total shock, in the worst state I've ever been in. I was put straight in the hospital. I could only just function. The governor called Dr James to see me and she was wonderful. I'd never been anywhere near a prison before and I had no help apart from her. I had nobody to talk to—the nurses were too busy. I felt I should be isolated, dealt with. The guilt was dreadful. I thought, I won't be able to survive this.

Women remanded, or sentenced to life, for murder are routinely put onto the hospital wing on reception for observation in case they make an attempt on their lives, though many who had been through this experience said they felt isolated and disorientated. Those returning to the prison from court after being given a long sentence desperately missed friends they had made on remand on the wing and needed their support—yet they were put in the healthcare centre where they knew no-one. Hilary stayed in the hospital for three months before being moved to 'normal location':

> I was terrified when I had to move out of the hospital to this wing and it really knocked me back. Like I said, I'd been in there three months and these officers suddenly came in and said to me "Pack your bags, we're going!" This really frightens you. You have no time and you've no idea what you've done to have to move—they don't tell you anything.

> Dr James sees me once a week and she's available at other times too if I'm feeling bad. I was devastated when I came back from the plea.[24] You want to kill yourself. Jane, the probation officer, was very good when I was upset on the date of Robert's birthday. I kept crying and saying, "It was his birthday".

31

Prison staff use the term 'anniversary syndrome' to refer to times when prisoners may harm themselves or attempt suicide when the date of some emotive event comes round.

In mid-July 1997, home secretary Jack Straw announced that—after a lengthy period of consultation—the prison and probation services might be merged into a single 'Department of Corrections', as in Australia, Sweden, Canada and the USA. The possibility had already been raised a few months earlier with the appointment of Joyce Quin as minister for both prisons and probation, and Jack Straw stressed the importance of closer integration between the services to deal more effectively with offenders. But during the discussion that followed, opponents of any such merger spoke of the entirely different cultures of the two services. They pointed out that the first probation officers in the 1870s were 'court missionaries' whose job it was to interview petty offenders and assess their potential for reform. The Criminal Justice Act 1948 stated that it was the responsibility of probation officers to 'advise, assist and befriend' offenders.

In future even less advice, assistance and friendship is likely to be available to prisoners who come from the courts in a state of crisis. Richard Tilt announced in November 1995 that prisons would be expected to make a reduction of 13.5 per cent in their unit costs over the three years from April 1996 to 1999. With budgets now devolved to individual prisons, it is up to each governor to decide what services should be 'bought in', and services like probation and psychology may be among the first to be cut. Some prisons have already reduced the size of their probation departments, and some will employ no probation officers at all in future. As I write, the probation officer at Risley women's prison is being redeployed in the community outside. Risley's annual throughput is between 4,000 and 5,000 women and now they will have no probation officer to enable them to attend to their immediate problems.

Most prison probation officers I interviewed regarded themselves as the last bastion of the probation service still working in terms of its original social-work base. Yet they fulfil a different role from social workers, whom many of the prisoners I interviewed mistrusted and feared, because of their power to remove their children from them.

Jane, the probation officer who helped Hilary through those first days in prison, is saddened by recent developments:

There are so many crises. It's important that psychologists and probation officers work together because being in a state of crisis recalls other crisis situations, especially previous abuse. At the same time I have to try and help women with all the practical problems of being in prison, mainly childcare, accommodation and dealing with social services. I would like to get involved more but I have been pulled off a lot of this work now and they are cutting back on probation officers seconded to prisons. I'm afraid I may be pulled out at any moment.

A woman's first experience of prison is of course the most shocking: the remand period is one of particular instability, which can end either in freedom or a further period in custody. Women appealing against conviction also find it difficult to settle, though the delays involved in the process soon seem to reduce most appellants to a kind of resigned acceptance that they will be waiting for a very long time. But there can be great trauma too in a woman's next move, from her remand prison to the one where she expects to serve her sentence (though if the sentence is a very short one, she may stay in the first prison.)

Even for those willing to accept that they 'did the crime so must do the time', one of the most psychologically damaging aspects of prison life is its inherent instability. At any point, sometimes for disciplinary or security reasons but more often simply for reasons of operational pragmatism (usually these days because of overcrowding) a prisoner may be 'shipped out' to a new prison. It is common to hear staff discussing 'bed swaps' or 'body swaps' as if prisoners were mere commodities to be shifted about like baggage.

Elizabeth

Elizabeth is a young prisoner nearing the end of her sentence at Foston Hall. She was moved there from Brockhill at very short notice, just after hearing of an unexpected 'parole knockback' which meant a further year in custody and for a while was shocked and depressed. She has embarked on an Open University law course, and is undertaking an important research project, entitled 'The Negative Consequences of An Unstable Prison Environment'. Her outline for the project begins:

Women in prison are exposed to an environment that is unstable and uncertain. They are moved from one prison to another and given little or no warning as to the reasons why. Due to lack of staff and resources, prison regimes are changed at a moment's notice. Prisoners suffer because they lose stable relationships and have no visits. These are serious matters because they do not know what is happening in their lives from one day to the next. Prison is a woman's home for whatever the period of her sentence. She needs an environment she can settle into, trusted friends, goals, continuity, familiar figures to maintain or gain identity and security. The ongoing results of such conditions can cause women to become violent and abusive, to self-harm and even commit suicide.

33

Caring for the Suicidal in Custody[19] recognises the continuing risks during further prison moves. In a paragraph headed 'subsequent receptions' it advises staff to 'identify significant changes in circumstances and needs.'

The Inspectorate review particularly emphasised the need for a quite distinct form of reception for women moving from one prison to another. In fact the inspectors remarked[25] on the lack of 'any coherent sense that transfers between establishments are part of a plan'.

A move of prison can mean severing prison relationships which may have been hard enough to establish in the first place, losing a prison job which may have supplied a little much-needed cash, or breaking off in the middle of an educational or skills training course—though the inspectors recommend that education and training should be continued in the new prison as part of an established sentence plan.[25]

A prison move means leaving a cell which, however spartan to begin with, will usually have been humanised with photographs, plants and ornaments into some kind of home. Even a move from one wing to another in the same prison can be shocking enough, because each wing has its own culture and a prisoner newly arrived on the wing is once again the outsider. It can be quite devastating to have to start from scratch and fight to re-establish some sort of status in an entirely new institution. One life-sentenced prisoner kept a daily diary for the first four years of her sentence. When she moved from her remand placement to her 'first stage' prison, the entries for the first few days are full of phrases like 'missing X and Y so much', 'feeling desperately lonely', 'nobody to talk to here', 'nobody I can seem to get on with'.

Another woman had changed prisons several times during her sentence but the process was still no easier: 'Even now I feel terribly nervous at the idea of changing prisons. I was physically sick and shaking when I first got here.'

Alison, who described above her reception into Risley, spent just five days there before being moved to her current open prison. Although she was grateful to be moved, she was horrified to find herself without any possessions:

When they moved me here[26] they found that my property bag which should have come here with me hadn't arrived. It had everything—my clothes, phone cards, my stamps, letters—everything. It's a two-and-a-half-hour journey from that prison to this one and they told me I'd have to wait till the next ship-out[27] in ten days' time. I had only the clothes I stood up in. They did buy me three new pairs of knickers but I had to manage for the next ten days by washing the clothes I had on. I shed many bitter tears alone in my room.

Particularly frustrating for women is the inconsistency between prisons regarding items allowed 'in possession'. Officers described the problems this causes them on escorts when they are unable to tell incoming women the rules of their own establishments because, as one officer said wryly 'The rules change almost weekly!' The Inspectorate review recommended the development of a standard list for all the women's prisons, as well as an adjustment of the rules on volumetric control, which limit property to the amount that will fit into two 'prop [property] boxes': these again vary in size from prison to prison. (The rules have in any case been made for male prisoners who wear uniform and need fewer clothes).

Despite the pressures of overcrowding, staff shortages and expenditure cuts, two features of these moves seem unnecessarily harsh: the suddenness and the speed. The prison authorities insist that for security reasons prisoners are never told in advance that they are to be moved to another prison. This precaution may be vital in the case of category A high security prisoners who may have resources outside to plan an escape. But few women are in this situation, and for women unable to let their families know when they are moving the effects can be disastrous.

Numerous women spoke of visits too late to cancel, of expensive wasted journeys and weeping children, of the frustration of knowing your visitors are struggling towards the prison on a wet Sunday afternoon while you sit in your new cell a hundred miles away. It is difficult to believe that there would be any real risk to security if a woman were informed late the evening before of a move the following morning. If she then remained locked in her cell she would have time to pack her belongings and prepare herself psychologically for the move— and there could be little risk of her contacting anyone before the following morning.

There should also be some way of prison staff informing relatives of a prison move. One telephone call to the family (made for security purposes immediately after a woman has been moved) could avoid unnecessary travel and inevitable disappointment and anger. I have stood behind angry families at the Holloway gate at visiting time:

'Sorry, love, she's not here—she's been shipped out.'
A grandmother with two children in a double buggy stares at the gate officer in disbelief: 'Where to?'
'Bullwood Hall.'
'Where's that?'
'Down Southend way—nice day out by the seaside for you!'

35

The speed of the 'shipping-out' process itself can be terrifying and shocking. Kaley, with children of eleven and three, described what happens:

> You get skulldragged out of bed and before you know it you're being shipped out. My room was full of the kids' photos and all the cards they've sent me. I was still in bed asleep and this officer marched in shouting, "You're on the ship!" She wouldn't tell me where so I thought it must be right far away and I wouldn't get any visitors in a million years. I had loads of stuff and I had ten minutes to pack it all into those prison bags.

The Inspectorate's report particularly stressed the importance of the reception and induction periods in setting the tone of the whole prison sentence. But most women's experiences got them off to a very bad start. Some described having to leave precious mementoes because of the speed of the operation. Yet they would then find themselves waiting in a holding area or a transport van for long periods. Unsurprisingly they began the next stage of their sentence bitter and resentful, making a nonsense of the whole sentence plan.[28]

The plight of the pregnant Irish prisoner Roisin McAliskey in Holloway drew public attention to a process rarely referred to in induction information material. This is one of the most degrading parts of the reception system—the strip search. Roisin's mother, Bernadette (née Devlin), the former MP, complained that her daughter had been strip-searched 100 times in the few months since she was sent to prison. Ann Widdecombe, then prisons minister, corrected her: the figure, she said, was just 75. The irony of the correction seems to have escaped the minister.

Many women—particularly those who have suffered past sexual abuse—find it so shocking that they prefer not to re-live the degradation by talking about it, or they defuse the pain with some euphemistic description like the common expression: 'I had to do a twirl'. Cathy, who described the reception process earlier in this chapter, had no such reservations:

> It's very degrading the way they do it because they treat you like cattle. You stand in a cubicle and you're told to remove all your clothes and then you stand there naked while two female officers go through all your stuff in front of you, go through your bra and they even turn your knickers inside out. I think that was the worst bit.

None of the women remembered being given any preparation for the strip search or for any part of the reception process: as recently as 1992 a woman sent on remand to HMP Pucklechurch (later closed) described being deloused as even more degrading than the strip search. The security measures to try to prevent drugs being smuggled into prisons have made the strip search much more common, and it has become part of the regular routine not just on reception into a woman's first prison, but when she moves from one prison to another. (It is also now used when women are required to provide a urine sample as part of the mandatory drug-testing process, and at random after visits).

A woman brought up strictly in the Muslim faith described her revulsion when she was strip-searched at her second prison:

> You have to strip naked and lie on your back with your knees in the air, then let your legs flop apart like you do for an internal examination when you're pregnant. Then they look inside you but thank goodness they're not allowed to touch you. It's horrible having those officers look at you like that. Then you have to stand up naked and bend forwards so they can look at the other side.

This refers to a particularly degrading variety of the strip search: women call it the 'squat search'. A few women described being entirely naked, but most said they had to remove trousers and underwear and bend over, feet apart, for female officers to look inside the vagina and anus to see if drugs are concealed there. Sometimes this is called 'the mirror test' because the prisoner will have to stand over a mirror, underwear removed, legs apart. Officers are not allowed to touch the woman as this would be classed as assault, but one woman, a rape victim, told a prison doctor that forced strip-searching of this kind felt like another rape. 'He agreed. He said "Yes, it's statutory rape."'

The Inspectorate review, while accepting the need for searches as part of the reception process, contains a strong recommendation to the Prison Service to investigate some form of electro-mechanical detection device to replace the strip search, and suggests Prison Service officials consult HM Customs and Excise who use such methods successfully to detect drugs coming through ports and airports.[29] In the meantime, strip searches should be carried out sensitively by specially trained staff, and staff behaviour should be carefully monitored.[30]

• • •

Following on from the initial reception stage, some of the prisons I visited were attempting to run meaningful induction programmes of the kind recommended by the Inspectorate, though in none did I see any differentiation between first-time prisoners and others.

At one open prison new arrivals stay on a special induction wing for a week before being allocated to one of the other wings. A 20 page introductory booklet explains the daily routine of the prison, its rules and other information. A young male officer took me through the combined reception/induction process for convicted women sent from other prisons:

> We got three in from Holloway this afternoon. They get an induction pack and a reception letter with a second class stamp, plus a book of prison information. They also get an advance of tobacco and a phone card and one free reception call which they've got to use after 6 p.m. as it's cheaper then. First of all they go into a room where we give them a verbal explanation of the procedure. We explain things like their wages, the fire alarm drill and so on. Then the doctor fits them for work on Labour One, Two or Three.[31] Then the chaplain comes in and talks about the religious services on offer. Then we have the Reception Board consisting of an officer and a probation officer. The officer sorts out the legal side and will talk about outstanding fines, further charges, the possibility of an appeal, time spent in custody, days knocked off and special diets. The probation officer sorts out the social side and will ask about childcare, accommodation, social problems. Then we explain the induction programme to them. They'll be watching videos on Aids, drugs, the prison itself and a fire video. Until a month ago we were also doing one-day courses, for instance on the dangers of stereotyping. But the women weren't getting much out of it because there was too much disturbance.

Disturbance there certainly was. This explanation was interrupted at least ten times as women knocked on the door of the induction office with questions ranging from requests for shampoo sachets (doled out incongruously from an office filing cabinet drawer) to enquiries about whether cash had arrived from previous prisons (delays in transferring money had caused serious problems for many women I interviewed). My officer interviewee and his young female colleague replied with the kind of banter reminiscent of a girls' boarding school: 'Oh no, not you again!' (The officer was in her twenties, the prisoner over 50). 'If I've told you once I've told you a dozen times—nothing's come through yet!'

'It's like that the whole time we're in here', the officer complained. 'It's like a treadmill. We've got eight induction officers and we take it in turns. You do get used to it because the questions are always the same.'

Even the best-designed programmes are only as good as those who implement them. A prisoner on this same induction wing told me later, 'When I first got to the office to ask something they shouted at me to get out. If they tell you anything it's all in quick garbled answers and they all tell you different things. If they'd give us respect they'd get it back. The young officers are the worst.'

Other women reported being bombarded with too much information on the first day when they were too shocked or disorientated to take it in. They described the videos as irrelevant: they were too generalised. 'What we wanted was information about what goes on in this prison, not advice about Aids.' One said she was terrified by rumours about intimidation and bullying by other prisoners, especially as there were no locks on the doors of the induction wing which was next to the lifers' block. The theory of an induction wing is to keep all newcomers together and prepare them before they go on normal location. But one women was so scared she pushed the wardrobe in front of the door every night that first week.

Zara, the induction wing orderly in this prison, feels that new prisoners are confused by the mass of information thrown at them. She says more practical help is needed, and agrees that other prisoners should be trained to introduce newcomers to the ways of the prison. She was pleased to have been invited to have some input into a new information leaflet: 'I said you must ensure that it's easily understandable because a lot of women coming in here are lacking in literacy skills. So you need three levels of literacy for the leaflet—low, medium and high. It's no good pitching it in the middle—they tend to talk to us all at the middle level.' It is obviously vital that any literature should also be available in the native language of non-English speakers, and that interpreters are available to help. The Inspectorate report suggested adding audio-taped and video-taped materials.[32] These issues are further discussed in *Chapter 10*.

At one of the closed prisons I visited, the induction process had almost ground to a halt because of staff shortages. Women serving longer sentences, including life imprisonment, come to this prison for the first stage of their sentences. The induction officer showed me a wall chart setting out the full induction programme the women should be receiving. On paper it looked good. There were timetabled briefing sessions on health, education, PE, religion, probation, the library, women's centre, access to the Samaritans and the Board of Visitors. The officer was pessimistic: 'The women should have one week on this wing but even that's not always possible. The idea is they should sort out any problems and if the unit was run properly they'd have the full programme and see all the people on this list. But we are not properly staffed so they can't'. The duty governor later confirmed that this induction wing was the first to be closed down if the prison was short of staff: in that case newly arrived prisoners were put straight on to normal location.

Sheila, a wing cleaner on the induction wing, had almost completed her week there: 'I've seen probation and the priest and had a tour of the prison but that's about it. I'm still waiting to see what's available in education. The only good thing about being on this wing is you can ring out when you want as long as you've got enough phone cards. At least I've been able to sort a few things out myself.'

Most women want to be enabled to sort out their own problems. Many expressed their profound frustration, once they emerged from the first shock of imprisonment, at being unable to take hold of the reins of their lives again. One woman I interviewed was still on remand for killing her male partner: she had spent months in a state of shock in the hospital wing, and now felt she should be given some responsibility for her own destiny: 'Even now, six months after I got here, I feel I am totally out of control. I would like to change my lawyer and if I'd been outside I'd have been doing all this myself. I'd have the ability to pick up a phone.'

The Inspectorate review underlined the statutory rights of remand prisoners to be given help in obtaining legal aid, and of convicted prisoners to apply for leave to appeal. The same applies to applications for bail, and the inspectors emphasised the importance of prisons setting up staffed legal aid and bail offices provided with telephones, especially as women prisoners are usually held far away from the courts where they were dealt with, and from their own solicitors. These bail units are said to be working very successfully at Holloway and Eastwood Park: trained staff collect information from the women which often results in their being bailed. Apart from the obvious advantage of relieving pressure on women's prisons, this has enormous implications for the women and their families.

Christine, one of the three probation officers in a closed prison, emphasises the importance of giving women back some responsibility:

On practical issues we try to empower the women to do things themselves. They can have special letters[33] to write—there's no limit to the number we can give them. But I must admit I'll sometimes just hand over the phone to a woman. We're not supposed to but it's so ridiculous to have a woman sitting next to you and to have to relay everything to her, then relay her answers back, so I'll often say, "Oh, for God's sake—just speak to her yourself!" We don't have quite such problems here as they do at remand prisons because some things will have been sorted out there before the women get here. But there are still terrible ongoing difficulties. We liaise with the family, with social services, with housing departments.

One of us sees every woman that comes in and we play up issues about how to keep their accommodation and so on. Though there are some things neither we nor the women can do anything about. If a woman loses her house because of being sent to prison and has nowhere to live on release, she can't possibly hope to go straight. The new rules on housing benefit have caused *chronic* problems.[34] I did some research monitoring the first three months of the new regulations and found that 15 of our women and 33 of their children became homeless at a direct result. This is outrageous.

Other probation officers confirmed that because single mothers' homes are in their own names they are more likely to lose them and, as one emphasised, 'we must not forget it is the children's home as well: one of our women has seven children split up in three different locations.' Imprisoned mothers whose homes have been lost in this way often have to agree for their children to go into care. Another probation officer said, 'Women are destroyed when the children go into care: so often it recalls memories of their own childhood in care, where so many of them were abused.'

Endnotes

1. HM Inspectorate, in their thematic review *Women in Prison: A Review*, July 1997, referred to the shared escorting of male and female prisoners in the same vans, but I did not come across this in my own research.
2. HMPs Holloway, Risley (Cheshire), New Hall (West Yorkshire), Low Newton (Durham), Brockhill (Worcestershire) and Eastwood Park (Gloucestershire).
3. The rest of the prisons are: Askham Grange (Yorkshire), Bullwood Hall (Essex), Cookham Wood (Kent), Drake Hall (Staffordshire), East Sutton Park (Kent), Styal (Cheshire), Durham, Winchester, Highpoint (Suffolk), Foston Hall (Derbyshire). See *Epilogue* for new women's prisons created in 1998 to 1999.
4. See 'Wayward Sisters', Lucia Zedner, in *The Oxford History of the Prison*, Oxford University Press, 1995.
5. It was so described by David Jessel, *Trial and Error*, Channel Four/Headline Book Publishing, 1994, p.161.
6. Though at Durham officers from the male prison are often sent on duty in the female H wing, without any training for working with women prisoners.
7. Male prisoners are placed in one of four security categories, A, B, C or D, and allocated to prisons according to the nature of their offence. Women are categorised simply for open or closed conditions apart from a few women designated as category A. The current categories were defined in the Mountbatten Report (1966). The definition of category A prisoners is as follows: 'Prisoners whose escape would be highly dangerous to the public, to the police or the security of the state, no matter how unlikely that escape might be; and for whom the aim must be to make escape impossible'. At the time of writing, there are only a few category A women prisoners. In their thematic review (1997) the inspectors advised against further categorisation of women: 'Allocation should be based on issues including health care, proximity to home, facilities for children, work or educational opportunities, and access to counselling'.
8. 'On the ghost train' or 'being ghosted' means being spirited away to another prison, often without warning, sometimes as a disciplinary measure but often for pragmatic operational reasons.
9. A report on women prisoners commissioned in 1995 by the Home Office found that more than half had not expected a prison sentence: *Managing the Needs of Female Prisoners*, Allison Morris *et al*.
10. By the time I interviewed her, Cathy had been transferred to an open prison. The Inspectorate recommended that a free phone card be given to every new prisoner on reception and access to a telephone to deal with urgent personal affairs outside prison.
11. 'Crutching' is prison slang for hiding contraband goods like drugs or money inside the vagina.
12. Under the Incentives and Earned Privileges Scheme (IEPS) introduced in 1995, prison regimes are divided into Basic, Standard and Enhanced levels, and prisoners move from one to the other according to their behaviour. Those on a Basic regime are allowed to spend only £2.50 a week

and their visits and phonecalls are severely limited. Some women's prisons house Basic regime prisoners on the bottom landing, known as the Ones.

13. Phone card units: phone cards are used as a form of currency in prison.
14. The canteen is the prison shop; the word also refers to purchases made there.
15. Private cash sent into prison by relatives or friends. A certain sum is allowed to prisoners each week for small purchases from the prison shop, such as cigarettes, snacks, phone cards, batteries and toiletries.
16. Every new prisoner is allowed one free phone call, usually within 24 hours of arriving in the prison. See note 10 above.
17. *Asylums*, Erving Goffman, first published by Penguin in 1961.
18. Dr Enda Dooley, a consultant psychiatrist at Broadmoor special hospital, who examined the suicides in prisons between the years 1972 and 1987 found that: 17% (51) of the suicides occurred within one week of reception into prison; 28% (84) within one month; 50% (151) within three months; and 77% (227) occurred within one year of custody. Quoted in Howard League 'Fact Sheet' No. 19, *Suicide and Self Injury in Prisons*.
19. *Caring for the Suicidal in Custody* was a statement of the Prison Service's new policy published in 1994 in response to two earlier documents: a report by Judge Tumim, then HM Chief Inspector of Prisons, 1990; and a research report published by the Institute of Criminology, Cambridge University, 1993.
20. Prisons ban lending or borrowing on the grounds that some prisoners might 'tax' or intimidate others for goods.
21. See above Note 1: Executive Summary 24, 27.
22. *Panorama*, BBC TV, 20 January 1997.
23. The *National Prison Survey 1991* (HMSO, 1992) found that 47% of women prisoners had dependent children living with them just before they were taken into prison. In my sample 51% (77 out of the 150 women) were in this situation.
24. Hilary must have been returned to court to be asked if she pleaded 'guilty' or 'not guilty'.
25. See Note 1 above: 11.01
26. I interviewed Alison in an open prison.
27. Movement of prisoners.
28. Each prisoner serving a sentence of 12 months or more, and all young offenders, in consultation with prisoner officers and probation officers, are obliged to plan their sentence with a view to ensuring they make the best use of their time in custody.
29. See above Note 1: 5.26.
30. See above Note 1: 5:30.
31. Classification of work prisoners are judged to be capable of. Labour 1 is any kind of work, however heavy. Labour 3 is the lightest, thought suitable, e.g. for pregnant prisoners
32. See Note 1 above: 6.18.
33. These are letters which a prisoner is allowed to write free of charge to professionals, e.g. legal advisers.
34. The Housing Benefit, Council Tax Benefit and Income Support (Amendments) Regulations 1995 ended the previous practice of using housing benefit to meet rent payments of convicted prisoners serving up to a year in custody. The change applied in respect of new prisoners entering prison from April 1995 onwards. The regulations limited to a maximum of 13 weeks the time for which housing benefit can be paid in respect of an empty property from which a sentenced prisoner is temporarily absent. Under the previous regulations, prisoners serving sentences of up to two years were eligible for assistance. Under the changed system, assistance is now confined to prisoners serving sentences of up to six months who receive conditional discharge subject to good behaviour after 13 weeks in custody. These changes were bound to increase homelessness among released prisoners by causing a substantial number of prisoners to lose their homes during periods in prison of between 13 and 52 weeks. A report, *Housing Benefit and Prisoners*, Penal Affairs Consortium, November 1996, estimates that 5,000 additional prisoners could be released homeless each year as a result of this change. Women prisoners are disproportionately affected because they are likely to be given short sentences.

CHAPTER THREE

Mums Inside

They should never put women like me in prison. I've got little kids. I'm not selling drugs and I'm not a desperate woman that's a danger to the public.

Bernadette, aged 27, six months for DSS fraud

Now and then a news story revives interest in the debate about whether pregnant women or those with young children should be sent to prison at all. In September 1997, a pregnant teenager, jailed for stealing four shirts from Marks & Spencer, provoked such a public outcry when a Gloucester judge ruled she should be separated from her child at birth that the ruling was rapidly quashed.

At emotive times like Christmas the media are keen to print stories about mothers facing the festive season behind bars. At such times the spotlight will be on the woman's mothering role rather than the nature of her crime. When in December 1996 Debbie Smith was sent to prison for nine months for attacking her estranged husband's girlfriend with a stiletto heeled shoe, the *Daily Express* ran a campaign for her release, with pictures of her three young children over the caption 'Please Set Mummy Free for Christmas'. When the Court of Appeal released her one week later, Lord Justice Beldam praised her as 'a hard-working mother and good wife' and an *Express* leading article rejoiced that for this act of seasonal charity he would be 'even more popular than Santa.'

Cases like Debbie's are a source of constant irritation to feminist commentators. They condemn stereotyping remarks by judges who send women away with a rap over the knuckles for their misdemeanours, announcing that they are showing them mercy and putting them on probation because they are 'good' wives and mothers.

Since the 1960s, criminological studies have dealt extensively with the issue of the stereotyping of women at all stages of what has been described as 'a patriarchal criminal justice system'. Some have focused specifically on motherhood and its place in sentencing logic, with feminist criminologists taking the view that by dealing leniently (or more accurately, *claiming* to deal leniently, because sentencing is said to be erratic and to depend on the whim of the courts) with women who are—or try to be—'good mothers', the system is prejudicial to those women who are deemed 'bad mothers' or who are not mothers at all.[1]

On the other hand, the Howard League for Penal Reform has long campaigned against mothers of young children being sent to jail, except in the rare cases of high risk women, and then only as a very last resort. In support, they have shifted the focus from the mother to the child, citing the UN Convention on the Rights of the Child which says that the best interests of the child should be paramount. In a 1995 report the League stated: 'The psychological, emotional and material damage done to these women's children, and subsequently to society, surely outweighs any perceived benefit enjoyed by the state when imprisoning mothers'.[2]

Nearly all the prison officers I spoke to said that the fact that women are mothers should not affect the decision of the courts whether or not to impose a custodial sentence: that decision should be determined solely by the nature of the offence. The views expressed by one principal officer were typical:

I know women have children but men have children too. A woman knows she is breaking the law and that crime shouldn't be taking place. Lots of men have a bond with their children too. I know a lot of women's crime starts with need not greed. Women "plead the kids" as a case for not coming into prison. But I see no difference between women and men. If women did the crime they must do the time even if they did the crime for money for the kids.

Many officers however deplored the jailing of women, whether they were mothers or not, for 'economic' offences like fine default. Prison officer Doris Briggs, quoted in *Chapter 1*, makes every effort to get immediate bail for fine defaulters with young children. She regularly contacts the Wise brothers, lawyers Ian and Richard, who have established a formidable reputation for getting bail for women remanded in custody for minor offences. Quite aside from the obvious humanitarian implications, this also makes good economic sense. As a governor grade at a remand prison said 'Of course we'd rather a woman like that was bailed. Apart from helping her it saves us a fortune in escorts.'

Probation officers were more likely than prison officers to feel that courts should consider the ripple effects of sending mothers of young children to jail, and should be prepared to look at alternatives to custody. The moral debate may never be resolved, but it can at least become a more informed debate by considering the reality of imprisonment for the mothers of dependent children and its effect on the children themselves.

The last chapter looked at the shock of being sent to prison, especially for women who are there for the first time,[3] and particularly for those[4] who did not expect a custodial sentence. For any woman the

44

emotional damage is devastating, but for a woman with children left at home, the suddenness and speed of the operation causes enormous problems.

Bernadette, the prisoner quoted at the beginning of this chapter, is a pale, thin Irish woman with children aged nine, eight, five and two. She was grim and bitter as she described her experience:

> It never occurred to me I'd go to prison. I'd left my two year old with my friend to come to court and the others were all at school. When I was sentenced I had no chance to make any arrangements for them. The fucking judge—God forgive me—he knew I had little kids, but I was shipped straight to Holloway. You can't even make a phone call to your kids. I never even kissed my kids goodbye because I thought I was coming back, and now they've been without me for six months. For three weeks my kids kept asking to see me, crying for me. My sister had to manage the four of them, and she's got five kids of her own.

As with any woman absent from her children for whatever reason, childcare will be the immediate concern of an imprisoned mother, and it can be a major problem. The *National Prison Survey*[5] found that almost half (47 per cent) of women prisoners had dependent children living with them when they were taken into prison, compared with 32 per cent of men. The difference of 15 per cent seems at first fairly small but the statistics mask the nature of the problem for women. The survey also showed that 91 per cent of the fathers in prison leave their children in the care of the child's mother or another female partner, while only 23 per cent of the mothers in prison said that the child's father or another male partner was performing the same role.

A further study of mothers in prison was conducted in November 1994 by the Home Office Research and Planning Unit. Of the 1766 women interviewed, 43 per cent had dependent children.[6]

HM Inspectorate's 1997 review of women's prisons[7] found even higher rates, with two-thirds of its sample having at least one child under the age of 16.

My own sample of 150 women prisoners showed a similar pattern to that in the national survey. Just over half (51 per cent: 77 women) had dependent children living with them when they came into prison. The total number of dependent children left behind at home was 171.

Who was caring for the children? In my sample only 27 per cent—21 women—said the father of the child or another male partner was looking after them. This corresponds closely with the figure in the National Survey (23 per cent) and with the Inspectorate's findings (25 per cent). Nearly half, 32 women (42 per cent), said they relied on other family members (52 per cent said the same in the *National Prison Survey*). The prisoner's mother or sister usually filled the caring role, though I was amazed at the stories of dedication I heard from the seven per cent of women who had female friends committed enough to undertake the very demanding task of looking after their children, sometimes for many years, and often alongside their own young children.

When no family or friends could be found, some form of temporary care or fostering arrangements had to be made, and there were women whose children had been adopted. Only about one seventh—14 per cent—of the mothers in my sample had had such arrangements made for them, perhaps unsurprisingly, considering that most women are serving short sentences. In the *National Prison Survey*, ten per cent of female prisoners had dependent children living in foster care, compared with just one per cent of male prisoners. The authors of the survey draw the perhaps predictable conclusion from these figures that 'there is greater disruption to family life when mothers are imprisoned than when fathers are'.

Leaving the children with a known and trusted carer is of course a woman's primary concern. Charley, a prostitute, was sent to prison for non-payment of fines. The judge showed little sympathy: there were no words of praise for Charley like those of Lord Justice Beldam for Debbie Smith:

> I've got a little boy of two and I really miss him. His dad's from Jamaica and he's in prison as well. The judge didn't seem to care what happened to my baby. He was very sarcastic and asked who was looking after him when I was on the game! Well—I was looking after him myself or I'd have a close friend in. Just because you're a prostitute those judges think you'd leave your kids with anybody. I was very careful indeed who I left him with. I had a really good friend who loved him.

Not all women are lucky enough to find such support. Many without family or close friends have to allow temporary custody to the children's fathers or other men—men they may despise and who may in the past have abused them. Margaret got into debt and joined her female neighbour to burgle antiques. She was given a six year sentence: 'My whole world is falling apart. I've got three kids—a boy of 13, another of five and a girl of four. They're with my husband and I hardly see them at all now. He's sleeping with my sister and he's started divorce proceedings. He won't bring them to see me. I pleaded guilty but the judge just said "Six years, take her down!"'

Adrienne had a daughter by a married man who obsessed her for seven years and who had abandoned her again and again as she suffered a series of miscarriages. She was serving a five year sentence for threatening to kill her lover's wife, whom she accused of ill-treating the baby. By a strange quirk of fate, the lover and his wife were now caring for the child:

> Kelly was three when I came in here and she had to go to her dad and that wife of his. It's not good but it's better for her than being in care. I won custody of Kelly. The judge said her father was the reason I was in prison and so he gave me custody. Her father wants me to mess up in here so I won't get my parole and then I won't get Kelly. He wants her himself.

As Bernadette's story quoted earlier shows, it is often the *manner* of the separation that is so devastating. There is now general consensus among childcare experts that children cope much better with a period of separation from their parents (if, for example, either parent or child has to spend time in hospital) if there is careful preparation and the child is told the true situation well in advance. Few imprisoned mothers will have had time for any such preparation. Their shame leads many to try to conceal the fact that they are in prison, but children often discover the truth and their trust and confidence is further undermined.

An experienced prison education coordinator felt that much of the trauma could be avoided by more careful planning:

> Taking the mother out is cruel without a key meeting first to decide what should happen to the children. This should be set up *before* the woman comes into prison on remand. The authorities will have a problem with this because they'll say, "She may walk [be released] so it's not worth going to all that trouble." But think of the damage done to the family when the mother is suddenly removed from them.

Many problems could be solved by a short period of home leave soon after a woman begins a custodial sentence, so she can see for herself that her children are well cared for. This used to happen before tougher security rules designed for men were applied also to women. Claire was jailed for seven months for selling a small quantity of drugs. At first a girlfriend agreed to look after Sam, her eight-year-old son, but after a few weeks the friend felt unable to cope, and Claire was forced to call in an ex-boyfriend: 'He had been violent to me in the past though he'd always been OK with Sam. But still, I wanted to check him out.' Luckily Claire was sentenced quite quickly and was allowed two short periods of home leave, now known as temporary release: 'I went home and saw that Sam was fine, and I managed to sort out my child benefits and everything. You could stay out two or three days and they gave you a travel warrant to get home and back again.'

The problem is that the vast majority of imprisoned women are remand prisoners and such a sensible arrangement would not be available to them: remand prisoners are automatically classed as category B and cannot be risk-assessed until they have been sentenced. Ironically, in view of the fact that women are much more likely than men to be primary carers of children and elderly relatives, women have always been disproportionately disadvantaged by the rules on home leave (temporary release), because most women are in prison for a very short time. Only 29 per cent of women remanded into custody in 1994 subsequently re-entered prison as sentenced prisoners, compared with 44 per cent of men on remand. Home Office figures[8] show that nearly three-quarters (71 per cent) of these remand prisoners were acquitted, given non-custodial sentences or that the case was not proceeded with. In Holloway, for example, nearly half of the women are remand prisoners, and 60 per cent of prisoners in Holloway serve an average of 28 days in prison.[9] The disruption caused to families, especially to very young children, by even a short sentence should not be underestimated. Courts could perhaps be asked to consider 'fast-tracking' the cases of women with pressing family commitments.

Sentenced women's access to their children has been adversely affected by changes in the rules on temporary release which came into force in April 1995[10] as a result of tighter security following the escapes of male prisoners from HMP Parkhurst and HMP Whitemoor, and the recommendations of the Learmont and Woodcock Reports on these incidents. The new regulations replaced the old home leave and temporary release systems. The revised system, known as 'release on temporary licence', allows three new types of licence: compassionate licence, facility licence and resettlement licence. Any form of release on temporary licence is a privilege and requires a prisoner to pass a risk assessment before being approved. Compassionate licence is the kind most likely to be helpful to imprisoned women because the rules state that one of the criteria under which it will apply may be childcare: 'If you are a primary carer, that is a prisoner who, on release, will have *sole* responsibility for caring for a child under 16 or an elderly and infirm or seriously disabled close relative'.[11]

Some prisons do try their best to interpret the rules to the prisoners' advantage. Joan is 40. She and her girlfriend Rachel are in the same open prison, jointly accused and sentenced together for social security fraud. Joan is registered disabled and the women were convicted of making false claims for transport costs to and from the swimming baths where Joan took therapeutic exercise for an industrial injury which left her unemployed. Together they care for Rachel's five children, aged seven to 15. Joan described what happened when both women were sent straight to prison:

> One day Rachel and I were at home looking after five kids, then the next day we found ourselves in prison with the kids left at home. We were in the middle of decorating and the place was in an awful mess. But the prison leaned over backwards to get me an overnight so I could go home and sort things out and I got a compassionate overnight soon after we got here.

> There are things only *you* can sort out if you've got kids. Like there's things that only *you* can sign, so they can get some money to live on. If only I could have gone into town and got money out to send them. But I was only allowed to go home. Some people can't even get home, and the kids need things like shoes. Kids want something different each week. I'm only half an hour from home here but it's so frustrating because you're so near and yet so far if you can't get out to do anything for the kids. When I did get my overnight compassionate and went down my road at home I felt terrible—I thought everyone was looking at me because I was in prison. But it was worth it for the kids.

Ellen is in the same prison as Joan and Rachel, but prison staff were powerless to help her: she cannot be classed as a primary carer because her three sons are all adults. But the youngest, aged 20, was discovered to have Hodgkin's disease, a potentially fatal form of cancer, soon after she began a five year sentence for conspiracy to murder her violently abusive husband, the boys' step-father:

> The changes in the rules on temporary release did have an effect on me. When I first came here at the end of 1994 there was the expectation that I'd be able to go home to see my sons. After three weeks under the old system I could have gone on town visits every week and every fourth weekend I could have gone home. But they started the new rule just one week before I came here and now I'm waiting to be risk-assessed.

Few mothers suddenly stop worrying about their children when they reach the age of 16, but Prison Service rules assume that they do. As Ellen says sadly, 'I'm not sure that I could get compassionate leave. You don't get that unless your kids are under 16.'

The new rules are as unpopular with most staff as they are with prisoners, especially in open prisons. As the governor of one open prison told me:

> Under the old system, if a woman had been here six weeks she could go out on an overnight visit once a month. This was the philosophy of an open

prison and was an attempt to overcome the distance away from home for some women. Now that has been stopped. Temporary release is now tied into IEPS[12] and we now have what are called 'earned community visits' where a woman can go within a 20 mile radius of the prison and of course, those lucky enough to live within that radius can go home and see their children. But for others the problem remains that the families still have to travel long distances in order to take the woman out. We get a lot of disappointed women coming to us, because they will have equated open conditions with permission for temporary release and this is a wrong equation. It means that some women come here with unrealistic expectations and this can lead to disappointment and anger because by no means all of them will have a successful risk assessment.

The governor's views were confirmed by a prisoner at another open prison, who sees at closer quarters the effect on women's behaviour:

Women coming here from a closed prison have to be risk-assessed and this can take up to nine weeks. People come here under the impression that they will get out to see their kids in a matter of days. Their hopes are built up before they come, then they are dashed and this causes terrible mood swings and disappointment and even drives some of them back onto drugs.

Even for those women who are bailed after arrest, the final parting when it comes is inevitably painful. Lorraine was jailed for two and a half years for importing amphetamines from Amsterdam. She says she thought the parcel she was given contained Rolex watches. When she came into prison her four children were aged six, 12, 15 and 17:

I was out for eight months on bail and I went through hell because although it did give me time to make arrangements for my kids, prison was always hanging over us all. The kids knew I was going to have to go away and the waiting had a very bad effect on both me and them. When I had to tell them, my eldest boy, the 17 year old, went mental. It was all, "Why didn't you think of us?" and so on. I tried to explain that I was doing it for them.

Lorraine was of course grateful when the prison arranged for her to spend a week at home after she had served half her sentence. In practical terms she managed to sort out a lot of problems, but emotionally it felt like a mixed blessing:

I found that very traumatic. By the time I'd settled it was time to go and it really upset me and the kids. The first night I was home I wanted to cook the dinner for the kids and I couldn't do it. The meat was tough and the gravy went all lumpy. I'd forgotten how to cook! You know how it is — it starts off with a real celebration—Mum's home. Then after two days it's back to normal: "Mum—tell him, he's hitting me!" Then you have to go away again and everybody's crying. You tell them it won't be long now but that's not much help when you know you've got half your sentence still to do.

Most women's worries about their children are both practical and emotional. One life-sentenced prisoner with an 18 year tariff summed up the feelings of many:

I worry a lot about my children and my home: my house is giving problems with the hot water and there's no heating. Women in prison are always worried about their children. As long as they have clothes and food we're all right, but if we hear they are sick or anything we all get very emotional because we want to be with them and we feel so helpless. This time of year [Christmas] we're all very sensitive. The screws just don't realise the pressure we're under.

Debt is another worry constantly assailing many imprisoned women. Debts may have been the reason for their initial offence, and will have been mounting up in their absence. For some women beleaguered by money worries, prison may even have come as a welcome respite from the loan shark and the bailiff. But as release approaches the worries begin to close in again. Bernadette, quoted at the start of this chapter, was to be released the day after I interviewed her. Her sense of panic was palpable:

I've got bills up to my eyeballs, the electric's been cut off and when I get home tomorrow I've got to get the kids back to school—they've not gone to school since I've been in prison. And I'll have to manage all on my own because Liam's got three more months to go in the Scrubs. He's never done anything bad before. He's a trained chef but it's very hard for the Irish to get work in the London restaurants. They can get jobs as waiters but the money's scabby.

Such fear, recrimination and resentment serve only to deepen the guilt of women who may already hold themselves in very low esteem. Whatever the length of their sentence, none of the women I spoke to reported getting any advice on the best way of limiting the damage for their children. Nicki, serving life for murder, has sons aged six and seven: 'I keep telling them it'll be a long, long time I'll be in here. They should give you advice on how to tell your kids about a long sentence— but the only person that could do that is someone who's done a prison sentence and come out the other end.'

Few mothers, even those who have never set foot inside a prison, escape a sense of guilt and failure at some point in the child-rearing process. The women I spoke to were desperate to make up to their children for their absence. Deirdre has a five-year-old daughter. She was at the end of a five month sentence for pension book fraud: 'I did it to survive. I haven't got a big posh house or anything but while I was doing it the cupboards were full and it was nice to have those things. My little girl, she's two, she's with my sister and when I get out I'm going to do two things—put my house in order and spend some time with her to make up for the time I've missed.'

Many recorded sadness and guilt at missing landmarks in their children's lives. 'I felt so bad,' said one, 'because I missed Jordan's first day at school. He's changed so drastically since I came in here.'

For imprisoned women this sense of emotional failure is exacerbated by the inability to offer their children even the most basic level of practical day-to-day care. Most women I interviewed were wracked by frustration and anger because they could not deal with urgent matters for their children and were every day reminded of the ripple effect on the whole family of their being in prison. As one woman put it: 'It's really terrible being inside if you've got kids. It's so difficult to get things done by letter and you can't make enough phonecalls to arrange things. You have to put in apps[13] for everything and you have to do it so far in advance.' Often these are women who, despite their desperate home circumstances, have managed to keep hold of the family reins, and they feel a terrible sadness and anger at losing control.

Prison-based probation officers try to help women with their practical problems. As one of them explained:

> Childcare issues are now one of our priority targets. Women make private fostering arrangements and some have gone for adoption. Then there are all the practical problems. I have come in each morning to find a pile of apps varying from "Can you fix for my child to have a new pair of shoes?" to "Please can you make sure the hole in my roof is mended?" These days all this should come through the personal officer though the first port of call should be the wing officer. Then the officers decide if they can cover it and if not they pass it on to us. In practice we do a lot of this stuff because the officers are so overworked. If the issue is the safety of a child they will always come and see me. The officers won't bother ringing us about the new shoes but they realise we will move in on the heavier issues.

Overcrowding means that valuable opportunities are being lost for officers to build up positive relationships with women while helping them with these practical matters. But of course the best solution is to give women the means of solving their own problems themselves.

Some probation staff recognise this: as one probation officer said: 'If there are childcare hearings I try to get the woman permission to attend. She should be able to go out on compassionate leave and she may have to have an escort.' But the new rules on temporary release are in danger of reducing imprisoned women's effectiveness as participants in custody hearings.

A former governor with long experience of women's prisons described what happens:

> The women won't go to these custody hearings from some prisons now because they have to go handcuffed to two officers. This they feel — probably rightly — would give a very bad impression to the panel hearing the case. They are scared by the panel anyway: they are often not all that articulate and they feel they couldn't possibly win custody of their children because of the image they present, handcuffed to two officers. It is the job of the panel to decide on some arrangement in the best interests of the child and they are not about to give custody to a woman they are bound to regard as potentially dangerous because she *looks* dangerous, *handcuffed to two officers.* Temporary release to attend child custody hearings is vital under the terms of the Children Act and I used to send an "accompanying officer" who was not a security escort, but often the woman's personal officer. It meant that in traumatic circumstances, especially if the hearing went against her, she had someone to support her, instead of turning to drugs or alcohol or absconding. You were giving these women responsibility for their own actions and the women were making a conscious decision to behave properly.

HM inspectors acknowledge such concerns and recommend that handcuffing is only used for women prisoners in exceptional cases.[14]

Some of the saddest conversations I had were with women who had lost custody of their children, or had had them taken into care or sent for adoption. Annette, quoted in *Chapter 2*, killed her common-law husband ten years ago and is reaching the end of a life sentence. Her children were aged three and five when she came into prison and are now 13 and 15. She decided early on that they should be adopted and though her face clouds over when she speaks of them, she does not regret her decision: 'At first they were in temporary foster care as my solicitor advised, but that meant they were moving all round the place. So I decided to sign their adoption papers so they could get settled. When I first came into prison I had quite a lot of visits from them with their adoptive parents. Then I told them not to leave me their address. It's not fair on them.'

Women prisoners have traditionally had a reputation for behaving badly in prison and the figures show that they are twice as likely as men to be punished for breaking the 'GOAD'—good order and discipline—rules of the prison. Theories for the reason for this abound—from the infantilising disciplinary regimes imposed upon them, through the ubiquitous pre-menstrual tension and other 'hormonal' explanations, to sexual jealousy and 'the natural stroppiness of women'. These are discussed in more detail in *Chapter 5*. One of the more plausible theses was put forward by an experienced female prison governor: for the average working man, she says, prison life replicates to some extent his daily life outside prison, with meals on the table, a regulated workplace, a game of pool with mates and TV in the evening. But for imprisoned women with families, life outside is very different. However straitened their circumstances, they usually have some autonomy, some sort of management of their children and the running of the home: 'Their lives are made up of multiple choices: it's the woman who decides what the kids will wear, what they eat. It's often said that men leave their home problems at the prison gate, do their bird, then go home. It's *never* like that for women.' For women prisoners the institutional regimes that replace their pre-prison existence are totally unfamiliar and disempowering.

Perhaps this theory paints too rosy a portrait of the family life of many women, but for those with children the reasons for anger and stress within prison are at least easier to identify.

A senior officer who has worked in both male and female prisons gave her views succinctly:

> There's a lot of women still running the home from inside prison. All men care about is their baccy, their meals and whether they're top dog in the prison. But the women are still running the home and I've see women in here [an open prison] write shopping lists every week to give their fellas when they come so they get the right food and things for the kids.

Most prisoners agreed. One, a mother of four children, said:

> A major problem is that so many of the women are mothers. Women are usually the backbone of the family and when they are gone their partners and their children are very much affected. They can do their bird OK but when things are going wrong outside and they can't be there to deal with it, that's when they get very depressed. That's why their moods change so dramatically. They might be OK one day, then the next day they might be in a stinking mood because they've heard something has happened at home and their hands are tied.

A female education coordinator described graphically how impossible it is for women to be able to take advantage of any form of positive prison regime—to concentrate on work, education or training, or even on 'getting their head round their sentences'—when they are being torn apart by the agony of speculation about their children's wellbeing:

> That's why I'll get a woman coming into the education department and slinging a chair across the room because she's just been taken out of class and told by a probation officer that her kids have been given to the grandparents. Her grandfather's abused her and she knows all this background that was hidden from the social workers — but the woman herself has never been consulted.

Understanding the effects of disempowerment and the resulting anger and frustration is important for prison officers. If they are given appropriate training, and if the personal officer scheme is working well, it should be easier for women to talk about the outside problems causing their current feelings, and for staff to be less likely to dismiss mood swings as 'hormones' or 'bloody-mindedness'. Most anger is caused by fear and cannot be defused unless the fear is understood.

Even those women who know their children are well looked-after at home may find it hard to hand over responsibility to other carers. I remember accompanying a family of young children to see their mother for an all-day children's visit. Working as an escort on a charity bus I was counted as a carer and allowed to take the children in to the visits room where the mothers were waiting. As 'my' children rushed up to their mother, I followed them and began to tell her how well they had behaved on the bus. The woman did not say a word either to me or to the children. She immediately picked up a hairbrush and set about vigorously brushing the eldest girl's hair and re-styling it in braids. It was as if she was re-establishing her authority and status in the family. Several women explained why, although they welcome all-day visits, they find them so difficult to handle: they feel torn between their desire to make the visit 'nice' and their need to reprimand the children if necessary to show they are still in charge.

A tiny percentage of imprisoned mothers are permitted to keep their babies with them in prison, though of course not all women want this arrangement and would rather families or friends cared for them as they care for older children. But this is not always possible. As one principal officer said: 'It's OK if a woman's sister or her auntie can take the child, but the sister may have five children of her own. The women don't want their children put in care because of the fear of never getting them back, specially if there are problems with accommodation and they lose their homes, as many women do when they come into prison.'

There have always been babies in prisons—Dickens' descriptions of debtors' prisons in novels like *Little Dorrit* show the incarceration of the whole family including servants and children. In the early mixed-sex convict prisons, women commonly took in their babies and infants and if they were pregnant were allowed to keep the new baby with them till the end of their sentences, though the children often died. In the 1850s there was dormitory provision at Brixton and Tothill Fields, the first prisons exclusively for women, for mothers to keep with them children under the age of two, and some stayed till the age of four. They wore prison uniform like their mothers and women working under the 'silent congregate' system were allowed to speak to their children, though they were banned from communicating with other women.[15]

The nineteenth century journalist Henry Mayhew was concerned about the effect on the children. He reported that in one prison he found 'one little thing that had been kept so long incarcerated that on going out of the prison it called a horse a cat.' There were always fears that children would be drawn into a criminal lifestyle and the Industrial Schools Act 1866 provided for the children of twice-convicted women to be removed to attend industrial schools. The Prevention of Crime Act 1871 applied this to mothers with just one conviction.[16]

Many present day reformers consider the imprisoning of mothers with small children to be a barbaric practice: the Royal College of Midwives has joined the Howard League in stating publicly that no pregnant woman or mother of a small child should be behind bars, with or without her baby.

Rule 9(3) of the Prison Rules 1964 states that: 'The Secretary of State may, subject to any conditions he thinks fit, permit a woman prisoner to have her baby with her in prison, and everything necessary for the baby's maintenance and care may be provided there.' There is similar provision in Rule 22 of the Young Offender Institution Rules 1988, though currently no separate female YOIs exist.

There are four prison mother and baby units—commonly known in the Prison Service as MBUs—one at an open prison (Askham Grange, near York), and three at closed prisons (New Hall, near Wakefield; Styal, near Manchester; and Holloway). At Holloway and New Hall the babies can stay until the age of nine months. At the other two units they can stay till 18 months. At the time of writing there are places for 68 babies.[17] Provisional Prison Service figures for 1996/7 show that 90 women were transferred to hospital for the delivery of a baby and 88 of these returned to custody following the birth—which means that 20 of those women would not find a space in an MBU if they wanted to keep the baby with them.

The criteria for entry as stated in the Prison Service booklet *Admission to Mother and Baby Units*[18] make it clear that the decision whether or not to allow a woman to keep her baby is 'made in the best interests of the child', but it will also very much depend on the behaviour and attitude of the mother. Schedule one offenders, convicted of offences against children, are excluded and HM inspectors emphasised in their review[19] that this policy should be 'watertight and consistent'.

But even this seemingly straightforward exclusion can mask tragic anomalies. At one prison a probation officer told me that a girl of 17 was unlikely to be accepted into an MBU with her baby because her offence was an attack on another girl of the same age. As the victim was a minor, technically this made the perpetrator (a minor herself) a Schedule one offender, likely not only to be separated from her baby but also possibly to be attacked by other prisoners who would suspect her of child abuse.

Once a woman is deemed suitable to enter an MBU, her local social services have agreed and her application has been accepted, she will have to sign a compact—Prison Service jargon for a contract—to agree to take responsibility for caring for her baby, to submit to regular random drug testing (all MBUs are classed as drug-free units), and to agree to having the baby searched from time to time (though this can only be done by a female officer in the presence of the mother).

Officers say that at first the MBU is regarded as 'a bit of a cushy number'. The rooms are more attractively furnished and on the face of it there is more freedom: it is never permitted for a prison to lock a baby in a cell so a woman's door will remain unlocked while the baby is in the room with her. But some women feel there is added pressure on them to conform to prison rules and to meet expectations. If a woman's behaviour or lack of care for her baby give cause for concern, she can be removed from the unit. On the rare occasions when this happens the prison arranges what is euphemistically termed an 'emergency handout' for the child to be cared for outside the prison.

Mothers in MBUs are also required to work in other parts of the prison during the day, except for a small number who are employed as nursery assistants and stay behind in a creche to care for their own and other women's children.

• • •

In the creche kitchen of one MBU, I meet Sherry preparing the babies' morning snacks. She is casually dressed in jeans and sweatshirt and carries Jake on her left hip as she mixes the food. Jake is a strapping ten month boy with a round face and red curly hair like his mother's. One by one the other mothers bring in their babies and strap them into high chairs. Sherry seems unfazed by their yells and feeds each one calmly as we speak:

> I had Jake two weeks before I came into prison. Everybody said they'd never send me to jail, but they did. I got two years for drugs offences and I'll have to serve half of it, so I'll be out just before his first birthday. When I first went into prison I lost him for a while because there were no places in any units. So my sister had to have him. But after three days I got into an MBU. They had to put me in a emergency room at first just so I could get back with Jake. Now I work part-time here in the creche but I'm doing an NVQ in the education department as well. I like being with Jake but it's important for me to get qualifications. Jake's dad's in prison too. I'm 28 and I've been a traveller since I was 16 but now it's time for me to settle down because I want Jake to go to school. Having Jake and coming into prison was a big turning point in my life.

The babies have all been fed and another prisoner takes over to change their nappies. Sherry takes a break to show me 'Jake's book'. All 14 of the babies in the creche have large albums to commemorate these first months of their lives. They are full of memories: photographs of tea parties, notes on the first smile, even tiny hand prints in reds, blues and yellows. 'I never knew you could do painting with a baby!' says Sherry.

Diane joins us. She is one of the three qualified NNEB nurses on the unit who have been contracted in by the prison from local social services. In the past, MBUs have been criticised for failing to employ qualified nursery staff, but now all the units are staffed by NNEB nurses:

> We try to provide what we can while the babies are in here, to make their lives as happy and full as possible for these first 18 months. If the mums see what we can provide, we hope they'll try to do the same sort of thing themselves when they leave prison. We want to try and give them the best start we can, even though their mothers mightn't be able to afford this kind of provision outside.

The women like Diane and they feel she understands some of their problems as she is herself a single mother with two small children. For Sherry, the good relationships between staff and women make all the difference. At her first prison MBU she was not so happy: 'The nannies were really bitchy and they were younger than me. They were always right and us mothers were always wrong. We weren't even allowed to pick the babies up when we wanted to. The women got no respect from the staff.'

Helping women care for their own children is always a minefield—especially if they are vulnerable incarcerated women who may have been damaged by their own childhood. Some very young women need special support: as HM inspectors said in their review, they are 'children looking after children'.[19] Some will already have several other children and will bitterly resent any hint of patronising by staff.

Mrs Burns is the manager of one MBU. Though a trained prison officer she deliberately chooses not to wear uniform. She is conscious of the sensitivity of the work:

> We try not to impose our own ideas of child-rearing on other people, specially women from a different culture. We're only strict on the child protection issues, like having your baby in bed with you at night which is forbidden for safety reasons. And we do come down hard on them if they try to prop-feed the baby, leaving a bottle propped up in the buggy or pram. We do frighten them a bit about the dangers of that sort of thing. If the women kept on doing it we'd bring a local health visitor in. The women like the health visitors because they don't feel threatened by them as they do by social services, because they have the power to take their children away.

One of the problems with child-rearing in a prison environment is ensuring that babies get enough stimulation. A recent Social Services Inspectorate report on another prison MBU recommended more stimulation both for the mothers and the babies. The prison took this on board and employed qualified nursery staff. The chaplain now arranges for women in the local community, often members of groups like the Mothers' Union, to take the babies out of the prison regularly, to the shops and the park. Now things are beginning to change in the unit: the new MBU manager is delighted:

> We see women learning to play with their babies and talk to them. The nursery officers are already seeing the difference in the way mothers interact with the babies. At first they couldn't understand why you would want to play on a tambourine to little babies, or talk to them. They were amazed at the idea of reading to them. But then we find if we walk past the unit a while later, the women will be playing the tambourine and reading and talking to their babies. This can happen even if the woman's had umpteen children before. Having a child can be a very powerful motivation in making a woman want to change her life.

When the new manager took over this unit she found 'a bad case of the goldfish bowl syndrome'. Perhaps because they are more accessible than other parts of the prison system, and because there is a natural curiosity about the effect of jail on the babies, MBUs tend to act as magnets for research studies by individuals and interested agencies: 'We had three different baby massage classes but no birth control advice—and we've got a woman of 26 in here with six children! So we rationalised the programme and now there are postnatal parenting classes, basic health care and yes, we still have *one* baby massage class! A local NHS health visitor runs a weekly clinic here, just as she does on the outside, which makes women feel more part of the local community'. Interestingly, research[20] has shown that babies reared in prison show no developmental differences from those raised in the community outside.

The case of the pregnant Irish prisoner Roisin McAliskey put prison mother and baby units in the limelight in March 1997, when, as a category A prisoner facing IRA bombing charges in Germany, she was initially forbidden to join the Holloway MBU. Another prisoner in Holloway at the same time described how the lights remained on in McAliskey's cell 24 hours a day, a security camera mounted on a roof outside was constantly trained on her window, and she was guarded day and night by two officers posted outside her door. She was not allowed association with other prisoners, and meals were brought to her in her cell. Other prisoners reported seeing her in a wheelchair: one of her legs was so swollen she could not stand and it was feared she risked thrombosis. It is not surprising that after her daughter's birth she suffered severe post-traumatic stress disorder and had to remain in the psychiatric unit of the Maudsley Hospital, too ill to attend any of the court hearings about her case. When she was finally told by Jack Straw she could go free, her solicitor Gareth Peirce said she was in such a weak mental state she was unable to take in the news.

Sadly, new security measures have extended into mother and baby units, even for low-risk prisoners. In one open prison mothers regularly used to take their babies to join a local playgroup in the nearest village. This has had to stop. The female deputy governor of this prison was one of the many staff who resented the application of the new measures to women's prisons:

The new rules have caused us great practical problems, especially on the MBU. What are the babies to be fed on? Some need baby milk and the jars of baby food once they are weaned. And the disposable nappies, how are the mothers supposed to get hold of them? All the mothers used to go into town for baby shopping[21] but now only those who have been risk-assessed can go. The new rules try to treat all prisoners as if they were at Parkhurst, and because the men were running rackets there, we are now told that prison officers can't do any shopping for women prisoners, though obviously mothers with babies are in an entirely different situation.

Even fluffy toys are banned for 'security reasons'. A charity called Babies in Prison gives funds for much of the equipment for prison MBUs and each year provides every baby with a Christmas present, but cuddly soft toys are gifts the charity's workers are unable to accept. BIP does other valuable work liaising with local groups so that babies can occasionally be allowed out of prison to meet other children. But the work goes largely unnoticed as the charity deliberately keeps its public profile very low. In our current punitive climate there are many who would wish to deny the children of imprisoned women a better start in life. There are prison officers who share this view. Some of the female officers at Styal felt the MBU mothers were 'spoiled': 'My children never had toys like these,' said one officer. Her colleague shared her disapproval: 'Prison is no place for babies. If a girl knew she'd lose her baby if she committed an offence maybe it would make her think twice.'

The time has to come when these babies must leave their mothers and however carefully the staff try to prepare them, most women find it a heartbreaking experience. Though one of the criteria for admission to a unit is a realistic expectation that mother and baby will soon be reunited, there have been cases where the mothers were serving longer sentences.

Dawn was given eight years for importing cocaine from the Caribbean, her first offence, carried out with a friend 'because I'd never been on a plane before and the idea sounded exciting.' She felt sick on the plane and discovered she was expecting a baby. She was three months pregnant when she was sentenced. Her daughter Corin was born in prison and stayed with her till she was 18 months old. When women have to hand out their babies they also leave the unit where they may have lived for many months and made close friends. The MBU manager sympathises: 'There's nothing worse than having to hand your baby out, and you can feel very isolated, but we do try to support them. Rachel used to be nursery assistant while her baby was here, so when she had to hand out the baby she lost her job and had to move to live on normal location in the main prison. She comes back to see us now and then and brings pictures of Corin to show us.'

Remand prisons like Risley have no facilities for women to keep their babies, and there is no mother and baby unit nearby that will take them: Styal only takes sentenced women. New Hall prison in Yorkshire has a mother and baby unit that would be suitable, but new mothers who are 'weekly remands' have to report to court and could not, for example, travel across the Pennines. Most women on remand are separated from their babies, though as the figures quoted earlier show, three-quarters of women remanded into custody are not finally given a custodial sentence.

A Risley officer described the trauma experienced by women whose babies have to be handed to social services immediately after the birth:

> One woman with a nine-week-old baby was sent to prison for stealing a Cabbage Patch doll. She was breastfeeding and when the baby was handed out of the prison to the carer it could not settle to the bottle and was becoming undernourished. Meanwhile here in the prison the mother had to express her breast milk and was in dreadful pain.

Prison reformers are now considering whether such a child could not in theory bring a test case against the Prison Service under the Children and Young Persons Act 1969 for the deprivation caused by separation from its mother during this vital bonding period.

Women deprived of contact with their babies in this way may be doubly disadvantaged by being sent to closed conditions though their sentences warrant only less secure open prisons. At one remand prison I sat in on a Risk Assessment Board where prison and probation officers were discussing whether a 17-year-old mother whose baby was with foster carers could be sent to an open prison. The principal officer was concerned: 'I think she'll do a runner: the baby was only born five months ago. She's in depression, the carers keep letting her down and not bringing the baby to see her. If she goes to open prison she'll abscond to be with the baby. We can't risk it'. HM Inspectors found[22] that the most common reason for women absconding was to resolve a domestic situation, often involving children.

The current climate in the USA is even more punitive than in this country, and there has been a five-fold increase in the number of women in American jails since 1980, from 12,000 in that year to nearly 65,000 in 1996. Between 75 per cent and 80 per cent of them have children under 18. Research has shown that these children are six times more likely than other children to end up incarcerated themselves.

Only two states, Nebraska and New York, allow any mothers to keep their babies in prison or to have regular intensive contact with them. But some interesting experiments are taking place there. At the Bedford Hills Correctional Facility, the only maximum security prison for women in New York State, children of imprisoned women are allowed one week each year at a summer camp run at the prison. Mothers spend all day, every day, with their children, who return to local host families each night. At the Nebraska Center in York, most mothers are allowed to keep their children with them up to the age of one, but some are allowed to have older children (boys up to nine, girls up to 12) staying with them in the prison for up to five nights each week. The programme, called 'Mother-Offspring Life Development', is justified by the warden on the grounds that it is best for the children. It also makes economic sense: to keep a child with its mother in prison costs $11,000 a year. To keep the same child in foster care costs $18,000.[23] Unfortunately the Center is becoming seriously overcrowded and now holds 50 more prisoners than it was designed for, with women three to a cell.

Other countries are also experimenting with similar schemes: in summer 1997 the Czech Republic drew up a Bill which would allow female prisoners to keep children up to three years old in special creche facilities in Prague's new Repy prison.

The female Regimes Manager of one open prison in this country has worked in the Prison Service for 27 years, and feels that similar programmes should be set up here:

> Babies are regarded as a problem in prison but I don't see any problems. I think young children should stay longer with their mothers. They should stay till they are five and ready to go to school. It's even better now we have male officers working in the women's prisons. Before that we found the babies used to cry when their fathers came to visit. So in one prison we used to wheel the babies in their prams round to talk to the workmen in the works department! I'm sure if we put enough resources into having more children in prison it could be managed.

Not everyone agrees that this would be desirable. The Styal officers quoted earlier had grave reservations. Styal's MBU has been praised as an example of good practice, but the officers said they feared for the babies' safety when their mothers got into fights. One, they said, had thrown a bowl of hot soup at another and babies had been splashed, though fortunately there were no serious injuries. When I asked a senior Prison Service official why MBUs could not be attached to more women's prisons his reply was unequivocal, though for different reasons:

> Because the more MBUs there are, the more the judges will fill them up. In my view, prison is not the right place for a child. You only have to look around Europe. In Spain and Portugal children can stay with their mothers to the age of five or six and that means you can have children coming into prison more than once. That can't be right. Even by the time they reach 18 months they are really noting their surroundings. I accept there is a need

for a few MBUs and it's OK in a place like Askham Grange with open conditions. But closed prisons are no places for children.

Frances Crook, Director of the Howard League, would go even further: 'We should be petitioning judges not to send women with children to prison at all. I would prefer all prisons to refuse to take in babies under the Children Act. Then something would have to be done. There needs to be a stand on principle'.

The best option is of course some kind of alternative to custody in the form of community service for all but the most serious offenders. But because women are in such a minority, most community service orders are geared to male offenders and offer only heavy manual work, mainly male residential placements, transport difficulties and poor or non-existent childcare.[24]

I interviewed one Holloway remand prisoner, a woman in her fifties, bailed to a hostel in Kent. She described to me her distress at being the only woman housed with 24 men, three of them self-confessed paedophiles. Several others were also sex offenders. Although she had her own room with a lock on the door, she had to go to the communal kitchen area for meals and to make herself drinks in the evenings. She had to put up with sexist gibes, and one man insisted on describing to her in graphic detail the sexual offences for which he had been arrested. When the hostel had to take in six more men—three rapists and three paedophiles—for Christmas 1997, the woman was finally sent to one of the few all-female hostels. But it was 100 miles away from family and friends and she spent a lonely Christmas far from her 14-year-old daughter.

Several mothers said they would prefer electronic tagging if it meant they could be with their children. With improved technology this may be an option the government is prepared to consider to take the pressure off overcrowded jails. If so, women with children might be the first candidates, though it would have to be recognised that tagging is certainly neither a cheap nor simplistic solution.

Until such alternatives are accepted, it seems as if women will continue to be imprisoned at an increasing rate and, especially with more and more drug misuse, many of them will be pregnant. Even if they are allowed to keep their babies, most will be sent far from their other children, family and friends. The Inspectorate's review[25] found that for over 25 per cent of the women they surveyed, lack of contact with their children and other family members was their greatest concern. The Inspectors recommended[26] that a key factor in the allocation of women should be to locate them as near as possible to their homes. But in view of the current geographical spread of the 16 prisons holding women, how can they manage to maintain these vital links?

Endnotes

1. For fuller discussion of this topic, see *Women, Crime and Criminology: A Feminist Critique*, Carol Smart, Routledge, 1976; *Women on Trial*, Susan Edwards, Manchester University Press, 1984; *Sexism and the Female Offender*, Lorraine Gelsthorpe, Cambridge Studies in Criminology, 1987; *Women, Crime and Poverty*, Pat Carlen, Open University Press, 1988; *Offending Women*, Anne Worrall, Routledge, 1990; *Eve was Framed*, Helena Kennedy QC, Vintage, 1993; *Doubly Deviant, Doubly Damned*, Anne Lloyd, Penguin 1995; *Women and Crime*, Frances Heidensohn, 9th edition, Macmillan, 1996.
2. *Prison Mother and Baby Units*, Howard League, 1995.
3. In my sample, 99 women (66% of the whole sample) had never been in prison before.
4. A report on women prisoners commissioned in 1995 by the Home Office found that more than half had not expected a prison sentence: see *Managing the Needs of Female Prisoners*, Allison Morris *et al.*
5. The *National Prison Survey 1991*, OPCS/SSD, report SS1329, HMSO, 1992.
6. Quoted by Yvonne Wilmott, HM Prison Service Directorate of Health Care, in *Understanding and Working with Young Women in Custody*, Trust for the Study of Adolescence/HM Prison Service, 1996.
7. *Women in Prison: A Review* (1997), 2.04.
8. *Prison Statistics, England and Wales 1994*, HMSO, 1996.
9. 'HMP Holloway: Basic Fact Pack for Visitors', July 1996, p. 2, p. 6.
10. The rules on temporary release do not apply during the remand period: so although remand prisoners have certain privileges (like being allowed more visits than sentenced prisoners) they have never been eligible for home leave.
11. *The Prisoners' Information Book*, jointly published by the Prison Reform Trust and HM Prison Service, 1996 edition, p. 95.
12. Incentives and Earned Privileges Scheme (IEPS): since 1995 prisoners are placed on one of three differential regimes. These are Basic, Standard and Enhanced. According to which regime they are on, prisoners are allowed certain privileges, including the chance to 'earn' community visits.
13. Applications. Prisoners have to make a written application on a form addressed to the governor for anything differing from normal day to day activities, e.g. items to be brought in or sent out.
14. See Note 7 above: 5.23.
15. *The Imprisonment of Women*, Dobash R, Dobash R and Gutteridge S, Basil Blackwell, 1986.
16. See *The Oxford History of the Prison, Chapter 11*, 'Wayward Sisters', p. 344, by Lucia Zedner Oxford University Press, 1995.
17. At the time of writing, Holloway has up to 17 places; Styal 22; Askham Grange 20 and New Hall 9.
18. HM Prison Service, 1996.
19. See Note 7, above: 9.49.
20. At a conference on imprisoning women held at HMP Styal in October 1997, criminologist Dr Sylvia Casale described this research by Lisa Cotton of Sussex University. Mothers from Styal's MBU attending the conference told delegates they had done their own research and found that their babies were in fact developmentally ahead because of the extra time their mothers could devote to them in prison.
21. Mothers in prison qualify for the usual child benefit which they must spend on the baby.
22. See Note 7, above: 5.02.
23. 'Mothers Behind Bars', *People* Magazine (USA), 11 November 1996; and 'Babies Behind Bars': *LIFE* magazine (USA), October 1997.
24. For further discussion of this topic, see 'A Better Service for Women', Marie Edmonds, in *Advanced Probation Studies*, Somerset Probation Service, July 1994; *Women Offenders and Probation Service Provision*, Report of HM Inspectorate, July 1991.
25. See Note 7, above: 2.15.
26. See Note 7, above: 3.08.

CHAPTER FOUR

Green and Friendly[1]

It's 7.30 a.m. and the mid-December morning mist rises over the Hackney Marshes as the minibus cruises the streets of the sprawling East London estate, the driver squinting at the numbers on the tower blocks. 'There they are!' The driver brakes and Cathy jumps out and hurries towards a group of five children, four girls and a boy. The eldest is 13, the youngest six. Despite the early hour they are all dressed up in party clothes, the girls in sequined tops and frilled skirts, their hair braided, bunched and ornamented.

'Hi Cathy!' The eldest girl hugs the young student and they all clamber onto the bus where a few of the other children yawn a sleepy greeting. There are ten of them and some are fast asleep. A toddler is wriggling dangerously. His nine-year-old sister asks if he can use a toilet in the flats.

'Can he wait till we get to the garage, Leanne?' says Cathy as the bus pulls away. She leans over to me: 'That last family live in a crack house—did you see the steel doors, the fortifications?'

This is the last pick-up call of the morning for a special bus taking children to see their mothers at a closed women's prison. The scheme was the brainchild of two women who discovered the difficulties of using public transport to visit their partners in jail. They started a minibus scheme and in 1994 were asked by social services to run an escorted bus service for the children and disabled relatives of prisoners. Cathy, a childcare student, is one of the regular escorts. Abel, the driver, is a retired London bus driver. Like all the workers, myself included, they had to undergo strict security checks to make sure they had never been involved in child abuse offences. These children join the bus once a month and without it, many of them would never see their mothers at all.

Chapter 3 considered the importance to imprisoned women and their children of keeping up family links. Research in the USA indicates that a prisoner without family support is six times more likely to re-offend than one who has maintained close family ties. Yet the prison we are visiting is one of only a handful of women's prisons to run all-day children's or family visits. Today is a special visit because the prison has organized a children's Christmas party. Most of the children have dressed up for the occasion. Under her flowered anorak Stacey is wearing a golden shalwar kameez covered with embroidery, made for her by her aunt. She first wore it yesterday for her tenth birthday party

66

and was careful to keep it clean to show her mother today. Mark and Mat, brothers aged five and six, have had their crewcuts specially gelled. They lie curled up together, fast asleep, their breakfast crisps scattered over the seat. They were the first pick-up, catapulted out of bed at six and fighting all the way until now. 'They're usually dreadful,' says Cathy. 'We're the only bus that'll take them.'

Two hours and hundreds of I-Spys later we are at the prison gates. The journey has not been without its dramas. One nine year old girl got upset when Stacey mentioned prison. 'Shhh—my little sister thinks Mum's in hospital!' Cathy had to be firm when Leanne and one of the Hackney girls undid their seatbelts and stood up to practice their Spice Girls dance routine in the aisle: 'But we're practising for our mums!'

Now we help the children down from the bus. Mat has made a Christmas card and has written in large letters 'I love you Mum. I miss you lots and I love you. Come back soon. Love Mat'. His mother is serving a life sentence for murder and he may be 16 before she is home again. He and his brother live with their aunt and her own two daughters. Stacey clutches a present wrapped in Christmas paper for her mother. Cathy and Abel exchange worried glances: 'They mightn't let you take that in, Stacey.' Stacey frowns and clutches the parcel more tightly.

In the visits complex two young officers have replaced their uniform with party gear. They carry out the search procedures efficiently and as sensitively as possible, making jokes as each child stands, arms raised, for the pat-down and scanner search. As each child is processed, the door into the visits room opens and we catch a glimpse of a mother waiting with outstretched arms, her eyes shining. Now it's Stacey's turn and the officers shake their heads: the parcel can't be allowed. The woman officer explains and cajoles. Stacey looks mutinous then retreats in tears to a bench in the corner. Her mother waits just feet away behind the door but Stacey will not move. The minutes tick away.

Finally the officers reach a compromise. If Stacey will leave her parcel in a locker and go in and join the party, they promise to unwrap it and show her mother the present through the door. Then Stacey can take it back and keep it till her mother comes home. Stacey looks unconvinced, but reluctantly agrees. It will be a year before her mother sees the little silver vase again.

The party ends at three and the bus returns to collect the children. It trundles away loaded up with plastic bags of gifts and gold and silver balloons which pop disconcertingly all the way back along the London-bound motorway. We hear about the conjurer and pass the parcel.

Father Christmas has given them all a toy. 'I don't think that was the real Santa was it? He had a black moustache,' asks Mark. 'No', agrees Mat thoughtfully, 'I think he was really the Old Bill.'[2]

The mothers have made teddy bears and cakes, tapestry pictures and cushions lovingly embroidered with the children's names. The joy and warmth of the party fills the bus as the children compare presents and lose all their puzzle pieces under the seats. There are no tears, only contentment. There are still ten days to go before Christmas but few of the mothers will see their children again until mid-January. The return journey takes much longer because the children all need help carrying their Christmas presents from the bus to their homes where their carers—grandparents, aunts and friends—greet us with relief and gratitude. It is past nine when we drop off the last child.

• • •

A few days after the Christmas party I went back to the prison to interview some of the women whose children regularly come on the charity bus. To them, they all agreed, the bus was 'a Godsend'. Marie, a lifer and the mother of Mark and Mat, enjoyed sharing the party with her sons:

> I only see the boys once a month because of that bus. It makes all the difference because it's the only thing I've got to look forward to each month. These kids haven't got a clue why their parents have been taken away suddenly. I think Mark and Matthew are doing very well really. Usually when they come here on an all-day visit we talk and draw and make things and go outside and play.

Lydia is serving four years for 'sticking a knife in someone who owed me money'. She never knew her own parents and has spent her whole life in care. She became a crack addict at 14 and at 16 she gave birth to Luke, a bright eight-year-old whose permanently anxious frown was transformed into smiles on the party bus as he unwrapped Lydia's presents, saved for the journey home.

> Before the bus started up I hadn't seen Luke for three months. I'm really grateful for that bus. Now I see him once a month and I wouldn't see him otherwise as his father doesn't have a car. On the whole-day children's visits we play football and table tennis and we talk a lot. You really made me smile today, talking about Luke opening his presents. Cheers for looking after him.

All the women I spoke to agreed this had been 'a good visit'. Five years spent listening to prisoners have taught me the difference between a good visit and one that is not so good. A good visit can sustain a woman through many grim prison days: a bad one can dash her fragile self-esteem and make her angry and 'difficult'. Sensitive officers quickly pick up on this and act accordingly; the less sensitive ones are not interested.

Even a good visit can be damaged by the way officers handle it. In Summer 1997 a group of ten organizations working with prisoners' families carried out a survey of 300 visitors in 50 prison visitors' centres.[3] One area particularly mentioned was the attitude of prison officers. One visitor commented: 'The attitude of the staff could make the whole degrading procedure a bit more bearable. What the staff must realise is we the families are innocent victims too. We have done nothing wrong'. Subsequent enquiries by the Prison Reform Trust reveal that the treatment of prisoners' families is not included as part of the training provided at the Prison Service Training College.

At one prison I visited, a group of women were unanimous about late calls to visits. This woman's words were typical: 'If the officers take a dislike to you they can really make your life hell. They can get back at you tenfold. For instance an officer can hang about and not call you when your visitors arrive.' Other women corroborated her allegations:

It's terrible in here the way they handle the visits. You've been looking forward for ages to your visit, then you're sitting there waiting to be called, getting more and more frustrated. Then you find out your visitors arrived ages ago and they never called you. Once I lost half an hour of my visit—that was a third of the time—because they forgot to call me. My sister was bringing my little boy. He's four and I can see him twice a month. She arrived 20 minutes early but they called me nearly half an hour late. Visits are from 2 p.m. to 3.30 p.m. and most officers won't let your visitors in if they arrive after three, however far they've travelled.

Women in the group also described other petty meannesses: 'The screws do nasty little things, like closing the curtains of the visits room at the end of the visit so you can't wave goodbye.' 'They make you walk back to your room the long way, so you can't wave goodbye—but what's the harm in waving goodbye?'

Another woman's graphic account showed how a positive experience can be turned sour:

In this prison they can treat you badly in front of your visitors. I'm 50 and a grandmother but they made me feel like a dirty little teenager because I

69

kissed my fiancé in the visiting room. They made me feel terrible. I was very embarrassed anyway when he came because the visits room here is very small and there are two officers in there with you and no music playing or anything. So the officers can hear everything you say.

Most degrading of all of course is the strip search, described in *Chapter 2*, which any woman, whatever her age, offence or behaviour may be liable to undergo following any visit. Judy described her experience:

I had a very good visit recently from this girlfriend. She was visiting me with her little boy. Throughout the visit these two gay officers were watching us and they could see we had no chance to pass anything between us. After the visit they strip-searched me and one of them was really ogling me. It was so embarrassing. First they made me take off my top, then the bottom half, and the way they touch you, you can tell. They even looked under my watch strap. It was disgusting and although I'm gay myself I felt degraded. I'd had such a good visit but they humiliated me and they ruined it so I went back to work in the kitchens in tears.

This sort of behaviour[4] sits uneasily with the Prison Service's own rules. Standing order 5 in the Prison Service Rules states:

It is one of the roles of the Prison Service to ensure that the socially harmful effects of an inmate's removal from normal life are as far as possible minimised, and that contacts with the outside world are maintained. Outside contacts are therefore encouraged, especially between an inmate and his or her family and friends.[5]

Most prisoners, male and female, whatever their age, benefit from keeping up links with friends or family. Numerous research studies have shown that such links can reduce recidivism. The Woolf Report[6] recognised separation from family, friends and community as the worst aspect of imprisonment, and this view was endorsed by HM Inspectorate of Prisons who further expressed their opinion that barriers to children's visits contributed to high levels of depression among female prisoners.[7]

The most obvious contact is the physical presence of a prisoner's family or friends in the form of regular visits. The Prison Service Rules also state the number of visits permitted to people in prison. Remand prisoners are allowed a maximum of one and a half hours of visiting time each week. Most prisons allow this to be split up, with one short visit of between 15 and 20 minutes each weekday. Once convicted, a prisoner's right to visits is cut to one-sixth of the remand allowance. He or she is allowed only one hour of visiting time a month, which can be taken as two half-hour visits on separate weekdays, or a full hour at weekends. Young offenders are allowed one hour each week.

These rules were further complicated by the implementation in 1995 the Incentives and Earned Privileges Scheme (IEPS),[8] which links the privileges allowed to prisoners with the way they behave during their sentences. For instance a prisoner who because of his or her behaviour has been promoted to an 'enhanced' regime may be allowed a privileged visiting order[9] to send out to family and friends for extra visits, some of which can last up to two hours. Each prison has different rules: one prison for instance offers well-behaved prisoners two extra visits every 28 days. Privileged visiting orders can also occasionally be granted if a prisoner is seriously ill or has severe family problems. Sometimes a foreign national prisoner may be granted one if relatives have come from overseas and are only in the country for a few days.

Such concessions may appear to be a sign of a humane attitude on the part of the Prison Service but it can also be argued that the IEPS is an internal control mechanism[10] to monitor and change the behaviour of prisoners, and should be unrelated to the number of visits allowed. Visits affect members of a prisoner's family as much as the prisoner: should they be made to suffer for lapses in their relative's behaviour?

Indeed, as standing order 5 implicitly acknowledges, any severing of family ties may be potentially harmful, and the logical rider to that theory is that lapses in a prisoner's behaviour may be less likely to occur if links with family and friends are strengthened. IEPS rules also determine the amount of 'private spends' a woman is allowed, and this in turn limits the number of prison phone cards and stamps she is able to buy in the canteen.[11] Women in one prison were furious to discover that books of first class stamps bought into the prison canteen at 25p per stamp were being sold at the new rate of 26p—and pennies mean a lot to prisoners.

As the women's comments on a 'good visit' show, contacts with family or friends are of vital importance in helping prisoners get through their sentences and some of the bitterest complaints came from the many women whose visits had been affected for disciplinary reasons. 'Blackmail' was a word very frequently used.

Jessie, aged 40 and in a closed prison, has six children: 'In here they blackmail you all the time if you've got kids. There's nothing you can do about it. It's the kids that are doing the sentence, not the mothers.'

For another woman, being a mother in prison is 'like treading on eggs all the time. You have to be careful not to upset any of the officers specially if you've got children. If you step out of line it means your VO[12] won't be sent and you won't get a visit from your kids.'

71

Rebekah has no children of her own but observes the effect on those who have:

> Women get a raw deal in prison because they don't usually have the power to change things by rioting like men. A lot of women in prison have kids and if they step out of line, it's so easy for the authorities to stop their kids' next visit. It happens all the time. They always have that hold over people, so women are afraid to protest against anything. If it was me I'd tell them to fuck off, but these women can't do that. I've seen women suicidal because they're not getting to see their kids. So there's this terrible lethargy in female prisons.

Stacey's mother Andy enjoyed the Christmas party, but at other times she has been suicidal at losing touch with her daughter:

> I only see Stacey once a month when the bus comes. This was a good visit, after we sorted out that problem with the Christmas present. But usually I'm crying when she leaves and she's crying too. I tell her it's not even a year left now. It's only eleven months then it'll be only ten months, and one day it will end. I'm doing five years and there's been months when I haven't seen Stacey at all. I was accused of supplying drugs in another prison though I wasn't involved. But they didn't believe me and I got shipped up north. I had no phone cards, they took my letters away and they wouldn't give me pen and paper to contact anyone. Stacey was starting to cut up[13] – she takes it really bad if she can't see me. And I get suicidal if I can't see her. In here if I get association[14] I ring Stacey every night but sometimes if I'm banged up and can't get to the phone, then she'll cry all night. I've tried to commit suicide twice since I've been here. I sit in my room and I cut up and think a lot. Two years before I came into prison I was expecting a second child but it was an ectopic pregnancy and I lost the baby. Sometimes I still get a lot of pain from the operation. Stacey is all I've got to live for.

Brenda is 27 and half way through a six year sentence for major fraud. Her children were aged one and three when she was first sent to Holloway. She is currently at her fourth prison in three years. Some of them she has been in twice:

> I've been shipped out from one prison to another and back again, accused of having drugs. I admit I was caught with pot in Holloway but that was all. If you're black they assume you're on drugs all the time. Since I've been in prison I have never spent a whole day with my daughter. I was kept on closed visits for 14 months. I didn't get to hold my baby till she was two.

72

> You sit in this box behind a glass window and all I wanted was one open visit for her birthday so I could hold her. But they kept issuing me with NOS.[15]

The governor of a closed prison showed me the kind of visits box Brenda meant. It stands in the corner of the main visits room, a large structure rather like a double-kiosked church confessional, with one kiosk larger than the other. The lower half is wood-panelled, the top half glazed. The prisoner is taken into the smaller side and sits on a chair with the door locked behind her. The visitors go into the larger, unlocked side where there are two or three chairs. Between them there is a reinforced mesh screen, though the governor told me she has known the wooden frame to be prised away from the mesh just far enough for drugs to be passed through on a pinhead.

The inspectors were deeply concerned about such preventive measures. While recognising the need to try to stop drugs coming into prison, they recommended that 'only for exceptional and well-documented security reasons should women prisoners be denied the opportunity to embrace their children and other relatives'.[16] In February, before the Inspectorate's thematic review was published, Sir Donald Acheson, the former chief medical officer, had recommended that closed visits should be ended for all prisoners, but his recommendation was turned down by Michael Howard, the then home secretary.

Brenda's story of being moved from prison to prison is a common one, and it is commoner still if, like Brenda and Andy, the woman is black. The most recent Home Office survey[17] of imprisoned women found that of the 1,766 women surveyed, black women were much more likely to be mothers (76 per cent, compared with 57 per cent of white women). Yvonne, a black woman serving seven years for intent to supply drugs, has nine children. The seven of them who are under 15 came to the prison Christmas party:

> Before that I hadn't seen any of them except the baby for months because I've been moving round. He's three and my mother's been bringing him from Birmingham to see me, whatever prison I've been in. They stopped my children's visits because they said I had sold drugs. I've spent a lot of time down the block.[18] My family were too scared to come and see me in case they got involved too. In the end I cleared my name with the help of people from the Home Office who came and supported me.

The fear of being 'shipped out' as a reprisal means that women with children are reluctant to make complaints. A young lesbian prisoner strongly objected to the way prisoners in the prison kitchen were treated by the male civilian officers:

They'll shout "Oi you—come over here, you tarts!"—insults like that all the time. I decided to put in a formal complaint about the way we were treated and I said to the other women "If we put in a collective complaint they can't scapegoat any of us". They all agreed with me but when it came to sign the app[19] for the complaint, in the end the only two signatures on the form were mine and my girlfriend's. Most of the women in here have got kids and they think they'll be stopped seeing them. But it's only the women's fear—if a woman asks for a visiting order to be sent out, the officers have got to do it, whether they like it or not.

Real or imagined, the fear certainly existed in every women's prison I visited that officers might refuse to allow women's children to visit, or that they would arrange for 'troublemakers' to be shipped off to a prison far away. At a different prison a woman complained that there were hardly any toys in the visits room for children to play with. I asked why she and others did not put in a formal request for more. She stared in disbelief at the naivety of such a question:

Why don't we ask for some toys in the visits room? We're frightened to ask for *anything*. We have to get the unconvicted women to ask for things for us. We don't open our mouths in case we get shipped off away from our kids. We don't try *nothing*. You can't even complain about the food because if you do you get sent back to a closed prison.

By no means all prison moves are linked to breaches of discipline. I have sat beside governors and overheard telephone conversations where swaps are arranged and deals done as if the prisoners were so many packages—which is what they are increasingly becoming as the numbers to be processed grow by hundreds every month. Many moves are pragmatic decisions based on where there is 'a bed for a body.'[20] But for the prisoner shipped out with little or no notice, the repercussions can be devastating. A woman with an eight year old son said: 'The way people get moved round the system is totally arbitrary. I had my son's visit booked for a Sunday and they told me I was going off to another prison a few days before. I had no idea when I'd see him again'. That was my most distressing day in prison.

Even for those women who stay in the same prison for the greater part of their sentence, it is difficult to maintain family links. Because of the geographical spread of the establishments that hold them, imprisoned women are much more likely to find they have problems. Styal governor Madeline Moulden has said[21] that though women prisoners are much more likely than men to be the sole carers of their children, it is much harder for them to see them. The term 'dislocation' was coined by the criminologist Dr Sylvia Casale to describe both physical and psychological distance from home. It is much harder—in terms of time, distance and expense—to visit a woman in prison than a man. Most women's prisons are far off the beaten track and public transport is poor or non-existent, especially on weekends when it is most convenient for working partners, carers and children still at school to visit. It is not at all uncommon for friends and relatives to make a four hour round trip for a 45 minute visit. The most recent survey, carried out by the Prison Service in 1994, found that prisoners' relatives had to travel an average of 62 miles to visit them. For young offender institutions the figure rose to over 100 miles.

According to both officers and prisoners, it is mainly other women who visit women in prison. There was much anecdotal evidence that male visitors are far less reliable. One male principal officer could scarcely contain his disgust:

> This prison [Brockhill] is next to a male prison [Blakenhurst], and the wives and girlfriends will trudge up this long road through all weathers to bring the kids to see the men. But if there's a drop of rain, the men will ring us up here and say, "Sorry, can't make it today". Or they just don't turn up and the women will be desperate, thinking there's been an accident. Yet they still keep faith with these men, and we have to pick up the pieces.

In the visits room of one prison, I noticed a woman's distress at being forbidden to leave her seat, whatever the needs of her five children. After the visit this young mother wrote to me: 'You saw for yourself how they didn't want us to play with our children. That is a crime. My children need to feel things are the same even though I'm not there for them. They have done a survey at this prison and many women signed in favour of full-day children's visits—but they still say 'no'. Why? Don't they know how important it is?'

The women were petitioning for full-day children's visits like the ones run by Holloway. There the visits are on Sunday and the prison's gym, swimming pool and education department are all made available to mothers and their children for the whole day. The idea is in principle an excellent one, but at less accessible jails the logistics for bringing children to such visits can be almost insurmountable, without the help of some service such as the charity minibus. Prisons have decided that imprisoned mothers need to spend 'quality time' with their children, rather than chatting to the accompanying carers. So the carers are allowed to hand the children over at the start of the visit but must then leave almost immediately, to return only to collect them at the end.

The theory is perhaps admirable, but it leaves the carer, often accompanied by her own young children, abandoned for five or six hours, usually in the middle of the countryside where many women's prisons are situated, and nowhere to go if it rains. Holloway is of course the exception, because of its convenient location at the centre of good rail, road and underground links. But visitors to other women's prisons will often have travelled on public transport for most of the journey and the last few miles by an expensive taxi. They will be lucky to find two buses a day running anywhere from the nearest village, especially on a winter weekend. Even if they manage to reach a town with cafés and cinemas, the extra expense of food and entertainment can be prohibitive. After one or two experiences like this, many carers simply give up, and the mother cannot see her children at all.

Some prisoners now have visitors' centres with toilet facilities, but most are very basic. According to HM Inspectorate, this is a lost opportunity, and they recommend comfortable facilities and the appointment of Family Contact Development officers to offer information and help.[22]

Nor can all mothers in prison cope with having their children for a full day. Those who would condemn them need to understand the build-up of tension inside a prison, the withdrawal from the outside world into the world of the institution, the lives some women have led before they came inside, and the emotional damage some of them have sustained in their own childhood. Kaley has reverted to short weekly visits:

I couldn't handle the all-day visits. You can have one of those every three weeks and your family have to go away and leave the kids. My sister used to bring Damien in. He's only three so she'd get him pop and crisps and a little toy to keep him quiet. But they all got took off him by the screws — so of course he comes in screaming the place down and she leaves him with me and I have to try and sort him out. There's not enough toys here for them to play with and it's too long for him and me. I didn't like him running round screaming spoiling the visit for everybody else.

A more effective arrangement is the kind of family visit allowed at New Hall, one of the closed women's prisons praised by the inspectors.[23] A life-sentenced prisoner I interviewed was looking forward to her move there for this reason:

You can have your normal visits but they've also set up some portakabins where they hold special family visits — so your family can come in and stay with you and you can have all day on your own with them. You can cook them a meal and there's places for the kids to play. They run the system every weekday from ten in the morning till three in the afternoon so all the

76

women get a chance. And as it's such a long journey for some people, the family can stay locally overnight and come two days running if you'd rather have your two visits close together.

Media eyebrows have already been raised at the idea of conjugal visits. One wonders what the *Sun* would make of Canadian women's prisons which have family visiting facilities in all their new establishments. Their Private Facility Visiting Program can enable a woman to spend up to 72 hours with close relatives. But this successful scheme has resulted in a strange anomaly: two lifers have become pregnant as a result, yet there are no mother and baby units in any of the prisons. In America, only eight states allow conjugal visits: there, too, imprisoned women have become pregnant.

Whatever the arrangements, there is always the cost of visits to consider. Anyone on a low income may be eligible to claim travelling costs for the two visits permitted each month and may also get help with meals expenses (though there are strange anomalies which exempt, for instance, very young children, as if they did not require food). The Prison Service's Assisted Prison Visits Unit (APVU) publishes a leaflet stating that prisoners' parents, brothers, sisters, children and partners can apply, if they are on income support or family credit. Visitors unable to travel alone may also receive help for an escort's travelling costs if they can provide a health certificate.

Although the costs of public transport are paid in full, the allowance, like most claims of this kind, is retrospective. When I rang the APVU in Birmingham on 15 January 1997 a pre-recorded message stated: 'We are currently processing claims received on the thirtieth of December. We are asking that you allow two weeks for claims to be paid'.

Many prisoners' families are living on the edge of poverty, and it may be quite impossible for them to find upfront the large sums of money needed for public transport. If they are just outside the eligibility bands, as many surely must be, the costs can be prohibitive. When in June 1996 I travelled by train from London to HMP Drake Hall, an open women's prison in Staffordshire, the return journey, booked on the cheapest ticket possible (an APEX return) cost £23.50. But that required pre-booking at least a week in advance and families are not always able to make this early commitment. The standard saver return ticket cost £36.50 for one adult.

Because most women's prisons are so difficult to reach by public transport, the cost of a taxi must often be added. The taxi fare from Stafford station to Drake Hall was £10 each way, adding a further £20. So the total cost for one visitor might be over £50, of which £20 would have to be found from the visitor's own pocket (the APVU does not pay taxi fares unless there is no public transport available and even if this is the case, prior permission to use a taxi has to be sought). The woman taxi driver who drove me to the prison said she often picked up prisoners' families and she sympathised with them. That week, she said, one prisoner's visitors—her mother, sister and child—told her it cost them £100 each trip. No doubt all these costs have increased in the two years since I made that journey.

Because of the distances involved, visitors may also have to apply for a day off work, and elderly parents may not feel able to make the journey. So it is not surprising that some women never have any visits at all. Morag is 23, and a professional 'dipper'—a pickpocket—from Leeds, serving her sentence at Bullwood Hall in Essex. She has no children. She was in care between the ages of 12 and 15 then returned to her mother and still lives with her. 'When I get out next April I'll go back to live with my mum. I was in New Hall first [in Yorkshire] so my mum used to visit me. But now I get no visits at all.'

About half the women in prison are mothers and it is understandable that more attention is generally given to their problems and the way prison affects their children. But this leaves the other half who have no children to visit them. Some of them are indeed little more than children themselves. The average age of people in prison is much lower than that of the population outside prison: the *National Prison Survey*[24] found that 32 per cent of women prisoners are under 25 compared with 16 per cent of the population outside prison. Over half of women prisoners are under 30 years of age. About one seventh of them are young offenders under 21.

A woman officer who has spent 17 years working in women's prisons in the north of England felt young prisoners were particularly vulnerable:

Some of them are a very long distance away from home. We have lots of Southerners up here and it's very expensive for their families to travel. When the younger girls' fathers came to visit them for the first time I always used to take a box of tissues because the fathers took it very hard. I have supervised visits and spent the whole time crying with the women and I'm not ashamed of that because the women know I feel for them. They know it's genuine, that there's a heart behind the uniform, because they can pick out a fraud a mile off.

Some women have been jointly accused with male partners—husbands, boyfriends or even sons—and each is sent to a different prison. Other women correspond with male prisoners and end up marrying them. Both groups can be allowed inter-prison visits. Women feel that male prisons are more relaxed about security and that the men know the timing of the visit before they do. Kaley explained: 'Terry and me have an IPV every three months. His prison is very good to him. He can tell me I'm coming to see him before I get to hear of it myself.'

A woman sent to one closed prison for accumulated inter-prison visits with her husband in a nearby men's prison said the whole experience was ruined by the four strip searches she had to endure every day, one before and after each visit, morning and afternoon: 'I was there for six days so that made 24 strip searches. It was ridiculous— we were both in jail, not coming in from the outside'.

In any case such visits are becoming more infrequent because of staff cuts: Florence, jointly convicted with her 19-year-old son, was very upset when I met her:

> I'm supposed to have an IPV with my son in Brixton prison every three months but I and another girl who was waiting to go and see both her brothers in prison were told there were no staff to take us so we couldn't go. I was told I was going to see my son in Brixton tomorrow. I woke up all excited but then they told me I wasn't going after all because there were no staff. Now I only see my son twice a year. They've stopped him coming to me although Brixton has got the staff for an escort, because they say this prison can't facilitate it.

Nearly one third[25] of the women in my own sample had been in care for part or most of their childhood. They may never have known their families or have lost touch with them. The male prisoners I interviewed in an earlier research project were much more likely to have female partners or mothers outside to support them. Many of the lone women I spoke to had no such support.

There is a well-established system of official prison visitors who offer to visit women like this, usually weekly or fortnightly. They are volunteers who may have heard of the National Association of Prison Visitors, or who may have a friend already doing this work. Prison chaplains usually act as liaison officers, processing applications and following up references, though the final decision on who to accept is made by the prison governor.

Holloway, for instance, currently has 20 prison visitors who regularly visit about 60 of its 500 or so prisoners. This may seem a small number, but there is little demand from the short-term prisoners who make up two-thirds of that prison's population. Overseas prisoners serving longer sentences are most in need of visitors, and there has been a drive to recruit more black and ethnic minority volunteers, and those able to speak a foreign language.

There is no shortage of volunteers for a prison like Holloway, though the expected commitment of a weekly or fortnightly visit over two years is quite a considerable one to undertake. They are usually local people from all walks of life—Holloway's current visitors include a teacher, a doctor and a community psychiatric nurse—and they can be any age between 21 and 70 on appointment, though chaplains often say their average age is much older than that of the average prisoner, and they would like more younger volunteers. Any woman can ask to have a visitor by approaching a member of the chaplaincy team, who will try to match her with a suitable visitor.

Newly-appointed visitors are given a *Prison Service Handbook* with advice on how to conduct themselves. It suggests they should see their role as 'simply an attempt to form a friendly relationship in circumstances and surroundings which are unnatural and far from ideal'. The visitor's value to the prisoner lies in the fact that 'he is a representative of the outside world . . . who demonstrates to him that he is neither forgotten by, nor isolated from, that world.' (The handbook uses the male personal pronoun throughout and makes no reference to women prisoners as such). Although most of the advice is positive and sensible, it is a pity that the guidelines' authors found it necessary to reinforce the prevailing view expressed by most prison staff that prisoners are naturally manipulative and devious: 'Be cautious on the other hand of the prisoner who may attempt to make use of you, to do him favours or to fight his battles with authority; some have had long practice in trading on the sympathies of the unwary.'[26] Such sentiments also seem patronising to volunteers who will, one assumes, have thought carefully about the issues before coming forward.

Some women choose to have no visitors because they feel such shame that they want nobody to see them in prison. Young women—specially those who have become involved in the drugs scene—are frequently estranged from their parents.

Many mothers tell their children they are in hospital, college or staying with family abroad. A Ghanian woman with family in Africa told me her children, aged eight and 12, believe she is there:

> The children don't know I'm here. They live with my husband and I ring them every Wednesday night. They think I'm in Ghana. I don't want them to think I'm a criminal. I don't see why they should find out unless someone's really spiteful and tells them.

Adrienne shared her feelings:

My daughter's living with her father in Cornwall. She's 400 miles away but that suits me because then she won't know I'm in prison. Every Wednesday her father takes her to the phone box at six o'clock and they wait so I can phone her up. She thinks I'm in hospital. That's why I don't want her visiting me here.

The officers had helped Adrienne keep up the pretence:

She did come once and they let me go down the road outside and meet her at the garage. I cuddled her as we walked back past the prison sign and when we got to the hospital wing where the visit was, none of the officers were in uniform so she had no idea it wasn't just a hospital.

These ruses are not always so successful. Another woman explained:

At first I tried to pretend this was college I was at. But one day my daughter said she wanted the TV on during the visit and I said we weren't allowed. So she said, "Can't you ask the officers?" I'd always called them teachers and she looked really ashamed of letting it out and I realised she knew this was a prison. I was amazed how she'd picked it up—she's only five!

Other women object to their families being subjected to the kind of security now in force on visiting days at most prisons—or the families themselves, especially if they are black, fear accusations that they are trying to bring in drugs. Visits procedures have been tightened as prisons wage a losing battle against illegal drugs. Women who have never used drugs resent the tightening of security measures caused by 'the drugs girls' and the resulting indignities inflicted on their own visitors. One, a grandmother jailed for fraud, never sees her granddaughters because her daughter refuses to subject the little girls to 'manhandling by the screws': on their first and only visit they had had to remove their shoes and socks. Newspaper stories describing children having their clothes removed have fuelled such fears. Babies' bottles cannot be brought in: they can be left in a locker and a prison officer will usually go and collect them on request. But by this time the baby is usually screaming. Visitors to Holloway (and some other prisons) can no longer bring cut flowers because drugs have been found hidden in the stems: now flowers have to be ordered from one of two approved florists and delivered by them to the prison: for many women the extra expense (the minimum charge is £15) has ended this small treat. It is also forbidden to bring family snaps to show the prisoner.[27]

The first visit to a prison can be a daunting experience, both for the visitor and for the prisoner. The process begins with the prisoner asking the prison to send her chosen visitor a visiting order (VO) on which the visitor's name and address have been written by prison staff. Three adult visitors are allowed on any one visit, and any of the prisoner's or visitors' children up to the age of 16. Young people under the age of 18 are not allowed to enter a prison unless accompanied by an adult.

• • •

Visiting a busy prison like Holloway[28] can at first be intimidating to the uninitiated, especially as everyone else seems familiar with the procedure. A convicted prisoner must send a VO to anyone wishing to visit her. When you receive your VO you must telephone a special number and book your visit—a fairly recent development added as an extra security precaution which in theory should speed up the process. But the phoneline is almost invariably busy and people without a telephone at home may have to make many trips to a public phonebox.[29] (A VO is not necessary to visit a remand prisoner, but visits still have to be pre-booked).

If however visitors despair and set out for the prison without booking, they are unlikely to be admitted, not least because nobody will have told them to bring some means of proving their identity. This must contain their current address as shown on the VO—a driving licence or recent gas bill will do. Without this, visitors may well be turned away. There is invariably a problem of this kind which holds up the whole queue. Leather-jacketed boyfriends bang angrily on the window; loud-voiced barristers with red-ribboned paper bundles explain to their moon-faced pupils that the queues are even longer to get through Security at the Old Bailey; babies scream; old-stagers shrug in resignation. The Holloway officers are impassive—they have seen it all before, day after day, year after year.

Once through this hurdle you move through electronically controlled glass doors and wait while they close behind you. For a few moments you are held in a narrow glass compartment like a fish tank, until identical doors slide open in front of you and you join other visitors in the waiting room. High on the walls some beautiful oils painted by prisoners make a forlorn attempt to civilise the room, but somehow fail to compete with the large red drinks-vending machine in the corner and the sum total of human misery on the long benches below. There is inevitably a delay as people borrow pens, fill in small white forms, try to hand in Tesco bags of clothes and mumble insults at the receiving officer in his kiosk when he refuses because the prisoner already has too many items 'in possession' or has not put in an app.[19] The receiving officer wears plastic surgical gloves as he sorts through incoming goods, reinforcing the sense that prisoners and their visitors are unclean pariahs. The minutes tick on and you feel your long-awaited visit being eaten away. However late the visit begins, it must end promptly and you may have travelled from Blackpool to London for just 20 minutes with the prisoner.

At last an officer calls, and you all shuffle through a door and leave your possessions in a locker, keeping out a small sum of money for refreshments—nothing else is allowed, apart from your locker key. You get in line—one queue for women, the other for men. Ahead you see male and female officers begin the routine search. You reach the front of your queue and are told to take off your scarf and your jacket (because it has pockets) and leave them in the locker. You return to the back of the queue and start all over again.

The 'pat down' search is fairly innocuous, like the familiar airport security checks. But you begin to feel a little threatened when the officer asks you to unlace your boots, then to open your mouth and throw your head back while she peers inside. If you have long hair you will be asked to hold it up and turn your head from side to side. Some officers smile, explain and apologise and that makes all the difference. Others remain unsmiling and inscrutable. Your left hand is stamped with an invisible mark. At last you are clear to pick up your locker key and your small change and head up the stone stairs towards the visits room. Some days you will meet further officers with a large sniffer dog. You will be told to walk straight along a blue line painted on the corridor and not to stop whatever the dog does. If you are carrying drugs the dog will find them, unless you have hidden them inside your body. If you have a cat at home, the dog may set about sniffing you alarmingly.

At the visits room door you wait while an officer bawls out 'your' prisoner's surname. Meanwhile the woman you have come to see will be sitting waiting in a 'holding area' on the other side of the visits room. If you are late, or even if you never turn up at all, she may continue to wait there during the whole visiting period, hearing officers shout other women's names, watching through a crack in the door as they hurry towards their visitors, listening to the greetings and finally the farewells.

Holloway's visits room was given a facelift in 1996 and is now quite welcoming, though cramped for Western Europe's largest women's prison. It is carpeted, with colourful fibreglass furniture (at each square wooden table are four chairs riveted to the floor: one blue chair for the prisoner, three red chairs for the visitors), a children's play area in one corner, sometimes staffed by volunteer supervisors, and yet more impressive examples of prisoners' artwork on the walls. At a kiosk—when it is open—two prisoners sell drinks, chocolate and crisps. You

83

buy a couple of Kitkats, hoping your prisoner will be able to eat both—
she will not be allowed to save them for later. As you weave through
the fixed chairs and tables with your tray you stop to admire a tiny baby
brought down by one of the mothers from the prison's mother and baby
unit. An officer moves you along: you are here to speak to one prisoner
and one alone.

It is only now that you realise how many officers are present. Two
sit at a large desk on a raised platform. Two more stand at the entrance
door. Others are stationed on seats round the room. Next to the
prisoners' exit stand the Dedicated Search Team (DST), the officers in
their red and black uniforms known by prisoners as the 'swoop squad':
they soon begin wandering around, on the lookout for drugs being
passed. Still more officers pace about and stand close by. Are they
listening to your conversation? You begin to mind your words as the
paranoia of the jail seeps through the colour and camaraderie. The
couple at the next table are oblivious as their kisses become more
passionate. An officer taps the woman on the shoulder and she
disentangles herself and slumps angrily back in her chair. At the table
beyond, grandparents struggle with a fractious toddler exhausted by
the long drive to the prison. He escapes their grasp and heads off to
another table. His young mother, the prisoner, sits helpless: she is not
allowed to leave her seat.

The officers begin checking their watches and soon they are yelling,
'Visit over!' Your half hour is through and there's so much you've
forgotten to say. A beautiful tanned teenager clings to her parents: the
father is a City type in pinstripe suit, the mother in Laura Ashley frock
looks prematurely aged by the worry of it all; their daughter, the
prisoner, looks like a supermodel and it shocks you to hear she's just
been given an eleven year sentence for importing drugs. A baby
screams as his young father prises him from his mother's arms. You join
the others near the exit as the women walk sadly away towards the
waiting officers. Some wave and smile for their children. Some walk
slowly backwards, their eyes fixed on their visitors' faces till the door is
closed behind them. The pinstriped father wipes a tear from his eye. At
the exit door you all hold your left hands obediently under an
ultraviolet lightbox. The invisible mark turns into a mauve stain which
shows nobody has swapped places with a prisoner.

Suddenly there is shouting and a scuffle among the bright tables
and chairs. In seconds the officers have wrestled a prisoner and her
visitor to the ground and are holding them there, six officers to each,
clinging to their arms and legs as if for some bizarre birthday-party
bumps session. The woman is kicking and fighting back. Children
scream and draw back from her flailing arms and legs. Everyone seems

to be shouting and the departing prisoners stop in their tracks. Some scream abuse, others shout catcalls. The exit door is slammed, the handcuffs are out, the woman is dragged struggling away and her visitor bundled behind her between two burly male officers.

The visitors stand shocked and silent at this sudden flash of violence, some shrinking back against the wall. It is as if for a few seconds a curtain has been drawn back to reveal the true nature of the prison. It is some minutes before the exit door is opened again. 'I saw it all', says an old man as you all tramp downstairs to the lockers, 'she put her hand in his pocket. Passing drugs, that's what he was up to, and that officer caught them at it. Now they're in the shit!'

The visitors pass through the electronic doors into the oblong fishtank where for an unpleasant three or four minutes all stand jammed together. Nobody says a word. Then the doors slide open. Out on the Parkhurst Road the stale London air has never seemed fresher.

• • •

Grim Holloway may be, but it is paradoxically the most popular women's prison. 'All the women say they hate Holloway', a Holloway officer told me, 'but they all want to be here rather than any other prison because it's ten minutes' walk from the tube and that makes it very accessible. Everyone in the country can catch a train to Euston.' Such is the effect of 'dislocation' on women and their families.

For those whose families are unable to visit them, links have to be maintained by letter or telephone. Although all letters must pass through the censor's office to be checked for contraband goods, only a random five to ten per cent are supposed to be read by staff—with the exception of letters sent to category A prisoners which are all subject to scrutiny. But prisoners commonly express their doubts. There is much anecdotal evidence that officers read any letters that interest them and women report staff teasing them about the contents. 'They always open your letters in here and read them. My mate caught one of the officers reading her letter and having a giggle with her friend.'

At one closed prison I visited, a young officer newly arrived on detached duty from another jail was routinely slitting open prisoners' Christmas cards with a paper knife, removing cash and cheques and quite properly entering the sums in the wing cash book. He was about to hand them out to the women when the female wing officer intervened: 'Hang on a minute, don't hand them out yet. I like to have a read of them first—I must admit I'm a bit nosy like that!'

Perhaps incidents like this one prove that the Code of Conduct[30] demanded by groups like Women in Prison is long overdue.

Many women and their families are poor correspondents and for them the next best thing to a visit is a telephone conversation. Prison phone cards look identical to the standard BT green cards but have a stamped message saying they can only be used on prison telephones. The ability to use an outside telephone line has proved a wonderful practical and emotional lifeline for women in prison. For a short time a few years ago prisoners were allowed to receive incoming calls, but this practice was stopped in 1996 as a result of new policies following the Woodcock Report on the escapes of male prisoners from HMP Whitemoor. Now the only incoming calls allowed are usually from a prisoner's legal representatives. The Inspectorate regretted this change[31] as such calls helped maintain links with families. Humane officers can of course bend the rules. In one prison the kitchen women tell their families the kitchen's extension number so they can ring through at any time of the day, and the officers will willingly pass on messages.

Sometimes however the ability to use the phone can become a mixed blessing:

> I ring my kids four times a day. My little girl got hysterical once when we were banged up and they wouldn't let us out to make our phone calls. That night my mum rang the prison and said, "Is there anything wrong with my daughter because she didn't ring?"

Prisoners are desperate to find ways of financing what can be an expensive service and the phone card, like tobacco and drugs, has become another form of currency, with vulnerable women being bullied and exploited to hand over their cards. In August 1997, Prisons Minister Joyce Quin announced that within the next two years she intended to introduce new 'smart telephone' technology into all the jails in England and Wales. Each prisoner will be given a PIN number enabling him or her to pre-pay for calls by a credit account system. The main purpose of the change was to prevent jailed male stalkers from continuing to contact their victims from inside prison. But the new scheme should also do away with the kind of bullying described by women I interviewed. One woman told how on her first day in prison she was targeted for her 'units' by another prisoner resorting to emotional blackmail (see *Chapter 2*). A recently released Holloway lifer said she even had to take her precious phone cards to the bath with her to stop them being stolen.

At another prison the governor became so concerned about this sort of activity that he took possession of all the women's phone cards and they are now held by officers in alphabetically ordered filing boxes and handed out to the women at evening association. But the women I met there were enraged: some cards had gone missing and this seemed to them the last straw in what they saw as a repressive regime:

Now they've taken away our responsibility for our own phone cards! You can't keep them yourself any more. You have to go along and apply to get them from the staff. I feel I am a responsible enough person to keep my own phone card. If it goes missing out of the office you've got no hope of getting it back. They treat us like children!

They keep the phone cards in boxes divided up with cards like a doctor's file and the screws can't be bothered to read the names properly so they may easily give your phone card to someone else. If a card goes missing they blame it on the other prisoners stealing it but if the officers are there all the time sitting at a big table with the cards in the box in front of them, how can the prisoners get them?

The governor dismissed these allegations:

Phone cards are a currency and put the vulnerable under pressure. Some of the inadequates were being bullied and they were also bullying others. This is our way of maintaining control over the number of phone cards people have and of keeping in touch. Sometimes there just has to be an adult-child relationship in a place like this.

When adult women are incarcerated, can such adult-child supervision ever be justified? Or is it calculated to goad the women into such a fury of frustration that they are bound to 'kick off'?

Endnotes

1. Prison slang for a phone card.
2. A policeman.
3. Reported in 'A Better Service for Visitors to Prison', Diana Ruthven: *Prison Report*, Issue No. 40, Autumn 1997, Prison Reform Trust.
4. Meda Chesney-Lind in *The Female Offender* (Sage Publications, 1997) recounts how video cameras were installed in some US prisons to monitor the behaviour of guards involved in strip-searching. In the women's Albion Correctional Center in New York, fixed cameras were replaced by hand-held cameras and 15 women prisoners filed complaints that the videotapes were being used for pornographic purposes. Some were granted substantial damages and the practice was stopped.
5. Quoted in *The Voice of a Child: The Impact on Children of their Mothers' Imprisonment*, a report by the Howard League for Penal Reform.
6. *Report of an Enquiry into Prison Disturbances*, Woolf and Tumim, CM 1456, HMSO, 1991.
7. *Women in Prison: A Review*, HM Inspectorate, 1997: 8.01 and 9.27.

8. Under the Incentives and Earned Privileges Scheme (IEPS), prison regimes are divided into Basic, Standard and Enhanced levels, and prisoners are moved from one to the other according to their behaviour. Those on a Basic regime are allowed to spend only £2.50 a week and their visits and phone calls are severely limited. Some women's prisons house Basic regime prisoners on the bottom landing, known as 'the Ones'.

9. Usually known as a PVO.

10. Erving Goffman in his 1961 book *Asylums* (Penguin) maintains that prisons create and sustain tension between home and institution and use this as 'strategic leverage in the management of men'.

11. IEPS allows for £2.50 per week for a prisoner on Basic regime, £10 for one on Standard and £15 for one on Enhanced. A prison phone card costs £2 (20 units) or £4 (40 units), the same as phone cards outside prison, though most prisoners are convinced they get less time for their money.

12. Visiting order, sent out by the prison to relatives and friends specified by the prisoner in advance of a visit. It must be produced on the day of the visit together with some form of identification so that the address can be checked.

13. Self-mutilate.

14. Association is the time when prisoners are allowed out of their cells to meet, talk, watch TV, go to classes etc. It is regarded as a privilege and can be withdrawn as a punishment, for security reasons or due to staff shortages. Prisoners not allowed association have to remain locked in their cells.

15. 'Not off sanctions notices': Certain sanctions can be imposed on prisoners regarded as misbehaving—one such sanction is closed visits. Women can apply for the sanctions to be revoked, but if their requests are refused they are issued with NOS notices.

16. See Note 6, above: 5.35.

17. *Imprisoned Women and Mothers*, Diane Caddle and Debbie Crisp, Home Office Research Study 162, Home Office, 1996.

18. Segregation unit used for punishment.

19. Application: prisoners have to make an application to the governor for anything differing from normal day to day activities, e.g. to get a 'request and complaint form'.

20. Prison officers commonly refer to prisoners as 'bodies'. When I first began researching in prisons I was taken aback to hear officers making remarks like: 'Come on, let's get those bodies downstairs into the yard'!

21. Interviewed on *Prison Britain*, BBC Radio Four, 5 August 1997.

22. See Note 6, above: Executive Summary 50; also 5.32.

23. See Note 6, above: 8.25.

24. *The National Prison Survey 1991:* A report to the Home Office of a study of prisoners in England and Wales carried out by the Social Survey Division of the Office of Population Censuses and Surveys, HMSO 1992. Women prisoners, though, are older than men prisoners on average: 41 per cent of male prisoners are under 25.

25. 30 per cent of the 119 who gave this information.

26. *Handbook for Prison Visitors*, p. 8-9, Prison Department, Home Office, 1987.

27. This is because drugs have been found on the back of photographs. Photographs can be sent to a Holloway prisoner in the post, as can a taped message on a cassette, as long as the tape is put in a clear perspex case.

28. A new visitors' centre was opened at Holloway by Princess Anne at the end of November 1997 though it did not become operational until the following year. It is situated outside the prison building and has a children's play area, baby-changing facilities and refreshments. Staff from the Prisoners' Wives and Families Society supply information about support groups for families. The building is basic—like a long narrow community centre—but it has toys for the children and is less intimidating for the new visitor than the uniformed prison officers they used to meet on their first visits. The rest of the visiting process is unchanged from my description above.

29. See Note 6, above. The inspectors recommended a dedicated phone line for booking visits, and for consecutive bookings to be permitted on the same call. At present, for instance, Holloway will allow visits to be booked no more than one week in advance.

30. *Women in Prison Campaigns*, 1995, calls for a Code of Conduct for prison officers.

31. See Note 6, above: 8.08.

CHAPTER FIVE

Kicking Off

On the weekend of 13 July 1996 Operation Tornado was activated for the first time in a women's prison, HMP Cookham Wood, making a small piece of British penal history. A squad of 21 male officers in riot gear arrived in response to a call from the prison to deal with two black women from a 'Yardie' drugs gang and their white 'runner' sent there from Holloway. The Prison Service maintains a Tactical Support Unit where there is a command suite and six duty officers ready to deploy manpower and intervene if there is a riot in any prison in the country. Operation Tornado is the process whereby control and restraint teams from six different prisons are sent to quell a disturbance. But until 1996 it was unheard of for them to go to a women's jail. In the event the riot squad was not deployed at Cookham Wood but waited on alert in the reception area.

The Cookham Wood prisoners only heard about the incident later through their own network of contacts in nearby male prisons. To the women this was just another case of over-reaction by the authorities, yet another example of women in prison being treated like men—'cons in skirts'. Prisoners in fact regard this particular prison as fairly stable, compared with the shifting and volatile nature of remand prisons like Holloway and Risley.

I was first told of the Cookham Wood incident the Monday after it occurred by a senior female officer at another prison: 'They are covering all this up because it's too embarrassing to make public.' She could only recall one similar incident in the 1980s, when a male MUFTI squad—the team known by the acronym for Minimum Use of Force Tactical Intervention—was sent to Styal prison to release a hostage taken by one of the prisoners. 'They charged in on the prisoner and she immediately stripped off[1]—so they were very embarrassed and there was a real fuss about why a male intervention force was sent to a women's jail. That incident was hushed up too.'

The UK Prison Service might perhaps be warned by events in Canada in 1994 when a similar squad from a male prison burst into the Prison for Women (universally known as the P4W) in Kingston, Ontario, to quell a disturbance in the segregation unit. Because a male emergency response team had been used, a commission of enquiry under a woman judge was set up, and the result has been a major shake-up in female incarceration.

All the statistical evidence shows that women prisoners do not riot.

This is not to say that they are incapable of direct action, but it is rarely sustained, partly because so many women have dependents outside prison and fear reprisals.

Women do not organize themselves into the sort of protest that leads men to climb on to the prison roof with banners. This excerpt is from the diary of Sheila Bowler when she was imprisoned in Holloway. It is dated Saturday 3 August 1996, a couple of weeks after the Cookham Wood incident. It recounts a Holloway disturbance which, although it took place in the heart of London, did not make even one paragraph in the newspapers. The account gives some insight into the kind of frustrations that lead women to 'kick off'[2] and into the nature of women's protests:

> I am writing this at 10 a.m. on Saturday. We have been locked in since 12.15 p.m. yesterday and we discovered this morning the cause was that something went missing from the craft workshop. Whole of prison locked in until items are found so you can imagine the racket being produced from all the rooms—screaming, shouting, banging of windows, sheets and clothes of all sorts being sent out of the window alight which set fire to some of the trees. The officers as well as continuing their search are now employed directing hoses on the areas outside the windows. Even mattresses and blankets have been thrown in addition to the usual food, sanitary towels, plastic cutlery, bowls, plates and cups . . . There is now furniture being broken and thrown out of the window . . . We were told at breakfast as it was handed through the hatch that the last time something was missing all inmates were locked in for four days. Bright prospect as Simon and Susan [her son and best friend] are visiting Tuesday and I need cash brought in . . . It is now midday and I have just been strip-searched and had a room spin.[3] Apparently it is a pair of scissors and a knife that are missing from the craft workshop. If the officers had done their job properly there should have been nothing missing as the class finished Friday morning and they should have checked.

What caused this mini-riot was resentment at the imposition of a blanket punishment for what the women regarded as officer inefficiency. Tension was heightened as women worried about missing visits and became bored and depressed at being locked in for hours on end. Inspectors recognised that 'a key to good order is a consistent, active regime' and condemned erratic regimes leading to the cancellation of activities.[4]

• • •

There is a popular misconception that incidents like this are increasing

91

because women in society are becoming more violent, and those sent to prison are the most dangerous of all.

There was much alarm and media hype with the publication in March 1997 of Home Office figures which showed that violent crime had increased by ten per cent in 1996 after a year in which the figures had remained static. Offences of violence make headlines though they are still only a small fraction of the totality of recorded crime. But the figures given the greatest media coverage were those showing that violent offences by women had doubled: in the decade from 1985 to 1995, the number of women cautioned or convicted of violent offences rose from 5,715 to 11,692. During the same period, the corresponding increase among men was 20 per cent. The figure of 11,692 has of course to be seen in the context of the total number of violent offences: women constitute over half of the population, but according to these figures they are still only committing one-fifth of the violent crimes. Interestingly, American statistics show a *fall* in the percentage of women incarcerated for violent crimes, from 41 per cent in 1986 to 32 per cent in 1991.

Four months after the publication of the Home Office statistics, the National Association of Probation Officers (NAPO) produced a paper called *Women and Crime* which analysed the figures more carefully, and found that the number of violent offences committed by women remains very small, most are domestic and acquaintance-related and between half and three-quarters are related to the misuse of alcohol or drugs. NAPO found that despite a 76 per cent increase in the number of women prisoners *convicted* in the four years between 1993 and 1997 there has been 'no discernible increase in the number of females involved in criminal activity, but there [is] ample evidence of a harsher sentencing climate'. The report estimated that two-thirds of women serving short sentences for non-violent, less serious offences would probably have been given community penalties in 1993. Unlike the earlier Home Office report, the NAPO report rated only a few short paragraphs in the newspapers.

I looked at my own sample of women prisoners in the light of these two 1997 reports—because the nature of the 'clients' has obvious implications for the way they are held in custody.

Of my sample of 150 prisoners, 117 (78 per cent) had been sentenced. This compares almost exactly with the proportion of sentenced prisoners in the female population (77 per cent). Of the sentenced prisoners, 33 women—28 per cent—had been convicted of one of the more serious crimes referred to in the reports. But this figure was bound to be inflated by the nature of some of the prisons where I was permitted to undertake research: HMP Durham and HMP

Bullwood Hall, for instance, are the only two women's establishments that take first stage life-sentence prisoners.

A closer examination of the violent crimes of these 33 women reveals that 16 of them were convicted of murder or conspiracy to murder; four of manslaughter; five of robbery; five of ABH or GBH; two of wounding and one of a sexual offence.

As the numbers are small, it is worth looking in a little more detail at the background to these violent offences. In 12 of the crimes (36 per cent) violence by a male partner was involved. Ten of the women (30 per cent) who had committed violence had a history containing one or more of the following factors, all involving some form of abuse by men: abuse in childhood; early pregnancy; early initiation into drugs by an older man; involvement with criminal men; violence in the home or employment in the sex industry.

In seven (21 per cent) of the 33 violent offence cases, misuse of drugs or alcohol was implicated. Three women (nine per cent) had received treatment for mental disorder before the offence occurred. Two women (six per cent) who killed their own babies were suffering from severe post-natal stress at the time.

Statistics may show that there has been very little change in the profile of female offending and that few women commit violent crimes. The problem is that media stories highlight the most dramatic crimes by women and this skews perceptions of all female crime. Prison officers are not immune from these influences. Of the 60 disciplinary staff I interviewed, nearly two-thirds (64 per cent) said they felt that women coming into prison were more violent now than they used to be.

In this group of officers, 41 per cent attributed the growth in violence to increasing misuse of drugs and alcohol. Twenty-nine per cent felt that greater economic and social pressures—unemployment and debt, leading to family breakdown and violence in the home—were to blame. Another smaller group of 20 per cent blamed women's liberation from the confines of domestic work and their entry into areas traditionally regarded as 'a man's world'. The remaining one-third of officers saw little change over the years. Their views were encapsulated by a veteran in the field. Joanna Kelley was governor of Holloway from 1959 to 1966 and then (until 1974) was assistant director of the Prison Service with special responsibility for women and girls. She says things were not really very different in what some now regard as a golden age of stability and calm:

> There were always some very violent women in prison and indeed in those days we wanted to bring male officers in to deal with them because women officers felt they couldn't restrain them physically.

The prisoners I interviewed shared officers' views that the most violent behaviour in modern women's jails is caused by drug misusers fighting over their drugs, and by mentally disordered women. Rosemary King, head of psychology[5] at Holloway, says that women on C1, the psychiatric wing, make up only one-tenth of the prison population, but are responsible for one-third of the assaults. But histories of women's incarceration show that women have always fiercely resented and resisted prison discipline. A former governor of two women's prisons in the fifties and sixties said:

> When they do kick over the traces women just don't care what happens to them. You can starve them and you can beat them but they don't give a damn. Men seem to have more sense of self-preservation. When my women got angry you could do nothing to stop them — they simply did not care.

Statistics[6] show that women prisoners are nearly twice as likely as men to be punished for infringements against prison rules. These statistics hold no surprises for students of penal history. Ever since they were incarcerated separately from men, women prisoners have always been considered 'harder to manage'. The Oxford penal historian Lucia Zedner quotes a report on the Ohio state penitentiary in the 1840s which claimed that its nine female prisoners caused more trouble for their jailers than all the 500 men in the prison put together.[7] In their exhaustive and fascinating review[8] of the history of women's imprisonment Rebecca and Russell Dobash describe the regimes in nineteenth century Millbank, the earliest of the English national penitentiaries, where women prisoners were sent for the first stage of their sentences. They were held alongside men, though in separate quarters guarded by female warders. The Millbank women are recorded as receiving between three and five punishments each a year, compared with only two punishments received by men, and the punishments were also more severe. Though it was as rare then as it is now for women to mount an organized collective protest, there were occasional riots, known as 'breaking out', like the 1825 uprising when the Millbank women, like the Holloway women 170 years later, smashed the windows and vandalised bedding and clothes.

They may not have burned down their prisons, but as individuals imprisoned women have always been perceived as far more 'difficult to handle' than men. They have always challenged the system and when frustrated turned their rage on their own cells, or internalised it by self-mutilation.

Penal historians like Zedner and the Dobashes record many instances of women's subversive reactions to austere regimes, ranging from overt and noisy protests such as drumming on their cell doors with their feet, to developing secret modes of communication such as knocking on their walls when confined to silent labour in their cells. They made fun of preachers in the prison chapel by loudly mocking the sermons, throwing hymn books around and shouting abuse at the preacher.

Nineteenth century commentators, even reformers like Mary Carpenter,[9] put this kind of behaviour down to women's 'irrational feminine personalities'. It seemed not to occur to anyone to blame it on the nature of the prison regimes rather than the nature of the women confined there. One rare exception was a medical officer at Brixton Prison, converted for women prisoners following the Penal Servitude Act of 1853. This official described women prisoners as 'anxious and restless' and blamed not feminine characteristics, but the way in which female prisoners were treated. Their prison regimes were certainly harsher, minor breaches of rules were punished more severely and it was felt that female warders were harder than male warders on their charges.

The modern equivalent of 'feminine irrationality' is the 'hormonal' explanation: pre-menstrual tension, the menopause and post-natal depression have been used as mitigating factors in court cases over the past few decades. In my research these factors were cited by both male and female officers[10] as a possible reason for women prisoners' bad behaviour. One female officer said:

Women are certainly a lot more volatile than men prisoners and that could be PMT—I know I feel more unstable myself at that time of the month. I have been assaulted by both male and female prisoners but with the males it only happened because I had to intervene when they were fighting among themselves. The women will come straight at you face to face— specially at that time of the month.

Feminist commentators have long voiced their objections to such physiological explanations for women's criminal offending, because by being described in such terms, women are 'defined by their biology'. It is rare, they say, to find the courts, prison officers or imprisoned men themselves blaming testosterone entirely for male criminal offending.

Whatever the influence of their hormones, it has long been recognized that women in prison—as in society—have always been subject to stricter moral requirements than their male counterparts. Set on a pedestal by men, their fall from grace has been harder to accept. Victorian commentators like the journalist Henry Mayhew were shocked by the 'depravity' of female convicts and found it difficult to countenance such behaviour in those 'whom we are apt to regard as the most graceful and gentle form of humanity'.[7]

According to the female deputy governor of an open prison, these moral demands are partly self-imposed:

> Women prisoners set higher standards for themselves and when they fail they kick off. We have lots of adjudications here for failure to return on time from temporary release. We do understand but we have to punish them.

I asked all the officers and prisoners I interviewed why they thought women prisoners were almost twice as likely as men to be in breach of GOAD (the acronym for the quaintly arcane phrase 'Good Order And Discipline' of the prison). The officers offered a variety of explanations—all of them very different from those given by the prisoners.

The officers were almost unanimous[11] in their view that women prisoners were more likely than men to challenge orders. Male officers' comments were generalised, reinforcing the stereotype of the bloody-minded woman prisoner and paying scant attention to women's individual circumstances. The most frequent comment was that women prisoners 'will never take no for an answer': invariably, said the male officers, they will challenge an order and demand an explanation for a punishment. Unlike men, who were said to 'get their head down and do their bird', women 'always want to know *why*'. Even when they were given an answer they would continue to seek further reasons. As one male senior officer said:

> No woman likes to feel she should be inside. Lots of males accept that they have done the crime and now they should do the time. Women don't feel that. They tend to say it's not fair. Even if they admit their guilt they'll still say "It's not fair because some other woman did worse than me". They think they should be doing community service.

Some staff did qualify their responses. The male governor of an open prison said: 'Women do challenge officers when they tell them what to do. But I find they respond better to reasoned answers. They will listen and then do what you tell them. Whereas male prisoners will go off saying "That's a load of crap!"'

The male deputy governor of a closed women's prison felt that officers, especially male officers, needed special training to prepare them for women's reactions to discipline:

I think you need to warn officers about to start work with women that they will challenge them all the time. The officers will either have to jolly them along or give them a good explanation even if it's only a brief explanation. It's no good just saying "Do it because I say so". If they ask why, there *should* be an explanation, or you shouldn't be asking them to do it in the first place. Some staff just can't accept that. They find this job attractive because to them it's a power trip and they are in charge.

Do women challenge the rules out of sheer bloody-mindedness? Or could it be because the rules in women's jails are seen as over-prescriptive, and sometimes so pointless that they *need* challenging? Is the perception that women are bound to be more 'difficult' simply another self-perpetuating prison myth? Or is it just stereotyping again? As one life-sentenced prisoner said 'Women aren't supposed to show anger or be aggressive, but it's acceptable for men to be like that.' Another lifer nearing the end of a long sentence spent in a number of prisons feels that prison has an empowering influence on some women, which gives them strength to challenge the system: 'Women do ask more questions than men do. And some abused women are away from their partners for the first time and this means that prison makes them stronger.'

Several prisoners with children of their own objected to being infantilised by puerile rules and regulations. Certainly the language used by some officers reinforced this perception. There was frequent talking of 'the girls playing up again'. 'Occasionally we have to impose a bedtime curfew', said a senior officer in one open prison, 'if they start playing up.' HM Inspectorate[12] acknowledged that 'pettiness is often reported to be a feature of women's prisons' and condemned the practice of unnecessarily taking away responsibility from women.

All prisons operate under a combination of various sets of Rules: those set out in the Prison Act 1952; those listed in the Prison Rules 1964; and those in the Young Offender Institution Rules 1988. There are also large numbers of local rules peculiar to each establishment. Rule 47 sets out the offences against prison discipline which can be summarized[13] as follows:

1. assault; 2. detaining another person; 3. denying an officer access to part of the prison; 4. fighting; 5. intentionally endangering health of others; 6. obstructing an officer; 7. escaping/absconding; 8. breaking rules of temporary release; 9. possessing an unauthorised article; 10. selling an article to another prisoner; 11. selling one of his or her own possessions; 12. taking another prisoner's belongings; 13. setting fire to the prison; 14. destroying or damaging property; 15. not being in the right place at the right time; 16. being disrespectful to an officer or visitor; 17. using abusive

threatening or insulting words/behaviour; 18. refusing to work/work properly; 19. disobeying orders; 21. offending against GOAD; 22. committing/inciting others to commit any of the 21 offences already set out.

Rule 47 also sets out the punishments that can be inflicted on a prisoner who commits any of the above offences. There are seven main punishments:

1. caution; 2. loss of privileges for up to 42 days; 3. stopping wages for up to 42 days; 4. confinement in cell for up to 14 days; 5. up to 42 extra days in prison; 6. exclusion from work; 7. loss of right to wear own clothes (for unconvicted prisoners who escape or try to escape).

Though there are only seven of them, these punishments are broad enough to be a catch-all covering most eventualities. It was revealing to observe how they were being interpreted in practice. I remember one long-term male prisoner beginning an essay on prison life with the weary words: 'Prison is rules, is rules, is rules . . . ' It is this unrelenting obsession with the enforcement of a vast number of *minor* rules, and the ongoing danger of infringing them every moment of every day, that breaks the spirit, induces paranoia and wears the prisoner down, as indeed it is designed to do.

Worse still, many of the rules are local to individual prisons, so something that may be permitted in one prison is forbidden in the next (as I described when writing about reception processes in *Chapter 2*). Women find this inconsistency endlessly frustrating: a typical example is the 'volumetric control' of items allowed in possession. This can mean that women sent to one prison may be given 'property boxes' much smaller than in another prison. This may mean they can no longer keep in their cells books they need for study, art and craft materials and so on. Women, who do not wear uniform, use more toiletries and keep more family mementoes, are yet again disadvantaged by rules made for men. For long-term prisoners, anything that will not fit in the 'prop box' is now sent to the North of England to a central Prison Service depot for all prisons, and women worry they will never see valued possessions again. It is not surprising they feel like challenging the rules.

• • •

In the young offenders' wing of a closed prison I visited, the young women were certainly challenging the justice of the punishments given them. Some complained bitterly of days added to their sentences (which would be covered under punishment number five in the above list). But according to the women these ADAs—additional days added—were handed out for the most minor misdemeanours.

They also complained about fines, presumably imposed by stopping money out of wages as in punishment number three in the list. The male wing officer ignored the women as they wandered in with their grievances. A wing cleaner leaned on her broom in the wing office doorway: 'You writing about this prison, Miss? Ask him why he fines us 20p every time we sit on the stairs! Would you believe you get a day on to your sentence for not having a potty in your cell? Ask him about that!'

Marcia was equally keen to talk: 'I'll talk to you, Miss! I'll tell you how they add on extra days for eating too slow!' Later in the wing TV room Marcia explained:

I should have gone home on 27th December in time for New Year which I've been looking forward to more than Christmas. But I've had extra days added and now I won't be out till the third of January. I lost five days and got a £3 fine for eating too slowly in the dining room. You have to queue for your food then you've only got about ten minutes to eat your meal before you have to hand in your tray and get out again – and you get nicked for being in there too long'.

Marcia's friend Morag joined in:

I was with her and I eat slowly anyway – the screws know that. We both sat there and then we went out and we didn't know anything was wrong. The next day this officer comes in with a report sheet and says we was nicked. I should have gone home in October but now I'm not going till April, I've lost that many days. I lost two days for smoking on the hospital corridor, four days for being where I shouldn't be – I was outside another wing gate talking to my friends in there. You need to chat to a friend if you're feeling down. Then you can lose a day if you get to your room late when they call you to be locked in. So it was a lot of stupid little things like that and I've ended up losing six months altogether. Losing days is the worst penalty they can give us, specially the women with kids. We'd rather go down the block. I put in an R and C[14] about getting nicked for eating slowly.

I did not stay in that prison long enough to find out whether Morag's complaint was upheld. But my conversations with most of the women suggested that though they might go through the motions of putting in request and complaint forms, they did not expect to get any satisfaction.

• • •

At one open prison, I interviewed a sociology graduate in her late twenties who was serving nine months for theft from her employer. As one of the few highly educated prisoners, she made it her business to galvanise the other women into pursuing their legal rights:

> The officers are threatened by me because I am aware of the complaints system and I encourage the women to use it. The officers' reaction is to stay clear of me and I do the same to them. They can't stand people like me. They block out challenges by endless subtle things which in fact amount to harassment.

Prison rules are complicated and intimidating, but those who persist can sometimes triumph over the system. I witnessed just such an instance at a different prison where a group of four well-educated remand prisoners, jointly accused of a human rights protest, had decided to conduct their own defence in court. The women were well aware that in the absence of legal visits, they were allowed certain rights of access to law books and other information and—more problematically for the prison—frequent access to each other, if they were to rehearse their case in time for the trial.

The female governor knew the law as well as they, and was determined to uphold their rights:

> They must be given resources to prepare a proper defence and to practice their defence together. They just want to act out the court scene, decide how they will present it. We must allow them any facilities they need. That is their right.

The male officers were plainly disturbed: 'I'm sorry but I've got a problem with this', said one, 'I don't see why they should have what the other women don't have.' They repeatedly expressed their opinion that law was a job for the professionals—for qualified solicitors and barristers. This was an interesting *volte-face:* I had earlier observed these same officers actively uniting with other women who had complained about the standard of legal aid representation. The officers joined these other women in condemning the shortcomings of the legal profession. But now they were being asked to support educated middle-class women taking on that same profession single-handed. This was quite another matter.

The four co-accused women insisted on their civil rights to the letter. Each day they marched purposefully round the exercise yard together, using up every minute of their allotted allowance. Whenever they addressed any officer, they wrote verbatim notes of the officer's response on the small notepad that each of them carried everywhere. The male officers shifted uncomfortably from one foot to another as they reluctantly gave them the information they sought. 'I can't *stand* the way they write everything down', one officer told a colleague, 'It really gets me!' They plainly found it easier to deal with challenges to their authority from other less articulate women whom they could scathingly dismiss as 'stroppy cows'.

In fact, because this prison was seriously under-staffed, meeting the women's requests caused considerable operational problems. The woman governor accepted that they needed some quiet time together. At first they tried to congregate round a table during normal association times. But the other prisoners found them a source of endless fascination. Some interrupted, wanting a letter read or written; a few jeered; most offered their support and wanted to join in the discussion. The noise made proper consultation impossible. Had the governor bent the rules and allowed them to congregate in one cell there might have been jealousy among the other women, and a precedent set that could be exploited by some to bully others. The library was empty but no staff were free to supervise. Finally the governor made the controversial decision to move the women to the privileged wing. This enraged the male officers. They felt it had taken 'ordinary women' months to earn this right.

I interviewed one of the four women:

> They don't like us defending ourselves. Arranging meeting times is very difficult. We are supposed to be accorded the privilege of legal visits, which we would get if we had engaged lawyers. That would be twice a week. There is a lot of pressure against people doing it themselves.

After six months on remand the women won their case in the courts and were released. The governor rang to tell me they had sent her a letter of gratitude. She had upheld the women's rights, but at the risk of alienating her staff.

The Inspectorate review expressed grave concern at the high levels of staff sickness absences in women's prisons—much higher than in men's.[15] During my research period in that prison, the governor had only 17 officers to control 151 women. Seven of these officers were pregnant, two almost at full-term: they could hardly have been fully operational in any disturbance. There should have been 33 officers on the day shift, but many were sick, some had been suspended pending allegations and a few, joked their colleagues I was interviewing that sunny Friday afternoon in June, had decided to 'swing the lead' and play truant.

Maybe because this prison was so short staffed, the officers tried to maintain a very heavy show of discipline and supervision at mealtimes. At 11.30 a.m. the women were let out through their wing gate to file along to the wing kitchen, collect their lunch and take it back to their cells, where they were locked in to eat it. A group of six officers flanked the gate where it led to the kitchen, formally ranked three on either side, forming a narrow corridor for the women to pass through. They stood straight, arms folded, shoulders squared, summoning six women through at a time. The line-up felt threatening, though it was perhaps understandable with so much hot food and large serving implements around.

One officer wielded a strange device—a wand with a metal disk at the top. It was a metal detector but, the officer confided to me, it didn't work: 'I think the battery's gone down or something. Still, it looks good!'

A male officer shoved a woman back in line, shouting at her, 'Do as I tell you! Why d'you think I've got these stripes on my shoulder?'

The women filing back to eat lunch in their cells seemed docile enough. So what is it about prison regimes that so regularly goads female prisoners into 'kicking off'? Could it be the kind of deliberately confrontational behaviour shown by some officers? Kate Donegan, appointed governor of Cornton Vale after a spate of prison suicides, told a conference at HMP Styal[5] that while prisoner-on-prisoner assaults at her prison remained high, prisoner-on-officer assaults were non-existent: 'That is a staff training issue', she said.

In *Chapter 3* I described the worries women expressed about their problems at home. One female governor felt strongly that this was the reason for the disturbances in many women's prisons, and that male staff did not understand it: 'There is no acknowledgement from male staff that everyone who comes here comes with some sort of emotional baggage. The summer holidays are when the women get very edgy and we have more disciplinary problems because they don't know where their children might be. I make sure they get a free phone call in the summer holidays—that helps a bit.'

In *Chapter 4* I examined the problems caused by dislocation from family and friends and the distress of women unexpectedly cut off from their children, their visits often cancelled for disciplinary reasons. Sometimes of course the cause can be purely operational and pragmatic. But so jagged are the emotions in prison life that it takes very little for a situation to become volatile. Here a life-sentenced prisoner records events one November evening in a closed prison:

Chaos this evening. Discontent all round as the incoming phone call equipment had been fitted but no box as yet, though we all expected it. No

102

organization for incoming phone calls and great ructions when newcomers to the wing monopolised the phone. Two young officers on the wing should have been aware of the risk in not taking control of the situation straight away. Net result was a near riot with lots of screaming and shouting and rushing up and down the wing. Three were taken to the block.

The same prisoner described a similar incident when electrical points were installed in every cell in her prison and the women were led to expect that they would be allowed to pay to rent a television set out of their prison wages. (Women in Durham's top security H wing are allowed to rent television sets for use in their cells: one male officer told me that TV sets were 'useful for the inadequates who can't get to sleep without it'). But no sooner had the work been completed than the plans were abandoned and raised hopes were dashed. 'We can have our music off the electric, but no TV. The screws said it was Michael Howard's fault, not theirs'.[16]

Broken promises and nonsensical bureaucracy were mentioned by many women as a reason for discontent and frustration: 'If you ask the officers something, however small, they won't bother to do it for you. They may promise, but they won't do it.' In view of current staff cuts and more overcrowding, complaints like these will inevitably increase: 'Us YOs are supposed to go to gym one hour a week but of the 125 or so girls in here, only about three or four go to the gym. We're banged up 17 hours a day.'

At one open prison, lifers approaching the end of long sentences are given their own kitchen so they can cook for themselves as part of their pre-release preparation. They can buy ingredients by ordering them in the prison shop:

> But we have to buy a whole commercial pack of twelve packets of pasta or twelve tins of tuna! When we ask why, they always say "Just because!" It's what I call the "broken record syndrome." Everything here is taken to the max. The amount of paperwork caused here by disciplinary matters is amazing. The rules are petty and puerile and the officers enjoy enforcing them out of sheer badness.

Both officers and prisoners felt that an entirely new phenomenon—drug abuse—was the root cause of many disciplinary problems. In attempting to deal with drugs, prison officers are in previously uncharted waters. But it is clear that the presence of drugs has certainly made prison discipline much harder to maintain.

New specially trained search teams were introduced in 1996 and caused a mixture of hilarity and fear when they first appeared on the wings, clad in black trousers and matching red T shirts with the letters DST printed on them (see *Chapter 4*). 'I've no idea what the letters mean,' said one Holloway prisoner, 'they won't tell us. But they don't half look daft. They carry these little cases around like vanity cases. They won't tell us what's in them either.'

The letters in fact stand for Dedicated Search Team and the cases contain tools to help the teams remove panels and unscrew furniture in their search for hidden drugs and other contraband. The refusal of the prison authorities to explain to the women the function of the teams is symptomatic of poor communications throughout the whole Prison Service. Staff from senior management to new recruits complained about it just as angrily as prisoners.

Drugs were said to be part of the reason for the serious riot on 20 January 1997 at the male prison HMP Full Sutton, where drugs barons, angry at the disruption of their prison rackets, incited other men to rebel. It would be naive and foolish to believe that parallel activities do not also go on in women's prisons, or that they can be dealt with wearing kid gloves, and obviously the teams have to respond rapidly to a tip-off. But there also seems to be little excuse for the kind of officially-sanctioned vandalism described by an outraged Holloway prisoner who telephoned me the morning after the DST team carried out one of its searches in the prison:

> They've almost wrecked the library — they pulled lots of the books off the shelves and left them lying round the floor with their tickets all fallen out. You know that little courtyard outside the library? They dug up the paving slabs and didn't put them back properly, they broke a flowerpot and dug up some shrubs and they've left the whole place in an awful mess. In the cells they tore people's family photos off the walls without removing the drawing pins, so they were split down the middle. It was real vandalism — what an example to set to the young offenders! The women are going mad!

Of course, not all search teams behave in this way. In another closed prison a woman showed me her cell. She apologized that it wasn't as tidy as usual, 'because I've just had a room spin'. Though her clothes and books were stacked on top of the bed and the cover still pulled up, she felt the officers had treated her belongings with respect and was grateful. She understood that they were doing their job and any resentment was defused.

The DST teams have—for obvious reasons—been nicknamed the 'swoop squads'. But in women's prisons they also have a more unpleasant name—the 'squat squads'. This refers to the degrading process described in *Chapter 2* where women are ordered to remove their underwear and bend forwards in a semi-squatting position or stand over a mirror (though Sheila Bowler said she 'would sooner be sent down the block than submit to such humiliation'. Thankfully she never had to). Women also report being required to undergo a strip search[17] each time they are randomly selected for a urine test under the terms of the Mandatory Drug Testing scheme (MDT) introduced by the Prison Service in 1995.

In March 1997 Sir Peter Woodhead, the Prisons Ombudsman, complained that prison officers carrying out strip searches were going 'way beyond the requirements in their own security manual', and the Director General of the Prison Service, Richard Tilt, warned prison governors not to abuse the guidelines on strip-searching inmates: 'I am reminding governors that squatting and bending must only be done where there is reasonable suspicion'.[18]

Three months later, at the beginning of June 1997, the media reported a scandal at HMP Highpoint, a former male prison and the most recent addition to the female estate. Four male officers were alleged to have strip-searched a female prisoner forcibly, three of them holding her down while a male doctor performed an internal examination. Women's groups expressed their horror and the Prison Service launched an enquiry. It was said that the woman was suspected of internally secreting illegal drugs.

But whatever the reasons behind the incident, the level of force used seems indefensible. Prison rule 44 says that 'an officer in dealing with a prisoner shall not use force unnecessarily and, when the application of force to a prisoner is necessary, no more force than is necessary shall be used'.

The wide-ranging effects of drugs in prison are discussed in more detail in *Chapter 9*. But drugs are mentioned here in the context of offences against prison discipline for a number of reasons.

First, some drugs are liable to make users more aggressive and therefore more likely to 'kick off' and breach prison rules. Opponents of mandatory urine tests point to the increase in hard drug use in prisons, because soft drugs like marijuana can remain detectable in urine testing for up to 30 days, while hard drugs are out of the system in two or three days and are therefore far less likely to be detected. While marijuana has a calming effect (and is therefore claimed by some prisoners to be secretly welcomed by prison officers), the crack cocaine which is replacing it in some prisons has the very opposite effect.

Second, the desperate craving for drugs leads prisoners to desperate measures to get them, including violent attacks on other prisoners, leading to further disciplinary procedures against them.

Third, the indignities described above, imposed on non-drug users during random testing, makes this group angry too. Refusal to undergo the test is itself a disciplinary offence and the degrading nature of the testing process heightens the antagonism both against the officers carrying out the tests and the drug-using prisoners perceived as the cause of the problem. There is also widespread scepticism about the accuracy of the tests, and a perception that results are fixed to show the prison in a good light in Prison Service 'league tables' (see *Chapter 9*).

Fourth, the whole raft of further security procedures enforced in the attempt to prevent drugs entering prisons has severely curtailed the activities of all prisoners. As I described in *Chapter 4*, those without any involvement in drugs feel particularly aggrieved.

Another reason given for the Full Sutton disturbances was the introduction of a new incentives scheme, which angered the male prisoners by forcing them to earn privileges that hitherto they had taken for granted. The Incentives and Earned Privileges Scheme (IEPS), introduced in 1995, places prisoners on Basic, Standard or Enhanced regimes depending on their behaviour. The effect of the system on the efforts of women prisoners to keep in touch with their families were discussed in *Chapters 3* and *4*. The frustration of women whose links with their children are curtailed for what seem to be petty reasons has certainly been identified as a common cause of anger and consequent indiscipline.

A major problem with IEPS lies in its administration by officers whom prisoners feel can be personally biased against them. Women commonly described being demoted for what they regarded as trivial offences or false accusations: 'Abolish the incentives scheme as it's unfair: if a member of staff doesn't like you then you are unlikely to be placed on Enhanced, even if you have earned it—or you may even be put down to Basic.' Another major cause of resentment is the system whereby a move to a new prison usually means demotion, certainly down from Enhanced to Standard, and sometimes back to Basic, until prisoners have 'proved' themselves. Ten per cent of the letters sent to the Prison Reform Trust by prisoners are complaints about the unfairness of the scheme. It has been criticised by the Prisons Ombudsman, who recognised the 'considerable potential for injustice. There is a danger that prisoners can be removed from higher levels to lower levels for arbitrary reasons or as a punishment'.[19] Reports from the Inspectorate have also expressed concern. The Styal inspection report in November 1996 found 'many examples of incomplete (IEPS) review forms in the prisoners' personal files . . . We felt that many aspects of the Incentives and Earned Privileges Scheme indicated the need for a review'.[19] And at Highpoint in March 1997 the Inspectors found that 'the scheme was introduced sooner than expected and very few staff had received adequate training'.[19]

The most vehement critics of the pettiness of prison rules were women held in open prisons, where, paradoxically in establishments supposed to be preparing prisoners for release, the regimes can seem even harsher than in closed establishments. In theory there are no gates or fences, though increasingly barriers are being erected—ostensibly to secure the women against prowlers. Perhaps because of the absence of external boundaries, the internal regulations can seem highly prescriptive and repressive.

Young offenders—in the female estate generally mixed in with older women—feel the restrictions particularly acutely. Vicky, at 17 the youngest woman in her open prison, gave a graphic account of her daily life, first in a closed prison, then in her current open establishment:

> The rules change all the time. A lot of the time in my last prison I was on 24 hour bang-up. The officers there kept saying I had "a bad attitude". I was nicked first for pressing the buzzer three times to go to the toilet.[20] I lost three days' association[21] and seven days' pay and seven days' canteen. Here you are on edge all the time. There's no list of rules. You have to pick them up from the other inmates. The screws suspect you of everything. Like if you go into association all happy and jolly you get piss-tested for drugs! They are supervising you and watching you all the time. I do get very happy sometimes and I know I'm very loud. Sometimes I just want to SHOUT! And there's nowhere to shout in here. There's a load of petty rules. If you look further than your nose you're nicked. YOs like me have to be in bed by 11 p.m. I'm in an eight-bedder with an overhead light so I can't even read a book if the older women want to go to sleep.

At a different open prison, an 18-year-old told a similar story of how she got into trouble for what in other circumstances might be regarded as youthful exuberance:

> One time I did a dance because the music was loud and I just felt like dancing. If the music's wild you've just got to dance! This woman officer was screaming at me and she put me on report. She never asked me why I felt like dancing — it was only to cheer myself up.

The dress code imposed on women in prison causes problems because of the stereotypical assumptions made in society outside as well as inside prisons about what women choose to wear. Everyone must by now be familiar with the criticisms levelled at judges who make comments about rape victims being partly culpable by 'asking for it', wearing mini-skirts or other 'provocative' clothing. One woman who

107

had worked in the London sex industry told me it was common knowledge that police officers are more likely to arrest a woman if she is not carrying a handbag—presumably a mark of such respectability that the lack of one can place a woman under suspicion of criminal tendencies! Female officers often criticised women prisoners who allegedly dressed provocatively to inflame the passions of male officers.[22] Women held in shared-site prisons were not allowed to wear cropped-top tee shirts out on exercise because they might have a similar effect on male prisoners looking out of their cell windows: 'It's just not fair on the men', they were told.

Sometimes however the aggravation was caused by rules that the women regarded as unnecessarily intrusive. A middle-aged prisoner complained that she was 'hassled for wearing gym trousers round the prison'. The wing cleaner in an open prison explained: 'I like to get up early in the morning and get on with my work cleaning the prison. You're supposed to get dressed but I get on with it wearing my nightie. Why shouldn't I? There's nobody to see me, I'm getting the work done and it's only cleaning the prison so why get dressed up?'

Bending the dress code rules is nothing new. Nineteenth century women convicts,[7] like their male counterparts, had to wear a sober uniform, but this only strengthened their resolve to retain some individuality. Matrons in charge of the Millbank women reported that they powdered their faces with distemper scraped from the walls, made rings from the foil under their dress buttons, and stiffened their stays with wire from their dinner cans.

Most convicted male prisoners are still obliged to wear a uniform of some description, even if it only consists of jeans, identical striped blue striped shirts and the same coloured sweatshirts. But women can now wear their own clothes, though prisons impose limits on the number of garments they are allowed 'in possession'. On the face of it, this is one area where women appear to get a better deal than men. But the situation is by no means as simple as it sounds.

Women in open prisons expressed outrage at some of the penalties imposed for breaches of the prison dress code. At one open prison, three women were particularly irritated by the 'slipper rule':

It's like a boarding school, full of petty rules and regulations. You can't wear slippers for coming to meals. If you are staying in the TV room after 9 p.m. you must be in your "night attire". The awful apathy is because of the control imposed by the petty rules.

There are a lot of petty rules—for instance there's even a rule about shuffling your feet! I saw an officer put a girl on report for that and some officers report you for wearing slippers round the prison.

> There's this stupid slipper rule. They book you for wearing slippers round the prison. But then this prison's supposed to be our home, and we'd wear slippers at home!

The illogicality of the rules causes most frustration. Women may not be able to wear slippers, and in one prison they are not allowed nose rings ('because in case of an accident their breathing would be impaired'— though one wonders how women in the community outside prison manage) but they *are* allowed to wear gold jewellery. Paradoxically this may be a case where stricter rules are necessary: women used to be able to wear only a partner's gold ring and a cross or St Christopher medallion but now they can use jewellery and designer clothes to do deals and buy drugs.

A senior officer in the 'slipper' prison said:

> We did have a rule restricting jewellery but we were being told by a lot of women that this rule was not being imposed elsewhere so the restrictions were lifted. But I think a lot of wheeling and dealing does go on and we'll soon have to pull back on that one. There's a lot of bartering and you can't tell if bullying or taxing[23] are going on.

Prisoners' reaction to the 'slipper rule' is typical of their reaction to the whole raft of seemingly petty rules by which their daily lives are governed. Every woman I questioned in the three open prisons I visited regarded the rules with contempt. 'Pathetic' was a word commonly used. Their frustration, expressed in the following quotations is palpable:

> The whole problem of the rules is their pettiness. If you ever question them the officers get angry. And they are such *pathetic* rules. Prisoners never get to see any list of the rules though they're supposed to show you a list.

> There are a lot of petty rules like not walking on the grass, or being out of bounds. You can get three extra days added to your sentence after three warnings. I have to count to ten five times a day to survive.

The male governor of the prison where these women were held felt that seemingly petty restrictions could be justified both on security and health and safety grounds:

> If the women wandered round in slippers and dropped hot food on their feet we'd be in trouble. It's the same with sunbathing. We had quite a few

women going topless so we have had to insist on a certain standard of dress. They can't go round in cropped tops and they can't wear shorts. You have to realise that not a lot is really demanded of the women here. All we ask is that they turn up on time so we are not chasing them round all the time, wear reasonable dress and behave reasonably well.

Because this is an open prison some things may seem petty to the women but in fact they are very important. One of the issues that causes them a lot of trouble is being punished for turning up late at meals. They get three warnings about this before they have an adjudication[24] but we have to explain to them that mealtimes are our main security check. So if they are late they get a formal warning and if they get three warnings they are put on report and then they might get a quite heavy punishment. The point is that these security checks are vital to the running of the jail and without them the regime would fall apart.

I was given a mass of conflicting information about the enforcement of the 'LA [Lesbian Activities] rule'. Officially, women publicly showing affection to each other can be put on a disciplinary charge under the GOAD prison rule which enables any prisoner to be removed from association with other prisoners, usually for the maintenance of good order and discipline in the prison. One officer explained: 'The rules are that homosexual activity in private among consenting adults is not against the law. But a prison is not a private place so there is nowhere in a prison where this should be allowed. Having said that we only really challenge predatory lesbianism because that amounts to bullying.'

In women's prisons, homosexual relationships have historically been tolerated or ignored. Lucia Zedner[7] recounts that in nineteenth century male prisons the authorities, worried at the extent of 'unnatural practices', meted out severe punishment for homosexual activities. But they refused to accept that female friendships could ever be of a sexual nature, and women were free to indulge in what they called 'palling-in'. Although well aware that lesbian relationships exist, most prison officers I interviewed said that unless the 'display of affection' was very overt, they were prepared to turn a blind eye to it:

LA is a case of good order and discipline. If two prisoners were found in sexual congress we would do something about it but otherwise we'd turn a blind eye. They can go to each other's rooms because this is an open prison. But it is of course unhelpful to have close sexual relationships in closed societies like prisons or the forces. I would say the rule is that if it is going on to the discomfort of others sharing the same room, we would have to put a stop to it, if they are found at it three or four times a night.

Male officers commonly said they did not like displays of affection between gay women on visits: 'I warn lesbian women not to get too tangled up with their girlfriends when they come in on visits. A quick peck on the cheek at the beginning and the end of a visit is all we allow. Visits are mixed company and you get little kids and old grannies in here who get very shocked.'

Another male officer, one of the many 'Hindley name-droppers', said 'Most of the staff turn a blind eye to lesbian activities as long as they are not so overt that they offend others. I remember some of the staff being very upset at Myra kissing a woman visitor—so I told Myra just to give the visitor a peck on the cheek in future.'

How far is 'kicking off' caused by the *manner* in which prison rules—petty or otherwise—are enforced? In all prisons the extent to which rules are enforced depends on the staff doing the enforcing. In the end it depends on the quality of staff-prisoner relationships and empathy further discussed in *Chapter 6*. As one experienced and popular woman officer said, 'You need rules to run any establishment: you can get round problems by having good relationships—lots of them.'

A male governor said 'You will never get an entirely cohesive group of officers. Some will be flexible but some will go exactly by the rule book, and they're the worst kind. Prisoners must be dealt with flexibly: some will have developmental retardation and if they act like children they must be dealt with firmly. If they act like adults they should be treated like adults.'

Male officers coming from male establishments to work in women's prisons for the first time were surprised at the punishments handed out for small misdemeanours (like swearing) that would have gone unremarked in male establishments. Most put this down to female officers' greater harshness against their own sex. As one male head of sentence management said, 'Women officers are harder on women prisoners. Male officers have a lot of abuse to start off with but 99 times out of 100 the women will apologise. There's a lot of petty stuff on both sides'. The female Regimes Manager of another open prison agreed:

The statistics do show that women are twice as likely to kick off and the statistics are the same whether it is an open or closed establishment. The records certainly show that we do see more inappropriate behaviour than in the male prisons. Women do take more advantage of the situation. On the other hand women officers do spend more time observing the women than male officers do and I think we also expect a higher standard of behaviour from women prisoners.

A young male officer said 'I would only give a direct order as a very last resort. That's the stage before being put on report. Any officer should have worked out the problem before it reached that stage. There must *be* a problem. It could be that a woman was under pressure from other women, or she has lost some property, or there's a personal problem at home. It's all about keeping your eyes and ears open. I have had training in hostage negotiation and I learned that there is always an opening, no matter how hard it seems.'

According to the women prisoners I interviewed, such understanding from officers, regardless of their gender, is very rare. On the contrary, a number of women described deliberate 'winding up' of women by staff, though rule 44 of the Prison Rules states that 'no officer shall act deliberately in a manner calculated to provoke a prisoner.' An animal rights protester nearing the end of her sentence in an open prison was allowed out to work in the community: 'To officers you are always a jailbird. Officers begrudge me going swimming to work with autistic kids. I get back exhausted and I have to listen to them saying "We've got to work while you go swimming". In my head I'm a bit anarchic and that does my head in more than anything. It really winds me up and I could lash out.'

Sheila Bowler was waiting anxiously to go to court to hear the judgement for her first appeal (which was to fail, though her conviction was quashed at the second appeal). She had endured a tense three-week wait after the appeal was heard. She described a cruel joke played by a senior officer at Holloway:

> He came into the office and said to the wing officer "Have you told her that Friday [the date of the judgment] is cancelled?" I was shocked and asked if that meant I was to phone my solicitor in Birmingham. "That won't be necessary," he said, shrugging his shoulders. I asked him if it was a wind-up, to which he laughed. How insensitive can you get? I told him he can have no idea what I am going through just now but he should try to develop some sensitivity and a little imagination.

In another prison, a woman described delays on visits days, a complaint echoed by several others quoted in *Chapter 4*: 'One of the worst wind-ups is when they don't call you to visits in time: some officers do it deliberately because they are on a power trip.'

Prisoners were not alone in making such allegations: a recently-retired education officer had the job, while Rosemary West was on remand, of taking needlework for her to do:

> She's very good at sewing and makes things for her grandchildren. She was held in isolation in the hospital wing while she was on remand and I had to

take the materials over to her. One day when I got back there was a group of women waiting for me. They were out to get me for taking things to her and they were in a very nasty mood. I calmed them down and I asked them if they'd like me to assume they were all guilty too. I told them that while Rose West was on remand she was as innocent as I was. I found out later that the officers had wound them up and told them to say all that rubbish. They love setting prisoner against prisoner.

Although women will challenge the system informally, driven by their frustration to fight back verbally and sometimes physically by 'kicking off', they rarely take advantages of the rights of appeal available to them because they fear reprisals. This especially applies to those with children, because of their fear of visits being cancelled and of being 'shipped out' far from home and family (see *Chapters 3* and *4*). Paradoxically, it is perhaps the frustration of feeling that such formal complaints methods seem unavailable to them that leads them to lash out and kick the system from time to time.

It is generally felt that the word of an officer will invariably be accepted against the word of a prisoner, whatever the evidence. Although in theory the right to appeal against an adjudication verdict exists, the procedure is complicated and prisoners fear reprisals from officers who can make their life very difficult while they await the outcome of their appeal.

Sadly, few of the women I interviewed expressed much confidence in the Boards of Visitors at their prisons. They claimed that BOV members were difficult to access because 'they always get taken round by the governor'. In practice BOV members are usually given keys and have access to all parts of the prison. They are obliged to carry out weekly 'rota' visits to certain areas including the segregation cells, the kitchens and the rule 43 areas.

But many of the prisoners said they distrusted the BOV because they are seen as part of the prison establishment. Though since 1992 the Boards no longer have any disciplinary function, older prisoners recall that they used to carry out their own adjudications. Perhaps more work could be done to communicate to women that this duty has ceased. BOVs do, however, still have an input into the parole process. The chair of one board said she could understand prisoners' reservations:

I agree that as we still have this function, inmates might watch their step in what they say to us, because they don't want to be labelled a complainer or a troublemaker in case it affects their parole. We have got to be seen to be independent of management.

Most women I interviewed had no faith at all in 'due process'—the statutory prison procedures which enable them to appeal against alleged injustices. Their perception of prison justice is that the officers hold all the cards, they close ranks and whatever the official rules, it makes no difference to the result of an adjudication. A 19-year-old in a closed prison described the system:

> Adjudications are terrible — they act like you're back in court. You get taken off to the block first to wait for your adjudication then you get brought up to the governor's office and you've got one officer on either side of you, and the governor's got one officer on either side of her and there's a long table in front of you so you can't do nothing.
>
> Nobody ever bothers to say they're not guilty at an adjudication — well, hardly anybody — because you know it's your word against theirs. The staff all stick together and even if you're proved not guilty they *never* say "not guilty" — they just say "dismissed". It says in that Yellow Book[25] that you can get a legal representative at adjudications. But I don't think that ever happens.

Ceri is now 21 and her first experience of a governor's adjudication terrified her:

> I'll never forget when I had an adjudication. At my first [closed] prison I was given 20 Regal Kingsize by my mum at visits and I didn't know I couldn't take in cigarettes. I didn't try to hide them or anything — I just didn't know. Though the fags were there for everybody to see I was still given a strip search. I had to take all my clothes off in front of two women officers. It was very degrading, *very* degrading it was. Then they told me to get dressed and I had to go in front of three more officers and the governor. It was terrible, it was like being back at court. They asked me "Have you anything to say?" so I told them the truth. I had nothing to hide. I was given seven days extra on my sentence. I think it would be a good idea to have an outside person[26] at adjudications to see fair play.

At another prison—an open establishment—an older woman agreed:

> I think there should be an outside person brought in for adjudications. A girl the other day at one adjudication got three days' loss of remission and a fine for nicking a pint of milk. Another got two days' suspended sentence for coming back drunk. I think the second offence was much worse and you've got to have a fairer system.

The summary justice administered in prison adjudications has long been a cause of concern among penal reformers and civil liberty

114

campaigners. The veteran criminologist Pat Carlen described at a 1996 conference a non-punitive method of dispute settlement she had seen in New Zealand prisons where outside arbitrators are brought in to deal with disputes between officers and prisoners.[27]

Some vulnerable prisoners said they were sent for adjudication when they were in no fit state to withstand the stress. Hilary (see *Chapter 2*) killed her abusive partner and her mental state was so severely disturbed that she had to spend the first three months of her remand period in the prison hospital. She had just been moved onto normal location on one of the wings and started her job as a wing cleaner when she was put on report:

One day an officer said to me "You're nicked! You're on report!" I didn't know what he meant. It devastated me. I cried. It made me ill. Next day I found myself taken to the seg[28] for adjudication. They came and got me after breakfast and said I had had 'numerous warnings' about my cleaning from the officers. I had had none—I'd only just started the job! From the seg I couldn't even ring my son. They told me what to write down so I wrote it. I wrote, "I am sorry if my work is not up to standard. I would never be knowingly rude to anyone." The governor dismissed the case. I think I must have been set up, or confused for someone else, and I still don't understand why this happened. This incident showed me just how fragile I still am. I have got no confidence since that happened to me.

It was shocking to meet some of the women who had recently been sent 'down the block': they must have gone through an adjudication process, though it was plain they were seriously mentally disturbed. It is against prison rules for prisoners to be sent for adjudication if they are incapable of a full understanding of the rules. Most shocking were the incidents where self-harming women had been sent to the segregation unit, at a time when they were so desperately in need of support. Officially self-mutilation is a reportable offence, amazingly placed in the disciplinary category of assault, and thus a breach of prison rules. In *Chapter 12* I examine in more detail the incidence of self-harm in women's prisons.

The strip cell and the strip dress[29] are meant to be used only to ensure the prisoner's safety, and then only in the health care centre, not the segregation block—like the padded cell and straitjacket in Victorian asylums. But like these discredited methods, there is growing anecdotal evidence that they are being used for disciplinary purposes.

A female officer currently serving in a closed prison confirmed that the strip cell is becoming accepted as part of the normal control and restraint procedure:

115

These women won't back down if they are kicking off. They will fight and you have to restrain them. We don't know how far to go and we have asked for instructions. For instance there may not be time to get other female officers from other wings and you may have only two officers, one male and one female, to take a woman down to the strip cell. We have to make her take off her clothes and put on a paper dress and if a male member of staff comes in there can be allegations.

In February 1997 a prisoner in a closed prison wrote to the Board of Visitors and the Ombudsman alleging misconduct by prison staff. Because she was refused a request she had smashed up her cell in retaliation. The female governor was off duty, and, according to the prisoner, the male staff ordered her to be put in a strip cell, made her remove her clothes and told her she must put on a strip dress. The prisoner refused, and remained naked (she was menstruating at the time), and the officers withheld any food or water for 48 hours. This constituted an offence because illegal restraints were allegedly used on a prisoner. Unusually—and unluckily for the officers—the prisoner was an articulate, intelligent woman jailed for fraud, who was determined to take the matter further. The Ombudsman upheld her complaint and a formal enquiry was conducted by a senior governor from another prison, though many reformers feel that such incidents should be subject to independent external investigation rather than an enquiry held within the Prison Service. A year later, in March 1998, a senior member of the prison's staff told me the woman had been awarded damages of £150,000 though at the time of writing, there have been no media reports of the award.

Few visitors to prisons are shown the cells in the punishment block, unless, like members of the official Boards of Visitors, it is part of their duty to inspect them. For any thoughtful visitor this is an area which therefore remains as an uncomfortable question mark in the back of the mind.

In one closed prison, an avuncular principal officer wonders whether I might be interested in seeing 'the block'. On our way towards the punishment cells I try to imagine what it would feel like if instead of my engaging in civilised conversation with this large cheerful man, he was one of a team of four or more officers dragging me along the low corridor. 'When a woman's in full C and R',[30] he is explaining, 'we've got hold of her arms in such a way that if she fights it could break her wrists, but if she cooperates it'll just make her arms ache'. Some women, he tells me, 'fight all the way to the strong box'.

Now we have reached the strong box itself, a roofless room within another room. The brick walls of the inner room stop about two feet short of the outer room ceiling and have ladder rungs built into the outside so that officers can climb up and peer down over the top at the woman inside. In the space between the outer door and the inner room walls is stored a strange contraption that looks like a very large fire extinguisher. The officer explains that this is useful for smashing down doors 'if the need arises': it is a kind of pressurised battering ram. The strong box walls are painted strawberry pink. The inner room is empty but for a raised stone platform used as a bed, and on it are two neatly folded items. One is a long padded jacket, the other a thin padded bedcover. They are made to match in a shiny red and purple striped material. The juxtaposing images of violent coercion and contrived femininity are too unpleasant to contemplate and I ask to leave. A few weeks after my visit to that prison the inspectors ordered that this same punishment block should be taken out of service.

• • •

On the final day of my research visit to a different women's prison I am again invited to see the block, this time in the company of the governor. With us is a young black prisoner, remanded from the courts the previous day on a charge of assaulting a bus conductor. She tells me she has a small baby left at home. The governor is allowing her to visit her even younger sister, held in the block because she is said to be dangerously violent, probably on crack cocaine. The governor opens a desk drawer and produces some large coloured photographs. They show the upper arm of a female prison officer, bitten deep on the underside into a gaping red wound. This, the governor tells me, was inflicted about six weeks earlier in this very prison by the woman we are going to see. She was suffering from the effects of substandard crack cocaine. 'She was HIV positive: I sent one of these pictures to Ann Widdecombe when she was prisons minister'.

The young woman and I follow the governor down a metal staircase to a row of punishment cells. Each cell has an outer set of double wooden doors, then a small vestibule, then a maroon-painted metal door with a hatch. The governor wedges the double doors open and calls to the woman inside: 'Here's your sister come to see you! Now do this visit well and I'll let you have it again.'

There is silence, then suddenly the woman's face appears at the hatch. The sisters kiss through the bars and embark on an animated conversation. They speak in a *patois* we cannot understand. The governor and I stand back from the door. 'Five minutes!' says the governor.

A gate at the end of the corridor slams shut and keys rattle in the lock. Along the corridor walk five figures. They make a chilling spectacle. An angry-eyed, dishevelled woman shuffles slowly along with four uniformed officers, two male and two female, flanking her, two on either side. The prisoner is probably in her late thirties, her blonde hair with its dark roots half covering her face. Her mascara is smeared over her cheeks. She wears a short pink skirt and white sweatshirt. The officers do not touch the woman at all, though one of them has handcuffs ready. Nobody says a word. It is as if we were not there. The woman wears bright gold sandals with very long laces, undone. She slops along in them and the four shining thongs, each about 18 inches long, trail along behind her. Somehow the sandals speak more movingly of her plight than the faceless escort beside her. The group disappears into one of the punishment cells.

The governor bangs on the maroon metal door: 'Time's up!' she says, 'Kiss your sister goodbye!'

Endnotes

1. In his report of an inspection of HMP Brockhill, published in February 1998, the Chief Inspector of Prisons noted that women prisoners were stripping to prevent male officers entering their cells. Only 40 per cent of the Brockhill officers are female and he called for the ratio to be increased to 80 per cent.
2. 'Kicking off' is the prison term for a violent disturbance by an individual, for instance smashing up a cell.
3. A room spin is an unexpected search of a prisoner's cell.
4. *Women in Prison: A Review*, HM Inspectorate, 1997; 7.17.
5. At a conference at HMP Styal, 'Imprisoning Women: Recognising Difference', organized by the Institute for the Study and Treatment of Delinquency (ISTD), 23 October 1997.
6. See *Women, Crime and Criminal Justice*, Allison Morris: Basil Blackwell 1987. She quoted 1985 figures which showed that violent incidents were two and a half times more likely in women's prisons than in men's. Women prisoners were also twice as likely to be punished for breaches of prison discipline. In 1985 there were 335 punishments per 100 women prisoners for offences against the Good Order and Discipline (GOAD) of the prison compared with 160 per 100 men prisoners. The Howard League quotes similar figures. Its Fact Sheet No. 2 gives more recent 1994 figures as 460 punishments per 100 women compared with 368 punishments per 100 men. See also NACRO Briefing No. 91, *Women and Criminal Justice*.
7. *Oxford History of the Prisons, Chapter 11*, 'Wayward Sisters', Oxford University Press, 1995.
8. *The Imprisonment of Women*, Dobash R, Dobash R and Gutteridge S, Basil Blackwell, 1986.
9. *Our Convicts*, Longman, 1864.
10. Though only seven (12 per cent—four women and three men) of the 60 officers mentioned hormonal problems as factors in violent behaviour in prison.
11. 90 per cent of male officers and 83 per cent of female officers.
12. See Note 4 above, 7.08.
13. See *The Prisoners' Information Book 1996*: Prison Reform Trust and HMP Prison Service, pp. 37-43.
14. An R and C is a 'request and complaint' form which prisoners wishing to make a formal request or complaint must complete. Perhaps significantly, prison officers call them 'CARP forms'. The process may begin with a verbal communication to an officer, followed by an application to see the governor, then, if necessary, a written formal request or complaint. If the prisoner is still not satisfied with the way prison staff deal with her problem, she can appeal to the governor, and then the area manager, by the process of 'confidential access', writing a letter in a sealed envelope. Certain more serious matters, called 'reserved subjects' can only be dealt with by the area manager or by staff in the Prisoner Casework Unit at Prison Service Headquarters. This unit deals with requests and complaints either about issues which cannot be dealt with at prison level, such as adjudications; or they will be appeals against an unsatisfactory reply from the governor. The Prisons Ombudsman can only investigate a complaint which has already been investigated at Headquarters level. However, a prisoner may

address a complaint to the Board of Visitors at any stage. Prisoners tell of long delays in the process of R and Cs: one Holloway woman said she had waited six months for a reply.

15. See Note 4, above: 4.15.
16. When Michael Howard was Home Secretary he announced in April 1996 that he would be phasing out portable television sets in cells, as part of his determination to introduce more austere regimes. But his plans were later scrapped when governors warned of widespread rioting: in January 1997 Whitehall sources confirmed to *The Sunday Times* (26 January 1997) that implementation of the policy to remove TV sets had been 'delayed indefinitely'. The decisions at the prison described — first to install in-cell TV points, then to withhold permission for the sets — were made while these moves were under discussion. Then in August 1997 there was yet another change, when the Home Office asked the Prison Service to offer one in three prisoners the use of colour TV sets in cells as part of the Incentives and Earned Privileges Scheme. (IEPS). (*The Sunday Times* , 17 August 1997).
17. See Note 13, above. The *Prisoners' Information Book* gives information on MDT and strip searching. In its explanation of the procedures for random urine testing, there is no mention of strip-searching. But in the section headed *Searching of Prisoners*, it states that any senior officer, principal officer or governor has the right to strip-search a prisoner at any time: 'A strip search may take place each time a prisoner enters or leaves a prison; immediately after a cell search; on entry to the segregation unit; and at random after social and legal visits. High and exceptional risk category A prisoners must be strip-searched after each visit.
18. Quoted in *The Independent* (7 March 1997). His comment was in response to an investigation by BBC 1's *Nine O'Clock News* which found that the practice had become routine as part of a security crackdown.
19. 'Incentives Scheme Begins to Unravel', by Nick Flynn, *Prison Report*, Prison Reform Trust, December 1997.
20. In prisons which have not installed 'integral sanitation' — toilets inside cells — prisoners are allowed out of their cells to go to the wing toilet. They can summon officers to unlock the door by pressing a call button.
21. Association is the time when prisoners are allowed out of their cells to meet, talk watch TV, go to education classes etc. It is regarded as a privilege and can be withdrawn as a punishment, for security reasons or, e.g. due to staff shortage. Prisoners not allowed association are locked in their cells.
22. See *Chapter 6*.
23. Prison slang for bullying and extortion.
24. An adjudication is a disciplinary hearing — the day to day process whereby governor grades deal with disciplinary matters.
25. *The Prisoners' Information Book*, 1995 edition — the latest 1997 'Yellow Book' has a blue cover.
26. There is legal precedent for a prisoner at an adjudication, or any party to legal proceedings in court, to request and be granted the assistance of a friend, often called a McKenzie Friend.
27. Pat Carlen: speech at a seminar *Women in Trouble with the Law*, 28 May 1996, organized by Criminal Justice Associates.
28. Segregation unit — the 'block' where prisoners who break prison rules are kept apart from others.
29. Untearable garment worn by prisoners in strip cells, officially so they cannot harm themselves with the material.
30. Control and restraint: a method of restraining prisoners taught as part of prison officers' training.

CHAPTER SIX

Screws and Cons

The women in the workshop are very angry: their canteen has been taken away. Canteen is an important highlight of the week for most women in prison. It is the name given to the prison shop where limited amounts of credit—'private spends'[1] and wages paid for prison work— can be used to purchase toiletries, make-up, food, stamps, greetings cards. Such things may be taken for granted on the outside, but they make life a little more bearable in prison. Now, the women tell me, the shop has been replaced by 'bagging'—a system where the prisoners tick boxes on an order form and the goods are put in plastic carrier bags and delivered to their cells the following day.

Later I am granted an audience with the governor. We meet in his vast office high above the cell blocks, with its imposing desk and acres of carpet. I ask about the shop: isn't this removing from the women a valuable socialising experience that at least went some way towards replicating life outside? Is it not like the removal of the phonecards in the same prison,[2] yet another responsibility taken from the women, another step towards total institutionalisation?

The governor raises his eyes to the ceiling, stretches his long fingers out in front of him then clasps them behind his head before answering. The gesture is one of long-suffering exasperation—he is used to questions like this:

We're not talking about *Observer*-reading middle-class women here. Women like these live very isolated lives before they get to prison and most of them will only shop by mail order anyway. A lot of them can't go out of their houses.

'You mean they've never taken their shopping trolleys down to Kwiksave?'

'I mean that NACRO and the Prison Reform Trust are made up of people from the chattering classes who impose their own values on prisoners, many of whom are gross inadequates. Bagging is partly to stop women intimidating the inadequates and making them hand over their goods. But it's mainly about cost reduction. It's much more cost-effective to buy in the goods and distribute them to the women than to have an officer standing around on duty in the canteen.'

This explanation and the manner in which it is given encapsulates much that is wrong with the provision of custody for women—indeed for all prisoners—in nineties Britain.

What is wrong is the stereotyping of prisoners by many of the staff who control them; the lack of understanding of, or empathy with, their individual circumstances; the disregard for rehabilitative, resocialising measures in the face of pressures to cut costs; the dismissal of reforming agencies as namby-pamby do-gooders. Of course these attitudes do not apply to all prison staff, but they do seem to be worryingly widespread. Although in recent years the Prison Service has been forced under the spotlight of public scrutiny, and although its officials and prison staff now speak of public accountability, partnership and multi-disciplinary teams, I can still find myself sitting here in the presence of a man with the power of an autocrat over the women in his prison. It is the power to send them hundreds of miles from their families, to confine them alone for weeks, to humiliate and degrade—or to raise up, restore and respect.

Christine Duffin, former governor of Cookham Wood, told me she always used to display pictures of her own children on her office wall.

> When people asked me why, I used to tell them "Because I'm scared of the power I have. Every decision I make can have an enormous effect on these women and their families. I have the power to recommend parole or I can keep them another month in prison. I need to look at my own family and remind myself of that."

• • •

Working in prisons, whether as a governor or basic grade officer, has always been a stressful job, never more so than in these increasingly punitive and dangerous times when the prison population is at an all-time high, jails are filling up at 1,000 extra prisoners every month and when cost-reduction is expected to take precedence over humanity. All these problems are exacerbated for staff working in women's prisons because they are trying to implement unsuitable policies in inappropriate establishments, which are also under-staffed. Kate Donegan, governor of Cornton Vale, said at a 1997 conference on women's imprisonment[3] that she was shocked how few officers are employed in some English prisons. At Cornton Vale, she said, the Scottish Prison Service employs 236 staff for a prison holding a maximum of 212 women.

Many officers felt that relationships between staff and prisoners were deteriorating. One experienced woman officer said:

> Women prisoners used to have respect for officers if they were strict but fair. They might not like you, but if you were someone they respected they would back you if you were in real trouble—for instance if a group of

121

violent women ganged up on you. I wouldn't like to say they'd do that any more. Now it's more us versus them.

This hardening of attitudes sits uncomfortably with recent Prison Service initiatives to develop an 'interpersonal skills' element in its initial training package. The training of prison officers is discussed in greater detail in *Chapter 7*, but an indication of a will to change the culture is found in the 'Care' section of the Prison Service's *Visions and Values* document. Prison officers are told to involve prisoners' families as much as possible—a complete reversal of earlier rules when it was a disciplinary offence for them to contact families in any way.

Many of the prisoners I interviewed were sceptical. Josie O'Dwyer, who had spent years in prison before she took her own life in 1997, described her feelings about the staff at Bullwood Hall:

I was in this prison 20 years ago and then you knew where you were: now you don't. The officers let you go too far then you find they'll turn round and nick you. Familiarity breeds contempt. The officers try to chat to you and be your friend but I don't want them as friends. They are not friends, but they needn't be the enemy either. I want them to go back to where they were. There used to be a definite line and if you stepped over it you were hammered. Now they keep moving the goalposts. The reason I don't want them to be my friend is they get too intrusive, they find out about you and they retain that knowledge and use it against you.

A first offender in an open prison expressed similar views:

I don't want to interact with them. I won't be their friend. I am not into getting on with officers. The reason is self-preservation: I don't want to reveal to them what I am—I have to keep my identity. I feel very distrustful of officers. In this prison they are very authority-happy and I don't want any of them to be my friend. If you ever challenge them, however politely, if you ask them quite civilly the reason for anything, they'll say "Why have I got to tell you? I don't have to give you a reason— you just do as I tell you!" And before you know it you are put on report.

Erving Goffman, in his seminal study *Asylums*,[4] said that in any total institution, 'each group tends to conceive of members of the other in terms of narrow hostile stereotypes, staff often seeing inmates as bitter, secretive and intrinsically evil, while inmates often see staff as condescending, high-handed and mean.'

The language used by officers and prisoners to describe each other is a key to their mutual attitudes. Whatever they have been taught at training college, officers frequently reveal their true opinions of female prisoners with expressions like 'convicts', 'people like these', 'inadequates', or the patronising 'girls'—words which enable prisoners to be depersonalised and banished to the realms of the 'criminal other'. Mr Mackay, the power-crazed prison warder in the TV comedy series *Porridge*, described the Ronnie Barker character Fletcher and his mates in similar terms: 'They're the dregs of society—you can't judge these people by *our* standards!' Perhaps the routine description of women who mutilate themselves as 'slashers, cutters, slicers and scratchers', and the dismissal of them all as 'attention-seekers' is a self-preservation mechanism to help staff bear the horror and the pain, to still the conscience so that they sleep peacefully at nights. Workers in other stressful jobs, from surgeons to mortuary attendants, resort to similar strategies.

Prisoners respond with equally dehumanizing names for officers: when I was compiling a dictionary[5] of prison words I collected more than 30 different words for prison officers, ranging from the affectionate rhyming slang derivatives *kanga* and *scooby* to the abusive *shit parcel*.

Goffman[4] described the staff of institutions as feeling superior and righteous, making the inmates feel inferior, weak, blameworthy and guilty. Social mobility between the two groups was, he said, severely restricted, and even conversation was conducted in a special tone of voice. The officers in my sample, especially the women, often described themselves as coming from the same background as the prisoners. But as if further to detach themselves from their charges, and to emphasise the differences between themselves and this criminal 'other', they stressed that unlike the prisoners they had 'made good' instead of 'going to the bad'. Prisoners said some officers took every opportunity to make this point to humiliate them.

Joanna Kelley, governor of Holloway in the fifties and sixties, feels this shared background was an advantage:

> A lot of officers were unskilled, uneducated people but they could still learn how to handle people with patience and integrity which are the main qualities needed for a good prison officer. A lot of them came from the same background as the prisoners. I remember one prisoner who blamed everything on her background, her father had never had a job and so on. In fact, one of the officers commented to me "I was brought up in her village and I went to the same school and I had the same background as she did."

There are indeed interesting parallels between women prison officers and those they have to control. Many of the disciplinary staff I spoke to appeared to feel threatened by the daily sight of the women they themselves might so easily have become. Far from empathising with prisoners who started out with similar problems, they prided themselves on having overcome their disadvantages rather than succumbing to temptation, and felt that this set them as far apart from their weaker sisters as if they belonged to a different species. In some, this kind of moral triumphalism was an unedifying spectacle.

Senior officer Jane Merchant—not her real name—exudes anger from every pore in her body when she speaks of the women in her care. She is a young blonde woman—tall and athletic, with a jawline hard as flint:

> No, I can't be compassionate to people in here. I had a very bad childhood too but I decided very early on that I wouldn't be like that. In my view we've got to look at the difference between 'need' and 'want'. In this country there are no people in need enough to steal and rob. There's nobody in this country without clothes to their backs. OK—they may not be trendy clothes. OK—some of these people might have been homeless somewhere along the line. I was homeless myself, and jobless, for two years when I first came to London. But I didn't rob and steal. This is what makes me totally unsympathetic towards the women in here because I could have done the same things as them. That's why there should be more of an element of physical hardship in prison. We should supply their basic needs but no luxuries. They certainly shouldn't have a swimming pool.

Another senior officer, an older colleague of SO Merchant in the same open prison, echoed her words:

> We get girls in here in their twenties who've never worked. They'd rather live off the state. I left school at 16 and went straight into a job. It's no good them saying there aren't the jobs around—the local papers are full of jobs. The women in here get far too much. I'm asking you—is it doing them any good to have their babies looked after in a creche? Is it any good for them to have two nursery nurses paid an exorbitant wage to look after their babies? They won't get that on the outside, will they! In that MBU[6] they're just dossing around all day. We're not giving them life like it is in the real world.

I was interviewing this officer in the prison Centre—the central area where officers congregate. The three or four other female officers on duty there joined in a rowdy cheer at the SO's closing words: 'They've got it too good in here. I tell them "If you don't like it here why don't you just piss off back to a closed prison"'

Resentment, even envy, of the facilities available to prisoners was commonly expressed by officers. Over a third of the male officers[7] and nearly half of the female officers I interviewed said that they felt the women were lucky to have access to the prison's facilities. Most of the education coordinators described, to a greater or lesser extent, the divisions between themselves and the disciplinary staff. A frequent criticism was the number of computers available to prisoners—better provision, many officers claimed, than those available to their own children at school.[8]

There was also resentment that prisoners were allowed to better themselves at daytime education classes: 'The rest of us law-abiding citizens', said one male officer, 'have to work all day and attend night classes if we want to improve *our* career prospects!'

Stereotyping of officers by prisoners is perhaps inevitable. To prisoners, officers are 'them': the enemy, the daily visible barriers to their freedom. 'They are all two-faced', said one woman I was visiting in Holloway. 'They look quite nice when you're all here on visits, but they can be very cruel to us when nobody's around to see them'. The stereotyping is often mutual: to officers 'a con is a con is a con' and never to be trusted: I heard the words 'manipulative' and 'devious' used over and over again every working day. Within these overall stereotypes there are sub-groups: the prisoners will soon identify the 'safe screw' (one whom the cons can bribe or manipulate); or the hard officer, given a nickname like 'Daddy Bangup'. The officers, like Mr Davies of the Reception Board described in *Chapter 1*, are quick to pigeonhole new prisoners as the 'good wife fallen on hard times', the 'respectable girl from a good family who got in with a bad crowd' – or the 'scumbag'.

Though the remarks of these officers are by no means typical of all the staff I interviewed, they do represent the feelings of a substantial proportion, and it is this immature, petulant and unprofessional 'them and us' approach to important and sensitive issues that gives the job a poor reputation.

The Prison Service claims it is attempting to address this damaging image by incorporating in its initial and in-service training new programmes designed to develop interpersonal skills. *Chapter 7* examines such training programmes in more detail. But it is clear that young officers emerging from their training equipped with these skills will need to be very strong to put them into practice. They are going to need a lot of support if the new training is to become anything more than an expensive public relations exercise. Older officers are all too enthusiastic to exert their influence on new staff and 'put them right' from their own experience, and only the most robust will be able to resist. As Tessa West wisely points out in her book *Prisons of Promise*:[9]

To resist the message of what can happen—prisoners *not* responding like most human beings would do—in the face of colleagues saying "I told you so" is difficult. Some new officers abandon their original intentions and the official message of their training under these circumstances, and are at best silenced and at worst persuaded to act offensively themselves.

This is why, when I interviewed a woman senior officer with 20 years of service, she recalled nostalgically: 'I was so green when I came in here—I was as green as grass—but I soon learned better.' Prisoners are familiar with this process which turns humane officers into 'screws like the rest of them'. Another interview with a younger female officer was depressingly typical:

> I wanted to work in a women's prison because I felt I could be more useful there. In week five of the nine-week training course you get lessons on interpersonal skills, body language and so on, but they didn't address the particular problems of women prisoners who have children, and one training officer kept using the expression TNB: "Trust no bastard". Still, I first came to this prison with high ideals. It was terrible. There were some awful officers working here and they made me feel very unwelcome. But since then I'm afraid I've had to realise that that training officer was right. I came in here quite green but I've had to accept that with the vast majority of inmates you get lied to all the time. They are so manipulative.

One long-serving woman officer, a veteran of both male and female prisons, would probably have given that young trainee a similar lesson:

> If you have to say 'no' to *these women* about anything at all, you'll be one of the 'bad bitches'—that's what they call us. The women will bear a grudge in the way male prisoners won't. I have done similar favours to help both men and women prisoners—like getting a man a valentine card to send to his wife—he was embarrassed to ask a male officer for fear of being called soft. I've done the same for a woman, like getting a card for her sister's new baby. But like I said, if I had to refuse that woman something I'd still go back to being one of the 'bad bitches'. That's what *these women* are like [italics supplied].

Prisoners I interviewed confirmed how quickly 'good screws' can change: 'One nice officer used to be an accountant and in the end she went back to that job because she couldn't handle the hassle from the other screws. She reckoned she'd only come into the job to try and help people'. Other women were more cynical: 'Most of the screws blatantly admit they only work here for the money. Prison officers get good wages and they want to pay their mortgage or buy a new car.'

As well as its efforts to improve officer training, the Prison Service has taken other initiatives. One was the attempt, beginning in 1993, to introduce name badges for officers so that instead of being mere ciphers of authority—the ubiquitous 'Miss' or 'Boss'—the prisoners would be able to address them civilly by their names. The decree was issued from Headquarters that all prison staff should in future wear a name badge. But the Prison Officers' Association disputed the order. One male principal officer thought the union was wrong: 'The POA stance is that we should not wear name badges because the prisoners don't wear them! But I think that's a dreadful attitude. Patients in a hospital don't wear badges whereas the nurses do. Customers in Marks & Spencer don't wear badges but the staff do!'

Officers also said they feared reprisals: they claimed that if prisoners knew their names they could look them up in the phone book and get their mates outside to threaten their families. But most prison officers' numbers are listed ex-directory, and in any case, the prisoners most likely to seek revenge are those involved in adjudications—when officers bringing a complaint have to sign their names for all to read.

In fact the name badges were superseded in 1997 by new security passes which must now be worn by all staff. Information on the passes includes the holder's name and photograph. But the name badge fiasco was important in terms of staff-prisoner relationships if only because it has made officers think about the issue of how prisoners and staff should address one another. As an older prisoner protested: 'I hate being yelled at by my surname. I'm old enough to be their grandmother!' Another woman, old enough to collect her old age pension, resented being addressed by her first name. To her it suggested undue familiarity.

One senior officer said:

Some of the staff do patronise women and call them "lasses" which is Yorkshire for women. You do have to keep watching yourself. I have started to call them "residents" because they must be sick of being called inmates and prisoners. I call the women by their first names but I tend to call the older women Mrs So and So. In the men's prisons there is more readiness to call both inmates and officers by their first name. I don't object to being called by my first name but I know very well the women won't do that—they tend to say "Miss" and "Sir". The male prisoners are much readier to call officers by their first names though it can be for a variety of reasons—to ingratiate, torment or cement a good relationship.

As Tessa West says: 'The issue here is *respect*. Respect is tied in to terms of address and disrespectful terms are the result of impersonal and disinterested attitudes.'[9]

Another innovative move was the introduction of the personal officer scheme. Each prisoner serving more than 12 months has one designated officer to look after her interests and help with her sentence plan. The personal officer is meant to suggest suitable courses of education, training and preparation for release. He or she should also prepare parole reports and court reports and supervise compacts—the name used for a written contract between prisoners and staff whereby prisoners agree to good behaviour in return for certain privileges. Inspectors found, however, that more than half the women prisoners they surveyed did not even know the name of their personal officer. Of those who had one, 90 per cent described their relationship with him or her as 'all right'. The inspectors recommend a much greater input by personal officers in the.management of review processes.[10]

Most women prisoners felt the scheme would work better if they had a pool of personal officers to choose from instead of having someone imposed upon them: that way clashes of personality would be less common. But the main problem they identified was the lack of trust. As one young prisoner said of her personal officer: 'He's always saying "Tell me your problems", but I keep my problems to myself—you can't trust them.'

Joanna Kelley approves of the introduction of the personal officer scheme which she feels worked very successfully in an informal way in the past. She has always maintained that relationships between prisoners and disciplinary staff were seriously damaged by the introduction of prison-based probation officers:

> The dominant period of probation officers was in the early 1970s. During that decade they really stopped the prison officers doing any welfare work for the prisoners. The probation officers had their sociology degrees and thought that welfare was their job. Before that, the officers used to write dictated letters for prisoners and help their visitors with problems when they came to see them. They would show an interest in the women prisoners' children. We had spent the first half of the century trying to persuade prison officers that they were doing useful social services kind of work. But then it was decided that probation would do all that sort of thing and the officers would just be turnkeys. This was supported by liberal regimes. When the officers were suddenly told they were just turnkeys some of them began to say, "All right then, that's what we'll be"—and I think it was a pity.

Prisoners' support groups like Women in Prison agree that prison officers are nearer to the 'client group' in socio-economic terms than probation officers. But some deplore the introduction of the personal officer scheme, because of the difficulty of reconciling the disciplinary and the pastoral roles. As one ex-prisoner said, 'These people are turning keys on the women.'

The question of trust is vital: it is difficult to see how any member of staff with a direct input into the parole process can be trusted with intimate revelations that women fear might adversely affect, or at least delay, that process. For that reason, many women told me they had ceased to trust anyone at all.

There are of course officers who still regard themselves as turnkeys and the women as convicts, and some male officers are undoubtedly unreconstructed misogynists and proud of it. Women in Prison calls for gender-specific training for prison officers. Inspectors concluded that the work of officers in women's prisons was 'challenging and stimulating' but that 'the drain on emotional resilience was exceptional'. They said they were 'horrified by the lack of preparation which male staff receive for work in female establishments. All staff need far more training and support in working with women offenders, and male staff need additional preparation.'[11]

The Prison Service made a promising start with an in-service training course produced by the Trust for the Study of Adolescence in late 1996.[12] I asked male and female officers whether they felt there was a need for special training for those working with female prisoners. Half of the men and a third of the women felt that this would be helpful. The rest were sceptical. One male officer said in response: 'Training to deal with women prisoners? I've had it—it's called marriage!'

Older male officers were more likely to feel resentful when women prisoners failed to respond to their attempts at chivalry: they were far more likely to express horror and disgust at the behaviour of 'women like these', and to say they had never come across their like before. Younger male officers, who had grown up without any sense of putting women on pedestals, rarely expressed any such views.

If the Prison Service is to fulfil its mission statement which promises 'to help [prisoners] lead law abiding lives in custody and on release',[13] stereotypes must be challenged and good relationships somehow fostered between groups as disparate as the jailers and the jailed. And in any case, however powerful the security and discipline of a prison, a minority group can ultimately only contain a much larger majority group by some form of consent.

The training package for working with young women includes a paper on staff development and training written by Jo Harris of HMP and YOI Drake Hall who stresses the vulnerability of young female prisoners:

> For such people, the quality of the relationships they have with staff whilst in prison may play a crucial part in where they go from here. In many cases

past relationships with adults have been characterised by violence, rejection, distrust and—significantly in terms of this course—of feeling desperately misunderstood. It is surely by encouraging a greater understanding of where these young women are 'coming from' that all positive things follow: the building of relationships which offer support, which foster the growth of self-esteem and encourage young women to take responsibility for themselves and which, ultimately, empower them to move towards leading better lives upon release.[12]

The key to such relationships lies surely in the old adage, 'Do as you would be done by', which applies as much in prisons as in any other social environment. In the end the success of the kind of relationship-building advocated in the new training course will depend on staff commitment. Sadly the reality in many prisons still falls far short of these ideals.

• • •

In one young offenders' wing I watched as a girl of about 17 perfectly politely asked the wing officer—a man in his thirties—whether a parcel had arrived for her in that morning's mail:

'No, darlin'. No parcel of any kind whatsoever has arrived for you—unless it's a shit-parcel!'

As the girl walked off despondently he turned to me:

'Basically this is just a dedicated shitbag wing. Let's face it, a lot of these women are just shit-parcels—that's all they are.'

As if on cue, another young woman stormed into the office and demanded angrily what had become of a missing cheque. She was told the prison had no record of it: she went stamping off to her cell and slammed the door. This teenager's forearms bore many old scars and recent wounds of self mutilation.

The wing officer picked up the phone. 'We're having a bit of bother with Sharon the slasher this morning', he said. 'Can't you have her over in education?'

These dismissive views, and the callous manner in which they were expressed, were perhaps unsurprising considering the attitude of management in that particular prison. The acting governor that day had earlier endorsed this officer's sentiments entirely when he told me, with stunning insensitivity: 'The problem is that there are so few female prisons and very few closed prisons—so basically we take all the female crap in creation in here.'

The atmosphere on the young offender wing was confrontational and noisy, with the wing officer bawling orders peppered with swearwords at the young women whom he routinely addressed as, 'You lot!' and the women yelling back abuse. I told him that the constant noise was what particularly struck me when I first began visiting prisons: 'Yes', he agreed, 'and the women are a lot worse than the men! The first thing you notice about working in a female establishment is the noise. It took me about two weeks to get used to that. I wouldn't have this level of noise given the choice.'

It seemed not to occur to this officer, nor to many others I met, that noise levels are within their own control and that prisoners who are shouted at tend to shout back. But noise is part of the 'nick culture' and many officers seem to rejoice in it. A young male officer on detached duty in the same prison had come from a male establishment: he boasted that there they had no public address tannoy system: 'We just yell orders at the cons all the time—it's brilliant! But the women's prisons are worse,' he added. 'It's something to do with the tone of their voices—it really does your head in.'

•   •   •

So many of the women prisoners I interviewed had all their lives suffered unstable relationships with families and partners: yet more volatile relationships are unlikely to help repair the damage. Women commonly described officers who 'get in a mood' and officers themselves admitted to using 'mood' as a method of control. The catering officer in one prison smiled proudly as he showed me round the kitchens where women were working quietly preparing a meal: 'I'm in a mood with the women today and they know it—that's why they're working hard.'

Popular officers, like popular teachers or bosses anywhere, were those perceived as 'fair' and prepared to show the women some respect. In the busy laundry of a closed prison I met Mr Woods (not his real name), an avuncular senior officer and laundry 'boss' universally respected by the women. On a hook in his office hung the Santa Claus costume he had worn at the recent children's visits party. He has no need to resort to 'moods' to get the women to work: 'I find I build up a rapport with the women. I treat people with respect until they show me they don't deserve it.' A prison laundry, like a prison kitchen, is potentially a very dangerous area, with equipment that can be used to inflict injury on officers or other prisoners. Such areas are also frequently isolated from the main part of the prison, putting staff at extra risk. This underlines the importance of interpersonal relationships and of control by consent. Officers like Mr Woods are unworried by such problems:

> In the six years I have been here I've never had an incident. I could go out there and throw orders around but I find I don't have to scream and shout—the women just go and get on with things. As long as the work gets done that's fine with me. I've had quite a few women who ask if they can speak to me because they don't want to speak to their personal officer.

The atmosphere in the laundry was purposeful but relaxed, with the women working at their own pace, stopping for a coffee break when a task was completed.

'In your face' is an expression commonly used by officers to describe the women: 'Our job is very stressful but sometimes I think it's our own fault for allowing the women to be so demanding', a woman officer told me, deliberately slamming the wing office door in the face of a waiting prisoner as she spoke. 'The women are in your face all the time. They're very gobby.'

The women maintain that they only become 'gobby' and answer back in response to the kind of verbal abuse I heard in the young offenders' wing. Of the officer who slammed the door, the women said later 'She talks to us like we're shit. The officers are usually rude to us and you can't approach them. You try to but they shout at you and you get embarrassed and feel ashamed. Then you start getting angry and kicking off.'

Some of the older prisoners had learned how to play the system. A woman in her forties said: 'They like to show who's boss, so you have to do a lot of "Yes Miss, No Miss." Three-quarters of the officers are younger than me. But I find if you show them politeness you get respect back.'

The problem is that the officers are the ones who have to set standards of behaviour. Like teachers dealing with damaged and difficult students, they must first show tolerance and respect, if they hope to be given respect in return. One minor incident I witnessed in the Holloway social visits room may stand as a symbol of the lack of consideration which is the hallmark of so many officers' attitudes to prisoners. The prisoners with the job of serving refreshments had not turned up (one was in court, the other was ill) so no drinks or snacks were available for the whole visit, a two hour session for those with privileged visiting orders. Children were fractious, adults thirsty after long journeys. The officers on duty opened up the refreshments kiosk, only to put on the kettle and serve themselves tea and coffee before closing it again. 'That shows exactly what I'm always telling you about the screws!' said the prisoner I was visiting as we watched the officers strolling round the room with their drinks. 'That just about sums them up.' A former prison medical officer endorsed this view:

> You have to get the staff in a position of trying to behave well to the women, before the women will behave well to them. It's a small thing but at the prison I worked in we tried to get the staff to smile when they unlocked the women in the morning, and to ask "How were you last night?" There was a *tremendous* amount of resistance. The officers would say to us, "How do you expect me to be pleasant when yesterday afternoon she was calling me a fucking this and fucking that?"

Women officers can find themselves cast in stereotypical roles. In the privileged wing[14] of one prison a well-liked female officer was back at work after being on leave. The women gathered round her in the wing office to welcome her. 'Isn't it great, Mum's back!' said one prisoner, a woman in her mid-fifties. The officer was at least 15 years younger.

Several older women staff prided themselves on being 'motherly' to younger prisoners. Some of the women resented this approach: 'Mrs X is supposed to be the wonderful mother hen looking after us all: she just has her little pets, that's all!' Paul Rock in his book on the history of Holloway quotes prisoners describing officers who 'wound up the girls so that they could mother them.'[15] A former Holloway prisoner confirmed this behaviour as quite commonplace even now, describing such officers as 'demon mothers'.

Officers for their part commonly described feeling they acted as surrogate families for prisoners: at the funeral of a Holloway prisoner's baby, the young bereaved mother would have been entirely unsupported but for the presence of two prison officers—the only 'family' present.

Sheila Bowler's appeal hearing at the Royal Courts of Justice in 1995 was attended by an elegantly dressed young woman who smiled at the appellant in the dock and chatted to supporters, though she did not give her name. Family and friends were later surprised to discover that the mystery 'supporter' was a prison officer who had taken an interest in Sheila throughout her sentence, though she kept strictly to Prison Service guidelines and never acknowledged letters Sheila wrote to her. 'I didn't think the warders cared', said one of Sheila's supporters in the public gallery. The officer also turned up one day at Sheila's Old Bailey retrial.

• • •

It was not until the early nineteenth century that women prisoners began to be imprisoned separately from men. As a result of frequent sex scandals inside prisons, Sir Robert Peel's Gaol Act of 1823 also insisted that they must only be guarded by female warders. These first female prison officers, known as matrons, were, like many prison officers today, from the same social background as the prisoners and Elizabeth Fry remarked with surprise that 'Some of the Women [prisoners] are superior to themselves [the warders] in point of Power and Talent, so that they have scarcely any Influence over them.'[16]

Although historically women's prisons were run by male governors, women officers remained solely in charge of female prisoners from the 1820s until the mid-1980s when the then governor of Holloway, Colin Allen (now HM Deputy Chief Inspector of Prisons), brought in male officers.

It was important to nineteenth century reformers that the warders should be 'of good moral character' so that their example might influence the prisoners in their care. I found no evidence of this requirement in the job descriptions of modern female prison officers, nor did any suggest such a element in their job—though a few who had themselves suffered violence at home felt they could understand and to some extent sympathise with women who had killed violent partners.

Male officers, however, commonly defined for themselves a dual moral role. The first was rather worrying: as upstanding family men they could become 'father figures' to the women. Secondly they could play an important role in the process of 'normalisation'. This view is endorsed by the inspectors who commended 'the positive effect of the introduction of male prison officers into women's establishments in the last ten years. This has normalised the environment in most prisons'.[17] However, they strongly recommended that the ratio of male to female officers in women's prisons should never exceed 1:4. This is certainly not always adhered to in UK prisons, and in America the majority of corrections officers overseeing female prisoners are now male.

A male works officer in an open prison said 'The women treat us male officers better and talk to us and relate to us more because in here they're away from males and it gives them the opportunity to discuss personal things with men.'

Female officers sometimes shared this view, occasionally casting women prisoners in stereotypical 'men-pleasing' roles: one governor grade said, 'It's good for the women to have male staff around. It means they dress up in nice clothes, do their hair, put on lipstick. With male staff here the prison is more a reflection of normal society where you do get up, get dressed and get made up to go to work'. The assumption she seemed to be making was that women in the community outside never dress up for their own satisfaction, or for the commendations of other women. Officers at Styal said it was important for the babies in the mother and baby unit to see male officers: 'Before we had the males here the babies used to scream if a man came to visit'.

Male staff themselves felt they had a calming influence on the women because they were 'less hysterical and less bitchy' than female officers. Does the message being sent out to female staff and women prisoners reinforce ancient patriarchal assumptions that men alone can sort things out? A former female governor of a women's prison voiced her doubts:

> When they sent male officers into female prisons there was no screening for suitability and many of the men who went to work there were very patronising. I would be dubious of the motivation of some of the men who accepted these posts. In my view they were patronising males who wanted to play daddy to a bunch of girlies. Women in prison are *not* girls! The average age of women in my [closed] prison was 35! The male staff I inherited when I arrived were not all suitable by any means and I soon told them in no uncertain terms that they would be happier elsewhere.

Indeed, in the women's prisons I visited, relationships between male officers and women sometimes revealed a dangerous and unprofessional blend of contempt and over-familiarity. In the chaotic young offenders' wing described above, one young girl draped herself round the male wing officer then clinched him in a bear-hug. After a few minutes he disentangled her, shrugging with a self-deprecating smile as if to say 'Is it my fault if the women behave like this?'

Many women—both officers and prisoners—spoke of their contempt at this kind of attitude: 'My personal officer—he's *pathetic*! Some of the stupid girls look up to him and he knows it and he thinks he's gorgeous.' 'The male officers like to have a little joke with us—but only on their terms. I won't joke with them—I won't play their game.'

I found mixed reactions among all my interviewees as to the wisdom of employing male staff in female prisons. While 82 per cent of the male officers approved unreservedly, only 16 per cent of the female officers applauded the move.

But of the 125 women prisoners[18] who replied to this question, 80 per cent approved of male officers working in women's prisons. Older women prisoners and officers who remembered the all-female staffing felt that male officers had helped break down a pervasive lesbian officer culture—the sort of club culture which many said imbued Holloway staff relationships and which reputedly still exists in that prison. 'I've no objection to gay officers,' said one woman officer, 'but I do object when

135

pressure is put upon you if your sexuality doesn't conform to theirs. That's an abuse of power.'

Prisoners felt male officers were 'more likely to have a life outside prison' and 'a home to go to' (especially since the advent of local recruitment: see *Chapter 7*) and that they had brought in more relaxed regimes. Younger prisoners felt you could 'have a laugh' with the male officers.

The support group Women in Prison began by totally opposing cross-sex postings. But the organization, staffed by ex-prisoners, has always emphasised the importance of consulting imprisoned women and listening to their views, and that is why they have accepted that the women prisoners prefer mixed staffing. However they remain concerned about the potential for abuse by male officers, and the fear felt by women abused in the past. Their fears may be justified judging by a 1996 report on American prisons published by the Human Rights Watch organization. It found evidence in all eleven states it surveyed of sexual abuse of female prisoners by male officers.

A woman probation officer working in a male prison converted to a female establishment, retaining most of the male officers, stressed the importance of specialised training. She observed that those male officers who had worked with male sex offenders discovered that 'they found it easier to work with the perpetrators of the abuse than to cope with the victims. They had to be told that a lot of the women's bizarre behaviour was because they had been abused'.

Of the 25 women prisoners in the sample who said they opposed the employment of male officers in women's prisons, more than half[18] were victims of earlier sexual abuse. For them the presence of men was a constant threat.

Marie, serving life for murder, was abused as a child: 'Because of what he done to me it takes me a while to get on with men. I don't think we need men officers in a women's prison. They should all be women. At 7.45 in the morning they look in your room to see if you're up and I won't get up till they've checked.' Ann, who had recently survived a suicide attempt, was serving a sentence for arson. She feels the same: 'I don't think there should be male officers. I don't trust men since I was raped when I was 16.'

Dr Sylvia Casale feels strongly that, because of women like Marie and Ann, 'There should be a clear preponderance of women staff. I know this is a contentious issue and I know men *can* work well with women. But 49 per cent of all women prisoners have been abused in the past, mostly by men. So the only sensible way to deal with this is to assume any woman may have a history of abuse.'[3]

Paradoxically, there was almost universal approval among officers, both male and female, for the employment of female officers in *male* prisons. Here most interviewees felt they were on safer ground, because women officers in men's prisons are cast once again in their stereotypical role as carers and calmers. As a woman officer put it 'Sometimes it may help to have a woman working in a men's prison. I used to run a pub with my husband and I could often deal with a difficult drunk because he would not be so obnoxious to a woman.' Another woman said that all men—both officers and prisoners—behaved better when women staff were on duty: 'There's less swearing and the officers treat the men better'. Many male officers shared the view that male prisoners were better-behaved 'in front of the ladies', though only if these female officers knew how to behave as 'ladies'. The female deputy governor of one woman's prison stressed the importance of modest dress and behaviour codes for female officers working in men's prisons. Male prisoners, she hinted, had uncontrollable lusts which must never be aroused: 'Female officers have to be *ladies* to gain respect. They must not swear, they must not wear see-through blouses or tight short skirts. Some of these men are locked up for a very long time and it's not easy for them. So yes, a woman officer must behave like a lady.' Nobody at any point suggested that male officers must behave like gentlemen.

For the majority of female staff who disapproved of the application of cross-sex posting to women's prisons, the main reasons given were practical and operational rather than matters of moral principle. There were, they said, so many occasions where male officers were rendered operationally useless by their gender. They could not do pat-down, rub-down or strip searches. They could not supervise mandatory drug testing by urine sample. Women would not ask them for tampons or sanitary towels (many women confirmed they found such requests very embarrassing, especially with younger male officers). There were many occasions when they could not operate at all unless accompanied by a woman officer. This made the working-out of shift patterns extremely complex and by their own accounts the women officers ended up working twice as hard as the men.[19] A female officer who had worked in a women's prison for 14 years expressed the views of many of her female colleagues:

I feel very strongly against cross-sex posting being applied to women's prisons. It just doesn't work across the board. There are far too many areas in a woman's prison that a male officer can't cover. One third of our staff on this wing are male, as well as the principal officers and senior officers who are male too. So us women are run off our feet. If for instance a girl has to be restrained and taken down the block there has to be a woman officer with her. That may leave only male officers on duty on the wing which

137

causes more problems. Every time the women leave the wing or come back, they have to have a rub-down search which the male officers can't do. And of course they can't do strip searches, so if there's only one woman officer on duty she has to do it all. We have a cupboard on the top landing where we keep the Tampax and sanitary towels and the women won't ask a man for those, so we have to run up three flights of stairs to get them.

There was professional as well as personal resentment among female staff that so many women's prisons were run almost exclusively by male managers. Male officers criticised women colleagues for being pernickety and stolidly conscientious, inflexibly sticking to the rule book: a common view was the one expressed by this male principal officer:

> Women officers tend to be more dogmatic bureaucrats than men. They are much more concerned about documentation. I think they also experience greater discomfort when dealing with women prisoners. There is a big difference in the way people make easy relationships with prisoners. Men find it easier, women find casual relationships difficult. Training is supposed to address this, but I wonder if you can teach relationships?

Whether or not they were now relaxed in their work, both male and female officers recounted their initial fears at the prospects of working in women's prisons—an almost unanimous view. Their fears echoed the prejudices of the general public outside prison:

> I admit I was frightened when I first came here. I went round close to the walls all the time at first—I was sure I was going to be attacked by these dangerous women. (Woman officer, 14 years' service)

Men's apprehension centred mainly on concern about sexual innuendo, overt gibes or in some cases direct sexual attack:

> I had read what the newspapers said about women getting more violent and I had visions of abuse and thought I might be propositioned on a daily basis. I also feared I might be in danger of women making allegations about me. (Young male officer)

A former governor of two women's prisons said: 'Men are never entirely at ease dealing with women prisoners. They are always slightly frightened that they will be accused of abuse, of raping them or groping them.' Women officers were scornful: as a young female officer said:

> There are lots of myths around female prisons and male officers are very scared of working in them. They insist on thinking that the minute they

walk into Holloway all the women are going to tear their tops off and it'll be nothing but boobs! But I tell them "I don't feel this sudden urge to take my top off when you come into the room—so what makes you think the women do?"

All but one of the male officers I interviewed agreed that men working in women's prisons were certainly at real risk of allegations of sexual misconduct, though only half felt that they themselves were at risk. Their fears are probably justified. It is not uncommon to read newspaper reports of male officers in female prisons 'taking sick leave' or 'taking early retirement' pending allegations of harassment. At the time of writing, a Risley officer has been suspended and is facing a court case for alleged rape and three alleged offences of indecent assault on a woman prisoner.[20]

Many officers felt that the risks were heightened by the large proportion of prisoners sexually abused in childhood, a worrying assumption suggesting that allegations by such women were not only more likely but less credible than allegations from non-abused women. Doubt was often cast on male officers' ability to cope:

There can be problems of rivalry among the women for their attention and they may not realise this. The men find it difficult to detach themselves and to realise that there is an invisible line which you must never cross. (Experienced woman officer)

One female probation officer working in a closed prison said 'There is a lot of sexist talk by male officers here and the line is overstepped all the time. The women prisoners themselves overstep the mark all the time as well and you will get women accusing officers of touching them up.'

Another long-serving woman officer in the same prison endorsed this view, and blamed the men for sometimes courting danger:

The younger men can cope better than the older ones. The older men get too involved with the women and they listen to them too much, especially if they are their personal officers. We have a lot of problems with allegations against the men. They do such stupid things. For instance they will go and see their favourites in their cells and have a cup of coffee. We warn them not to sit in the cells or there will be allegations and indeed there have been allegations recently. The men now come up to us and say they wished they'd listened.

We often find that a woman's personal officer, if it's a man, will have his own opinion of an inmate which is totally different from all the other views in her parole reports. I've seen a male officer give a glowing report which gave a totally false picture of the most repulsive woman. These women aren't silly. They know how to behave impeccably if there's a parole review

139

coming up. The women really manipulate the men and the men just can't see it and if you warn them and point it out to them they think you're being bitchy women. There are plenty of other males around for the women to relate to without there having to be male officers. We've had male probation officers and there are the governors, the chaplain and then the women's regular visitors like boyfriends, fathers and brothers. Male officers have caused more problems than they're worth.

Dress codes have to be adapted to the presence of male officers (see *Chapter 5*) though one female chaplain felt this was unfair as the prison is after all the women's home. The governor of an open prison described the problems he had with women sunbathing and going round wearing 'those cropped tops'. The women themselves maintained that cropped tops were worn every day in the streets of London. Women staff blamed the prisoners for dressing seductively to entrap male officers: 'We have to keep telling them to fasten their dressing gowns', said one female officer, 'they love wandering round deliberately leaving them open'.

One male wing officer was used to dealing with such situations: 'If you are a male under 50 you get constant sexual innuendos. When you're new the women will try anything to embarrass you. The dressing-gown will fall open and the only way to deal with that is to have a laugh and say something like "Ooh—*lovely!*"' He was fairly sure that the word of an officer would be believed rather than the word of a prisoner: 'You are always open to allegations and you just have to hope that the people you work with know what sort of person you are. That's what matters, never mind what the inmates say about you. As long as your workmates and bosses know what you're like, if an allegation lands on their desk they will throw it out.'

A male deputy governor also subscribed to the stereotyping theory that mere males are at risk of manipulation by seductive female prisoners:

I do think female officers should be the dominant group. Women understand women's needs and women's wiles. We men get mixed up between needs and wiles. We had one female orderly who would always ask me if I wanted a coffee and she would come up close to me. I knew the vibes were wrong and one day she knelt down on the floor in front of me. She was wearing a very low-cut dress so I deliberately did not look down but I went to get somebody else to talk to her. I told another male officer and he said "She does it to me too." Male officers are certainly at constant risk of allegations. One woman had it in for me because I'd had to target her as a member of a group of women who were bullying others. I received an anonymous typed letter accusing me of sexually harassing the woman and virtually telling me to lay off the group or they would tell her husband.

So men have to be very careful. For instance they should never enter a woman's cell without knocking on the door first.

But a female officer in the same prison ridiculed this suggestion:

> If an inmate is on special watch, on the "at risk" register — which means you have to check her every 15 minutes, even at night, to see she hasn't harmed herself — what is a man supposed to do? If he knocks every quarter of an hour he'll wake up the whole wing as well as the woman herself! Cat A women routinely have to be checked by looking through the hatch in the cell door. If the women are in a proper state of dress that shouldn't be a problem. But in the summer the women wear next to nothing in bed and if the duvet falls off and a woman's nightdress rides up, any male officer looking in can see her half-naked. It's not right, specially as a lot of these women have a history of sexual abuse. Yet if the officer doesn't look in and something happens to that woman he could lose his job.

A prisoner in this prison suggested that night shifts should be entirely staffed by female officers—but it is doubtful whether female staff would share her enthusiasm. During the daytime, some male officers say they warn the women by shouting 'Man on the wing!' and some even sing at the top of their voices. But their presence does cause all sorts of daily problems, some of which could have been avoided by better planning. For instance in many cells the toilet is immediately inside the door, visible to officers whose duty it is to check by looking through the hatch. A simple remedy, the installation of privacy screens, has solved the problem in some prisons.

Women officers working in women's prisons are not immune to allegations of sexual harassment. The fear of homosexual molestation is less overt in women's prisons than in men's but it is certainly present. Many women spoke of their initial fears on coming into prison of being approached by lesbian officers or other prisoners (see *Chapter 1*), though in reality few had experienced such overtures. There was plenty of anecdotal evidence of lesbian advances, but only two of my 150 prisoner interviewees said they had experienced a direct approach from female staff. Candida, a heroin addict, was 25 with an six-months-old baby when she came into prison: 'A lot of the screws are gay. One of them came to my cell at night and made it clear what she wanted. Can you believe anyone could say things like "Call me Babs"!' Lorraine, jailed for importing amphetamines, has four children aged six to 17: 'The first night I was here I was propositioned by one of the women officers. She came into my room and started offering to get me stuff. She said, "I could get you packets of cigarettes." When I realised what was happening I said, "I'm sorry, I'm not interested." She said, "I don't know what you mean. I just thought you were a nice lady and I could get things for you." It was the first time she'd ever met me!' In nineteenth century prison incident books, sexual relationships between female warders and women prisoners were coyly recorded as 'tampering.'[16]

The Prison Service may send out directives on the way prisoners should be addressed and it has made its employees wear security badges showing their names. But successful relationships depend in the end not upon any such formalised structures but on empathy. I experienced and was told of so many incidents where staff seemed quite incapable of making that leap of imagination which could place them for a moment in a prisoner's shoes.

One woman, Ellen, told me the effects of being in an abusive relationship with her second husband, a violent alcoholic who became intensely jealous of her adult sons from her first marriage. She described how his power over her grew until she completely lost her confidence and even her sense of her own identity. An experienced driver, she became afraid to drive a car at all: 'And I even had to ask him whether or not I liked sugar in my own tea.' She was serving five years for her part in an unsuccessful conspiracy to have him murdered. According to Ellen, none of the officers, including her personal officer, seemed able to understand the nature of this kind of abuser-victim relationship. 'They say to me "You're a big strapping woman—why didn't you just walk off?" But they just don't understand the nature of power. I've given up trying to explain to them that he fills me with absolute terror.'

A few weeks before the end of her sentence, Ellen absconded from the open prison where I later interviewed her. 'I was doing well here. I had a hospital appointment and was trusted to go out on licence. But when I came out of the hospital there was my husband waiting in the car. He just said "Get in the car!" So I got in and we drove off.'

She was out of prison for eight months before she was recaptured, losing all her remission: 'He even shaved my head so I couldn't go out. I didn't want to abscond but people can't understand how frightened I am of him. When I got back the staff here said "Why didn't you tell him to just piss off?"'

Ellen's recapture was still recent enough to be a subject of gossip in the officers' mess. Not realising I had interviewed her, two female officers were discussing the incident: 'I can't understand how some of them think!' said one. 'For instance that woman who absconded, her husband was giving her a really bad time and what does she do? Only absconds and goes off with him again and loses all her remission. I just can't understand it!'

The most popular and well-respected officers are those able to identify with the women and empathise with their problems. Before this can happen they need to find out more about their backgrounds. As a former prison medical officer explained:

> The officers need to know the poverty of some women's circumstances, that they have never been employed, or if they had employment it was probably in the sex industry. That some have had no reliable educational background and at school nobody ever listened to them. And listening to these stories is not just about *being* there. If an officer can't empathise then he or she will never engage with the prisoner.

One officer of 17 years' experience said she had shared the fears of most of her colleagues on starting her first job in a women's prison:

> It was a real culture shock and at first I was very frightened of the women. Then when I got talking to some of the lifers I realised that for most their crime was their first offence and that in the same set of circumstances I could have done exactly the same thing. This prison ran its own brand of personal officer arrangement long before the launch of the official national scheme. Most of us women officers had families of our own and we understood the problems. We could make phone calls to their families unless they were cat A women. I'd been a battered wife myself so I found it quite easy to identify with women who reacted to stress and abuse by killing someone in a one-off crime. I also understand a lot about their background because my father battered my mother every Saturday night when he got drunk then spent all day Sunday apologising. I have never been insulted by the women because they know I understand them and I am fair. But they resent the younger officers here who have just not seen enough of life to understand.

Perhaps the commonest complaint coming from the women prisoners was about the way they were treated like children by the officers. Women who had run their own companies and women with adult children spoke of being lumped together with 16-year-old young offenders and treated like naughty schoolgirls. Some very young women already had several children and equally resented such attitudes. I often observed young mothers in MBUs being sent off to clean their rooms or look after their babies by officers behaving like bossy boarding-school matrons.

Officers for their part said the women behaved like schoolgirls and had to be dealt with as such. They claimed they acted up and 'kicked off', and one officer who had considered the reasons said she thought some women's emotional development[21] stopped at the age they entered prison—and as so many of them had entered prison as young offenders, this, she thought, explained the prevailing adolescent behaviour in women's prisons.

Ceri, 21, has sons aged two and three and was managing to bring them up on her own until she was arrested for shoplifting children's clothes: 'The hardest thing is being treated as if you've gone back to school. They don't treat the women with respect. They are always telling us to respect the officers, but they don't treat us that way. '

Vicky, 17, has two baby daughters, though she was so badly sexually abused by her father from the age of five that it was once thought she might never be able to bear children. She has been in three secure units since she began abusing solvents at the age of nine. As a minor, she is still on a full care order and her two children have been adopted without her consent, though she showed enough willpower to free herself of her amphetamine and Temazepam[22] habit. Though so young she has thought deeply about the reasons for her past behaviour and is making real headway in understanding and addressing it. But the prison appears to give her little credit: 'They treat you like little kids. One woman screw said to me "You need a smacked bottom you do, having children at your age." I'm the youngest in this prison and the officers never let me forget it. But I've had more experience of life than most of them have.'

Humiliation of prisoners, often by older female officers, is routine in many women's prisons. I found it revealing in the middle of a friendly and civil interview with a senior officer, to watch her expression change to one of extreme irritation when disturbed by a knock on her office door. A grey-haired woman in her forties, girlishly dressed in shorts, tee shirt and ankle socks, stood nervously on the threshold, feet together like a twelve year old, waiting for an opportune moment to make her request. The officer barked an order to 'put in an app' and the woman scuttled away to try her luck when the officer was in a better mood. It was a chilling experience.

The Prison Service claims that prison officers with such attitudes—'dinosaurs' in prison slang—are being phased out and that the 'nick culture' is gradually changing as the service introduces the new strategies for recruitment and training considered in *Chapter 7*.

Endnotes

1. 'Private spends' and 'private cash' are terms used for money sent into prison by relatives or friends, or any small amount of cash a prisoner brings in on reception. A limited sum is allowed to prisoners each week, in credit not in cash, for small purchases in the prison shop. The amount allowed varies according to whether the prisoner is on Basic, Standard or Enhanced regime—three levels fixed by the Incentives and Earned Privileges Scheme (IEPS). At the time of writing, prisoners on Basic are allowed £2.50, on Standard £10 and on Enhanced £15.
2. See *Chapter 4*.
3. Presentation at the conference 'Imprisoning Women: Recognising Difference', on 23 October 1997, organized by the Institute for the Study and Treatment of Delinquency (ISTD) at HMP Styal.
4. *Asylums*, Erving Goffman, Penguin, 1961.

144

5. *Prison Patter*, Angela Devlin:, Waterside Press, 1996: 'kanga' is short for *kangaroo*, rhyming slang for screw. 'Scooby' is an abbreviation for the cartoon character Scooby-Doo, also rhyming slang for screw.
6. Mother and Baby Unit: see *Chapter 3*.
7. 36 per cent of the male officers, and 45 per cent of the female officers.
8. The former education officer of a male young offenders institution, now closed, described a serious riot when she says she overheard prison officers inciting the rioters to smash up the computers in the education department. She claims she heard them egging on the youths: 'Go on, go on — you haven't got the bottle!'
9. Waterside Press, 1997.
10. *Women in Prison: A Review*, HM Inspectorate, 1997.
11. See Note 10 ,above: 4.08.
12. *Understanding and Working with Young Women in Custody*, Juliet Lyon and John Coleman, TSA Ltd, 1996.
13. The full statement, displayed at the entrance to every prison, reads as follows:

   Her Majesty's Prison Service serves the public by keeping in custody those committed by the Courts. Our duty is to look after them with humanity and to help them lead law abiding lives in custody and after release.

14. The privileged wing is the part of the prison where prisoners felt to be of good behaviour are housed. They are usually on an enhanced regime according to the national Incentives and Earned Privileges Scheme (IEPS).
15. *Reconstructing a Women's Prison: The Holloway Redevelopment Project, 1968-88*, Paul Rock, Oxford University Press, 1996.
16. See *Oxford History of the Prison, Chapter 11, 'Wayward Sisters'*, Lucia Zedner. Oxford University Press, 1995.
17. See Note 10, above: Executive Summary 14.
18. Of the 125 (out of 150) women prisoners who replied to this question, 80 per cent — 100 women — liked having male officers in the prison, while 25 did not. Of these 25, 13 (52 per cent) had been sexually abused in the past.
19. In the October 1996 issue of the POA journal *Gate Lodge*, the 'Branch News' section contains news from HMP Brockhill, then recently converted to a female establishment. The anonymous woman officer included the following paragraph: 'The females [i.e. prisoners] aren't the real problem; it's the lack of thought and communication with the re-role, with insufficient female staff in post. We (the female staff who are here) are being stretched to carry out our own work as well as assisting our male colleagues with tasks that they are unable to perform, e.g. strip search, MDT and rubbing down. We haven't the female staff to cover all the tasks involved and more female inmates keep arriving.'
20. Reported in *The Guardian*, 23 January 1998, and *Manchester Evening News*, 18 April 1998.
21. The Training Pack developed by the Trust for the Study of Adolescence (see Note 12, above) recognises developmental retardation in many prisoners, but acknowledges too the complaints of women propelled into early adulthood that they were 'being treated like little kids'. More than anything, the authors' introduction says, 'they want to be listened to and treated with respect.'
22. Temazepam is a benzodiazepine drug, used in the short term treatment of insomnia or as an anti-depressant. It is sold illegally under names such as tems, jellies or eggs.

CHAPTER SEVEN

Turning the Screw

In a glass cabinet labelled 'Warders' Weapons 1830' are three heavy swords, each engraved with the words 'City Prison, Holloway'. The next cabinet contains canvas punishment clothing stamped with arrows. 'This robust clothing', reads the legend with customary Prison Service understatement, 'was worn by prisoners who destroyed their normal prison uniform. The use of the broad arrow markings was abolished in 1921.' The gruesome exhibits are very much at odds with the comfortable carpeted reception lounge of HM Prison Service College in Wakefield, Yorkshire, where waiting visitors may relax in easy chairs, gazing at a large aquarium tank where fish take gentle exercise in their own watery prison.

How much of the old-style 'screw mentality' has been abolished, along with branded convict clothing, since the early years of the century? How successful have new strategies of recruitment and training been in breaking down the 'them and us' barriers between officers and prisoners described in *Chapters 5* and *6*? How far can these new methods equip officers to maintain discipline in prisons which, by their own accounts, are becoming increasingly violent places to work in? And, particularly in terms of this study, are they trained to meet the special needs of women prisoners?

When the Prison Service in the Fresh Start initiative of 1987 lowered the minimum age of entry to prison officer training from 25 to 20, the general perception outside the service was that this was a recruitment-boosting ruse for a job probably second only to being a traffic-warden in the public's mind. This view, perhaps coloured by those TV screws bested by *Porridge*'s wily Fletcher, or portrayed by Lynda la Plante, could not have been further from the truth. There has never been any shortage of applicants, including plenty of university graduates wanting to join the Accelerated Promotion Scheme (APS) for training to become prison governors. At present there are 30,000 to 40,000 would-be officers on the waiting list, and the APS attracts between 10,000 and 15,000 enquiries a year. The dropping of the age limit was simply an economic cost-cutting exercise to allow officers to get their maximum pension at the age of 60 after 40 years' service—and to put in that length of time they have to start work at 20. Middle-aged women prisoners with major life experiences particularly resent being ordered about by 'boys who are still wet behind the ears'.

'Who'd want to be a screw?' The women prisoners I interviewed

146

were scathing. 'They've got to be sick, let's face it!' 'It's an untenable job', said another who had read law at university. 'There's no way I could do a job that involves locking away other human beings', said a third.

Indeed, why *should* anyone want this difficult, demanding and often dangerous job, when hardly a week goes by without the Prison Service being rocked by some fresh scandal like the Whitemoor escape fiasco, or the incarceration of Roisin McAliskey with its veiled threats of IRA retaliation?

Staffing numbers were the same in 1997 with more than 60,000 prisoners as they were in 1992 for 42,000. Since Fresh Start, officers are eligible for the aptly named TOIL (Time Off In Lieu) instead of overtime pay, but such is the crisis in staffing that at the beginning of January 1997 they were owed a quarter of a million hours for the time they had worked. There has been a freeze on recruitment and thousands of experienced staff, exhausted by stress, sickness and directives from HQ, have decided to leave under the voluntary redundancy scheme known as VERSE (voluntary early retirement scheme).

One experienced governor acknowledged all these problems:

> Universally in the Prison Service everyone is shocked at the increase in prison populations. They are rising at a thousand a month, which amounts to two new prisons a month. *Nobody* in the Prison Service is convinced of the wisdom of this idea. We *are* convinced that there should be rehabilitation.

The Prison Officers' Association hoped for better treatment from a Labour government. They particularly expected Jack Straw to restore their right to take industrial action, removed in 1994 under Michael Howard's Criminal Justice and Public Order Act. In opposition, Tony Blair had written to the POA saying this was a totally unwarranted attack on the rights of prison officers.[1] Nine months into the new government's reign officers grew tired of waiting, and said they felt badly let down, voting to defy the anti-union law. Jack Straw has further angered the union by continuing his opposition to the right to strike, though he offered to set up an independent tribunal to settle disputes about pay and conditions.

Problems looming on the horizon do not yet appear to have affected recruitment. As one governor put it: 'We have become a much more professional service over the last ten years and this is a major attraction when it comes to recruitment.'

The reasons given by serving officers and trainees for joining the service are perhaps more prosaic. Many of the men I interviewed mentioned job security and prospects of promotion as a major motivation. A large proportion of the older men (and some of the women) had left the armed services and sought a similar disciplined and uniformed job. The modern Prison Service seems keen to discard this militaristic image, and in theory this new approach should have positive implications for the management and staffing of women's prisons. A training official told me:

> We are now recruiting different kinds of applicants from different backgrounds. There used to be a lot of ex-forces people who felt they needed the discipline of the Prison Service and used it as a sort of half-way house. They did a particular job in a particular way but there was a lot of bullying and violence in the prisons as a result and this is now changing and we want to recruit different people for different reasons.

'Back in the old days', said a female former governor, 'the majority of prison officers were ex-servicemen and women. The men had been boy soldiers from 16 to 25 and had more experience. Mind you', she qualified her enthusiasm, 'they had still been trained in male bigotry and intolerance!' A male principal officer expanded:

> Some officers recruited straight from the services came into the Prison Service because they wanted a uniform to make them feel safe. They tended to be subservient to the system and no good at interpersonal skills. They may have been well-travelled but they had very limited life experiences and poor social skills. It was a mistake to think they could step out of one uniform into another. If you put some of them in tee-shirts and jeans they would find it impossible to do their job. It's taken us a long time to get these attitudes out of the system. Now we want to recruit people with varied life experiences.

In fact, many of the serving officers I interviewed—both male and female—had commonly done a range of other jobs before joining the Prison Service. Theoretically these wider experiences should give them greater empathy—especially with women prisoners, whose own life experiences have sometimes been extensive. But decisions to work in prisons were often presented to me as negative choices made through lack of other employment opportunities. Several male officers told me frankly that they had been made redundant and had to find work fairly rapidly to meet family and personal commitments:

> I was a works foreman—I had gone through the whole traditional bonded apprenticeship in carpentry since I was 15. Then I had bad luck and was made redundant when the whole company I worked for closed. I wanted

148

security for my family so I really appreciated the opportunity to become a prison officer.

A woman in her fifties said she became a prison officer at the age of 36: 'I always wanted to join the police force but I had my children so I never did that. I was at home when they were small, then I was a hairdresser. Then I did a range of jobs, working in cafés and so on, and it was only when the children were teenagers that I came to work here.' Another officer in the same prison was 40 before she joined:

> I was a civil servant first, then I ran a golf club with my husband, then we ran a pub near this prison. The prison officers used to come in and I'd had enough of the licensed trade by then so I told my family I fancied being a prison officer. My son said "Mam, don't be silly—you're too soft!" But I said "They need all sorts in there, soft ones as well." I was very fit as I'd always gone to keep-fit classes and done sport.

According to the training officers I met at the college, reasons for applications are changing: 'People used to apply to this job for family security but now we find that most new recruits join because they really want to work in the Prison Service. The job is generally viewed as something a bit different—and there are lots of positives.'

A major attraction for people wishing to become prison officers has always been the lack of any minimum educational qualifications. In this regard the Prison Service used to lag behind the police who have for years insisted on a minimum number of GCSE or O level passes although in 1997 a new requirement of five GCSE passes or equivalent qualifications was finally introduced by the Prison Service. Pay is the other inducement. A 20-year-old starts at between £14,000 and £15,000 per year after only 12 weeks of training. A graduate accepted on to the Prison Service's fast track promotion scheme, the APS, can be a principal officer within a year or two, earning about £22,000 a year, and deputy governor of a prison within five years of leaving university.

Whatever the perception of prisoners and the general public about the quality of prison officers, training officials insist that the calibre of applicant now getting through the initial test is very high. One told me that between 1989 and 1992, for every 100 applicants, only two or three made it into the service. Over the last five years, it has been replacing its policy of national recruitment for one of local recruitment. Now an individual prison will advertise jobs in a local job centre or newspaper. The inspectors see this as a positive step because it means that staff applying specifically to work in women's prisons can be selected for their suitability. The inspectors recommend that the Prison Service should devise a special selection method, based on an analysis of the needs of women prisoners.[2]

I asked experienced prison officers now employed in women's prisons about the move from national to local recruitment. Older officers (both male and female) were more likely to disapprove. They especially regretted the loss of camaraderie, with evenings in the mess bar where 'lonely' men could seek solace in companionship and drink, and women emulated their bar-room behaviour. Now, they said sadly, officers are more likely to commute back home to the family every evening. Some officers felt that prisoners were also the losers, as staff rush off home at the end of their shifts. 'We used to have knitting and crocheting circles for the women prisoners at the weekends', remembered one elderly woman officer fondly, 'but nobody's interested in things like that now.' A male governor however had no regrets:

> There were negative things about national recruitment with people living in residential prison accommodation far from home. I can well imagine that was part of the reason behind the lesbian culture among women officers, and there was also for the male officers a club/alcohol culture. I think the closure of officers' clubs was a very positive step and local recruitment helped with this.

Although the Prison Service has moved over to a system of local recruitment, it still retains national training. At the end of the two-week observation period, every recruit will spend nine weeks at the Prison Service Training College in Wakefield, which is part of the training estate, along with the College at Newbold Revel near Rugby which now only provides in-service training.

The Wakefield College runs a flexible rolling programme whereby new recruits can join the course every fortnight. Normally there is an intake of 40 new trainees at the start of each of these two-week periods. The group of 40 is split into two sections and they will each have spent two weeks in their 'own' prison. They then embark on the complete nine week course into which all the initial training is packed. The system is one of weekly boarding with all trainees returning home at weekends. In 1996 the training package cost £4,300 per person, of which £3,700 went on the residential part.

In late 1996, when I was visiting the college, a general freeze on recruitment meant that there were, in total, only 44 students in two parallel classes of 22 each. There were roughly equal numbers of male and female trainees. Classes were given by a team of seven tutors. One of them outlined the aims of the course:

> We do have a lot of emphasis on interpersonal skills but we also do a lot of work on security and what you might call jailcraft, in the first four weeks.

150

Though we deal with interpersonal skills separately, this also comes into everything we do here. We also do racial awareness training and drugs awareness training. We teach control and restraint techniques too. Every student, male or female, has to do exactly the same training.

I was allowed to observe three classes, each 45 minutes long and given by different tutors, and then to interview students. I was looking at the training in terms of how it would prepare those trainees wishing to work with women prisoners. HM Inspectorate's review[3] said that 'a cause of the greatest concern is the paucity of specialised training for staff who work with women prisoners'. The inspectors said they were 'horrified by the lack of preparation which male staff receive for working in female establishments' and concluded: 'All staff need far more training and support in working with women offenders; male staff need additional preparation.'[4]

• • •

The first class I saw was a session called 'How to recognise and deal with mentally disordered offenders'. Having interviewed some deeply disturbed women prisoners, I was interested to see how the training would meet their needs. The 22 students, all wearing the standard trainee uniform of white shirt, black trousers and belt with chain ('No keys, it's just to get us used to wearing the key chain!') sit on upright chairs arranged against the walls around three sides of the room. Pinned to their desktop attachments are large labels printed with their surnames, initials and the establishments to which they are attached. In time-honoured jail fashion, each student is addressed by the tutor and by each other as 'Mr' or 'Miss'. Some mature students are married women but in the quaintly formal language register of the Prison Service it is common for 'Miss' to be applied universally to female staff by colleagues and prisoners alike.

It is plain from the outset that academically, socially and in terms of their experience, this is very much a mixed ability group. About one in three —15 out of the total of 44 trainees—are APS graduates destined for senior management positions. It soon emerges too that some have special areas of expertise. One student is a community psychiatric nurse—a fact publicly acknowledged at the start of this session by the tutor, a cheerful man also in uniform. Although his delivery of the lesson is relaxed, the session is organized quite formally with the teaching directed to a test of the knowledge which it is the tutor's job to impart. The students are given at the outset three main objectives, listed on a overhead projector slide:

151

1. Be able to state four of the main causes of mental disorder
2. Be able to state who may need to be informed if an offender displays abnormal behaviour
3. Be able to state three differences between physical health problems and mental heath problems.

The tutor tries to lighten a serious subject by interspersing facts and definitions with jokes: 'What's the definition of *anxiety state*? That's the thing I get before coming into this class with you lot!'

When the tutor asks the trainees for their understanding of the meaning of the term *mentally disordered offender*, answers are depressingly simplistic: 'Somebody different to the majority.' 'Sick people—mentally sick.' One student gives a demonstration, lolling his head about with his mouth open and banging it against the wall! When the tutor asks for a definition of *schizophrenia*, the same student grimaces: 'Ow'd d'you spell *that*? Oh yeah—it's like that bloke in *Eastenders*—he was brought up bad and subjected to abuse and he went schizophrenic so he could withdraw from all that.' The psychiatric nurse keeps his hand patiently raised throughout, until finally the tutor asks for his definition: 'Schizophrenia is a biochemical imbalance of the nervous system which makes some people less able to cope.'

The tutor's advice is also worryingly basic. On manic depression:

People quite often appear normal but they have mood swings from being highly elated to normal, then from normal to depression. You have no clue how to take them because their moods can change so much. You have to be careful how you deal with them. If they are very elated you have to be strict with them. Then next day they might be motivated to do something.

On affective disorder:

This means emotional disorder. It's just psychiatrist-speak—we all know those people who charge £500 an hour for their services because they've done seven years' training. (*Don't* write that down!) These people will be highly elated for a few days then highly depressed.

Some of the students are looking confused: 'Can they be both?' 'They don't do both, no', explains the tutor patiently. 'They are characterised by not doing both because if they did both they would be diagnosed as manic depressive.'

At this point the psychiatric nurse is moved to interject once more: 'That is not the terminology that is used at the moment'. His neighbour turns to him scathingly: 'What d'you mean? It's written in the book, isn't it?' 'Well—in that case the book's wrong. Manic depression is a bi-polar

152

affective disorder.'

There is a moment's stunned silence then a few giggles. 'Don't use words like that!' says the tutor 'You forget you're in Yorkshire now! What about persecution complex? I think I must have it—I feel Mr X over there [the nurse] keeps on persecuting me!' [general laughter]. Now, look at this last one: apathy, social withdrawal, not interested in what's going on around. Three out of two prison officers suffer from it! Right, let's take a break now. Please be back at 2.20 p.m. sharp.' The session on mentally disordered offenders is over. There has been no reference to the life histories of prisoners which may have contributed to the mental state of so many of the women I interviewed.

• • •

The other two sessions I observed were run on similar lines. One was called 'Supervising Prisoners under Punishment', the other was on writing parole reports for sex offenders.

The tutor of the first group introduced this session with the words: 'We often have to deal with the inadequates who have been put in the seg.'[5] Much of the session was about the rules governing prisoners under punishment—for instance, the number of times the governor, the prison medical officer and the Board of Visitors are obliged to visit the segregation unit. The students would be tested, said the tutor, on these rules and procedures: how often prisoners in the seg should be observed, where their activities should be recorded, the minimum number of officers required to unlock and so on. Again, there was no mention of women prisoners, nor any suggestion that the level of physical restraint required for them might not be so great.

As in the first session, the tutor then moved on to what could be loosely interpreted as 'interpersonal skills'. He was reassuring about officers' likely involvement in supervisory work: 'It's important to say about the seg that the majority of people in there are OK. Only a minority are violent or truculent. But with these kinds of prisoners we have to resort to non-medical restraints. So we have to get the body belts on and put the offenders in the special cells. What is your feeling about putting a prisoner in restraints?'

A female trainee attached to Grendon Underwood, Britain's only (male) therapeutic prison, was not happy: 'I would feel uncomfortable though I can see there are instances where you would have to. But I wouldn't want to stick them in a body belt. It seems like a return to the days of the straitjacket.'

The tutor said he had only had to use a body belt three times in his 25 years of service: 'The last time I had to use MUFTI[6] was probably 12 years ago—now that was just a matter of bodies jumping on someone to restrain him if he was violent. You just had to sit on him and grab his arms and legs.' He asked the group for their views on control and restraint: 'Once they've gone to the seg unit it's one of our last resorts and we have to use C and R techniques. How would you feel about that?'

A Gazza lookalike skinhead in the far corner guffawed: 'I'll *enjoy* it!' The tutor's smile was tight-lipped: 'Playing to the gallery again Mr Y! I'm talking about *supervision* skills. You've got to be prepared to handle feelings of aggression and anxiety—you'll have those feelings as well as the prisoner. 'The students were divided on the subject. One thought, rather worryingly, that 'You'd have so much adrenalin rushing around it would get you over it.' Another was more dubious: 'If you don't feel frightened when you hold up that riot shield there's something wrong with you.'

• • •

The third session—on writing parole reports—was half way through when I arrived and the tutor had moved from the rules and regulations to the 'interpersonal skills' section. Though the session had a practical end in view, the brainstorming methods used were the same as in the earlier classes. Again, it was entirely male-oriented. The students were preparing for a role-play which would be videotaped. They had to imagine they were interviewing a sex offender called O'Mara to write a report for his parole review. O'Mara's personal officer had 'gone off sick' and they had a few minutes to interview him and take notes for reports to the Parole Board. They were told to consider the offender's future employment were he to get parole: 'As a convicted sex offender his job prospects are going to be limited', said the tutor. 'Job prospects are even limited for the three million law-abiding people without work. You also have to think if his expectations are realistic. If he wants to be an airline pilot that's not very realistic is it?' The students guffawed.

Asked for other questions they should ask, the students volunteered their suggestions: 'Does he feel ready for release?' 'Is he afraid of being released?' 'What about his attitude to prostitutes? Does he feel he's been stitched up by prostitutes?' 'What about his attitude to authority?'

The tutor nodded, 'Yes, if he goes out and hits a policeman over the head it's not much good is it?' He gave the students a warning:

Prisoners are extremely good at telling you what *they think* you want to know. Any officer will back me up on that. Your prisoner may have done his GCSEs, but when you try to examine his attitude to women he will clam

154

up and you might find this embarrassing. But if he keeps beating about the bush you've still got to go on asking him questions. One important thing to remember is *never* to tell him whether you are going to recommend parole. You might give him a good report, then you could find that all the other reports on him will knock him back. Just tell him that lots of other people have got to consider his application, and say he'll get to read his parole report at some stage. Another thing to remember is that you can take notes of the interview but be careful what you write—*don't* write down things like "lying bastard"!

'Why not? Why can't we write what we really feel?' 'Because if you did, you'd be on the defensive in case he tried to look and see what you've written. These days we've got open reporting, so you want to try and make any criticism a constructive criticism—like how he can improve. As long as you can justify the things you've written you'll be all right. But if you write down something like "untrustworthy character" he can turn round and say "On what do you base that judgment?"'

• • •

I have quoted extensively from these three sessions because they reveal some important aspects of modern prison officer training. Despite the attractive physical environment and the generally fair quality of the course materials, the course was an odd mixture. The elements of old-fashioned rule-book learning sat uncomfortably with the bolt-on interpersonal skills training, which in the classes I observed served little useful purpose other than to allow tutors and trainees to voice their own stereotypical prejudices and have them publicly confirmed. Crass remarks were treated with tolerant indulgence and although there were more or less equal numbers of men and women, the whole ambience of the place was of a laddish, macho culture. I saw this replicated in the 'nick culture', or 'canteen culture', endemic in all the prisons I visited. Women staff on duty with men were frequently chaffed with puerile sexist comments—though it is only fair to say they usually responded in like fashion.

Above all, the training seemed to reinforce the old adage that 'a con is always a con', manipulative and devious. One of the women APS trainees, a 24-year-old law graduate, found this confusing: 'The training does teach you to see the prisoner as a person and to try to develop relationships. However, we are getting mixed messages because at the same time we're being told "Never turn your back on an inmate", and for us women, "Watch it round the men prisoners"'.

In none of the sessions I observed was recognition given to the very different needs of women prisoners. Indeed all the theoretical case histories described in the classes were about male prisoners, and women's prisons were *never* mentioned until I raised the question with students after the classes were over.

Some of the female APS trainees I interviewed seemed to be just the kind of thoughtful, intelligent governor grades needed in women's prisons. Why, then, did they share the men's reluctance to work in them? HM Inspectors have expressed concern that 'moving into the women's estate is not seen as a career move. Working predominantly in women's prisons should be regarded as a legitimate and valuable career path and selection and promotion should reflect this.'[7]

Serving officers told me there is inevitably less opportunity for promotion within the small female estate, which is regarded as a career backwater. The Prison Service operates an equal opportunities policy. But at the time of writing, only five of the 16 women's prisons have a female governing governor.[8] Some women officers said these jobs are perceived as high-risk, no-win positions. They mentioned Janet King, who was replaced at Holloway by a man, and Sally Swift, who did not go on to govern another woman's prison after Pucklechurch closed.

All but one or two of the students I interviewed were less than enthusiastic at the prospect of working in a women's prison—though gut reaction rather than concern with their own career prospects seemed to have informed their decision. Some seemed to have fallen for the usual stereotyping, mythologising and demonising of female offenders. Once again I heard the old adages paraded, depressingly as much by women trainees as by the men.

One woman, a former bus-driver, had been put off by seeing increasing aggression among women shoppers fighting over turkeys at Christmas in Marks & Spencer—though in the same breath she described being held hostage by an armed gang of boys on her bus till the police arrived. Another woman said she felt 'female prisoners would be questioning you all the time. They have to be dominant and I think they can be fairly envious of women officers and of each other. They will fight each other to have something'. A third was ambivalent:

My first reaction to the thought of women's prisons is that they frighten me far more than men's. I think I might also be torn between doing my job and sympathising with the women because they are there for very different reasons from the men. Many are victims and are there for debt and abuse. In some cases it's outrageous. They shouldn't be there at all and this shows the completely abhorrent nature of the criminal justice system. Women are victims of their own socialisation. However, I still think women in prison are far more frightening than men and the thought of them makes me shudder far more than men prisoners.

This woman would not have been reassured by another who had spent her two-week observation period in Holloway and was concerned about the increasing use of restraints: 'I found that the new SOs used control and restraint more: it's very frightening using the C and R gear. The visors get steamed up and you can't see what you're doing. Here we're about to do advanced C and R—how to deal with petrol bombs etc—so I suppose they think it's going to get worse.'

One woman trainee felt 'there should be training for male officers about the psychology of women prisoners. They are always saying they don't understand what makes women tick, and going on about the manipulation they are afraid of. They should be taught how to deal with difficult women who may well make allegations against them.'

The men expressed almost identical views to those of most of the male serving officers I interviewed, and it was depressing to hear that seven of the nine weeks of training had done nothing to change their minds. This trainee spoke for most of his colleagues when I asked him why he did not plan to work in a woman's prison:

I would find it intimidating. Quite honestly I wouldn't fancy it at all. I suppose I've got my ideas about women's prisons from the telly— *Cell Block H* and all that—plus what's written in the press. I can tell you, I'd want a good few years working in men's prisons before I'd consider a job in a women's!

Perhaps this reluctance is unsurprising when, for all their lip-service to interpersonal skills, the tutors themselves also rehearsed the old myths:

Why won't these new recruits work in women's prisons? Can you blame them? *I'm* scared to go into Holloway though I've been in the business for over 20 years! I'm even scared of the female officers![9] I think there is a feeling that prison is the last resort for women and they have to be pretty bad to get there. As a male you do fear being verbally abused.

His younger colleague agreed:

There's the idea that if women in prison fight, the fight will be much more vicious than men fighting. There is the male perception that females work in isolation, not like men prisoners who stick together, and that there is a certain amount of bitchiness among them.

To be fair, I was only able to attend one day of the nine week college course. But the tutors admitted that as yet no action has been taken to challenge these stereotypes and make sure trainees understand the background to women's offending. This has been a cause of concern frequently voiced by inspectors. In their report on Holloway,[10] published in 1997, they said 'We found that many wing staff had a very limited understanding of the type of problems experienced by prisoners. We found most wing staff unaware of the needs of women who had suffered abuse.'

Were there plans to introduce gender-specific training, as demanded by groups such as Women in Prison and by HM Inspectorate? The tutors said these plans were in the pipeline: 'The new courses will increase streaming. This means that there will be specialised courses for officers wishing to work in the women's prisons, the dispersal prisons and so on.'

The Trust for the Study of Adolescence, which had already produced training packages for staff working with male young offenders, was commissioned by the Prison Service to produce a similar course for work with young women, and in 1996, after pilot projects at Drake Hall and Holloway, it produced a detailed package called 'Understanding and Working with Young Women in Custody'. The package, designed for use in in-service training sessions, helps to demystify the problems which young women present when they come into prison. The modules look carefully at the reasons behind difficult-to-manage behaviour and quite properly attempt to get officers to remember their own adolescence and to empathise with young prisoners, especially those who have suffered abuse. The section on self-mutilation should put an end once and for all to its being dismissed as 'attention-seeking'—a favourite expression used by officers—because it explains the condition as a way for people to find physical release for mental anger they are unable to express (see *Chapter 12*).

However, a similar package is now needed to help officers understand the needs of older women, though at Cornton Vale the TSA package is being adapted for this purpose with input from the Samaritans and women's groups. Although the average age of women in prison is younger than the female population on the outside, there are closed prisons where the average age is much higher. Many long-term prisoners have been sentenced for a one-off offence, sometimes involving the killing of a violent male partner. Yet, apart from a few exceptions, the serving officers I interviewed seemed unable to understand the way power can be so grossly abused in a relationship that women are driven to take such desperate actions. It is not of course an officer's job to analyse sentencing policy, but an understanding of the reasons for offending is essential if an empathetic relationship is to be established. Some officers I spoke to had little sympathy with women who had stolen for economic reasons, still less with those who were drugs offenders. Carole Rigby of WISH (Women in Secure Hospitals) says there needs to be a radical shift in these attitudes. At a Liverpool conference in April 1998 she told staff working in prisons and secure hospitals, 'Don't be afraid to question your own beliefs and suspend your preconceived ideas. Believe the women in what they say about their pain and loss and recognise there is wisdom and value in what they have to say'.

When I discussed current initial training with serving officers, many expressed irritation with a form of preparation which in their view did not properly equip new recruits to do the job. 'It's all very well to be intelligent, but to do this kind of work you need to be trained in the skills of the job', said one older male officer. 'When I trained at the Wakefield college I knew all the processes of the prison. I knew what to do on reception, I knew how the gate manning worked. This new lot don't know anything like that. We have to teach them everything from scratch.'

Another principal officer I interviewed had come up through the ranks too. A small terrier-like man with a rugged face and solid stance he exactly fitted the stereotypical cartoon image of the old-style screw, and did not try to hide his contempt for modern training methods:

> The methods of training now are completely different from the methods when I trained 20 years ago. The syllabus is totally changed. The emphasis used to be all on jailcraft. You used to spend two or three weeks at the training school learning the rule book, then you'd be sent to an establishment where an old screw used to tell you the proper way to do things. Now it's all about *social studies*! Now the average age of the staff is much younger. They come straight from college and they may have been trained in "interpersonal skills" but they have absolutely no background in prison security. They have got to be told by us that security is of the utmost importance.

College tutors, however, think they have the balance about right:

> We do include jailcraft, but we teach them more than that: we teach them that gate officers will get a lot of abuse from visitors, so they need to learn how to cope with that and with the frustration of the job. We train them that no matter how abusive a person is, if you respond with abuse they will complain and you'll be the one who is punished, not them.

The principal officer remained unconvinced:

> Whatever they've been told at the college, new officers will find when they get here that they just can't do all this interpersonal skills stuff. They

can't talk to the women one to one, however much they may want to. These young officers come in here thinking they can give the women tea and sympathy. They have high expectations and when they can't do what they want, they don't like it.

He was joined by his superior, the male deputy governor, who endorsed his views: 'That's the hardest part, when you have to bring these young officers down to earth. This kind of attitude is wrong because it also gives the women prisoners high expectations of what they can get in prison and none of them like being told "No" either.'

'Going by the book', the passion for adherence to rules, is a prison attitude that is difficult to challenge. In a different prison the 'old' and 'new' approaches were epitomised by two male senior officers. The first proudly showed me his copy of *Operating Standards 1994*, a fat volume which, he said, covered every issue that could possibly arise in a prison: 'On this side of the page you'll find all the problems, and on the opposite side of the page you've got all the answers'. When I interviewed the second officer, he also showed me the manual, but was dismissive:

Look at this book. It can't begin to tell us how to deal with the problems we meet with women coming in here on remand. It won't tell me how to deal with a frightened woman like the one I found crouching at the back of a prison van yesterday. Nobody could get her out, she had wet herself, the agency staff who brought her didn't want to know — they were just the van drivers. I had to go and talk to her for ages and I finally persuaded her to come out holding my hand. I used her first name and I thought of my daughter. The operating standards book doesn't mention things like that.

If an attempt is to be made to break the mould, to 'turn the screws' and make sure serving officers, as well as new recruits, are up-to-date on current thinking, how can it be effected? For instance, is it compulsory to take part in in-service training? Do these courses have to be specific to the establishment, so that trainees planning to work in a women's prison would be obliged to take part in a course designed to look at the special needs of women prisoners?

When I asked a member of HM Inspectorate about compulsory in-service training, he gave a derisory snort: 'Compulsory? You're joking! They hardly have to have *voluntary* INSET!'

In their report on Holloway,[10] the inspectors commented: 'It is extraordinary that the governor, manager and staff at Holloway, as with those in other establishments for women, receive no special training or support for the particular work they are required to carry out. Every member of staff at Holloway should have appropriate training for working with women offenders within urgent but achievable time targets. Thereafter there should be ongoing support and refresher training available.'

In fact, I discovered, serving officers *are* obliged to undergo in-service training but it seems woefully thin, and the Prison Service official who told me the rules sounded sheepishly apologetic: 'Yes they do have to take part. For instance at least once a year they have to go on a control and restraint refresher course. They have to spend six days a year in in-service training.'

The new training courses may leave much to be desired, but at least they are a step in the right direction. So how far can the 'new breed' of officers and governor grades challenge and change the old 'nick culture' in the face of the determination of a body of older staff to keep things as they have always been? In the current punitive climate, with politicians of left and right vying with each other to occupy the vote-winning 'tough on crime' high ground, is it becoming easier for old-style officers to hang on to entrenched attitudes? It takes stamina to change a culture, and certainly I met several young officers who had made the attempt, failed, and ended up embracing old-style views.

In the new women's prisons in Canada, new staff have been employed. Marie-Andrée Drouin, Warden of the Grand Valley Institution for Women, opened in 1997, found it was essential to get rid of the old culture of the staff at the P4W, formerly Canada's only female prison: 'We are hiring new staff because it is easier to train than retrain'. Drouin spent four years before the facility opened, building up her team: 'You need the right staff doing the right job in the right way, and you need intensive training.'[11] In the end it all comes back to personal relationships. A senior Prison Service official observed:

The trouble with prisons and with all institutions—old people's homes, children's homes, anywhere with vulnerable people—is that they are run for the benefit of the staff and not for those living there. The trouble with Holloway in the early eighties was that it was not primarily about the prisoners at all. The staff were concerned about their own deprivations and their own needs, not about the needs of the prisoners. A lot of the problem lay in the personal backgrounds of the staff. All the officers were women and many of them had suffered from bad relationships with men. There was a strong lesbian culture and the trouble was that this was a culture of *self* which was reinforced in the way the women prisoners were treated, and it became a culture of fear where there was more and more lockdown with the women being handed all their meals through the hatches.

The inspectors have for many years been voicing these sentiments. Five years ago their report on HMP Bullwood Hall[12] complained that the prison's routine was run for the convenience of the staff, with prisoners spending little time out of their cells, and meal-times grossly distorted to fit in with staff shifts.

The senior official quoted above tries to retain some optimism in the face of current pressures on the Prison Service:

> Trainee prison officers may be better educated now, but you can't screen out all the unsuitable recruits. You do hope the training we give them will help. What is important is to create an awareness of the needs of the individual prisoner. Though it is very difficult to imagine how on earth you can maintain this level of interest in individuals when you are strapped for cash and resources, when a thousand new prisoners are coming in every month, and the time out of cell is being cut down more and more.

Staff training is, then, of the utmost importance. But if an establishment is to succeed, leadership is also vital. When Kate Donegan was appointed at Cornton Vale she immediately emphasised 'visible leadership': 'The managers used to sit on the top corridor smoking. Now members of the management team follow each other round the prison, talking to prisoners'.[11]

Women prisoners may be demonised by the media, but prison staff suffer demonisation as well, and the whole culture of prison life is a culture of mutual blame, leading to high levels of staff stress, sickness and absence. This culture goes right to the top: governors' heads will roll if there are embarrassing breaches of security. Governors with 25 years' distinguished service have been 'removed' for this reason—some a great loss to the profession.

Yet some of the 'fast-track' trainees I interviewed were still optimistic—perhaps even idealistic—about being able to make their mark: 'I know there are bad vibes about the way the Prison Service is being handled at the moment—I'm straight out of college and as yet I lack credibility. But I still hope we can change things.'

Endnotes

1. This quote from Mr Blair's letter was read out by Bev Lord, vice-chair of the POA, on *Breakfast with Frost*, 8 March 1998.
2. *Women in Prison: A Review*, HM Inspectorate, 1997, 4.09.
3. See Note 2, above: Executive Summary: 15.
4. See Note 2, above: 4.14.
5. Segregation unit: punishment block.
6. Minimum Use of Force Tactical Intervention: Prison Service jargon for forcible restraint. Prisoners speak of the 'Mufti Squad' and say they have been 'muftied' if they have been dragged by forced 'down the block'.
7. See Note 2, above 4.19.

8. East Sutton Park, Bullwood Hall, Styal, Cookham Wood and Foston Hall.

9. A young male officer had spent part of his training at Holloway: 'I was scared stiff when I was warned about the lesbian staff at Holloway. Us blokes were told to watch our step because there are certain comments you can't make in the mess when there are so many gay couples around. We were given a briefing and told there were a lot of attractive female staff but we shouldn't take anything at face value and we'd better not try anything, or their girlfriends would get us'.

10. *HMP Holloway: Report of an Unannounced Inspection by HM Chief Inspector of Prisons*, Home Office, 1997

11. Presentation at conference on 23 October 1997 at HMP Styal: 'Imprisoning w omen: Recognising Difference', organized by the Institute for the Study and Treatment of Delinquency (ISTD).

12. *HMP Bullwood Hall: Report by HM Inspectorate of Prisons*, Home Office, December 1992.

CHAPTER EIGHT

Twisted Sisters?

Sonya, in her fifties and serving life for murder in H wing at HMP Durham, travelled to the Royal Courts of Justice in February 1997 for her appeal. She has always maintained her innocence and was devastated when the three Appeal Court judges took just ten minutes to reject her lawyers' plea for a retrial. Alone, in one of the court cells from 10.10 a.m. until 4.30 p.m. that dark February afternoon, Sonya 'paced round and round, my wrists skinned and scarred from the double handcuffs Durham use. I thought I would go mad'. By the time a prison escort was free, it was too late for Sonya to return to Durham, so she was taken to Holloway.

> The Holloway prisoners were wonderful. I was at rock bottom, feeling I had nowhere left to go, but the officers allowed me on to a wing where I knew some of the women. I was with them from 5 p.m. till 8 p.m. when we were all locked in. We talked and talked and they were a fantastic support. I think I would have gone crazy without them.

Unlike Sonya, Sheila Bowler was fortunate enough to have her appeal allowed and she was cleared by an Old Bailey jury in February 1998 after two murder trials and two appeals. Sonya knows Sheila and wrote of her delight at the unanimous not guilty verdict. It would be natural if other life-sentenced prisoners felt some resentment, but Sheila heard later from one of the Holloway chaplains that her release 'lifted the whole prison' as women tuned in to the radio and TV news throughout the day until the verdict was announced.

These descriptions of groups of empathetic, supportive women is a far cry from commonly-held views about female prisoners. Public misconceptions about violent women prisoners were discussed in *Chapter 5*. The demonising of women in prison seems to cut across all the boundaries of class, gender and age. As I embarked upon research for this book I discovered a deeply-rooted revulsion in some quite unexpected quarters. The almost universal horror invoked by the very idea of women's prisons suggests that although an individual female criminal may repel (especially if like Myra Hindley she has been portrayed for decades as an icon of evil) it is the thought of *collective* female wickedness that people find so terrifying. Most frightening to outsiders is the concept of the coven, of weird sisters coming together to hatch their dark plots.

Women sent to prison are as susceptible to this terror as anyone else. Many—like two-thirds of my sample—have never been in prison before.[1] In *Chapter 2*[2] women described refusing to come out of their cells for fear of attack by other prisoners. One woman said:

> I didn't mind that I had to be put in the seg[3] at Risley for the first few days because there was nowhere else for me to go. I'd seen women with blacked eyes so I thought I was probably safer in there.

Among the most frequently voiced fears were having to fight off attacks by murderers and to repel overtures from lesbians—two groups in fact least likely to pose a threat. Many women serving life for murder have killed male partners who have abused them—a one-off situational offence which means they are extremely unlikely to be any danger to another woman or, indeed, to anyone else. The term 'predatory lesbian', bandied about by (mainly male) officers, perpetuates yet another prison myth. Imprisoned gay women, once they have 'come out', usually have no shortage of partners without having to resort to force, though fights between them may break out because of jealousy in the heightened tension of prison life. Some women seeking physical affection in a hostile environment also become 'prison-bent' for the period of their incarceration. One lesbian woman admitted:

> I was the one who was scared of being jumped on! I believed all the old stereotypes I was brought up on and when the other women were all so wonderful to me I felt ashamed of these misconceptions.

Media reports of women being 'raped' by other female prisoners are not borne out by the reports of women prisoners themselves. Although sexual abuse by women is not unknown, and isolated attacks do happen, it is much more likely that the vast majority of these so-called sexual attacks are not motivated by sex at all but are part of the organized system for smuggling drugs into prison, which I discuss in detail in *Chapter 9*.

The true reason for new prisoners' fears of other women lies deeper than simple preservation of life and limb. The most commonly voiced dread was of *contamination* by proximity to 'women like these'. *Newly* imprisoned women—as distinct from those who had served part of their sentences—would very forcibly make it clear to me that they regarded themselves as set apart from other groups whose crimes were worse than theirs. A woman jailed for the manslaughter of her lover said 'Being lumped together with the others, all regarded collectively as manipulative, devious, cunning liars—that's the most painful thing.' Women who had never taken drugs would distance themselves from 'those junkie girls, those crackheads'; white women distanced themselves from black women; all shrank in horror from baby-killers, child-molesters and those who have attacked the old and vulnerable. They are the untouchables of the prison caste system.

Women's prisons are subject to the 'nick culture' code, just as men's are. In December 1997, Denise Giddings made headlines when she was remanded to Holloway for allegedly snatching baby Karli Hawthorne. She was released on bail three days later, saying that she had endured 'a horrendous few days' being attacked by other prisoners. That same week a woman solicitor jailed for protecting her boyfriend—a police officer—from a drink-drive charge was moved from Holloway to an open prison for similar reasons. The prison authorities commented that former prosecutors and police officers were among those likely to face abuse of this kind. One of the lifers I interviewed admitted setting up a vicious attack on a woman convicted of killing an old woman. Her crime made her 'a beast, a nonce' and according to the attacker she deserved the broken jaw she sustained. An added impetus for the attack was the woman's 'superior' attitude. 'She thought because she was middle-class and had a few A-levels she could look down on the rest of us. As far as I was concerned she was the scum of the earth.'

New prisoners may also be shocked if (as frequently happens with women felt to be at risk of harming themselves at the beginning of their sentence) they are sent to the prison hospital, where they may find some seriously disturbed women. One woman was on remand for committing a one-off drugs importation offence for money to escape from an abusive husband abroad: 'I was in the hospital wing at first and I was really shocked by some of the women I saw in there. I couldn't cope at all when I first came in here.'

But usually this kind of reaction is temporary: the 34 per cent of my sample who had been in prison before, and those who had served even a month or two of their sentences, would soon look back ruefully to their first few days. Although relationships in prison are fraught, though there is intimidation and bullying, and though proximity may create unbearable tensions, the terrors do recede and prisoners do begin to see others as they really are, not according to some stereotypical image. Perhaps this is why several officers—and indeed a few of the prisoners—were of the opinion that two or three days in prison would be the most effective deterrent for minor offenders: this would 'shock them out of ever coming back inside again'. But a week, they said, would be too long: by then they would have 'got used to the place and made a few friends.'[4]

At Cookham Wood I met a 22-year-old New Yorker serving four years for importing heroin. Compared with what she had heard about

US jails, she said, Cookham was easy:

> When I heard I was coming to jail I expected to have to fight. As they were taking all my jewellery away I was allowed to keep one ring and I remember looking at it and wondering if I could use it to fight with. The first few days I was waiting for people to attack me. But it's not like that at all. Most of the trouble is over drugs.

Most women showed sympathy and understanding for those prisoners they felt 'shouldn't be in here'—especially fine defaulters and women with small children:

> There's one woman here with a big family — kids, grandchildren. She's got a drink problem, that's what's wrong with her. She did cheque books but she's not a danger to anyone, is she? (Woman jailed for defaulting on fines for prostitution).

> There are women here sentenced to nine months for shoplifting, though they've got several kids. The fucking judges haven't learnt anything. (Woman jailed for drugs offences).

In spite of outsiders' perception of women's prisons, and despite new prisoners' own fears, it would be wrong to underplay the good and positive relationships that can be formed in prison. There are women who for the first time in their lives have forged a close friendship with another woman, not necessarily based on a sexual relationship. There are women who with the support of other prisoners have found the strength on release to walk away from an abusive relationship and start a new life. Women outside prison have traditionally been better than men at supporting each other and forming self-help groups—perhaps because in the past their isolation in domestic and child-rearing situations has driven them to seek the help of other isolated women. Erving Goffman in his influential work *Asylums*[5] described the 'fraternalisation process' whereby people living in institutions of any kind start out with the usual popular misconceptions about other inmates, but soon develop systems of mutual support and common 'counter-mores' in opposition to the regime that has forced them into intimacy. Certainly many women told me they would leave prison with a little more understanding of the problems of those they had once vilified, and most were united by a sense of the injustice of their treatment by prison staff.

On prison visits there are always plenty of released women coming back to see those still inside. A woman governor told me:

> Lots of ex-inmates come back on visits: while the men have family outside

167

to come and visit them, the women might not have anyone in the world except the friends they have met inside.

I heard plenty of accounts of friendly supportive relationships like the one described by Sonya at the beginning of this chapter. The New York drugs courier had led a chaotic life until she came into prison:

> I've made three really good friends in here and my best friend's an excellent person—she's helped me a lot. When I was in New York I never had a chance to sit and think. I seemed to be living 24 hours a day. She made me sit and go over what I've done with my life. I've made quite a few wrong turns. I'm only 22 and I've already been in jail a year. I've grown up a lot in here.

Such friendships can be empowering and renewing: the senior probation officer in an open prison went as far as to say this was the most valuable aspect of prison life:

> In spite of all the fierce supervision and the silly petty rules, some women really like it here because for the first time in their lives they have become friends with other women. Some do well in here because of that, and get back their self-esteem.

In her powerful play *Yard Gal* (1998), Rebecca Prichard explored these friendship bonds after working as a writer in residence at Bullwood Hall. Friendship can be shown in small but important kindnesses—one lifer went to endless trouble to care for another lifer's pet budgie when she went to another prison on accumulated visits.[6] A woman in her twenties serving two years for a violent offence supported a new younger prisoner:

> She was only 16 and her head was all battered by her boyfriend. She was in a terrible state when she came in. I spent nights and nights talking to her and we're still good mates.

The Prison Service has tapped into this valuable source of help in the hope of preventing the growing number of prison suicides.[7] In most prisons there are now officially approved counsellors known as 'listeners' (or 'befrienders' as they are called at Holloway). These are prisoners trained by the Samaritans to help others: they can be identified by a special badge and can be sought any time of day or night. A nun attached to an open prison chaplaincy team praised the scheme: 'I have seen these listeners sit up all night with a woman who is very distressed.' Denise, jailed for animal rights protests, is a listener:

> Prisoners will never open up to an officer. Prison is sick — it's a very sad place. You need to talk to people one to one about all their problems. But this doesn't always happen and you hear people left alone, up all night crying their hearts out. Sometimes other women support them. But sometimes they can be quite horrible to people in distress.

Such interdependent relationships can of course lead to problems. One major difficulty is that a woman may be moved around the system for all sorts of reasons and will then lose hard-won friendships. After four months in Holloway Sheila Bowler was taken to Bullwood Hall for the second stage in her sentence. The first evening in the new prison she wrote: 'Desperately lonely without X: though we did not always talk a great deal, we knew we were always there for each other if necessary.'

Good inter-prisoner relationships also depend on the extent to which prison staff are prepared to support them. One open prison prides itself on the 'birthing partner' scheme whereby a woman going into hospital to have a baby can choose another prisoner to go with her for support. But however imaginative the idea, in practice it depends for its success on those who implement it.

Savita's best friend, Asian like herself but much younger, was in this prison expecting her first baby and was terrified:

> She went into labour and I would like to have gone to hospital with her as her birth partner. I could not go because I was not risk-assessed[8] — I'd only been here four weeks at that time. My friend was petrified, so I asked if someone else could go with her. The SO[9] shouted, in front of my friend "I can hardly find a licence for this bloody woman, much less anyone else!" This girl, waiting for her first baby, was made to wait 45 minutes in the visitors' waiting room though her waters had already broken in the middle of chapel that morning. They sent her off to hospital on her own in a taxi. She was shaking with fear. Early next morning I was summoned to the principal officer's room. He said "There's a rumour going round that you're complaining about Miss P going to hospital in a taxi on her own. If you're not very careful you'll be off to another prison — a closed one this time!"' He was livid — the man's face was bright red. Since I've been released I've had several phone calls from this friend, still there in the prison with her baby. I find them quite upsetting. You don't appreciate what close friendships you make inside. You meet a caucus of women you can identify with.

Some campaigning women take active steps to empower more timid prisoners. At Styal I interviewed Sara Thornton, later released after a high-profile campaign, two appeals and a re-trial. She was celebrating a

169

small but important victory when I met her in her cell in one of the houseblocks:

> I try to inspire women in here — anything I've done in prison I haven't done for privileges or for myself but I've done it to show them they can be powerful. This prison is run on patriarchal lines and the women still seek the approval of the male prison officers. But anger can be healthy and it can empower people. There was an officer in this house who was really terrible and everybody hated her. At 1.30 a.m. I called a meeting and I got about eight women together in this small room and we decided to protest to the governor about this officer's behaviour. We wrote a letter to the governor, saying this house would explode if this officer wasn't taken off duty here. I think the governor was quite shocked but we won and the officer was removed. When one of the inmates came back with the news the whole place erupted and we all had music on to celebrate. Women in prison are often frightened and there's a lot of bitchiness because of that.

Some women used blunter instruments to show sisterly solidarity. I interviewed Nadine in Pucklechurch remand centre before it closed down: 'We had a little riot in here last week. My friend's dad's dying and she wanted to be in a room of her own but the screws said she couldn't. So the girls smashed some stuff up, set fire to their blankets and that.'

Women living in small groups at such close quarters can of course become involved in dangerously intense relationships from which is difficult to escape. Simone, an older woman lifer, had always had problems making close friendships in prison until she met Eileen and found they shared many interests. But the relationship became one-sided with Eileen invading Simone's space, demanding constant attention, exhausting and draining all Simone's scant emotional reserves. Unlike on the outside there is nowhere to escape and if you protest there is the dual fear that you will cause lasting damage to the other person and that she will turn others against you. Luckily Eileen was soon to be moved to another prison but Simone continued to worry: 'People forget that crime doesn't stop when someone is sent to jail. Women still keep up their criminal links outside and have dangerous contacts they can use to get at your family.'

Another lifer nearing the end of her sentence had learned over the years to avoid very close relationships: 'I get on better with animals really. People take me as anti-social but I'm just very wary of getting involved. I'd rather talk to the prison cats. I'm not very confidential with inmates. I'll have a chat but you don't want to get too close to people'. This wariness is sadly sometimes born of experience. As another woman said: 'I have become a lot stronger since I came in here and much more cynical too, I'm afraid. I was brought up to trust everyone

170

but now it's more a case of I'll wait and see. I am much more wary because I have seen a side to people that I never saw before.'

Histories of women's imprisonment reveal how those who control incarcerated women have always tried to prevent women coming together in friendship. *Chapter 5* described how women prisoners have traditionally been subjected to closer surveillance than men, and how this continues in today's jails.

In early nineteenth century prisons there were two different disciplinary systems: the first was the 'congregate silent' system where women were allowed to work together in 'associate silent labour' such as laundry or needlework (usually washing, mending or making the clothes of male prisoners). They were forbidden to talk at all, except to their own small children incarcerated with them. The second type of regime was called 'continuous solitary confinement' where prisoners were physically separated, locked on their own in single cells.

The silent system caused enormous problems of supervision in both male and female prisons and was opposed by reformers because of the harsh punishments inflicted on those who breached the silence rule. But there were special concerns about women: it was felt that, being 'naturally more sociable and excitable than men' and 'lacking in self control', women were much harder to keep working silently than men. It certainly proved impossible for the female warders or 'matrons' to keep the women quiet: the older ones would respond to a reprimand with 'a torrent of obscene and blasphemous abuse', which in itself was regarded as corrupting to their younger, relatively, innocent neighbours.

The congregate system was replaced when the Penal Act 1839 brought in the solitary system. The chaplain of one prison was plainly relieved: women who 'under the old system must have gone out corrupted and ruined by the association with the most depraved and basest of their sex' were now leaving prison much more likely to 'become useful members of society'. In France as in Britain, women were held separate because 'women contaminate each other even more than men do'.[10]

This attitude still prevails in some quarters, and older officers still speak of 'contamination'. One very experienced woman governor grade who in the past had worked at Styal told me: 'We used to run the old 'star' status at Styal. This had only first offenders on it which meant they were not *contaminated* by others. I am not talking about ages. I approve of mixed ages. You can have first offenders aged from 16 to 60. But I don't approve of mixed offences. Some women come here on remand *uncontaminated* and we want them to stay that way.' [italics supplied].

Because only 16 prisons currently take women, allocation decisions tend to be based on operational pragmatism rather than the suitability of an establishment for a woman's age and offence. Prison allocation boards assess women as being fit for open or closed conditions, then send them where there happens to be an empty bed, in a prison as close to home as possible—though very often this cannot be arranged.

Allocating officers spoke openly of 'primitive allocation'. Male category A prisoners are dispersed among maximum security dispersal prisons—high security closed training prisons. But at the time of writing there are only a few women categorised in this high security bracket, and most of them are in Durham's H wing where 46 long-sentence women prisoners are currently held in the midst of a local jail containing 844 male prisoners.

With a few exceptions, prisoners in the other women's prisons or units live together, regardless of their ages and the gravity of their offences. The largest, Holloway, has about 500 women, of whom 60 per cent are on remand. The average stay of Holloway prisoners is only 28 days, but there are also some life-sentence prisoners, because Holloway is a second-stage lifer jail,[11] and a large proportion of foreign nationals, because it is also a designated centre for foreign national detainees. Holloway has in addition to cater for women sent there temporarily because of forthcoming appeals to the Court of Appeal which sits at the Royal Courts of Justice, and the many women sent for accumulated visits.[6] The open prisons—Drake Hall, Askham Grange and East Sutton Park—also vary in the way they accommodate prisoners. Drake Hall for instance has a separate induction wing and a separate block for lifers.

Other internal prison divisions exist in the four mother and baby units,[12] where, at the time of writing, 68 women live with their babies, separate from the main population (though they may work with other prisoners); in the hospital wings, where mentally disturbed women and vulnerable prisoners on rule 43[13] live alongside women who are suffering from short-term ailments; and in the drug-free units. Most prisons now have a drug-free block or wing, where women wishing to rid themselves of their habit gain certain privileges if they sign a compact[14] not to take drugs.

Penal reform groups are growing more and more concerned about the number of very young girls now being sent to adult women's prisons. Most Victorian accounts of prison life[10] describe the plight of young female first offenders finding themselves incarcerated next to prostitutes and thieves. Such girls were thought to be dangerously susceptible to contamination by older criminal women who might corrupt them and recruit them to a life of thieving and prostitution. The language of these criminal women was often mentioned as corrupting in itself, being 'full of blasphemy and ribaldry'. So the women's jailers made every possible effort to make sure they did not even speak to each other.

The average age of women prisoners is now 31, but this gives a false impression because there are a few much older women. The most common age for women prisoners is 20. Yet there are no dedicated young offender institutions in England and Wales for young women and girls as there are for young men and boys: presumably it is felt that the small numbers involved would not justify the expense. As it is, it costs £512 per week to keep an adult women in prison—£92 a week more than it costs to keep a man. There were only 139 sentenced female young offenders in the system on 30 June 1994, though throughout that year, 510 of the 4,100 YOs received into prison establishments were female.[1] The use of prison for girls aged 15 to 17 increased by 110 per cent in the period 1992-1995, despite a recommendation by the last government that only those juveniles who have committed serious offences should be sent to prison.[15]

The Criminal Justice Act 1991 included provision to end the practice of remanding defendants under 17 to prison but at the time of writing this practice still continues. More local authority secure accommodation was built to hold these 15 and 16 year olds, but these places are now to be used instead for 12 to 14 year olds under secure training orders included in the Crime and Disorder Act 1998 which lowers the age of imprisonment. Unless local authorities set up the planned youth offending teams in time to divert them, more 12-year-olds will go to adult jails. Already now, each year, more than 300 girls under 18 are sent to adult female prisons and the numbers are growing, despite the recommendations of the chief inspector of prisons that no child under the age of 18—because under English law they are classed as children— should be subjected to the 'corrupting influence' of prison.[16]

In August 1997 *The Observer* published the preliminary findings of a Howard League investigation into the experiences of girls held in British prisons. The report quoted researchers' horror at finding 15-year-old girls held alongside the most disturbed prisoners at prisons like Risley and Bullwood Hall. Several were victims of serious bullying, there were incidences of self-mutilation and some had attempted suicide. No special provision was made for their education and some had left prison addicted to hard drugs. The Howard League said that the conditions in which they were held were in breach of the United Nations Convention on the Rights of the Child.[17] The League's Director pointed out that the new detention and training orders could result in the home secretary having the power to send girls as young as 10 to adult women's prisons.[18] Also in August the High Court ruled in a test case that a girl of 17 could not be held on remand at HMP Risley, because it has no young offender wing.

The Howard League and other prison reform groups rejoiced: what business is it of the Prison Service, asked the Prison Reform Trust[19] to be caring for 15 and 16-year-olds at all? The trust pointed out that the mixing of young girls and adult women was regarded by the Prison Service as a positive virtue: 'The older women, we were told, acted as mother substitutes for the younger ones.' But when the Howard League's full report[20] was published in October 1997 it exposed bullying and sexual abuse by older women upon girls who should be protected under the Children Act. The report blamed the steep rise in the number of young girls being jailed on a media obsession with girl gangs in the wake of a gang attack on the actress Liz Hurley.

Doris Briggs, the officer quoted in *Chapter 1* feels there are other more complex reasons for the increase in the female prison population:

> I've worked in this prison for the last 20 years. The courts are getting worse and they're sending young and younger girls to prison. In the old days, if we had a juvenile girl in here it would be for a really serious offence. But now we get 16-year-old girls sent to prison for fighting! Well, teenagers *do* fight! Girls always did fight but now the courts send them to jail for it. We always had little boys in court for fighting and now we are treating juvenile girls the same way.

In October 1997, the same month that the Howard League report was published, the Magistrates' Association debated a motion calling for the decriminalisation of child prostitution—the result of a two year campaign by The Children's Society, which argued that under-age girls are not criminals but victims of child abuse. The Association of Directors of Social Services and the Association of Chief Police Officers joined the calls for child prostitution to be dealt with as a child protection issue, rather than a criminal offence. Many young girls now in prison would not be there if this were the case. Home Office figures show that between 1989 and 1996, about 4,000 young people under the age of 18 (most of them female) received convictions or cautions for soliciting.

One woman officer with 20 years' experience of women's prisons felt strongly that young girls should be kept apart from older women:

> The young offenders would be better on their own in my view. We get some very young ones in prison and they learn how to commit crimes better. A YO can come in for a fine and she is not a criminal. She might be on such little money that when she gets put with burglars she is told how to make money easily and it must seem very tempting. Some of the older ones do take the young ones under their wings and help them—but they can also corrupt them.

Prisoners and officers were in agreement about the destabilising effect of drug abuse on the prison community: the intimidation it causes is discussed in detail in *Chapter 9*. But they were ambivalent as to whether older women were more likely to recruit younger ones to their drug habit, or vice versa. A Bullwood Hall prisoner in her thirties, with young daughters of her own, said she was shocked:

> I've seen young girls of 17 coming in here and they've only smoked a few joints but they go out raving addicts because the older women get to them. It's true what they say about prison being a university of crime. This is definitely true when it comes to drugs. You see women exchanging phone numbers of dealers and they'll say "Go to so-and-so at this number. He'll sort you out and you can earn yourself a fifty." All prison does is spread the network further.

But a 50-year-old Holloway prisoner disagreed:

> In my experience the older women are not likely to encourage the younger ones to take drugs. I don't think the kids in here need any encouragement — most of them are deeply involved with their habit before they come here. I would estimate that 90 per cent of the young girls are here on drugs-related charges — that's including cases like shoplifting done to support a drugs habit.

Relationships, especially prison relationships, are never simple. There are certainly girls in prison who after a life in institutions have discovered in older women the affection their own mothers could never give them. Patsy's already tragic childhood ended when at the age of 15 she was sent to Bullwood Hall, which like Durham takes the more serious offenders, for a violent lock-knife attack on another teenage girl who had taken away her boyfriend:

> I came straight to this prison from court. I was the youngest in the prison and all the other girls were very nice to me and they kept asking me if I was all right. Before I came in here I thought everyone hated me. My boyfriend treated me like crap and everyone else was shit to me.

Bullwood Hall used to be a girls' borstal and in the past had a poor reputation for the bullying alleged to go on there. An officer explained the current arrangements:

> Here we combine YOs (some of them girls of only 15 and 16) and much older women which makes life difficult as you obviously can't treat them all the same. We have mixed accommodation and in the two main wings we try to keep the mix about fifty-fifty between YOs and adults. It can be

that the older women are a good influence but I have seen cases where the adults are more childish than the kids. In general though, the older women do calm down the younger ones because in prisoners' eyes the longer the sentence the more brownie points you get. So the older women become infamous. We don't mix remand and convicted prisoners because all our women are convicted. We do mix offences. Some of our lifers are here for their first and only offence. There's only us and Durham for people like that in the first stage of their sentences — that's the problem of the female estate. And alongside these very serious offenders we have 15-year-old girls who shouldn't be here at all — but there aren't enough female secure units round the country for young girls like them.

Sir David Ramsbotham described his horror in his second week as chief inspector of prisons at finding four 15-year-old girls in Holloway, one of them in the pregnant women's unit 'because the prison didn't know where else to put her'. His full report on women's prisons published in 1997 restated the Inspectorate's concern about juveniles in prison, but concurred with the mixing of older age groups, as long as 'greater care [is] exercised over which individuals are accommodated together.'[21] The inspectors deplored, for instance, the holding of YOs in Durham's H wing, where there are several schedule one offenders. They noted 'the serious child protection issues involved in mixing young prisoners with adults', and recommended that systematic procedures to deal with child protection issues should be urgently implemented.

● ● ●

There is an issue too about the effect on older prisoners. At present, as the Bullwood Hall example shows, older prisoners commonly live side by side with some very young women, and inevitably their interests will sometimes clash. Noise was mentioned by many women in their forties and fifties as a major problem: an older Holloway prisoner wrote in her diary: 'Incredibly noisy when we were let out after lunch today: stereos seemed to be turned up to maximum volume. Will I ever get out of this hell hole?' A prisoner in her forties explained:

It's not too bad on the lifers' wing but even here there are youngsters mixed in with us older women and there's a lot of music and noise and it's not easy. If there's bad behaviour and noise in the night you daren't tell the younger ones off or they'll give you bad language, an f . . . or a sh . . . and say "Who are you, my mother or something?" They're only about 15 or 16 years old but we can't tell them off because it just causes more disturbance. So I keep myself to myself. I try to keep out of it and I don't want to know anything about the bullying that goes on. I've got enough problems of my own.

176

This woman's prison does have a designated wing for young offenders, but in practice it is not used exclusively for younger women. The wing officer did not know why this was so:

> I'm not sure it's deliberate policy to mix YOs and older women: though this is supposed to be a YO wing, we always have a few women aged 40 to 50 on it. I suppose the theory is that the older ones will keep the younger ones quiet, but it may just be putting people where we've got the space. The fact is that we haven't got enough women's prisons to separate the different ages.

At one of the open prisons, a lifer in her thirties was nearing the end of a ten-year sentence. She endorsed the Prison Service view that older prisoners could have a positive influence over younger women:

> It's better to mix younger and older women together. It's chaos if it's just younger ones. The ones who are not on drugs can be condemned by the others who are. You overhear them being bullied and they are very frightened. You try and ask them questions and help them. Older prisoners should do more of that. If the officers intervene the girls tell them to fuck off but they are much more reluctant to cheek an older prisoner, specially a lifer. I think they're a bit afraid of us.

Anita agreed. She is 40 and has spent most of her life in and out of prison:

> I've seen girls in here [another open prison] who have never touched heroin but they fall in love with other women who get them on to it. Women should never bully young girls and I won't turn a blind eye to it, knowing what happened to me when I was abused as a child. Two weeks ago, let's say I was in the wrong place at the wrong time, I found out about an older woman abusing a young girl here. I went to an officer and she went out to get the police.

A prisoner in her mid-forties, on remand at Risley, said 'There is a core group of older women and they cleaned up a lot of the bullying. If we see it we confront it but I have just had an incident where I had to back down because I was in danger.'

But many older women told me they resented being *used* by the prison as part of its control mechanism. The inspectors' review[22] recognised that older women prisoners have 'become part of the strategy' to manage younger, more volatile women. One of the older prisoners on a mixed wing was Linda, serving two years for supplying Ecstasy. She is 39 and became involved with drug dealing through her relationship with a man 20 years her junior:

It's a nightmare in here. They keep me here because I'm good and they want me to influence the younger ones. I did think I might be able to have some influence on these girls, having a younger boyfriend and my own teenage son and daughter, but they're a different matter altogether. It's incredible in here. It's opened my eyes, I can tell you. It's like an awful boarding school.

A Holloway prisoner, aged 51, wrote me a letter putting the case for older prisoners:

I have no idea whether it may be beneficial for young offenders to associate with older women. Personally I would prefer to be segregated. This may sound selfish, as several of the young kids seem inclined to pour out all their problems to us older women. However, frankly, although in many cases I do sympathise, I am not an unpaid social worker acting on behalf of the home secretary. Older women have their own problems and often need the space to sort them out. This is difficult when you are confined on a wing with 40 volatile youngsters.

Many older women found it particularly hard to share dormitory accommodation and a common complaint was the lack of privacy. Most women—even long-termers—begin a sentence in shared dormitory accommodation, and have to work their way through the system before they are allowed single cells, though in some prisons dormitories are the norm. Life-sentenced prisoners are more likely to be given single cells at an earlier stage in their sentences.

A Holloway prisoner in her fifties said, 'I have to share a dorm and it's highly embarrassing to have to dress and undress in front of youngsters.' Another woman of the same age, who had recently undergone a major breast cancer operation, found herself sharing with much younger women who liked to stay up late, long after official 'lights out'. One of her room mates, aged 20, felt women of different ages should be separated: 'We all get on all right except you don't get much sleep–and there's a lot of bitchiness around because girls are tired all the time.' In one open prison a woman in her thirties described a similar case:

A lot of women in here are terribly depressed and the younger ones intimidate some of the older ones. There's an old lady here—she's in her late 60s—and she snores terribly. The young girls are horrible to her and keep telling her to shut up and making her life a misery. We all told them off and to lay off her. There is lots of bullying going on all the time here.

Another woman in her sixties was finally moved away from her young room mate and allowed to share a double cell in her open prison with a woman of 41:

> It's better being with a middle-aged woman, but still, the only time I can be alone to read or do my knitting or crochet is when my room mate has gone to one of the communal rooms. I never go in there to watch TV because they're always smoke-filled and it's always noisy with the younger inmates' loud music.

A grandmother in her forties felt fortunate that in her open prison she has her own room, though the wings are mixed-age:

> They put the older women with the YOs and it's not easy. I was really terrified of them at first in Risley and even in here I keep myself to myself. The young girls in here, they're OK, they're a laugh. But they do wind people up and they're only young so they're very loud. And of course drugs are rife in here. I'm grateful for the key in the door of my room and I don't mix much with other people. There should be more privacy for the showers. There's just the door off the corridor and shower curtains. I find it very embarrassing that anyone can just look in. I hated sharing a room, even for the one week I had to do it. I have one or two friends on this wing but I really keep myself to myself. If you say you want to be on your own, other women do respect your privacy.

Younger girls were said by older women to dominate association periods and mealtimes with rowdy behaviour ignored by the officers. Holloway women made the following comments: 'All hell was let loose today when a youngster had a radio cassette player handed in and it's been going full blast ever since. I tried to counter it by watching a 1952 TV film—but not very successfully'; 'It's always the younger girls wanting to watch rubbish so I don't bother'; 'I don't think older and younger inmates should be mixed together, the noise level is sometimes intolerable and they totally dominate what we see on TV— normally videos on sex and violence—and push and shove us around in medicine queues and meal queues. In the dining room we older ones have moved our tables to the end as we were being bombarded with chips one side and doughnuts the other side one evening.'

• • •

As I noted at the beginning of this chapter, newly imprisoned women voiced their fears of being approached by aggressive lesbian women, and indeed, 'contamination' to many means 'sexual homosexual contamination'. Victorian reformers chose to ignore the existence of prison lesbian relationships.[10] But contemporary accounts tell of

179

passionate jealousies and fights in nineteenth century female prisons, and the matron of the Petite Force, a women's prison in Paris, claimed that most of the inmates indulged in *commerce contre nature*, leading French penal reformers to condemn such institutions as dens of moral corruption.[10]

More than a century later, when 'the love that dared not speak its name' is now openly celebrated in most countries of the Western world, among new prisoners there still remains the abiding fear of lesbian seduction. Although as I discussed in *Chapter 5*, the lesbian activities rules are rarely strictly enforced, some officers still feel that young girls are at risk of 'corruption' by older gay women. Young male officers were the most likely to complain:

> I think in terms of sexuality it is not very good for the younger ones to be with older lesbian women. If a 15 year old child — yes, we do have them here as young as that — is out in the exercise yard and she sees two women kissing and groping each other, well — that's not very good, is it? Her sexuality may be influenced. There is an LA rule but it's not enforced and people turn a blind eye.

But many women were not so sure: a 21-year-old mother of two young children shuddered as she said 'You can get 14 days added for lesbian activities. I've been punished once by being sent to prison and that was enough. There's a lot of dykes in here. If one of them approached me I'd die! I'd say no!'

Another young prisoner in the same prison agreed: 'There's a lot of dykes among the officers and the prisoners. I never saw anything like this till I came into prison. I don't want to share a room with any of them. If you're gay you're all right in prison. If you're not, you can just get left out of conversations and that. I go to church to get away from it all.'

Sadly, fear of being labelled a lesbian can endanger a good friendship. One heterosexual prisoner thinks officers can foster this unhelpful attitude:

> There is a lot of pent-up frustration in a woman's prison. There is physical contact but it's a different type of contact from a sexual contact. Men try to keep a stiff upper lip — they keep themselves to themselves in prison. Here women might want to give each other a hug — it's about comfort not sex. I remembered giving my best friend a hug because she was very upset about something and an officer went past and sniggered and said "Are you enjoying yourselves?" Smutty stuff like that. I am separated from my daughter so you need comfort from other women.

Male officers certainly seemed to feel threatened by the presence of lesbian prisoners and constantly used clichés like 'the predatory lesbian', 'jail-dykes' and 'rampant lesbianism'. Both male and female officers said that sexual rivalries among the women can cause serious breaches of discipline, even in open prisons. But male officers were more likely to express revulsion:

> Sometimes lesbian affairs cause fights and this often happens when a new woman comes into this prison whom I would regard as plain both in personality and appearance—to my eyes she will be unattractive, macho and butch. Other women clearly identify her as gay and find her attractive and there will be jealous competition. The parallel in a men's prison is the effeminate young boy who comes into a male prison and attracts some men in the same way. This is the most disruptive thing that can happen in any prison and in my view it is more serious than drugs.

Another male officer could barely conceal his distaste: 'You can tell the lesbians by the love bites they have on their necks. They wear them as a trophy.'

Though newly-arrived prisoners said they felt threatened by the thought of lesbianism, most women accepted its existence as part of prison life: 'I've seen women commit crimes just so they can get back inside to be with their girlfriends. It happens all the time', said a prisoner in a closed prison. A middle-aged Bullwood Hall prisoner said:

> One of the young wing cleaners got very upset because of some mischief-making going on between her pen pal at the same prison as the girlfriend of another Bullwood woman. She was screaming that when we were next unlocked that this particular prisoner would get bashed. After 20 minutes screaming and shouting and crying I pressed the call button and the wing officer sent for another officer who tactfully played a game of pool and calmed the wing cleaner down. When we were let out the prisoner who'd caused all the trouble asked to be kept locked in her room for safety.

Both officers and women described some lesbian liaisons in prison as temporary replacements for heterosexual relationships outside:

> Women are more tactile. With sexual frustration men are more likely to hit each other. But men are also less likely to break the barrier into sexual relationships because of the taboos about male homosexuality. (Senior male officer, open prison).

> Women get involved in lesbian activities because they need the tactile contact. They can't have it with their partner or their children so they do it with other women. We do get the bullying but it's mainly to do with drugs and not the same kind of taxing and mugging you get in men's prisons. (Woman governor grade, closed prison)

181

Some women do become prison-bent because in the end it's down to you whatever you can do in your sentence to make it pass. Women miss their partners whatever sex they are, and they want love. When people become prison-bent it's usually just for affection, not real relationships. (Lesbian prisoner, open prison)

Gina, who served a sentence in Cornton Vale for the manslaughter of an abusive lover who robbed and raped her, described a lesbian relationship she developed in prison. It began as a non-sexual friendship but went wrong when it became physical:

I am not homosexual but in Cornton Vale there was a strong lesbian culture. A lot of the gay women were those who had been abused as children. I had a lesbian relationship and I found it soul-destroying. I was very vulnerable when I went into prison and this lesbian was a long-termer. She was someone I admired and had an affection for—though not a sexual attraction. I had a male friend I was attracted to but we were not allowed to kiss on visits. This woman was attracted to me and it took a while but in the end I went to bed with her. It was like being raped again, lying there watching this creature doing this to me, and I was filled with revulsion.

An ex-Holloway prisoner felt that far too little attention is paid to the influence of understandable sexual frustration in such relationships: 'There was a lot of sexual frustration and women became "prison gay" just for the comfort of it. There were lots of sex toys—dildoes—brought in, and the screws just turned a blind eye to it.' The former education officer at another prison agreed: she had helped the women make representations to management to be allowed to have plastic dildoes on sale in the prison shop:

I was in a meeting and I was asked by the deputy governor what I found was the hardest thing to deal with in my job. Everyone was shocked when I said it was the pent-up sexual frustration of the women. But it's true—these are young and sexually active women, many of whom have been on the game, and suddenly this part of their lives has disappeared. This is denied and these women are not supposed to have a sex life. The authorities won't acknowledge that women can be as sexually frustrated as men and that this is a major source of disciplinary problems. The women told the prisoner rep on the prison council that they wanted plastic dildoes to be on sale in the canteen and she asked me what I thought. I said it was a good idea and I was happy to support it. Of course the authorities would never accept such a thing because it would get into the tabloid press and the governor would have to take the rap of accusations that the women were having orgies at the tax payers' expense. But to me it seemed a pretty harmless way of defusing the tension. The attitude to female sex is absolutely medieval.

Despite new prisoners' initial fears of lesbian seduction, most soon become tolerant of gay women: 'When I told the officers I was gay they immediately saw me as a threat. The inmates didn't mind at all. A lot of them are prison-bent anyway. They said "Don't worry, we all do it in here anyway"'.

A lifer now in an open prison said that at her previous prison, Cookham Wood, 'lesbian activities were common because you are hardly seen by the staff and it wasn't unusual for two women to live together as "man and wife". Here [open prison] they have to be more discreet. So it's not too bad here because they have to sleep in a dorm and there would be more complaints from the other women.'

I interviewed another prisoner, Joan, in the prison gardens, where she works in the greenhouses. She is 40 and her partner is another middle-aged woman with whom she was jointly convicted of social security fraud. A male senior officer had told me the two women were in a long-term gay relationship and were respected by other prisoners. Joan confirmed this was true:

> I've had no problems at all in here about being recognised as being gay. I get on great with the girls in here. At the end of the day you've got to get on with people, you've got to associate. They've all been a hundred per cent towards me and Rachel. We are accepted because everybody knows we've been in a relationship for seven or eight years. We're sharing a dorm with three others and they could be nasty—though of course, though we share we don't—well, you know, we don't *do* anything. We show the other women in the dorm respect and they show it to us. My personal officer told me it's never been known before for two gay people to come into prison and share a dorm. Prisons don't really recognise gay rights. She said we were the first two for it to happen to.

• • •

In this chapter I have tried to illustrate something of the nature of relationships—both sexual and non-sexual—between women prisoners, some of them positive relationships. But no relationships exist without tension and it would be naive to claim that fear, mistrust, cruelty and intimidation do not exist among women prisoners: they exist in every society and are bound to be exacerbated when such disparate groups of people are held involuntarily at close quarters, often far from family and friends, sometimes for many years. Many imprisoned women and men are insecure, emotionally damaged and therefore volatile people with histories of abuse and loveless childhoods spent in care. All these insecurities are heightened in the unstable and paranoia-inducing world of the prison. Occasionally women reported violent fights—in one, boiling water was thrown in a prisoner's face, in another it was hot soup. That second incident was in a mother and baby unit and it was a miracle that none of the children were injured.

Most disturbing is the new element—drug abuse—which has had such a dramatic influence on the make-up of the women's prison population[23] and on the way women behave[24] towards one another. A study of drug misuse at Holloway found that more than a quarter of the prisoners had been pressurised by others to keep quiet about drug misuse and that 40 per cent of the young women were being bullied compared with 22 per cent of adult women.[25]

Penal historians have recorded the social control mechanisms that exist among inmates in any prison—indeed in any institution. Paul Rock's history of Holloway[26] describes a hierarchical structure with lifers and 'heavies' at the top and alcoholics, vagrants and child-neglecters at the bottom: the inmates 'exerted a limited control over one another and themselves, mediating disputes violently or peacefully, bullying and bribing, and all within the fabric of formal discipline exercised by the staff.' Such systems still of course exist, and the next chapter describes the formal hierarchy of the drug dealers and their 'runners'.

Women who have never lived with others may take some time to adjust to such communal living. A highly educated woman, newly remanded to Holloway, said:

There is certainly violence, both physical and verbal, amongst the prisoners. I think this is inevitable in a situation which throws together a group of women of diverse temperaments and backgrounds. The prison is certainly overcrowded which adds to the aggravation and at times we are banged up quite a lot. Recently they introduced a new timetable which gave us more time for association than before but during last weekend we were locked in our cells for about 42 hours out of 48. This is not conducive to genteel ladylike behaviour particularly in view of the volatile nature of many of the women here.

A woman recently released agreed:

There was lots of bullying and fighting in Holloway and the screws would leave the women to it. I remember two young girls who were sisters and for some reason everyone turned against them and used to call them fat slags though they were neither fat nor slags. It grew into a sort of hysteria as people invented things these girls were supposed to have done. They would throw piss under their doors and so on.

Many of the prisoners I spoke to at other prisons had spent time on remand at Holloway, and without exception they all said it was much the worst prison for bullying. This is unsurprising: it holds about 500 women, two-thirds of whom will be there only for about one month.[27] It is unrealistic to expect that steady relationships between the women or with the staff can be formed in such a shifting, volatile population: many will feel the need to assert themselves to establish themselves in the pecking order, and assertion can soon become aggression.

In the survey of women prisoners they carried out for their review of young prisoners,[28] the inspectors found that 70 per cent of their sample said they had come into contact with bullying in prison, and one third of these said they had themselves been bullied. However, against that, 87 per cent reported feeling safe from bullying. My own research indicates that most of the very serious bullying is drug-related, and this is discussed in detail in the next chapter.

In prison, as outside, female bullying can make use of social exclusion. At one closed prison a kitchen officer said 'Most of my kitchen girls stay working in here six months at least. The problem with this is that they get so close and form a clique and it's difficult for a new girl to fit in with them. I tried to put two more girls in with them separately and they each left within a day.'

Research both inside and outside prisons has shown that the nature of female bullying is very different from male bullying. It relies less on physical brutality (though this can be part of it) than on the kind of exclusion described by the kitchen officer—gossiping about a woman's sexual behaviour, making fun of her clothes and so on. Women being bullied in prison had usually been victims of bullying long before arrest: in fact they had sometimes been bullied to take part in crime. The most vulnerable are those known in both male and female prisons as 'nonces': the numbers of female child molesters and sex offenders coming into prison is increasing, perhaps because there is now less reluctance to report past abuse. If their crime is very serious they are sent to Durham's H wing where they can be held more safely. Otherwise they live in the hospital wing under rule 43.[13]

Paula, 19, finished her sentence in H wing. For two years before she left prison I kept up a correspondence with her. She had been convicted of the manslaughter of her baby step-daughter and many of her letters describe daily bullying by other women, until she was finally removed to the sanctuary of the hospital wing in her first closed prison. Pregnant at 17 she had married the child's father and came home from hospital to face caring for his three other children as well as the new baby. Her one-year old stepdaughter was sick and cried all day. It was too much for Paula and she smothered the child. Although many of the other prisoners must have experienced similar stress at home, and though many must have had daughters Paula's age, so powerful is the vilification of the 'nonce' in prison culture that she was constantly insulted or ostracised. In the even more punitive climate of some American jails, women like Paula are publicly labelled: at the world's largest female prison, Sybil Brand in Los Angeles, child murderers have to wear a bright red uniform and are terrorised by other prisoners.[29]

However, the profile of victims of prison bullying is a complex one: even those who outside prison have been very strong people can find themselves being bullied in jail, where they have lost all status and identity. Middle-class, educated prisoners who have in the past been in command of their situation may find themselves vulnerable in this new world which operates according to different rules.

Sheila Bowler always maintained her innocence and was ultimately released and acquitted. When she first arrived at Holloway in the summer of 1993, she heard women whispering 'bloody murderer' under their breath as she passed. Although she was unaware of it, being new to prison life, she was particularly vulnerable as she had been convicted of the murder of an old lady. She wrote in her diary: 'I overheard X telling everyone I was suffering from rigor mortis and making up all sorts of dreadful things about me. They have written silly remarks on my cell card outside the door. I don't know how to take this situation much longer.'

Sheila was eventually moved to Bullwood Hall but went back to Holloway in May 1996. She applied for a transfer to D2, the 'privileged wing' which houses only about 17 prisoners and where there is no lock-up during the day. Other advantages include access to a washing-machine—a rare privilege for prisoners. After only a week her application was successful and she was given a room on D2, sharing with three other women. But immediately she discovered the other women were openly hostile. She began washing her face in a bowl in the basin and was told this was unhygienic—the women never washed their faces there: 'You're supposed to go down the corridor to the bathroom!' All the surfaces were covered with the women's cosmetics and the only space left to her was a tiny locker beside her bed.

She tried to make conversation with the others but 'they completely blanked me. There was a horrible bitchy atmosphere all the time.' Sheila apologised but they turned away and she crept about, almost afraid to move. In the evening they brought in a huge frying pan of food (another D2 privilege is for women to cook for themselves) which they shared among themselves without offering her any. Sheila usually woke early each morning and tried to catch up on her correspondence. At 7 a.m. next morning she was writing a letter in bed when one of the women woke up and angrily told her to stop crackling the paper as it was keeping her awake. The following day Sheila asked for a transfer back to her old room on A5. Later the officers told her that 'nobody stays long in that room'.

Another much younger woman, the mother of five children, said, 'It's a big shock when you're in here [open prison] for the first time. The young girls start by trying to intimidate you. They'll order you to get them two Mars bars and you have to be strong to resist. If you don't, you'll find yourself giving them everything—including their drugs.'

As this woman indicated, intimidation can go further than demands for Mars bars. One of my most memorable interviews was with Carrie, a bright, witty woman in her early thirties, with four young children. It was hard to believe that, on her own admission, she had been 'shipped' to her current prison as a punishment for her part in a violent bullying incident: 'I held the door while five women attacked another woman to get her drugs. What you've got to realise is that women are so supportive of each other in prison—with one exception. That's when they get involved in drugs. I became addicted to smack [heroin] and you'll do anything to get it—99 per cent of the bullying in women's prisons is to do with drugs.'

Endnotes

1. *Prison Statistics, England and Wales, 1994*, HMSO, February 1996: 36 per cent of the population of adult female offenders sentenced to immediate imprisonment reported no previous convictions, whereas for males the proportion was 15 per cent. The number of previous convictions was not known for 10 per cent of sentenced female prisoners. Of the remainder, 60 per cent had two or fewer previous convictions. See also Penal Affairs Consortium: *The Imprisonment of Women: Some Facts and Figures*, March 1996.
2. *Chapter 2*, pp. 24-25.
3. Segregation unit, the punishment 'block'.
4. A male officer described how such a system would work: 'I'll tell you what I would do with young offenders, both female and male: instead of bailing them out I would send them to prison for three days only. They will have no friends there, they will be scared. Then I would bring them back to court and the judge would say to them: "If this ever happens to you again you will be sent to prison". They would know what that meant and I reckon it would divert them from crime. It would have to be three days, not five days. Five days is long enough for them to make friends'. This is the 'scared straight' method which has been tried in the USA. There was a high failure rate because it soon became a badge of hardness and honour for young offenders to boast that they had spent time inside. And the young female drug addicts I interviewed told me they already knew many other prisoners, also from the drug scene. One young offender in Risley said she knew 50 of the 150 women in Risley's women's unit.
5. Erving Goffman, *Asylums*, Penguin, 1961.
6. Visiting orders (VOs) may be stored up and combined if a prisoner is normally held far away from home. The prisoner will be moved to a prison nearer his or her home and family, and allowed several visits packed into a short period of time.
7. See *Chapter 12*.
8. Though the prison allows pregnant women to choose another prisoner to be their birthing partner, the chosen woman has to be cleared by prison security's risk assessment system — now much stricter since new rules on licences for temporary release came into force following the escapes from male prisons Parkhurst and Whitemoor. There is another 'birthing partner' scheme, run by the National Childbirth Trust. At present there are eleven trained NCT tutors available to undertaken this role. Known as *doulas* they are on call to pregnant women prisoners.
9. Senior officer.
10. *The Oxford History of the Prison*, Chapter 11, 'Wayward Sisters', Lucia Zedner.
11. There is a system for female LTIs — prison jargon for long term inmates — to serve the first stage

of their sentences at Bullwood Hall or Durham, the second stage at Cookham Wood or Holloway, the third stage at Styal or New Hall, then their fourth and fifth at one of the open prisons—East Sutton Park, Askham Grange or Drake Hall. But prisoners can also be 'shipped out' to another prison for disciplinary reasons. For some very short sentence prisoners it is more convenient if they serve their entire sentence at the prison to which they were first remanded, such as Risley or Holloway.

12. The four MBUs are at Holloway, Styal, New Hall and Askham Grange.

13. Rule 43 is listed in Prison Rules 1964 and deals with the control and restraint of prisoners. It enables a prisoner to be removed from association with other prisoners, usually to maintain the Good Order and Discipline (GOAD) of the prison. Many prisoners 'go on rule 43' at their own request because they are in danger from other prisoners, usually due to the nature of their offence, e.g. child molesting.

14. Prison term for a contract between a prisoner and the prison authorities whereby the prisoner promises to be of good behaviour in return for privileges.

15. Howard League Fact Sheet No. 16, 'The Use of Imprisonment for Girls'.

16. *Young Prisoners*, thematic report by the Chief Inspector of Prisons, November 1997.

17. *Observer* 3 August 1997: front page headline 'Nightmare of Teenage Girls held in British Jails'.

18. Letter from the Director of the Howard League, Frances Crook, to *The Times*, 16 December 1997, 'Crime Bill Attack on Civil Rights'.

19. 'Adults Only', *Prison Report*, Issue Number 40, Autumn 1997, Prison Reform Trust.

20. *Lost Inside: The Imprisonment of Teenage Girls*, Howard League, 27 October 1997.

21. *Women in Prison*, HM Inspectorate, 1997: 3.32-3.36.

22. See Note 21, above: 3.33.

23. The figures on 30 June 1994 showed that drugs offences were the largest group of all recorded offences at 30 per cent, though the figure is probably much higher, as many of the other recorded crimes may well be drug-related, *Prison Statistics England and Wales, 1994*, HMSO, 1996.

24. Discussed in greater detail in *Chapter 9*.

25. *Drug Use in Prison*, J Fraser (Unpublished, 1994). Available from the Psychology Department, HMP Holloway. Another study *Descriptive Analysis of Bullying in Male and Female Adult Prisons* (Unpublished, 1995) confirmed that female prisoners perceived younger prisoners as targets for bullying.

26. *Reconstructing a Women's Prison,The Holloway Redevelopment Project 1968-88*, p. 40, Paul Rock, Oxford University Press, 1996.

27. See *HMP Holloway: Basic Fact Pack for Visitors*, p. 6, 'Key Facts', July 1996.

28. See Note 16, above:2.16.

29. See the case of Susan McDougal, reported in *The Guardian*, 11 July 1997.

CHAPTER NINE

Drugs : A Conspiracy Of Silence

This chapter is about the terrible effects of drug abuse in prison. It is called 'A Conspiracy of Silence' because of an allegation made by a senior woman prison officer:

> Drugs are causing terrible intimidation and brutality in women's prisons as well as in men's. But it is all being hushed up. It's a conspiracy of silence. Why? Because male governors won't admit this is happening in the women's prisons they run. They can't face the fact that women will do such things to each other. But until they admit it, these terrible incidents will continue.

The officer's words are fuelled by anger at the complacency of her male superiors in the face of drug-related intimidation, and frustration at their continuing denial of its existence. Her own official representations have been ignored and every day she sees at first hand the worsening of the problem. Women prisoners in every prison I visited confirmed the officer's allegations. As one said, 'Bullying goes on because of drugs, and this will never be stopped until the prison governors admit that it happens.'

What certainly has to be recognised is that the presence of drugs in a prison changes all the rules. Women—and of course men—in the grip of serious addiction are desperate people who will take desperate measures to feed their habit. It is naive to expect them, without highly specialised help, to abide by the accepted rules of social intercourse. The inspectors recognised in their 1997 review that 'women prisoners with substance abuse problems have complex needs which are arguably different from the needs of adult male offenders'. They recommended a central detoxification strategy which would look at the reasons for women's drug misuse and provide appropriate intervention.[1]

The Prison Service's drug misuse strategy[2] is said to focus on three areas: reducing the supply, reducing the demand, and rehabilitating drug misusers.

Women's prisons are especially at risk. Home Office statistics published in 1996[3] showed that drug offences are the largest group of offences recorded for women under sentence: 30 per cent of all recorded offences by women fall into this category. By mid 1997 the figure had risen to 33 per cent though even this is probably an underestimate because so many other offences—like the 26 per cent for theft and fraud, and the 24 per cent for violent and sexual offences—will be drugs-related. The average heroin addict funding a relatively modest daily habit from crime will have to steal more than £43,000 of goods a year, because stolen goods only attract one third of their market value.[4]

Statistics of drugs *offences* are not of course entirely reliable to show the extent of previous drug *misuse*. Some of those remanded or convicted will be non-users, who regard the drugs industry as a source of income: many women in this category are those trapped in poverty. Some have other reasons: I interviewed one woman in her late thirties who found herself stranded in Portugal with an abusive husband. She tried to smuggle cannabis into Manchester Airport to finance her escape with her two young sons. There are also foreign national drugs 'mules', driven by poverty into drug couriering, and young British women sometimes attracted by the chance of fast cash, a free holiday and the buzz of the crime. This group of non-users is discussed in *Chapter 10*.

Of the 150 women in my sample, 21 per cent (32) were charged[5] with offences directly arising from drugs involvement—possession, supply, intent to supply and importing. But of the 130 of the sample who explained the background to their offence, 58 women (nearly half - 45 per cent) said it was drugs or alcohol-related. Because it is a 'legal' addiction, alcoholism is underrated as a cause of crime, but the charity Alcohol Concern estimates that more than half a million women now drink at 'very risky' levels, and the number of women drinking above recommended levels rose by 50 per cent between 1984 and 1994.[6]

It was estimated in 1992 that 23 per cent of women prisoners, compared with 11 per cent of adult male prisoners and six per cent of male young offenders, could be assessed as drug-dependent on entering prison.[7] A smaller but more recent survey showed that of 544 adult males, 206 male young offenders and 245 women on remand, 20.8 per cent of females were opiate dependent, compared with 12.1 per cent of adult males and 9.2 per cent of male young offenders.[8]

In 1996 the Advisory Council on the Misuse of Drugs produced a report *Drug Misusers and the Prison System*.[9] It acknowledged that drugs misuse is widespread in prisons, and recognised that it results in violence and intimidation (as well as the spread of HIV/Aids and hepatitis, and in continued drug-related offending on release.) It recognised that there was a need for a different approach to the treatment of female addicts, and that effective throughcare—the Prison Service term for the ongoing work throughout prisoners' sentences to prepare them for release into the community—was much more difficult for women as they are so often held far from home. Prison reform groups[10] have called for more staff training to deal with drugs. Drugs have made their job far more difficult and dangerous and their training equips them only in drugs awareness—how to recognise substances. One recently trained young officer admitted,

> I was amazed at the number of women in here [open prison] on drugs. I had smelt cannabis on my training to be able to recognise it but that's about all. I can't imagine taking drugs myself and I can't understand why people do it.

The Advisory Council's report recommended that 'extra resources be allocated to women's prisons, disproportionate to the number of prisoners they hold, to enable a wide range of treatment services that reflect their additional needs to be offered'. It also acknowledged that in all prisons 'bullying and violence often accompany the actual dealing' and that 'in recent years there has been a marked increase in the level and brutality of the associated violence, perhaps reflecting to a certain extent changes in the wider community.' But it made no specific reference to the nature of drugs-related bullying in women's prisons.

As I went from one women's prison to another, the jigsaw puzzle of gross intimidation, terror and cruelty in the prison drugs scene was assembled piece by piece. There were hints of it in the palpable panic of young girls at reception interviews at the prospect of being sent to prisons where they knew people were 'after them, waiting to get them'. It was confirmed by addicts themselves and by other women living close to them day by day.

A woman who has served 16 years of a life sentence in half a dozen women's prisons has seen the changes brought about in the last few years by drug misuse:

> Seven years ago I razored another inmate's face and that was the worst attack anyone in the prison had ever seen. Now people would just shrug their shoulders because that sort of attack is so common. Women make weapons and carry them around for self defence, because they know the screws won't defend them. When I attacked that woman it was at least an honourable attack in that it was just one to one. Recently I've seen eight women set upon one woman and fist-rape her. All these attacks are about drugs. These feminist groups make me sick. Some of them may have been in prison themselves years ago, but they're not here now — we are, and we see what's going on now, in prisons in the nineties. Everything's changed and by denying it they are denying us the chance to get something done.

Women bullying other women is nothing new. The bullying that women prisoners described in the last chapter, and the hierarchical systems that act as control mechanisms, is the kind of behaviour that has been known, analysed and understood for decades. Unpleasant it certainly is, but it falls within the boundaries of recognised patterns of human behaviour.

But the drugs-related bullying that is now happening in women's prisons is much more serious. Baroning and taxing[11] in male prisons is accepted as par for the course, but the brutality inflicted on women by other women is harder to accept. If male governors find it hard to stomach, so too do the women's groups which have since the early years of women's suffrage encouraged women to support each other in the face of a patriarchal and misogynistic society.

The particular activity that male staff find especially hard to accept is vaginal searching, known in the prisons as 'de-crutching'. The commonest way for drugs to be smuggled into prison by women is by 'crutching', whereby the drug, usually contained in a condom or in the finger of a plastic surgical glove, is internally secreted via the vagina. Women visitors use this method to bring drugs in, transferring them during the visit to the prisoner, who will herself crutch them. Of course this method is not unique to women: as one female officer put it: 'Men have orifices too!' Male prison argot contains all sorts of words for the process of anal concealment (*bottling, charging, chubbing, plugging*). But because of the stereotyping of women as traditionally gentler, more fastidious and more caring, it is taking longer to accept that internal concealment constantly happens in women's prisons too. Even harder to acknowledge are the vicious methods used by other addicts to seize the smuggled drugs for themselves.

The intimidation may begin at the end of a visit, because this is when the 'searchers' go to work to de-crutch those who have smuggled the drugs in from their visitors. Women told of the enormous pressure exerted, often on young, vulnerable prisoners, to supply drugs in this way. In many prisons there is a holding area on the 'prison side' of the visits room, where women wait at the end of a visit for officers to escort them back to their wings. This gives an ideal opportunity for the searchers. There is usually a toilet in this area, and the searchers, who may have been watching the transfer of drugs during the visit, will force a woman to admit she has crutched them, and if she denies it or refuses to hand the package over they will remove it forcibly, either by hand or with some improvised implement. A young prisoner newly arrived at Foston Hall, itself a prison newly converted for women, reported: 'I was in my first week here when I was having a shower and I heard a women being raped by other women in the next shower. It wasn't about sex, it was about drugs.'

A woman officer told me: 'They are unbelievably ruthless to get their drugs. They wear surgical gloves stolen from the hospital wing, or rubber gloves from the kitchens often lubricated with butter from the small individual packs they take from the prison kitchens. They also use plastic spoons or spatulas and the women are in terrible fear, specially if they were abused as children. There are often terrible results —miscarriage, severe physical damage—and it can end in suicide.'

A senior prison officer recently intercepted a threatening letter from a group of searchers to another prisoner. 'Any messing around' said the writer, 'and we'll bring out the marigolds!' referring to the Marigold brand of domestic kitchen rubber gloves. The victim is told that if she keeps quiet and doesn't make a fuss it won't hurt so much. The whole process can be carried out in less than a minute if the woman co-operates.

A female officer told me of an incident in her prison in May 1997 when the police were called to take a statement from a young prisoner given a forced enema by searchers using a washing-up liquid bottle. The officer was so shocked she told a local newspaper: 'The reporter could have asked the police and they would have verified it, but he told me it was too shocking to print in his paper'. Two months later in a different prison there was a similar attack using a broomhandle and a razor.

If the searchers are interrupted the victim may be released, but her respite may only be temporary. Later, in the wing toilets or showers, the attack can be even more brutal, especially if the woman resists. According to an informal survey carried out by staff at one women's prison, victims tend to be the younger prisoners, small in physique and timid in behaviour, with a confirmed drug habit and a history of minor offences of supplying and petty theft to feed their habit. They will tend to have crutched just enough drugs for their personal use. They have often been sexually abused in the past and will be afraid to tell the staff about the attack for fear of reprisals. Sometimes they will have been forced by stronger prisoners to send out a visiting order solely for the purpose of drugs transfer. A senior female prison officer at another prison described such incidents:

One woman had a Kinder egg[12] full of £120 worth of heroin. Another had £800 in cash stashed away inside her, another had gold jewellery to use for drugs deals. They often bring in syringes that way. They know we can't touch them—internal searching would be regarded as assault—and the sniffer dogs can't smell out the drugs through the skin. I have seen women smile at me as they pat the dogs.

Non-drug using prisoners confirmed these stories, explaining how easy it is to get past the dogs by wrapping drugs in mint leaves to disguise the scent:

> The drugs here are terrible. Some girls 'll take the clothes off you to get the drugs. The officers never see what's going on. It's worst in the showers — I've seen them in there making girls swallow shampoo to make them vomit and jump on their stomachs to hurry it up. Mind you the only people who get hassle on the wing are the smackheads.[13] Straight away they get asked "What you in for? You into the gear?"[14]

The inspectors noted that 'women's [drug] dealing is less organized and often based on sharing among acquaintances rather than on profit and intimidation'.[15] According to many women I interviewed, this gives rather too cosy a picture. One prisoner explained that on the contrary, the intimidation in Holloway is well-organized, in a terrifying travesty of the usual hierarchical systems:

> There are strong women at the head of the drugs rackets and they appoint others as middlemen figures, or 'runners', to do their dirty work for them. The weakest women are made to bring in the drugs. They pass them on to the middlemen, then the leader distributes them. The problems start when a woman doing the smuggling wants to keep the drugs for herself. Then the chain breaks down.

This woman had witnessed incidents of organized bullying:

> I saw two women standing guard outside a door while another two gave a girl a doing-over. I also saw an unprovoked attack on one woman who'd tried to keep her crutched drugs. She had very long hair and as she was sitting in the TV room, a 'middleman' woman came and yanked it so hard that a big lump was torn out. The perpetrator was shipped out immediately, but all she was doing was the dirty work for the top dog.

This eye-witness was angry at the blanket punishment imposed by the officers: 'Though it was lunchtime and half of us hadn't had any lunch, we all had to return to our cells and be locked in'.

What can a prison do when it discovers this kind of gross abuse? A woman officer was sceptical: 'We call the police because this is assault, but the trouble is that this is all anecdotal and the witnesses are often the perpetrators' assistants so their evidence is tainted.' The Advisory Council Report[9] stated:

> We were told by staff representatives that the investigation and prosecution

of prisoners for assault, whether drug-related or not, was seen as a low priority for the police and the Crown Prosecution Service. We have some sympathy with prison staff on this issue. Failure to prosecute cases of assaults on staff or other prisoners, where merited by the evidence, is unjust . . . and can only add to discipline and control problems.

The officer quoted above confirmed this lack of interest in the fate of women drug users:

If the victim eventually commits suicide — and it does happen — nobody cares very much. If a male prisoner hangs himself it's in the papers — but nobody cares about another poor female heroin drudge. A couple of weeks ago we found this poor woman had hanged herself by her own tights. She was on some kind of drug when she came in and didn't know what she was doing. But we should all care, not only out of common humanity but because they've got families and kids like the rest of us, and I believe we should be giving them a lot more help. The trouble is that people on a career path, the high-up people in the Home Office, are not at all interested in what happens here. They just won't accept that anything nasty is really happening in the women's estate.

The senior officer quoted at the beginning of this chapter has succeeded in rescuing some women by faxing their solicitors and getting them bailed quickly. Here are her own notes on two cases:

Inmate J: small stature; prostitute; drugs; well-versed in prison system. Transferred to open prison where attack took place. Led by a well-known recidivist bully, a group internally searched J, wrapped her in blankets, threw her down the stairs and one then walked on her face. Perpetrator given three years. J, now back in system, a complete physical and nervous wreck as she was told they would "get her wherever she went for grassing". I was so concerned I faxed to solicitor to identify containment problem we would have if J continued in custody. She was then bailed. She said she would commit suicide if she has to come back in.

Inmate T: 23 year old slight, downtrodden prostitute. In care all her life, ran away at age 13 and worked as a prostitute. Ran off from pimp who said she had kept money. Tops of all her fingers were chopped off and side of face burnt. Has not been in here for 2 years and was in complete trauma when arrived. Said the girls were here who had searched her vaginally and anally. Said she could not live if this was to happen again and she knew it would. Absolutely distraught. So again I wrote to solicitor outlining the facts and she too was bailed. However these are but two incidents. There are many more because nobody will admit to it.

There is no doubt that the Prison Service is aware of these attacks and is worried. On Monday 24 June 1996 a meeting was held at HMP New Hall, a closed women's prison in Wakefield, entitled *Female Estate Anti-Bullying Seminar*.

One of the delegates sent me the minutes of the meeting. Although much of the discussion was about bullying in general, one female governor referred to 'particularly unpleasant instances of bullying that have occurred recently, relating to concealment of drugs.' She said that prisoners were 'prepared to conceal internally drugs, money or jewellery' and that other prisoners were 'prepared to extract concealed items by force or with compliance'. She feared that there was 'a growing possibility that a pregnant woman could be internally searched without her compliance'. She had drawn up a code of practice for dealing with instances of intimate searching. Measures included reporting the incident to the police, informing solicitors and offering the victim the services of a rape counsellor (though the searchers' motive is not sexual, such attacks can have devastating consequences, particularly for those who have suffered past sexual abuse). The minutes note that two staff representatives of other women's prisons had also recorded incidents of internal searching. Further reference to the subject was made in the open forum at the end of the meeting, and the minutes record that 'Internal searching does go on and may not always be reported' and that 'This is the first opportunity to discuss a difficult and complex situation'. But my delegate contact was disgusted by the attitude of some male governors:

> The male staff just wouldn't admit this was happening. They were all scoring brownie points, saying there were no drugs in *their* prisons and no bullying went on. The governor of one women's prison stood up and said he'd worked for 20 years in the prison service and never seen any of this sort of thing. I was appalled! But I wasn't surprised because the men in my prison certainly can't handle the idea of what happens to women addicts. They can't cope with it at all when the women are lying round the floor withdrawing, vomiting and incontinent.

The inspectors, in their review of women's prisons,[16] referred obliquely to the June conference, noting that 'at least one national conference on bullying was held, to which governors of all female establishments were invited'. They regretted that 'no central policy exists to highlight the different aspects of bullying among women prisoners.' The review refers to assaults in two women's prisons: 'Incidents of very serious assaults, all connected to the trade in illicit drugs which forms such a significant part of substance abuse in women's prisons, have been uncovered by managers and staff at Risley and Holloway'. Later they note that 'a small number of serious assaults were reportedly carried out on women by other women prisoners searching for drugs that had been internally concealed.' In his highly critical report on Bullwood Hall, published on 10 December 1997, Sir David Ramsbotham mentions 'at least one suspected sexual assault by women on other prisoners as part of the illegal drugs trade'.

Such assaults are not confined to the remand or closed prisons. I made a preliminary visit to a women's open prison and was taken on a tour of the establishment by one of the chaplains. We passed a squat brick building in the middle of the campus, with an extra fence around it. The chaplain nodded towards it: 'And that's the block, of course'. I said I assumed a segregation unit was not much used in an open prison like this one. The chaplain looked uncomfortable. 'Well, it *is* used occasionally. Just the other day a girl had to be put in there because she'd gone absolutely berserk, smashed every stick of furniture in her room. She'd been the victim of a very serious sexual assault.'

He was referring, I supposed, to childhood sexual abuse, the memory of which had been triggered off by some incident, perhaps a rape before coming into prison. 'Oh no,' he said, 'it was while she was in here you know. They were after getting the drugs off her and—well, they'd used forks and all sorts of dreadful things on the poor soul . . . '. He hurried into the chapel and I felt unable to pursue the matter.

Six weeks later I was back in that prison for my three day period of research. Of the 23 prisoners I interviewed there, ten mentioned what they called 'the forks incident', some in passing, some in more detail:

> Some terrible things go on in here. You heard about the forks incident no doubt. Everybody knows about it. Some of the drugs girls got a woman in the showers and tore her up inside with forks to get her drugs. It could stop her having children. One of the perpetrators is still here and if she wasn't pregnant with twins I think some of the women would have gone for her. The forking incident shows the lengths to which women desperate for drugs will go. There's no problem getting heroin, whizz,[17] anything in here—for a few phone cards.

A male officer in the same prison hinted at the incident: 'The drugs girls do terrible things to people. We had to put one girl in a strip cell because of what they did to her.'

• • •

The overwhelming significance of drugs misuse in prisons is privately recognised—if not always openly acknowledged—by prison staff. But as yet the subject has received comparatively little public attention in the case of women's prisons. If reported at all, it has not been taken very seriously. On 23 March 1998, for example, the *Manchester Evening News* included one paragraph headed 'Women's Jail Roof Party'. The paper reported that six women prisoners, thought to be high on drugs or home-made drink, spent the night on the roof of Styal prison singing and dancing. The very public enquiries into scandals at Whitemoor and Parkhurst has raised the profile of baroning and taxing in men's prisons. But the implications of drugs misuse for imprisoned women are still largely unknown.

The figures quoted at the beginning of this chapter show how dramatically drugs have changed the profile of the women's prison population. Long-serving officers have observed the changes: at Risley women's unit, an experienced officer remembered: 'Back in the seventies we had very few drug users—it was mainly alcoholics. Now we are getting the children of addicts. The other day I counted five girls in here who were born to addicts in Styal prison.[18]

The officer described the drug-related crimes that brought such women into prison again and again:

Women will steal Marks & Spencer nightdresses and will get half the recommended retail price for them — that's the going rate at the moment. Principles stores clothes go for one third of the price. Everything is done on a commercial basis. Everything has its price. What worries me is that someone somewhere is buying all this stuff on from the dealers - you and I could end up buying it from a market stall.

In her recent book on women prisoners in the USA[19] the criminologist Meda Chesney-Lind calls the American 'war on drugs' a 'war on women' which has been a major cause of the explosion in the women's prison population. One in three women in US prisons are there for drugs offences, compared with one in ten in 1979. Though the American media interprets women's involvement in drugs as yet another version of the 'more women's liberation equals more women's crime' hypothesis, 40 per cent of American female prisoners have a history of physical and sexual abuse and many use drugs as self-medication, or as a means of economic survival.

My interviews with addicted women also commonly revealed a background of childhood abuse and of being in care. Of the 58 women who said their offence was drink or drugs-related, 20 (34 per cent) had a history of being in care as children. As a young former prostitute, who had been abused and spent her childhood in children's homes, explained, 'I got into drugs to belong, to be part of something. Then I needed drugs to give me courage and confidence and that's when I really got addicted'.

The 45 per cent of women in my sample convicted of drugs-*related* offences were either serving sentences for 'economic' crimes to finance their habit, such as shoplifting, theft or burglary; or sentences arising out of their habit, such as crimes of violence like actual bodily harm, grievous bodily harm, wounding, threats to kill, criminal damage and even manslaughter and murder. This group included women who had committed acts of violence such as smashing windows, affray and fighting. Of the 34 disciplinary staff who thought the number of women entering their particular prison for a crime of violence was definitely increasing, nearly half thought this was because of the growing misuse of drugs or alcohol.

Once women with so many problems are in prison there is little incentive to give up their habit. As an education coordinator in one prison said:

> So many have been trying through drink and drugs to escape memories of their own abuse and this continues in prison where things are even harder to bear. For instance they may get a letter from their solicitor saying things are worse than they thought. So little help is available to them and they are in an unsafe environment in prison. So it's not surprising that they want their drugs to help them get through their sentence.

Women are also far more likely than men to have been prescribed legal drugs like Valium and Temazepam in the treatment of depression and other conditions, which perhaps predisposes them to the misuse of illegal substances. 'Legal' addictions can be just as serious and the withdrawals sometimes even more traumatic. Women suddenly deprived of these props will seek out any other drug they can obtain to replace them.

Both staff and prisoners confirmed that the pattern of women's drug misuse is very different from men's. As one woman officer said:

> Unlike the men they are non-discriminatory: they will mix and match, take Ecstasy and Valium combined—anything they can get hold of. They don't know what they are doing at all and they don't think of the consequences. There's a particular group of women who can only escape the burdens of their lives by drug-taking and these women have no desire and no incentive to get off drugs. They talk about "numbing-out".

Another telling slang word used by women for heroin is "bird-killer"—

that is, a way of getting you through your sentence (bird).

Richard Tilt said at a 1996 conference on drugs in prison:[20] 'We have a duty to care for the prisoner and I believe a strong moral obligation to offer treatment. We have a strong practical incentive to do so if we are ever to get prisoners to break out of the circle of drug misuse which causes such problems both inside and outside prison and all too often turns the prison gate into the revolving door'.

Toyah, whom I interviewed in Risley, lives just a few streets away from the prison. Though she was expelled from school she was doing well in the hairdressing business bought for her by her parents till she became involved with a drug-using boyfriend. She is now 22 and has been addicted to heroin for six years:

> I go to British Home Stores and usually get some of them silk nighties and negligées. They cost £45 to £65 new and I can get £25 to £30 for them from the dealer. So each one'll buy me two bags of heroin.

Toyah said all her friends were into drugs and even if she could be bothered to get off drugs in prison, which was unlikely, she'd go back to the friends and start using again. She looked puzzled when I naively suggested that at least in here she was away from the influence of her drug-using friends. Of the 150 women in the prison, she guessed she knew 50, 25 of them well, and five or six very well indeed.

Toyah was on remand for stabbing a store detective with a syringe and thought she was likely to be given three years. I asked her whether anything could ever persuade her to give up her addiction:

> No, because it's my way of life. It's what I get up in the morning for and what I do every day. It's boredom that gets you into drugs and once you're into them your whole day revolves around them and it gives you a purpose to your life.

Toyah had viciously attacked the store detective who stood between her and her drug—in her present state she is undeniably a danger to the public. Unless some effective intervention is put in place to help her combat her habit and to give her skills leading to employment, she will leave prison, return to drugs and commit further crimes.

• • •

I considered the three main planks of the Prison Service's drugs strategy in relation to women's prisons: the detection of illegal drugs already in prisons (and the punishment of those who bring them in); the prevention of any more drugs coming in (and the prosecution of those who try to bring them in); and the treatment of addicted prisoners. My research suggests that—at least in the women's prisons—so much time and money is being expended on the first two planks that the third is being neglected. What is more, there is no coherent strategy, no protocol for diagnosis and treatment.

The most significant method of detection—in the sense that it has been universally implemented—is Mandatory Drug Testing (MDT)[21] which was introduced in eight pilot establishments in February 1995 and is now used in all prisons. The form of testing chosen was the urine test. Prisoners are selected at random by computer and required to provide a urine sample for testing purposes. The test, referred to by prisoners as the 'piss test' or 'taking the piss', is carried out under a degree of supervision to avoid substitute specimens being supplied.

Each prison is required to test at least 10 per cent of prisoners at random each month but the rules provide for other testing if there is 'reasonable suspicion' of drug misuse, or if prisoners are returning from temporary release. Prisoners are tested on reception to their first prison or transfer to a new prison and there is provision in the rules for persistent drug misusers to be tested more frequently. Women living in mother and baby units, and those in privileged wings or drug-free zones, may sign a compact[22] to undergo more frequent testing.

Grave doubts have since been voiced as to the effectiveness of the existing form of MDT. First, there have been allegations about the reliability of methods of testing and most of the women prisoners I interviewed feel the tests are rigged. Although staff maintain that prisoners are selected for drug tests at random by the computer, the prisoners are sure that from *this* selection, a further selection is made so that not too many drug users show up and give the prison a bad name. This is a very widespread view in every one of the prisons I visited, and though of course it cannot be proved, many women described other prisoners 'wandering round stoned out of their heads and nobody's testing them'. This seems to them a very odd way of showing commitment to stopping drug use in prisons. One woman in her twenties, was serving a sentence for fraud (unrelated to drug-abuse) in an open prison:

> There are women going round this prison like zombies. The officers know the ones to search—they know exactly who they will find with drugs. But when they do the MDT test they have to have so many negatives to outweigh the positives and stop the prison looking bad to the Home Office. So they are very careful to select some girls they know will test negative.

An older woman, a lifer in her forties who has never taken drugs, described a similar situation in her closed prison:

The MDT testing here is a farce. I've had five tests though they know I'll be clear. The officers will come up to me and say "We need someone quick—it's less paperwork if we have you!" I can see who's on drugs myself, and I'm not even trained for the job. But of course they don't *want* to find out who's on drugs because it would look bad for the prison that so many drugs are getting through. Anyway, having women on drugs keeps them quiet and gives the screws an easy life.

Another lifer at a different prison told the same story:

They test me every month, regular as clockwork because they know I've been "clean" for years. There's an old lady of 78 in here and they test her too!

As in so many other areas of life in the 1990s, market forces are at work. A former governor explained the system:

Everything is about KPIs—key performance indicators. This is the system whereby prisons have to show an improvement in certain areas, and the governor's own performance is judged on the KPI. There are alternative methods of testing for drugs: one is the hair test where they can take a strand of hair and analyse it. Prisoners fear that test, because on analysis it can produce the historical background of drug-taking—in other words they can tell exactly what drugs the person's been taking for the entire time that hair has been growing. Two, they can take a blood sample—which is all right as long as the prisoner can see where the blood's going to. The trouble is the prisoners don't trust prison staff. The third is the saliva test which the Prison Service doesn't feel is accurate enough. I think the truth is they bought in the urine test as a job lot and got it on the cheap. Everything is about managing finances and as I said, about key performance indicators.

The inspectors were equally scathing about KPIs: 'The Prison Service's Key Performance Indicator measures activity not results.'[23]

MDT is also very expensive: each prison has to pay for its own test and this diverts scarce resources that might instead have been used for more effective alternative programmes. It is estimated that for a prison like Holloway, holding about 500 prisoners, the cost per *month* of mandatory drug testing is between £16,000 and £23,000. Perhaps alternative ways of spending such sums could offer more hope to addicted women like Toyah described above. But there is anecdotal evidence that, on the contrary, rehabilitative programmes have been closed down because of the cost of the MDT programme.

Another major objection to the urine test is even more serious in terms of the effects on prisoners and, ultimately, on society outside. It is well known among prisoners that whereas soft drugs like cannabis can be detected in a urine sample for up to 30 days, hard drugs like heroin and cocaine only remain detectable for two or three. So prisoners fearing detection will move on to harder drugs.

In July 1997 Dr Pam Wilson, head of the Prison Service's order and control unit, quoted interim results from an Oxford Centre for Criminological Research study of prison drug testing programmes which was said to disprove claims of widespread drugs switching.[24] Yet in all the prisons I visited, there was anecdotal evidence of just such switching. Indeed, so concerned was the Prison Service about drug switching that in early 1997 it commissioned the National Addiction Centre at the Maudsley Hospital to carry out a study. Between March and September 1996, there had been found to be a fall in the number of randomly tested prisoners showing positive for cannabis, and a rise in the number found to be taking opiates.[25]

A number of women spoke of 'weekend' heroin use—if they take heroin on a Friday night it will be out of the system by Monday and they know it is extremely rare for MDT to take place at weekends. Once a prisoner has decided to switch to heroin, she will have little trouble getting hold of it. An ex-Holloway prisoner said 'It was always easier to get smack [heroin] in Holloway, but harder to get cannabis just because it's physically bigger to smuggle in.'

Heroin use has implications which extend far beyond the prison walls: the sharing of dirty needles is more likely to lead to infection, including HIV/Aids, hepatitis B and hepatitis C, and considering many women are on very short sentences the stakes are being raised for infection to spread faster in the community outside. In March 1996 Dr Rosemary Wool, director of prison health care, made a report to the home secretary mentioning fears about the spread of HIV in prisons, and Harry Fletcher, spokesperson for NAPO, the probation officers' union, said 'The public should be very worried: HIV and hepatitis are not confined by prison walls.'

Two years later, the Prison Service still appears to have an ambivalent and unresolved attitude towards prisoners addicted to drugs. Perhaps this is not so surprising, as British public opinion is itself ambivalent. Sir David Ramsbotham says the Prison Service has to walk a tightrope between accepting the problem of drug use without condoning it; and Richard Tilt admitted publicly in early 1998 that considerations of public health may force the issuing of sterilising equipment, clean needles and—in male prisons—condoms.[26]

Switching from soft to hard drugs also has serious implications for internal prison discipline. Marijuana has a mellowing effect, and prisoners have for many years believed that officers turned a blind eye to it because it calmed the prisoners down and made their job easier. One remand prisoner in her forties said she was shocked when she first came into prison: 'The staff in here don't really want to sort out the drugs problem. You can smell the hash wherever you go in the prison and it's just hypocrisy for them to say they don't know about it.' But crack cocaine, for example, has the opposite effect. As one prisoner put it: 'The girls have started going off dope[27] and on to crack which doesn't stay in the urine so long. The trouble is, crack makes you aggressive.' Indeed, many non-drug-using prisoners described 'those crackheads' as women they tried to avoid because of the volatility of temperament caused by crack cocaine.

Prisoners described the extraordinary lengths some will go to to avoid detection. One of the many women who wished to distance herself from 'those junkie girls' was shocked:

> It's terrible what the girls in here do to avoid being caught for drugs. They save up those little oil bottles they get in aromatherapy classes and get a woman who's not on drugs to fill them with piss. Then they crutch them and if they're given a piss test they substitute the clear piss for their own. I've known women keep bottles inside them for a week — what worries me is toxic shock syndrome.[28] If you can get that from Tampax, what'll you get from a bottle with germs all over the outside?

There is also doubt about the accuracy of the next stage of the testing procedure and the Prison Service has received many complaints. Urine samples may be mixed up, and if the prisoner is on other medication this can give an erroneous positive result.

It is currently a disciplinary offence to refuse to supply a urine sample, and various punishments can be imposed if the test is positive, though no punishment is imposed if a prisoner tests positive at the routine test on reception into prison. Punishments include loss of various privileges, the imposition of closed visits, fines, additional days added to a sentence and cancellation of home leave. Women in the open prisons I visited also claimed that so ludicrous is the scale of punishments currently imposed that it makes sense for prisoners to abscond rather than risk testing positive for drugs. The punishment most feared by women prisoners, especially those with children at home, was the imposition of extra days on the length of their sentences.

In May 1998, drugs minister George Howarth announced a change in prison drugs policy, arising out of concern that extra days added to prisoners' sentences as punishments, mainly for cannabis use, were adding to overcrowding problems. Governors were urged to reduce the amount of random testing from ten per cent to five per cent, and to concentrate resources on prisoners found to have used class A drugs. They were asked to use alternative punishments such as loss of privileges and restrictions on visits. But there was no promise of extra funding, and the approach is still punitive rather than therapeutic and rehabilitative.

A woman serving six months in an open prison for fraud said:

> The MDT has caused a lot of problems in this prison. That's why three girls absconded last week, because they would have tested positive for drugs and could have got an extra 28 days. But if they abscond they only get seven days!

A lifer nearing the end of her sentence in a different open prison agreed:

> MDT is an absolute joke. You get 42 days extra if you test positive for opiates, and 28 days for cannabis. So if you think you will test positive it's worth absconding as you only get seven days for that.

If what the women say is true—and this was the anecdotal evidence from several different prisons—it makes a nonsense of the whole process of mandatory drug testing and it could be claimed that the system poses an added security risk by encouraging women to go 'over the fence.'

Every year the number of deaths in custody increases, and many of the female fatalities are drugs-related. Some may be suicides, some may be accidental overdoses.

At one open prison a heroin addict had recently died and I spoke to some of the women who had known her. 'That Mary's case was a disgrace', said one:

> She was in this wing, and we all saw her going round hanging on the walls to stand up. They sent her to the medical centre and they gave her more medicine and everybody here reckons it was this cocktail of drugs that killed her. There was no counselling for the girl who found Mary dead. She was sharing a room with her and when she woke up and found her she was in a terrible state—because Mary was in an awful mess, lying dead in her bed. The officer who was called in was immediately put on sick leave and *she* got counselling to get over it.

Another woman in the same prison described the incident from another point of view:

> Mary was a drug addict who died from an overdose. She came into the dining room on the night she died and couldn't hold her head up — it kept falling into her meal. Only one of the officers showed her any compassion. He phoned up to the officers on her landing and asked them to keep an eye on her that night. But all they did was send her to the health centre where they gave her more medicine and she died of a cocktail of medicine. They've tried to cover it up by saying she took the overdose herself. Mary was a pest and she got on everyone's nerves. But she was a lovable pest and she should have been given help. She had three small children. Her death devastated me because whatever else it does, prison does bond women together. Women *do* need help for drugs. The prison should think what it's doing, specially as this is an open prison supposed to be preparing women for release. It has not learnt anything from Mary's death.

• • •

The most worrying aspect of current prison policies is that they may be creating more Marys, more Toyahs. In his report on HMP Styal in 1995, Judge Tumim, then HM Chief Inspector of Prisons, wrote: 'Inmates asserted, and staff agreed, that drugs were freely available in Styal. It was also firmly asserted that a number of inmates were introduced to drugs for the first time and became addicted in Styal'. Tumim commented: 'Enter a shoplifter and leave an addict'.[20]

The help addicted prisoners are given varies enormously from prison to prison. The inspectors' survey of women prisoners for their review found that three-quarters of their sample reported receiving no help at all, a few had light medication and only one in ten had any drugs counselling or help with 'detox and rehab' programmes. This lack is not peculiar to the women's estate. While mandatory drug testing is operational in all prisons in England and Wales, drug treatment programmes are currently available in only 59.[29]

Some women described being left 'down the block' for the first 24 hours, vomiting and crippled by agonizing stomach cramps. Heroin addicts said they were given just 5mg of Valium and Paracetamol and had 'gone through hell'. Addicts recently remanded into Holloway seem to be more fortunate. One said, 'I got a five day Methadone course and Chloral at night with a bit of Valium. That's only to help you re-establish your sleep patterns. It did help me get off smack [heroin].'

Methadone is a synthetic narcotic opiate used to treat opiate dependence. Some prison medical officers refuse to prescribe

Methadone, or to allow prisoners to continue on reducing prescriptions given to them in the community. They claim that Methadone is often traded for harder drugs, and that it is itself addictive, with even worse withdrawal symptoms than the opiates it is meant to replace.

The inspectors found that the variation between prisons was enormous. They estimated that the money spent on detoxification and rehabilitation for 33 women in Holloway made up 80 per cent of the *total* drug intervention spending for all women's prisons. Risley has to manage with one drugs counsellor for 150 women, though the governor estimates that 90 per cent are substance misusers, and Bullwood Hall, which takes many of the Holloway prisoners, is given no central funding at all for drugs intervention. And now that budgets are devolved to individual governors, provision is even more variable: not all governors see addiction intervention programmes as a priority.

To non-drug using prisoners it seemed to be simple common sense that detection and punishment alone will not work. Many made comments like this woman: 'I do think women on drugs should be given some treatment instead of just being sent to prison—because cold-turkeying[30] alone in your room doesn't help. If they have a sentence of less than 12 months they get nothing at all. The ones on drugs need detox and rehab.' It was certainly not the perception of drug-users I met that if detected they were likely to get any help, even at times of extreme distress. A Holloway prisoner wrote:

Last Christmas Day when I was in the open prison I nearly died of an overdose—heroin was very available there. I did try and speak to the nursing staff on Boxing Day but they were too busy to speak to me and I needed help—so I ran off out of the prison, thinking I could get myself away from it. But when I was out I was getting worse than ever. I was caught after a few weeks and sent to Holloway and now I've lost[31] 28 days.

The nature of regimes in women's prisons, with the paucity of provision for work, education, training and therapeutic programmes, currently does little to reduce the demand for drugs.

• • •

The first plank of the Prison Service's anti-drugs strategy, described above, has been to detect drugs that get into prisons, and to punish those who procure and use them. The other major and parallel plank has been to reduce the supply by bringing in a series of measures to prevent drugs entering prisons in the first place.

The view universally expressed by Prison Service officials is that the only way drugs get into prisons is by being brought in on visits. At a London conference in June 1997 the Prison Service issued figures showing that more than 1,300 visitors to prisons had been arrested trying to smuggle illicit drugs into prison during the previous year.[24] Outside every prison is posted a notice warning visitors of the maximum penalties of attempting this offence. Outside HMP Brockhill, for instance, the notice reads as follows: 'Class A (heroin, cocaine): Life; Class B (cannabis): 14 years; Class C (Valium): 5 years'.

The effect of anti-drugs security on visitors is described in *Chapter 4*, where women tell of family too intimidated to come to the prison at all, and children forbidden to visit because of the trauma of searching. Some officers were apologetic:

> People find it hard to accept that we have to search children but we have found drugs even hidden in nappies, and in sweets. One of these days a child is going to put a wrap of heroin in its mouth thinking it's a sweetie.

Other rules, though relatively minor, upset those who have never used drugs. Some prisons now forbid postage stamps being sent in because some have been found to be impregnated with LSD. The prison ban on cut flowers, mentioned earlier, is another example of increased security.

The prisoner herself will automatically be under suspicion after every visit and may be randomly chosen to undergo certain security procedures like the degrading strip searches and the 'squat test' described earlier. In *Chapter 4* women told how the effects of a 'good visit' could be destroyed if they had the misfortune to be picked, apparently at random, for a post-visit strip search. One woman recalled being strip-searched after her children had visited her: she said it made her feel dirty and seemed also to sully the innocence of her children. This woman had never taken drugs.

As for physical security: most visits rooms now have large mirrors positioned on the ceiling, and some have CCTV cameras which can be trained on known drug misusers if necessary. Prisons have installed leg barriers to prevent legs being intertwined and crutched drugs passed. One open prison has replaced its tables with much lower coffee tables for the same reason. But there have to be refreshments, often from vending machines, for visitors who have travelled a long way. The visitors may bring drugs in their mouths (most visitors are now required to open their mouths, but such a search can only be fairly cursory without causing offence) then share a drink and the drugs are passed that way.[32] One officer said, 'The women are very deft—they are much faster than the men'. And as another officer put it, 'The more you "up the anti", the more you also increase their determination to get their drugs in, whatever it involves.'

Certainly some ingenious methods have been discovered: as well as postage stamps, the pages of magazines and the backs of family photographs have been impregnated with LSD, which has also been found in women's hair extensions and the beads woven into them. 'What can we do if we see a woman pulling her hair extensions out?' said an officer, 'They're only supposed to keep them in for a few weeks at a time anyway!'

Plainly the tougher security becomes, the more people's civil liberties and human rights will be damaged. In one prison, prisoners on the way to visits are subjected to the degrading practice of being asked to lift up their skirts to show they are wearing knickers, and they are never allowed to wear clothes with holes, or jackets with pockets, to a visit.

Nor are the civil liberties of prison officers likely to remain immune from scrutiny. The Advisory Council Report[9] acknowledged that 'a very few prison staff may . . . be attracted to the prospect of considerable financial rewards from smuggling in drugs'. The Prison Officers' Association (POA) reacted angrily in March 1996 when the Prison Service confirmed it was considering forcing them, like the prisoners, to undergo compulsory drugs checks to make sure they were not smuggling drugs into prisons. Their spokesperson David Evans said: 'My members would react violently if this went ahead. It is a tremendous slight.'

In December that same year, the National Association of Probation Officers (NAPO) threatened to take legal action after intrusive physical searches by prison staff. It was alleged that probation staff were 'on the side of prisoners' and more likely to supply them with drugs. Sixty probation officers, mostly women, objected to rub-down searches, solicitors and barristers joined the protest and finally in July 1997 Joyce Quin MP, the new Prisons and Probation Minister, agreed that the practice should cease.

In an address to a Prison Service drugs conference in Birmingham in March 1996[33] Michael Howard, then home secretary, announced even tougher measures to try to prevent drugs coming into prisons. Four prisons would run pilot schemes whereby prisoners found to have misused drugs, or suspected of doing so, would be placed on closed visits (where visitor and prisoner are separated by a screen, often in a cubicle locked on the prisoner's side), or non-physical contact visits (where there must be no touching).

If universally implemented throughout the service, a closed visits system could have a particularly devastating effect on imprisoned mothers and their children. Already in Risley, for example, women can be kept on closed visits for 14 days on suspicion of bringing in drugs, and for 28 days if there is proof. The kiosks built in some visits rooms for this purpose are described in *Chapter 4*, where I also quote the Inspectorate's caveats about depriving women of physical contact with children. In the next chapter I quote from interviews with black women prisoners who have been subjected to these measures.

These, then, are some of the Prison Service's prevention strategies, and perhaps they could be more easily accepted by drug users and non-users alike if they were seen to be working. But the misuse of drugs in prison is known to be on the increase.

While new anti-drugs security measures imposed on prisons have had serious repercussions on drug-users and have, if anything, exacerbated the situation, the implications for non-drugs users are, in their way, equally serious. The security clampdown to prevent drugs coming in has caused animosity towards the 'junkie girls' as well as against the prison authorities, with a resulting heightening of tension all round. Women prisoners claimed that the tension is fuelled by some officers: 'Officers should view addicts as suffering from an illness: instead they foster the 'anti-junkie' mentality whereby these women are viewed as being the lowest in the prison, along with nonces [sex offenders and child molesters]. The staff like to encourage bullying as it divides the wing and sets the women against each other. It helps them control us by "divide and rule"'.

All women, but particularly those with no history of drug involvement, bitterly resent the way the urine test is carried out. It is accompanied by a strip search which women find degrading and unnecessarily harsh. In some prisons testing is done in the health centre in the presence of nurses, but some nursing staff have refused to hold it there on the grounds that testing is part of the disciplinary process with which they want no association. In such prisons testing may be done in the segregation unit, making the process all the more intimidating.

A woman in one open prison found this particularly upsetting: 'The block is used for drugs testing which is very humiliating. You have to take your bottom half off and they also do a strip search. It's supposed to be random but they get at you by having it in the block. The piss test itself is an infringement but it's a secondary invasion. They should do it in the health centre.'

To avoid the substitution of another prisoner's clear urine the door of the lavatory cubicle must be left unlocked, and—especially as male prison officers may be present—women feel embarrassed and insecure: 'The door is never properly shut and the officer's hand is always on the handle—and it may be a male officer'.

It is clear that the Prison Service's current drugs policy is woefully ineffective. A radical alternative is one favoured by most penal reformers, who argue that punitive and therapeutic regimes cannot work successfully in tandem. Such groups believe that unless they are a danger to the public, people addicted to drugs (including alcohol) should be diverted from custody altogether, and directed instead to drugs agencies in the community. Such methods have been successfully piloted in Germany, Italy and some American states, where judges directly supervise treatment schemes and can impose immediate sanctions on offenders who break the rules. American research has shown that for every dollar spent on such drugs treatment programmes, seven dollars are saved during the treatment period and for 12 months afterwards, largely from the resulting reduction in drugs-related property crime.[34]

As one of his first actions after coming into office, home secretary Jack Straw announced a number of pilot projects to test the effect of making available to the courts a similar new drug-testing and mandatory treatment order. Offenders would be treated in the community, being tested randomly, and would not be sent to prison unless it was clear they had no intention of giving up their habit.

But such alternatives are rarely used by the courts: although drugs convictions have trebled between 1985 and 1995 (from 23,000 to 80,000, fewer than 2000 drug and alcohol addicts each year are given treatment orders.[35] Courts may fear that the public will be at risk, or that the treatment will not work—or treatment may not be available. Yet prisons minister Joyce Quin MP agrees that such orders are a vital way of rehabilitating addicts into society: 'It is a vicious circle which must be broken', she says.[36]

Reformers have welcomed Mr Straw's initiatives, on economic as well as humanitarian grounds, and the Crime and Disorder Act 1998 will give the courts powers to impose the new orders. Drug treatment combined, for example, with a probation order, can cost as little as £3,000 per offender, compared with £26,624 a year to keep a woman in prison.

Most prison staff I spoke to agreed that their jobs would be made far easier if drug users could be diverted from prison. Most felt that women who had committed non-violent offences like shoplifting to fund their habit should be treated in the community. There is historical precedent[37] for treating addicted prisoners in a non-penal setting. In 1898 the Inebriates Act removed alcoholics from prisons into reformatories. Two kinds of institutions—local and state—were established. Most of the inhabitants were women, who made up 91 per cent of the local reformatory population and two-thirds of the state-run establishments. There are some parallels between these alcoholic women and today's drug addicts, in that like the alcoholics, the addicts constantly move in and out of prison for petty crimes and for breaches of public order; their sentences are usually very short and they disrupt prison discipline. The chaplain of Brixton, in the nineteenth century a women's prison, felt that the alcoholics, like today's addicts, were women who needed medical treatment 'in a special manner and in a special place . . . as their presence among other prisoners operates most injuriously upon those around them and constitutes one of the chief difficulties in carrying out the discipline of this prison.'[37] The reformatories had only a limited success in practice, because they were of dubious and idealised conception, built in remote rural settings designed to remove the women from their communities and from the temptations of urban life.

A more realistic but equally radical approach to drugs misuse would mean that the current judgmental attitude would have to be replaced with one of sensible pragmatism. Women addicts with dependent children so much fear reproach by the courts and even by social workers and the medical profession, that they are terrified even to admit they are drug abusers, let alone seek help. They know from the experience of others that their children are likely to be taken away. Many drug addicted prisoners told me they had lost custody of—and sometimes even access to—their children. This could still happen even after they had controlled their habit and were clear of drugs. The devastation of their loss had commonly driven them back onto heroin to 'block out the pain'. Ruth is 26 and her daughter Kelly, six, is being adopted:

> It was a mistake to admit the drugs because it led to Kelly being taken away from me. I had got my heroin habit down to only £10 a week and I was building up a nice little family life with this great bloke and there were just the three of us. I wanted to get right off drugs so I went to a DDU[38] and admitted my drugs problem and went on a course of Methadone. I only wanted help—but they took Kelly away. Once she was gone it sent me back to heroin. You drink and smoke and take drugs to ease the pain. Now I've just been done for three months and 14 days for possession.

Ruth showed me her diary, an exercise book in which she had written:

> Living every day feeling depressed. Bloody social services won't let me see my daughter, or even talk to her on the telephone, they say it makes her upset. What about *me*, *my* feelings? Today I was told that she, my darling daughter, my life, my reason for living, will be adopted. In the back of my

mind I think what is the point of stopping taking the drugs? Cos when I take that awful shite it stops the hurt, the pain, the tears. It seems that everything I've ever loved, cared for, wanted, needed, has gone. I feel the tears welling up in my eyes. Twenty-four seven I cry over losing my baby.

If Mr Straw's proposed new drugs treatment orders are to work successfully, they will have to be properly resourced and facilities specially designed to meet the needs of women offenders, e.g. child care, will have to be widely available. Until then it seems likely that addicts like Ruth will continue to be sent to prison. A few may be lucky enough to be on a programme that gives them the incentive to end their habit. Experts in detoxification may offer them supervised advice for a short intensive period, then different specialists may employed to offer rehabilitation programmes, with the main emphasis on throughcare and aftercare so that they are linked with agencies in the community on release. Here again women addicts are at a particular disadvantage when it comes to leaving prison: because of the geographical spread of women's prisons, it is much harder to set up links with support agencies in a woman's home community which can be maintained on her release.

Many prisoners' support groups and drug agencies remain sceptical about prison drug programmes, maintaining that there is little incentive for imprisoned people to give up drugs, and that therapeutic and punitive regimes are irreconcilable and cannot coexist. If ever the prop of a drug is needed, they say, it will be needed in the alien world of prison, where addicts, often emotionally and psychologically damaged to start with, are beset by loneliness and fear. As one prison psychologist put it: 'We treat prison drugs programmes as a kind of sheep-dip process: dip the women in while they are in prison, push them out the other end and they'll be fine. It just doesn't work like that'. Another said, 'Women in their forties and fifties who have been addicted for many years are going to need special help to believe they can ever change'.

I interviewed a woman serving the latest of many sentences for supplying drugs. She had been a heroin addict for over 20 years:

Drugs are a deep-seated illness – a mental as well as a physical addiction. Prison is not the right place for addicts. What they need is counselling because drug-taking is only a symptom of their real problem. There is something intrinsically very sick about pushing metal and poison into your body. At an intellectual level you realise it's ridiculous but you still do it because of the other emotional problems you have.

In the current circumstances the best that can be hoped for is damage limitation—Methadone and other substitute prescriptions, clean

213

needles, sterilising equipment and drugs advice and information programmes. Several European countries and the USA and Australia are now using such harm reduction techniques.

There are success stories, though they are often fragile: Lucy is 31 and a former heroin addict who had overcome her habit but was serving a sentence for shoplifting—a second habit she had learned as a by-product of the first, and found equally addictive:

> You need a terrific amount of support to get off drugs. You've got no chance of doing it on your own. One of the real problems is that when you are coming off drugs you need something to fill up that time—the time you spent grafting and scoring before. You need something long term to replace all that. That's one reason I would direct people out of prison and put them on a full rehab programme. What people don't realise is that drugs is a full time 24 hour occupation and people have to have something to replace it or they will go back to it.

As I was drafting this chapter, I received a letter from a young Holloway prisoner. She was already suicidal, and the new measures such as loss of privileges and limited contact with her family will further damage her chances of rehabilitation:

> I never knew what heroin was until I came into prison on my first sentence. I was sent to an open prison where the drug was easily available. All the prisons are full of drugs. When you come into prison you come to do your time, not to leave with an addiction. I came out of prison a heroin addict and due to that I am back in prison again, this time through my addiction. Now I find myself relying on heroin more and more and I've had to get my grandfather to send money into other girls' accounts so I could pay for it. He thinks the money is helping me to buy phone cards. I've tried to commit suicide as I know I'm losing everything and I've had no help.

Endnotes

1. *Women in Prison: A Review*, HM Inspectorate, 1997.
2. See Note 1, above: 11.39.
3. *Prison Statistics England and Wales, 1994*, HMSO, 1996.
4. As assessed by Peter Worden, a leading expert on drug misuse at a meeting of The Stapleford Trust at the Royal Society of Medicine. Reported in *The Observer*, 11 January 1998.
5. The Misuse of Drugs Act 1971 divides controlled drugs into three categories called classes A, B and C. For the possession of class A drugs the maximum sentence is seven years and a fine, but it is not widely known that for supplying the maximum penalty is *life* imprisonment, plus a fine and the confiscation of the offender's goods. For class B drugs the maximum sentence for possession is five years and a fine, and the maximum sentence for supplying is a hefty 14 years

plus a fine and confiscation of goods. For possession of class C drugs there is a maximum sentence of two years plus a fine, and the courts can still impose up to five years, a fine and confiscation of goods for supplying.

6. Quoted in *The Independent*, 'Girls Behaving Badly Pose a New Problem', Glenda Cooper, 7 November 1997.

7. A. Maden, M Swinton and J Gunn, 'A Survey of Pre-arrest Drug Use in Sentenced Prisoners', *British Journal of Addiction* 87: 27-33, 1992; and 'Women in Prison and Use of Illicit Drugs Before Arrest', *British Medical Journal* 301: 1133, 1990.

8. A Maden, C Taylor, D Brooke and J Gunn, *Mental Disorder in Remand Prisoners*, Home Office, 1995.

9. *Drug Misusers and the Prison System: An Integrated Approach (Part II)*, HMSO, 1996.

10. See Penal Affairs Consortium paper *Drugs on the Inside*, November 1996.

11. A drugs baron is a prisoner at the head of an extortion racket. Taxing means the extortion of protection money or tobacco.

12. A German-manufactured hollow chocolate egg — marketed in Britain as 'Kinder Surprise' — with a cavity usually containing a small children's toy.

13. Heroin users —'smack' is slang for heroin.

14. 'Gear' is slang for drugs, usually heroin.

15. See Note 1, above: 11.36.

16. See Note 1, above: 7.20.

17. Amphetamines—also known as 'speed'.

18. HMP Styal is one of four prisons to have a Mother and Baby Unit.

19. *The Female Offender: Girls, Women and Crime*, Sage, 1997.

20. Quoted in PAC paper, see Note 10, above.

21. The Penal Affairs Consortium paper *Drugs on the Inside* (November 1996) lists the five key components of the MDT system: (i) Initial testing on reception or transfer; (ii) Targeted testing on reasonable suspicion of having misused drugs; (iii) Random testing of about 10 per cent of the prison population each month; (iv) More frequent testing for inmates thought to be persistent drugs misusers; (v) Risk-related testing, e.g. for those involved in temporary release.

22. Prison contract whereby a prisoner promises to remain drug-free in return for incentives.

23. See Note 1, above: 5.36.

24. Quoted in *The Guardian*, 19 June 1997. The final report was published in May 1998. Researchers did not visit any women's prisons.

25. *The Independent* reported (21 February 1997) that among drug-using prisoners there was a fall from 25.97 per cent to 19.74 per cent in cannabis use, and a rise in opiate use from 5.01 per cent to 6.35 per cent.

26. Both Sir David's and Mr Tilt's comments were made on *Breakfast with Frost*, BBC 1, on 8 March 1998.

27. Marijuana.

28. A rare severe and sometimes fatal illness caused by a toxin produced by bacteria. First recognised in the late 1970s. About 70 per cent of cases are women using vaginal tampons at the time of onset. Recurrence is common.

29. See Note 1, above: 2.18, 11.43.

30. Giving up drugs suddenly without substitutes being prescribed.

31. Had 28 additional days added to her sentence.

32. One ex-prisoner told me how she had brought drugs into her former prison by mouth when visiting a friend still there. She purchased a cup of tea and transferred the drug from her mouth to the cup. Unfortunately for her it floated up to the top of the liquid and was seen by the WVS lady serving the drinks. 'It was bright blue and the old lady was most upset. "Oh dear", she apologised, "There's something nasty in that cup—let me get you another one!"'

33. 13 March 1996, Birmingham.

34. Quoted in *Clean Break*, Jonathan Rugman, *The Guardian*, 23 July 1997.

215

35. Quoted in Penal Affairs Consortium, *Drugs on the Inside*, see above, Note 10.
36. Quoted in *What the Dutch Can Teach our Minister about Cannabis*, Heather Mills and Andy McSmith, *The Observer*, 28 December 1997.
37. See Lucia Zedner, 'Wayward Sisters' in *The Oxford History of the Prison*, Oxford University Press, 1995.
38. Drugs Dependency Unit.

CHAPTER TEN

Poor Mules and Strong Fighters

I was accused of selling drugs in prison and I had 20 days added to my sentence. I was CCd[1] down the block for 11 days. In the end I took it up with my MP and he got the accusation quashed and deleted from my record. But that didn't stop the prison refusing my children's visits because they said I'd sold drugs. My family were scared to come and see me in case they got involved too.

Yvonne is 36 and one of many British-born African-Caribbean prisoners in my sample who reported being under constant suspicion of drug-dealing inside prison. She is also one of seven women (more than a third of the British born African-Caribbean women in the sample) who complained of brutal treatment by prison officers. In an account reminiscent of the terrible story of Joy Gardner[2] she described her ordeal:

I was in bed on a Monday morning about 6.30 a.m. when eight officers came rushing in. This woman officer said "Get dressed, you're being shipped out!"[3] I said "What did I do?" I couldn't contact my family to tell them and I had a visit booked to see my youngest child. Two officers grabbed me by the hands and pushed them behind my back. They pushed my head down—like this' [she bent her head down to her knees]. 'I was only wearing my nightdress and these shorts I've got on today. I was taken down to reception and they bent up my hands and put the handcuffs on me. When they released my neck and took the pressure off I was sick all over the place. I was coughing and a nurse asked me if I would like some water and if I was in pain. They gave me two painkillers—one for the journey and one to take when I got to the next prison. Some girls at the new prison told me later they'd heard the escort officers boasting how they had treated me.

The stereotyping of women prisoners, and its effect on the way they are treated, has been a recurrent theme of this book. Are black women doubly jeopardised by both gender and race? The percentage of black women in prison has more than doubled in the years between 1985 and 1997. The *National Prison Survey*,[4] found that black Caribbean prisoners were far less likely than white prisoners, black African prisoners or Asian prisoners to feel they were treated well by prison officers. The title of this chapter refers to two dominant stereotypical images of black women prisoners that I met constantly in my interviews with prison officers.[5]

I found distinct differences in the way black British women and foreign national black women are regarded. The term 'poor mules' exemplifies the patronising but often sympathetic attitude to foreign—in my sample black African—women serving long sentences for importing drugs from abroad. The term 'strong fighters' refers to the prevailing view among prison officers that British black women prisoners are physically strong, aggressive and often dangerously violent. This chapter explores the reality behind these two images.

I asked all the women in the sample whether they had noticed inter-prisoner racism.[6] Only six (four per cent of the total sample) could recall any such incidents. One white woman described ethnic minority women as 'sticking together too much' and 'wanting their own spicy food all the time'. A young black British woman said 'Lots of the girls don't like black women—you can tell by the way they behave. So we all stick together.' But when pressed for details she could not give any specific incidents—it was 'just a feeling you get'.

Two black woman drugs couriers reported having problems with other prisoners, but these were connected with their offence rather than their ethnicity. One was put in the hospital wing where drug addicts were undergoing painful withdrawal symptoms, and was vilified for 'making money out of others' suffering'. The other, serving 16 years for drugs importation, said: 'I have had a difficult time with both prisoners and staff. When I came into prison my English was poor and they did not make allowances. Now they all treat me as if I'm a leper.'

Several prison probation officers confirmed that most of the racism between prisoners was drugs-related:

> Some prisons used to be very dangerous places for black women but now there are more black staff and we have raised the consciousness of the problems of black women in prisons so it is safer. They used to be put among all the drugs girls and were blamed for all their problems, accused of being the ones to bring drugs into our country and so on. And at some prisons black women were so rare that people looked at them as if they had four heads!

Another probation officer agreed, but felt work was still needed to raise staff awareness. Sensitive handling by staff could solve many problems:

> There is racial prejudice, specially towards the deportees.[7] But it is really about drugs, not race. We had five young Turkish women in here recently—they'd been imprisoned for their involvement in a protest about

conditions in their country. All the other prisoners assumed they were drugs couriers. I had to fight very hard for them and I told the officers I wanted them kept on one wing because there was safety for them if they could stick together. But the staff wouldn't listen and they separated them on to different wings. In the end I asked one of the governor grades for help and we got them back together again. There's no reason why prisons shouldn't be able to manage to keep certain vulnerable groups like this apart from others.

In the following account a fifth prisoner, Shelley, a British-born African-Caribbean woman, describes a racist incident which she recalled because of its rarity:

They are racist in here [a closed prison] but not the inmates — I've hardly ever heard a racist remark and most of this wing are black or mixed race anyway. If there *is* racism the officers will ignore it or blame the black women. Once my friend — who's black — and this white girl had an argument and this girl shouted at my friend "You black c . . t!" She didn't just say it once, she shouted it really loud a few times. That was the first racist remark I'd heard in here for ages and my friend was so shocked at it that she punched this white girl for saying it. The officers came rushing in and they nicked my friend for punching the white girl but they never did nothing to the white girl for what she said. The officers pretended they never heard it but they must have because she shouted it twice and the second time she screamed it out really loud so the whole wing heard it. Yet they nicked the black girl for the punch, though they couldn't have seen it because they were down the other end in the wing office.

Asian women were never mentioned by officers as threatening: they are categorised by a different stereotype, and indeed the offences of the three British-born Asians in my study were all non-violent crimes. But according to the sixth prisoner (herself Asian) who mentioned prisoner-prisoner racism, they are still subject to prejudicial treatment by officers.

The staff encourage you to argue — it's the "divide and rule" principle. We do have a Black Women's support group in this [open] prison and I go to the meetings. But once I wanted to go to communion in the chapel and that clashed with the meeting. I was taken to task by the black woman who runs it and the officers were winding us both up. If you are intelligent and black they resent you all the more. I was told by a male officer that I had an attitude problem because I wanted to start up a magazine.

In my sample of 150 women prisoners, 21 per cent (32 women) were from minority ethnic groups. This compares with official mid-1995 figures[8] where 24 per cent of female prisoners are classed as coming from ethnic minorities, though later figures put the percentage even higher at 26 per cent. There is a disproportionately high percentage of black people in the prison population: minority ethnic groups make up only 5.5 per cent of the general population. While only 1.6 per cent of women outside prison are of African-Caribbean origin, 20 per cent of women prisoners come from this group. The Prison Service includes in this figure black foreign national women serving long sentences for the importation of drugs into Britain. But when these are omitted, the number of British black women prisoners still remains high at 12 per cent, compared with one per cent of British nationals aged 15 to 64 in the general population. This high proportion is not confined to the United Kingdom: in Canadian prisons, for instance, 18 per cent of prisoners come from First Nations aboriginal peoples, compared with just three per cent of those groups in the population outside prison. In my sample 19 women—13 per cent of the total sample—were black British so that the sample is fairly representative of the female prison population as a whole.

What lies behind officers' perception of *British* black African women —primarily those of African-Caribbean descent—as physically threatening? They were often described as 'big and strong', 'big black girls', 'violent' and 'difficult to control'. At the reception interviews[9] I observed, British black women were treated very differently from white women who had committed similar offences. Both groups were treated patronisingly, but white women, especially if they were young, attractive and well-dressed, were patted on the head and told to run away and behave better in future. Black women's crimes seemed to be regarded far more judgmentally and any attempt at assertiveness was quashed immediately, especially by male officers, who routinely used words like 'loud', 'mouthy', 'gobby' and 'noisy' to describe this group.

A young black woman in an open prison approached me with a specific point to make: 'I have to count to ten about five times a day to survive. They are really racist in this prison. They won't put four black women together to work in this prison, though four white women can. The gardens officer told us he wasn't allowed to put four black girls together as that was Home Office regulations. I suppose he thinks we'll turn round and attack him or something'. In fact this directly contravenes the Prison Services race relations policy statement which states: 'All inmates should have equal access to the facilities provided in the establishment including jobs.'[10]

The African-Caribbean women felt the officers commonly over-reacted, precipitating trouble when none would otherwise have occurred. Shelley, quoted above, is 19 and though she is serving a four year sentence for supplying crack she swears she has never used it.

> I know there is bullying around drugs, and the officers do try and stop it. But they do it in such a stupid way, by coming down hard on everybody regardless. Say you have a fight with your best mate: now that's not really bullying—it's not serious, it's a fight among equals, and if they left you alone you'd just make it up and that would be the end of it. But they say it's bullying and they bring in rule 43 and send you down the block. I've been in the block a lot—14 days at a time.

Women prisoners are generally recognised as being subject to closer surveillance than men prisoners. A 1994 study[6] showed that black prisoners, both male and female, were more likely to have been disciplined than white prisoners. They were more likely to feel that the discipline was unfair, and that there were racial aspects to the unfairness. From the evidence of the black British women I interviewed in a number of different prisons, it seems this group is subject to particularly heavy supervision, partly due to a lack of understanding of cultural differences. Young black women were anxious to point out that though they may appear assertive, noisy and physically tactile, these characteristics should not be misinterpreted as signs of aggression: 'That's just what we're like'. A black police officer I interviewed for a different research project described similar misapprehensions among his white colleagues when confronted by groups of young African-Caribbean men on Brixton street corners. 'They'd say "These lads are causing trouble, let's nick 'em!" But I'd say "They're doing no harm, just listening to loud music and hanging out. That's what happens back home in the Caribbean"'.

Eight of these 19 women (42 per cent) were indeed accused or convicted of violent crimes, but closer analysis[11] shows that more than half (five) of these offences were assaults committed when they were under the influence of drugs or desperately seeking money for drugs. Of the three life-sentenced black prisoners (two of them in their forties), one maintained she was innocent and the victim of a miscarriage of justice, another said she had been abused by the husband she killed and the third did not disclose the reason for her crime.

Though their accounts are impossible to verify so long after the incidents, it is significant that women felt that summary prison justice was meted out to them, often on trumped-up charges, and that if they tried to complain they would be made to suffer. Brenda was by no means anti-authority—indeed she spoke warmly of many of the prison staff: 'The Governor's so nice and so is Mr X—you can talk to them any time'. Of the deputy governor she said: 'Miss Z has so much respect for us and we have respect for her. I would never have a problem with her because she treats people with respect.'

But Brenda too fell foul of the system. In *Chapter 3* she described being kept on closed visits for 14 months because she was caught smoking marijuana—though the offence for which she was imprisoned was not drugs-related. In her next prison there was another incident:

> I sent a VO [visiting order] out and the officer wrote it in red pen. So when my friend tried to visit me they said the VO was forged and wouldn't let him in. This friend happens to be a barrister and he said he was taking this further. He said the idea that a VO could be forged was ridiculous because the officers write them not the prisoners. I was shipped out to another prison: they came along and got me out of bed in my bra and knickers and sent me straight off without any of my clothes. I had no shoes even. I had terrible marks on my wrists from the handcuffs and I showed them to the doctor. I told the Board of Visitors and my family phoned the Home Office. When I was sent back to the prison where there'd been this trouble, I was put down the block on a charge of "interfering with witnesses". The officers said to me "We don't want to hear anything from your solicitor".

Even if women admitted a breach of discipline, the punishments given seemed particularly harsh, involving a large number of officers. Yvonne's description of being intimidated by eight officers as she was 'shipped out' to another prison was by no means an isolated account. Black women in different prisons commonly described being violently manhandled by six, eight or even 12 officers, and of spending a lot of time 'down the block'. In the many months I spent visiting prisons there were enough separate accounts, corroborated by both black prisoners and white prisoners, to be convincing. Shelley, quoted above, was in prison for her second offence two years ago:

> I was put in the block because I assaulted an officer. I was only 17 and I was feeling victimised because the officers just used to blank me if I asked for anything. For instance I tried to tell them I couldn't have cheese or pork and the officers just blanked me again. I sat down a little while then I started getting really angry. I ran up to the officer and I pushed her and she fell down and was rolling on the floor. They rang the riot bell and locked all the doors.

> Then six officers—men and women—came along and shouted "We're taking you down the block!" They tried to restrain me by grabbing hold of my head and I'd already got a cut on my head from where they restrained me before on my last sentence in 1994, plus I had a bruise on my arm. So I

fought them off and they held me by the head and that was how I got cut last time. They told me "This is the usual procedure" and when they said that I kicked an officer I got 28 days added on for that, and ten extra days for pushing that first officer. I was the first YO ever to get 38 days added on. They manhandled me through that door. Once they get you through that door there you're done for, man. They twist your arms behind you and they really punch you.

As *Chapters 8* and *9* showed, there is no doubt that some young women —both black and white—do behave violently in prison and that some action has to be taken. But from these women's accounts, it seems that a policy of constant vigilance, accompanied by excessive control and restraint methods, simply serves to 'up the anti' and exacerbate the situation. Many young black women (and the young black men I interviewed in earlier research) expressed their need for 'respect' and their anger when they felt they were being 'dissed' [disrespected]. The greater emphasis on interpersonal skills in initial and in-service training of prison officers ought to be addressing these issues.

Because the offences for which African-Caribbean women are jailed are so often directly or indirectly drug-related there is, they claim, an automatic assumption by staff that they are all guilty of bringing drugs into prison, that they are likely to be using crack cocaine which will make them aggressive and dangerous, and that they are taxing other prisoners, particularly white women. One black woman said 'They single you out, and if you say something quite natural to a white woman, like, "Give us a roll-up", they'll nick you for taxing. But if you ask another black girl the same question, they'll ignore it. They love to create racism between us.' Many of the women were constantly aware of being under suspicion, and described the tension it caused: 'If you're black they just assume you're on drugs.' This, according to the women, led to their being blamed for bringing drugs into prison when they were not guilty, and even 'shipped out' to another prison, far from friends, children and other family.

If the government's radical plans to consider diverting large numbers of drug-users from prison were to be universally implemented, many black women would not be in prison at all, but would instead be offered detoxification and rehabilitation programmes in the community. Meanwhile, as mandatory drugs testing (MDT) in prisons remains such an inexact procedure, there is no reliable evidence to suggest that black women, even those imprisoned for drugs-related offences, are any more likely than white women to be bringing drugs in.

Andy told in *Chapter 4* of her suicide attempts when she was kept apart from her ten year old daughter. She is serving a five year sentence for supplying drugs, but she was so incensed by accusations and punishments that she was taking her complaint to the Prisons Ombudsman.[12]

> I was in Holloway for a year and had no trouble. Then I was shipped out to another [closed] prison because they said I was bullying and supplying. But I was not involved. Twelve officers sat on me though I'd had an operation on my stomach. The cut from where I had an operation for an ectopic pregnancy was hurting me. They accused me of bringing in drugs but I don't even smoke a cigarette. I had no chance to speak to my solicitor. I had no phone cards and they took my letters away and wouldn't give me pen and paper to contact anyone. I've tried to commit suicide twice. I've been through a lot and now I'm going to the Prisons Ombudsman about it.

What of the 'poor mules' for whom officers were more likely to express some sympathy? Of the ten black women drugs couriers in the sample, five were African nationals, whose average age was 34, one was a US citizen aged 21, and four were British citizens whose average age was 25. The average age of the whole group was 32 and the average length of the sentence they had been given was eight years.

It is interesting to compare this group with the five white women drugs couriers in the sample. One of these was a US citizen aged 22, the others were all British citizens: the average age of the white couriers was 30 and the average length of sentence was 5.8 years. Customs officers claim[13] that the cocaine trade is ruled by black 'Yardie' gangs who choose to use educated 'respectable' middle-class white women to bring cocaine from Colombia via the islands of the Caribbean. They are preferred because they are felt to be articulate enough to talk their way through if they are stopped. They will make £4000 plus a free holiday, and the dealers will make £200,000 or more on each trip. The traditional drugs mules may still be used, but often as a decoy to distract customs officials. They can even be set up to be captured by a telephoned tip-off after they have boarded the plane.

The younger white women in my sample are perhaps typical of this trend: two were young risk-takers from respectable but unconventional backgrounds, prepared to carry drugs for the 'buzz' and the chance of big money. One said, 'I'd never been on a plane before and it was exciting to fly to St Kitts [Caribbean] for the weekend. I would have made £3500'. The third young woman was enmeshed in a chaotic drug-ridden lifestyle and was set up by ruthless British male dealers to take the blame if their very amateur plan should fail.

A fourth young courier, an elegant and sophisticated black New Yorker, was ironically only captured because of the racist attitudes of airport customs officials. Lorelle, serving eight years for importing cocaine, makes no secret of the fact that she couriered drugs to maintain her already comfortable New York lifestyle. She qualified as a nurse and is married with a young son who is cared for by a nanny and attends private nursery:

> I was given a first class return ticket to London and told a hotel had been booked the other end. I was given a special suitcase with the cocaine sewn into it. It was in a flat pack about the size of a computer keyboard. They caught me at Heathrow by a random check. The suitcase got through the X-ray with no problem but they were suspicious of a well-dressed young black woman travelling first class. When the guy at Heathrow stopped me he said "What kinda job *you* got then?" I said "I'm a registered qualified nurse and I can afford to travel first class. I come from a country where there's freedom whatever colour you are." I was real shocked at the young black girls in jail over here. I'm telling you, half of them haven't got a pot to piss in.

But most of the drugs mules now serving long sentences in British jails have a lifestyle very different from Lorelle's. In 1996 there was a fivefold increase in the number of Jamaican women drugs couriers in UK jails and they come from very much poorer backgrounds. During the last decade two sister organizations have been set up to help women who become drugs mules. The Female Prisoners' Welfare Project was established in 1986 to support women coming into prisons. Its workers offer advice, advocacy, child care and employment to women of any race, not just black foreign nationals. In 1991 another agency, Hibiscus, was started under the FPWP umbrella, to help the disproportionate number of foreign nationals, mainly from West Africa and the Caribbean, among the British female prison population serving sentences for drugs offences. In June 1996, according to FPWP/Hibiscus figures, 31 per cent of the 459 women sentenced for drugs offences were foreign nationals. Hibiscus also works with Grupo Amiga, a group set up for Spanish-speaking women, now that more and more poor South American women are being recruited as mules. These are younger than the African women—in their twenties rather than their thirties—and are less likely to have children.

Those who do bring children are likely to be given such long sentences that a place in a mother and baby unit is felt to be inappropriate and the children have to be taken into care. Concern has been voiced about care provision. In November 1996 a Department of Health inspection of prison mother and baby units[14] asserted that 'social work arrangements for the care and discharge of children of imprisoned foreign national mothers were *ad hoc* and lacking in consistency'.

Prison officers were commonly dismissive and scathing about the 'stupidity' and 'greed' of the younger white women couriers for throwing away years of their lives by drug smuggling. But my interviews revealed a perception of foreign national African drugs couriers that was quite different from the attitude to the British black prisoners or to the young white couriers.

Officers frequently expressed some sympathy with 'poor black mules' because they were incarcerated so far from home and family. They were likely to believe the women's accounts of being duped to carry drugs, and regarded most as 'docile' and likely to cause much less trouble than British black women (and than some white prisoners). There was sometimes implicit post-Colonial racism in the reasons given for these views. For instance, staff at open prisons expressed regret that foreign nationals were no longer sent to them:[15] 'I used to like the African women because they had such nice personalities and were *so quiet and respectful*' [my italics].

Of all the women I interviewed during the course of this project, the interviews with the African nationals serving long sentences for drugs importation were the most harrowing. The universal term 'mules', though degrading, seems appropriate to their situation for they are regarded as little more than beasts of burden, cheap and expendable if they are caught. Despite the enormous street value of the drugs they bring in, the women see only a tiny fraction of the proceeds. The vast sums of money going to the drugs barons are in ironic contrast to the dire poverty of the women's backgrounds. Many of those mules who swallow heroin or cocaine in 'fingers' of rubber gloves have died on the planes or in the airports because they have a total of only 36 hours to reach their destination before the bags burst. The mules I spoke to had not used this method: all had carried the drugs strapped to their bodies or in their luggage, though probation officers said some Peruvian and Colombian women among their prison clients had been forced to swallow drugs with a gun to their heads.

Affua was a prime target to be set up as a 'mule'. She is 38, a Nigerian with a very sad story to tell. Her face often crumpled into tears as she spoke. Her language is pidgin and her English, though rapid, is not always easy to understand. She was married for 12 years but when she was unable to have a child, even after an operation, her husband left her for another woman. 'He had to, his family was giving him such a lot of pressure.' Affua remarried and became pregnant but it was an ectopic pregnancy and she lost the child. After that she spent all her money on everything from fertility pills to traditional African medicine: 'In Nigeria if you don't have any children you get no respect. 'It was at this point that 'a friend' offered to do her a favour. If she would bring a packet to England she would be given £2,000 which she could use 'to get a test tube baby'. Affua was caught with £60,000 worth of cocaine and given six years. 'You can't explain the situation. I was stupid because I was desperate. In my country they'd understand what it means if you can't have a child. But here nobody will help you. I've got no friends here. If only they'd send me back home. Some punishments are just too much, too much.'

These women usually leave home expecting to come back in a few days. All imprisoned mothers suffer maternal deprivation, but the plight of women so far from home is desperate. Hibiscus workers cite the example of five foreign nationals in Holloway on sentences of between five and ten years. All of them have daughters between the ages of 12 and 18. One of their greatest concerns is that they will not be at home for the younger girls when they have their first period. 'They worry, who will tell her about it, who will get the sanitary towels for her? Because in West Africa and Nigeria it is only the mother who will tell a girl about such things: it would be unthinkable to talk to the father or any other man about it'. The women are of course also very worried about losing their possessions and their homes: in most of their native countries there is no system of housing benefit or welfare help.

Every prison should have a special liaison officer to look after the needs of foreign women serving long sentences. A major problem is of course language. The Royal Commission on Criminal Justice (1993) acknowledged the importance of interpreters for prisoners, especially when they need to communicate with their lawyers.[16] All prisoners have a legal right to have the prison rules explained to them, but now such costs have to come out of individual governors' budgets. One principal officer told me he had had to engage an interpreter recently for a woman who spoke Gujarati: 'For one hour's work, plus travel expenses, the interpreter charged £200! The governor went ballistic!'

Yet the absence of interpreting services can be terribly damaging. One prison probation officer told me she had recently received a telephone call from the education department in the prison. Did she know anything about a young Turkish woman who had come into their classroom a week earlier and had never been seen again? The wing officers told the probation officer that the woman was a 'loner' and liked staying on her own in her room all day.

It turned out that the young woman was terrified. She did not understand a word of English and was confused by announcements like 'free flow'[17] over the tannoy. In fact she did not understand a word that was said. Worst of all, she had left a four-months-old baby at home, thinking—as many couriers do—that she would be back after the weekend.

The chaplain in the same prison was approached by a South American woman who had had her baby with her on arrest. The child was taken into foster care by social services and his mother, misunderstanding, had come to ask how far away was the town of 'Foster'.

A variety of resources are now available to help foreign national prisoners. There is, for instance, a special information pack, translated into 12 languages, for staff and prisoners to use. There is also an efficient telephone interpreting service: in 1993 the Prison Service announced that Language Line was available to all prisons. At the touch of a button the prison can access an interpreter in any one of 140 languages. But the service costs £1.50 per minute, a cost which has to come out of governors' own budget.

This service would be most valuable at reception interviews, where information about new prisoners needs to be accessed urgently if later problems are to be avoided: the reception period itself is known to be a time of high suicide risk. But receiving officers say the reception process is now so rushed, as more and more prisoners enter the system, that they have no time for such luxuries.

There is potential for real tragedy in such an omission: at the reception interviews I observed in one prison, a Croatian woman remanded the previous day from the courts could neither understand nor speak a word of English. As he ploughed hopelessly through the standard questions, the interviewing officer shrugged apologetically and said he spoke only holiday Spanish. I managed to dredge up my schoolgirl French, the woman could also speak a little, and together we discovered that no, she was not pregnant, and no, she had never self-harmed. The makeshift delivery of such crucial questions was alarming.

In fact what interpreting services there are at present are largely *ad hoc* and amateur, raising serious issues of confidentiality and accuracy of interpretation. HM Inspectorate's 1997 review of women's prisons[18] recognises the importance of translators, especially during the reception period, but accepts that specially trained prison staff who happen to be fluent in foreign languages may have to do the job if outside translators are not available. Hibiscus tries to arrange for ex-prisoners who have remained in this country to go back into prison to act as interpreters. They say the prisoners trust them so they can help with interpreting for an appeal, or talk about family problems.

Women jailed in a foreign country are specially vulnerable and need emotional support as well as practical help. Hibiscus has run group cultural awareness sessions in prisons with members of staff, trying to focus on the women's needs. But there is always the danger that after they have had a training session, staff will feel they have paid lip-service to solving the problem, then forget the importance of implementing what they have learned. When one women's prison ran a Foreign Nationals Day, they invited a serving judge to speak. One member of the prison staff who heard him commented wryly: 'He talked about the reason why judges feel able to give foreign drugs couriers such long sentences. He did not say it in so many words but you could see that the judges are unable to feel any empathy—they just regard these black drugs couriers as aliens and can't think of them as having children left at home who need them.'

Holloway is one of the prisons with a Foreign Nationals Group which meets once a week, with about 30 women attending regularly. Some of the meetings are information meetings, with solicitors and speakers on education coming in. On alternate weeks the prison invites in 'motivational' speakers—charismatic people who, it is hoped, will motivate the women. Sometimes the governor joins the meeting to hear the women's views. Sometimes ex-prisoners return to tell how they managed to cope with their sentences. They bear witness that there are ways of getting through and surviving, of dealing with depression and bullying, of setting goals and achieving them.

The small size of the women's prison estate causes problems for many prisoners in terms of integrated regimes and programmes. But for the foreign national, the options are further limited by the 1991 Home Office ruling that 'deportees' would no longer be allocated to open prisons following an alleged increase in the number who absconded. A spokeswoman for one women's group sees this as a racist: 'There were lots of absconds from one particular open prison, but there were just as many white as black women doing that. So it is mainly punitive'. HM Inspectors' review[19] pointed out that as foreign women have had their passports confiscated, have few contacts in this country and have not committed violent crimes, they are not a serious escape risk. The Inspectors conclude that 'their exclusion from open prisons compounds the harshness of their imprisonment.'

There is a tendency to allocate foreign nationals together in one prison. A large remand prison like Holloway will inevitably have large numbers awaiting trial: of the 500 or so prisoners there, between a quarter and one third at any one time are foreign nationals. Holloway is also a designated detention centre for alleged illegal immigrants. Many are asylum seekers who may at first be held in a detention centre but who are sent to the prison if there is concern about their physical or mental health, and if they are subject to a court warrant stipulating they must be held in a secure establishment pending deportation. Their situation is particularly poignant because they may have committed no crime at all and fear torture and death if they are returned to their own country. Many commentators feel prison is an entirely inappropriate place for them to be held.

Some closed prisons such as Cookham Wood and the women's unit at Winchester have a very high concentration of foreign nationals. Although it is desirable for women to have the support of others speaking the same language, there is also a danger of their being 'ghettoised'. One black woman prisoner felt this was a mistaken policy: 'They need to spread out, to learn more about different cultures.'

Just occasionally a woman will be lucky enough to have a visit from family members coming from abroad and her prison will usually try to make special arrangements so family can visit every day. But the authorities can also make life very difficult. An African woman serving a sentence of 16 years told me:

> I have been depressed as I am so far from my family. My twins were 14 months old and I was eight months pregnant when I was charged. I am very concerned about my husband. My mother came to see me once but they made it so hard for her, strip-searching her, following her and treating her so badly that it is not fair to put another member of my family through this ordeal.

In Spring 1997 the prison newspaper *Inside Time* printed a letter from Mercedes Barnett, a foreign national prisoner at HMP New Hall, a closed women's prison in Yorkshire. The letter complained that deportees could not earn privileges available to British prisoners, such as gate passes, open condition, town passes, temporary release or parole. The writer suggested that British prisons should emulate the US system whereby prisoners can earn up to 58 'good days' each year in return for good behaviour. Foreign nationals could then 'return home a little earlier'.

It is of course rarely possible for foreign nationals to have visits from relatives, so in some prisons in lieu of visits they are allowed one, two or three free airmail letters a month as part of the Incentives and Earned Privileges Scheme (IEPS). They used also to be allowed a free phonecall home once each month in lieu of visits, but this practice has ended and they now have to pay for the call themselves.[20] A probation officer said:

> The women are terribly isolated and now they have to pay for foreign phone calls, which eats into the money they might have been able to send home to their families. Occasionally if there is a special reason a woman might be granted a free phone call but this is now discretionary and no longer a statutory right.

In Winchester, according to the Inspectorate report, foreign women do now have a five minute phone call free each month, though probation staff said this was not nearly long enough to sort out serious family problems.

These policies, like the lack of interpreting facilities, are partly a question of economics. Prisons now all have devolved budgets and the governors should make allowances for the special needs of foreign nationals, but not all have the empathy and understanding to do so. Hibiscus sometimes simply sends funds to the women to make the necessary phone call. 'Women are suffering *now* so what they need is £5 a month *now* for that phone call.'

Another new rule which causes foreign national women particular hardship is the latest version of 'volumetric control' mentioned in earlier chapters—the rule which allows prisoners to keep in their cells only as many possessions as will fit into two standard size boxes. Each shallow box is about the size of a coffee table, and anything that will not fit in can no longer be stored in the prison's own property store but must be sent to a central storage depot for all the prisons in England and Wales. British long-term prisoners can arrange for property to be handed out to friends and relatives outside but foreign women, who during their very long sentences accumulate a fair number of possessions, have nobody to send them to and fear they will lose them altogether. The Inspectorate[21] emphasised that the policy on goods allowed in possession should take into consideration the distinct needs of foreign nationals, and indeed of any ethnic minority prisoner who may need items of cultural and religious importance, such as statues of the Buddha which the Prison Service permits[10].

How do black women—both British and foreign nationals—fare when it comes to work, training and education?

It has long been a tradition for black women prisoners, especially foreign nationals, to work in prison kitchens: those I interviewed said they preferred hard work to help them forget their troubles. Sometimes, however, even this dubious comfort is denied to them. I noticed in several prisons that most of the kitchen workers were white. One reason, according to probation officers, is that foreign women do not have a good enough command of English to fight for a better-paid prison job. But British-born black women said there was another reason:

> The kitchen officers couldn't get on with the black kitchen workers because they are very finicky: these African and Jamaican women are home-makers and they like things done properly in the kitchen. They are very thorough, while the officers of course don't care. So they have stopped putting so many black women in the kitchens. Kitchen work is hard and the

231

conditions aren't very pleasant—it's very hot and so on and the hours are long. But the pay is good and foreign nationals desperately need that money to send home to their children.

Another reason foreign nationals say they prefer kitchen work is that it supplies them with a uniform: wearing the white coat and hat gives them a sense of equality and they do not have to worry about competing with other women in the clothes they wear. Many 'mules' have only the light summer clothing they were wearing when they got onto the plane in their own country, thinking they would return within a few days. When a suspected importer is arrested, all her property is seized by Customs and Excise. If heroin or cocaine is found in a suitcase, customs officials may treat the entire contents as contaminated, even if the bags of drugs have not burst, and everything will be destroyed. So some women enter prison with nothing at all. Although they should be given a form on which to record their losses, many are too much in shock, or unable to read English, and officers said the forms rarely reached the prison.

Depending on the work they have done before, some foreign nationals are keen to improve their education while in prison. Many African-educated women have very good learning skills because of the traditional teaching methods in their own countries and because they have such long sentences some feel they could really achieve something if given the opportunity. Some are so keen to do computer courses that they have managed to pay for these themselves from their prison wages. There are women who have taken and succeeded in passing law courses while in prison. One education officer thought this was a better option than kitchen work:

> They may be earning the money for their children by working hard in the kitchens, and it is often said that they work so hard so they haven't got time to think and worry about their families. But in fact while they are doing this manual labour their minds are still free to worry. If they were concentrating on an educational course their brains would be occupied and the terrible maternal pain they suffer could be channelled into something positive in their training. They say they will go mad if they're left to their own devices but if their brains were engaged in this way it would be better for them. It does depend on what age they are. Maybe some are in their late 30s and they have always been traders. So to stand the discipline of an educational course they will need a lot of encouragement. Wages are a real problem because they desperately need to earn money to send home to their children. So I think the education department should offer the same wages as the kitchens as an incentive to encourage these women. The key is to equip them with skills they can use on release. One woman here is

planning to buy a special industrial sewing machine which she can take back to Africa to set up in business.

At the end of their long sentences, a further fear awaits foreign nationals. At three of the prisons I visited, I was told of cases where women had been held in custody months after their sentence had ended because the immigration authorities had not completed the necessary paperwork, or had failed to locate confiscated passports. One Race Relations Liaison Officer described how a woman's family waiting for her at an African airport were distraught when she failed to arrive. Her papers had not been processed and it was weeks before she finally left prison.

Food is a common cause of complaint from all prisoners, but because black women, and especially foreign nationals, are not accustomed to the food they are given, they find it even harder to bear. Three-quarters of the ethnic minority women (24 out of 32) mentioned poor food: many made comments like the following: 'They can't cook black people's food. There are no black people in the kitchen here. At least in my last prison, Cookham Wood, they did cater for every different nationality'. A long-sentence prisoner in a closed prison said: 'I am a Muslim and the Halal food is of a very poor standard and the facilities to buy it are not adequate.' One catering officer told me that all that prison's meat is Halal (which of course might offend non-Muslim prisoners if they realised it). Decisions about diet are made which are racist in their assumptions. For instance, at one prison rice was invariably served with a curry sauce which upset the digestion of the Colombian and Peruvian women until the kitchens were persuaded to serve the rice separately.

It is difficult to fit religious observances involving special diet into a prison regime. At Brockhill, for instance, staff said that during the 40 days of Ramadan, when eating is only allowed between sunset and sunrise, Muslim women have to take their supper into their cells in thermos flasks to be eaten later, and their breakfast has to be issued to them the previous evening so it can be consumed in the cell before sunrise.

Prisoners should at least be able to supplement their diets with goods from the prison shop—the canteen. The staff guide book[22] recognises that 'canteens should cater for different cultures and needs'. But poor canteen supplies were mentioned by all but two (94 per cent) of the ethnic minority prisoners as a cause for complaint, either because of the range of goods available, or because of the high prices.[23]

The commonest complaint was about products for hair and skin care. Items like hair relaxants and cocoa butter are not luxuries but essential to prevent serious problems. One young black woman

233

described the shop in her open prison: 'You can't get any skin preparations for black people, though they've just brought in cocoa butter. I bought all that sort of stuff in Holloway where you *could* get it, but I wasn't allowed to bring any of it here with me. I went to the prison doctor for skin cream but he said no, though I was prepared to pay for it. We can't wear ordinary white people's make-up.'

A white prisoner agreed:

> There are very few cosmetics for black women in the canteen. They have to slap *Lady Jane* cosmetics for white women on their skins and look like prats, or use nothing. They have started selling cocoa butter but at £3.50 a jar it's prohibitively expensive. The most we are allowed to spend is £10 a week and lots of women don't get anything like that much sent in. So no wonder some black women stick two fingers up to the officers because all this really pisses them off. All these subtle little things really get up their noses.

There is also great variation between prisons. Yvonne, quoted at the beginning of this chapter, said her current closed prison compared unfavourably with Holloway: 'I get £4.75 wages a week, that's all. Just now and again one or two friends send me money but a lot of my friends and family are in Jamaica. Everything in the canteen is expensive and you don't get much for your money. Black hair gel is £1.10 a small size here but it's only 90p in Holloway. Simba skin cream is 70p in Holloway and here it's £1.30 so we can't buy it.'

These problems are just one example of the effects on women's prisons of the harsh security measures following the Woodcock and Learmont reports.[24] Officers said they used to be able to go out and buy goods that prisoners needed from different stockists at the best prices. Now everything has to be ordered from a single approved supplier.

A few women felt angry that important prison race issues tend to become subsumed by such concerns. In one prison I was approached in the corridor by three separate groups of black women, all complaining about the need for a decent set of curling tongs. But the distorted value-systems of prison institutions mean that small issues are magnified and assume enormous importance.

One of the problems in the Prison Service, as indeed throughout the criminal justice system, is the under-representation of the ethnic minorities among prison staff. Prison Service figures for 1995[8] show that of the 1,020 governor grades, only 5 (0.49 per cent) are from ethnic minorities, and there are only 354 (2.4 per cent) ethnic minority officers out of a total of 19,325. The governor grade figures had remained exactly the same as the 1993 figures, though the officer figures had improved from 1.8%. In August 1997, Colin Moses, one of only nine

234

black officers to reach the grade of principal officer, put his career on the line by alleging that there is institutionalised and covert racism at the top of the Prison Service.[25] Not one black or Asian graduate had been advanced by the Accelerated Promotion Scheme (APS) described in *Chapter 7*. The two black people in my sample of 60 disciplinary officers actually *over*-represent the reality, as they stand at 3.3 per cent of the sample.

One white prisoner in an open prison was conscious of this glaring disparity: 'This prison is not a good place for ethnic minority women. About 30 per cent of the women are black and we have just one black prison officer'. A black woman in the same prison gave this officer limited support: 'There's only one black officer here, a woman. She's OK —at least she tries'.

Following a 1991 Prison Service ruling, governors are now required to set targets for the recruitment of prison officers from minority ethnic groups. I did not see any black trainees on the day I spent at the Prison Service Training College, but the tutors claimed that the service was keen to recruit more ethnic minority officers:

> In the Accelerated Promotion Scheme we are actively seeking ethnic minority recruits. But it is very difficult, though we advertise in journals like the *Voice* and *Asian Times* and we attend recruitment fairs aimed at that type of recruit. Those who have applied have not met the required standard for APS which is quite demanding. This is something echoed throughout the Prison Service. It's a cultural thing and unless society gets over it, I don't see how we can. The trouble is that historically the Prison Service has always been very insular.

I asked the two black prison officers in my sample whether their own communities had raised any objections to their joining a service which they might perceive as an arm of the Establishment traditionally resented by ethnic minorities. Only one of the two black officers I spoke to felt able to discuss racism, and she had not found it a problem:

> I have not experienced any racism but then I was brought up locally near this prison. There are very few black families in this rural area and I've always been used to being the only black person around. No, I didn't have any objections from my family when I decided to become a prison officer. It's not quite the same as black people joining the police: they do get more objections from their community who may regard them as traitors because they're so much more visible in public than we are as prison officers.

The Prison Service has embarked on a number of initiatives to promote good race relations in its establishments. The Prison Service race relations policy was first issued in 1983.[26] The statement is exemplary in every way, making it clear that the policy applies equally to staff and prisoners.

In 1991 in a further initiative the Prison Service launched a *Race Relations Manual*[27] stating its policies on everything from monitoring, access to facilities, work, education and training, allocation of accommodation, religion, diet and disciplinary matters, to racially derogatory language, complaints of racial discrimination and contacts with ethnic minority organizations outside prison. The potted version of the manual—the small pocket guide quoted earlier—is available for all staff.

In 1993 the service introduced widespread monitoring of areas within the control of Prison Service staff.[27] Training on race issues has been revived and updated throughout the whole service. An offence of racially discriminatory behaviour is now included in the prison staff disciplinary code.

All prisons are now required to appoint a Race Relations Liaison Officer whose job it is to help prisoners who feel that they have been discriminated against and to make sure the laws on race relations are followed.[28] Each establishment must also set up a Race Relations Management Team to monitor and investigate allegations of racial discrimination and make sure ethnic minority prisoners are give equal treatment to white prisoners. The RRLO and the governor must belong to the team. But none of the black prisoners I interviewed held a very high opinion of the RRLOs whom they regarded, rightly or wrongly, as much more likely to side with the establishment than with black women if a complaint is made.

The Prison Officers' Association has its own race relations policy[29] in which the following demand is made: 'The Association insists that race relations training be made more available by the Prison Department to all members in line with its own policy.'

Apart from informal events like Foreign Nationals days, are prison staff given any initial or in-service training in race relations or cultural awareness as required in the Prison Service policy guidelines and demanded by their own union?

A training college tutor said that the initial basic training contained 16 separate sessions on race relations: 'For instance we spend a whole group session brainstorming ways in which being racially aware could aid officers in their jobs'.

One young officer who had recently completed his training was unimpressed: 'I felt we spent too much time on race relations. We had a good crowd and none of us were racist but we still had to spend three or four weeks "doing race relations". It seemed to me a very long way round to see if we were prejudiced'. The need to be aware of cultural differences and to challenge Eurocentric stereotypes seemed to be lost on this officer: 'When I am talking to a coloured person I honestly don't notice what colour they are. But the tutors tell us what words to avoid and all that. It's not always about colour either, it's about accent. We were told about being aware, as you can stereotype people with a Scottish or Welsh accent as well.' Like this officer, Styal officers persisted in using the term 'coloured' which is now generally accepted as offensive.

An Asian woman in an open prison did not feel much had changed:

We have a race relations policy in force here but it's not easy to change attitudes. The other day a woman SO[30] was talking to a black girl waiting to go out on parole. She asked the girl "How's your baby, by the way?" The girl said "But you know I haven't got a baby!" "No?" said this officer. "Oh well, you all look the same to me!"

Endnotes

1. CC is prison slang for 'cellular confinement'. It can also mean 'cardboard city', referring to the cardboard furniture in segregation units ('the block') to prevent prisoners harming themselves.
2. In *Black Women's Experiences of Criminal Justice*, Waterside Press, 1997, Ruth Chigwada-Bailey says: 'The highly publicised case of Joy Gardner, a black woman of Jamaican origin who died in 1993 in London, lends support to the view that black women can be seen by the authorities as potentially violent. Joy Gardner had overstayed her visa and was visited by the Alien Deportation Group. Her wrists were handcuffed to a leather strap round her waist, bound by a second belt around her thighs, and a third one around her ankles. As she lay on the floor, 13 feet of adhesive tape were wound around her head and face. Mrs Gardner collapsed and died in hospital a few hours later.' Chigwada-Bailey comments: 'Three officers were tried for the murder of Joy Gardner and acquitted. In effect, the trial put the victim in the dock. As if to honour the standard stereotype and myth of the "big strong black woman", she was described by one of the officers as "the strongest and most violent woman" he had ever encountered. One of the officers said that the treatment she had received was "reasonable in all the circumstances"'.
3. Moved to another prison, often without warning.
4. The *National Prison Survey, 1991*. In *Chapter 5:* 'Relationships in Prison' the figures quoted are as follows: 43 per cent of white prisoners, 46 per cent of black African prisoners and 44 per cent of Asian prisoners said that prison officers treated them well, compared with only 29 per cent of black Caribbean prisoners. The figures refer of course to both male and female prisoners taken together.
5. I did not ask officers direct questions about the way they regarded black prisoners as this might have appeared as a slight on their professionalism and could have provoked a defensive reaction. I base the findings in this chapter on points that emerged in my conversations with them, and on my 'fly on the wall' observations during the months I spent in women's prisons.
6. Compare the findings in *Reported and Unreported Racial Incidents in Prisons*, Ros Burnett and Graham Farrell, University of Oxford Centre for Criminological Research, Occasional Paper No. 14, 1994. The researchers interviewed 501 prisoners of whom 373 were from ethnic minority

backgrounds. The number of black women in the study was small: only 29 of the sample were women and 41 per cent of these were white. Though the women were more likely than the men to complain about inmate-inmate incidents overall, they were less likely than the men to claim that incidents in which they had been involved had a racial aspect. Far more were likely to claim unfairness in respect of prison facilities or activities than to say they had been victims either of inmate-inmate or staff-inmate incidents. The study shows that black and mixed-race prisoners were more likely to have been disciplined than white prisoners during the previous three months (46 per cent of black prisoners compared with 34 per cent of whites). 35 per cent of the black prisoners thought they had been unfairly disciplined, compared with only 23 per cent of the whites. Whereas only two per cent of white prisoners claimed there was a racial aspect to the unfairness, 16 per cent of white prisoners made this claim. The authors stressed the value of a survey approach because 'although self-reports of victimisation cannot simply be taken at face-value as evidence of the extent of racial incidents, this approach is valuable in situations where the full extent of a problem is unlikely to be known.' They felt from considering other research that there are 'grounds for suspecting some under-reporting of racial incidents in prisons.'

7. Three of the African foreign nationals referred to themselves as deportees or detainees, a term more commonly understood to refer to illegal immigrants. Strictly speaking this is incorrect. Immigration is a complex issue because it is not easy to tell who is resident here and who is an illegal immigrant. If a foreign national has lived in Britain for many years and then commits an offence, a judge can recommend deportation as part of his or her sentence because he or she has breached the rules of residence. But such prisoners are allowed to appeal and during the appeal they may be regarded as an illegal immigrant and could be held at a British prison like Holloway while waiting to appeal — or they could be sent to a specially designated holding area.

8. Figures in this paragraph come from *Race and Criminal Justice*, Penal Affairs Consortium, September 1996.

9. See *Chapter 1*.

10. Quoted in *Race Relations and Religion: A Pocket Guide for Prison Staff*, HM Prison Service.

11. Of the 22 Black and Asian British women who were *not* drugs couriers: the offences/alleged offences were as follows (R = remanded; C = convicted):
    - TWC 1 (drugs rel) (C)
    - handling stolen goods (drugs rel) 1 (R)
    - violent attack (drugs rel) 4 (3R, 1C)
    - forging cheques (drugs rel) 1 (R)
    - DSS fraud 2 (both C)
    - possessing drugs 1 (C)
    - supplying drugs 3 (all C)
    - murder 3 (all C)
    - bank robbery (drugs rel) 1 (C)
    - not disclosed 1 (?)
    - kidnapping 1 (R)

    The 3 Asian women's offences were as follows:
    - false accounting 2 (both C)
    - robbery (jewellery) 1 (C).

12. The official appointed to deal with the final stage of any prisoner's grievance. The post was established in 1994.

13. *Daily Telegraph*, 23 January 1997.

14. *Inspection of Facilities for Mothers and Babies in Prison: Third Multi-Disciplinary Inspection by the Department of Health*, November 1996.

15. Following a number of absconds from open prisons, the Home Office decided in 1991 that foreign national prisoners should no longer be sent to open conditions.

16. For further details see *Interpreters and the Legal Process*, Joan Colin and Ruth Morris, Waterside Press, 1996.

17. Free flow: movement, usually lightly escorted, of prisoners from one part of the prison to another.

18. *Women in Prison: A Review*: 6.28.

19. See Note 18, above: 7.12.

20. Prisoners told me that in Holloway foreign national women may use higher denomination phone cards in special phones situated on every landing.

21. See Note 18, above: 5.47.

22. See Note 10, above: p.4.

23. Burnett and Farrell (see note 6, above) found that black-Caribbean prisoners (both male and female) were twice as likely as white inmates to complain about the prison shop (canteen). 44% of black Caribbean prisoners complained about the canteen, compared with 21% of white prisoners).

24. The Woodcock Report looked at escapes from HMP Whitemoor in 1994. The Learmont Report investigated an escape by three prisoners from HMP Parkhurst and also looked at Woodcock's recommendations.

25. 'Why Our Jails Have No Black Governors', Heather Mills, *Observer*, 10 August 1997.

26. Its aims are summarised by Burnett and Farrell (see note 6, above) as follows:
    (i) All prisoners, irrespective of race, colour or religion, are to be treated impartially, and must not be addressed with insulting or derogatory language.
    (ii) All must be given equal access to jobs, facilities and activities.
    (iii) Provision must be made, where feasible, for members of minority religious groups to practise their faith.
    (iv) All members of staff have a responsibility to ensure the race relations policy is carried out.
    (v) The policy applies to staff as well as prisoners.
    (vi) Prison governors must notify area managers of any racial incidents in the prison. (This is defined in the Prison Service *Race Relations Manual* as 'an incident where any of the parties involved, or dealing with an incident, alleges that a racial motivation is present or is perceived'.

27. The Penal Affairs Consortium paper *Race and Criminal Justice*, September 1996, summarises the manual's main points and the main points of the monitoring and training policies.

28. In the Burnett and Farrell survey (see note 6, above) very few prisoners — only three per cent — said they had involved the RRLO in dealing with racial incidents. Of those few prisoners who had made a complaint, eight out of ten were dissatisfied with the outcome. Most said they would not bother to make a complaint because they believed nothing would be gained by complaining. It would be interesting to know whether more complaints have been upheld since the appointment of the RRLOs. An obituarist of Sir John May, the former Lord Justice of Appeal who died in January 1997, pointed out his historic ruling in the Court of Appeal in 1988 when he raised the damages awarded to a black prisoner following a case of racial discrimination. The man had complained that he had been refused a job in the prison kitchen on account of his colour, *The Times*, 21 January 1997.

29. This was published in the union journal, *Gate Lodge*, October 1996, as follows: (i) The Prison Officers' Association is committed absolutely to a policy of racial equality and opposes any display of racial prejudice. (ii) The Association will work positively to protect all its members from racist or discriminatory behaviour, either by word or conduct. (iii) The Prison Officers' Association is committed absolutely to the law and will not tolerate discriminatory behaviour by or against its membership. (iv) Branch officials must deal promptly with complaints made by any member regarding any racial incident. (v) The Association insists that race relations training be made more available by the Prison Department to all members in line with its own policy.

30. Senior officer.

CHAPTER ELEVEN

In Sickness and in Health?

The shackling of prisoners in hospital turned the media spotlight on the plight of those unfortunate enough to fall ill or give birth to a child while in prison. The practice of shackling women in labour was relaxed in 1996 after a woman gave birth in chains. But pregnant women taken from Holloway to the Whittington hospital, North London, for ante-natal checks such as scans still have to endure the embarrassment of sitting handcuffed to an officer among local women in the waiting room.

In another of the prisons I visited, there was conflict between a long-serving woman officer and her female superior on the subject of shackling. The officer refused point-blank to put handcuffs on pregnant women on their way to hospital for ante-natal appointments or delivery of the baby. The senior officer regarded the practice of shackling as vital to avoid escapes: 'We have to use restraints in my view because pregnant women will escape. These women will do anything. They've been known to pour water on the sheets, then prick the inside of the mouth to produce a little blood, then they will say their waters have broken, so they can get out to the hospital and yes, they will escape.'

It is true that pregnant prisoners have escaped: on the very day the chief inspector of prisons published his review of women's prisons recommending the ending of handcuffing in hospitals[1] the newspapers also reported the escape from a maternity hospital of a remand prisoner transferred there from Brockhill prison for the birth of her baby. Rosemary Doherty, 20, who was charged with robbery, was not guarded by police or prison officers.

Although a woman about to give birth is unlikely to pose much of a threat to public safety, such escapes are highly embarrassing to the Prison Service. So the practice of chaining sick prisoners continues. Some of the most shocking cases have been those of remand prisoners, innocent until proven otherwise: in December 1996 Patricia Rayson, a remand prisoner at Holloway, was manacled to prison officers while being treated for breast cancer. A Prison Service spokesperson said: 'Our overriding responsibility is security and maintaining public confidence'.[2]

The media has since remained silent on the subject of shackling. But in October 1997 I interviewed a woman in her fifties, finally bailed after spending a year in prison on remand for fraud involving a sum of money amounting to hundreds rather than thousands of pounds. Before her arrest she had been prescribed hormone replacement therapy by her own doctor, and had found it successful to treat menopausal problems. But the prison doctor decided the medication should be changed to a higher oestrogen product. The result was that in the heat of August 1997 the woman collapsed at work in the kitchens and had to be rushed to a nearby hospital. A friend telephoned the prison and was told she was terminally ill. It transpired that she had developed blood clots in three parts of her body: behind the eye, behind the knee, and in the lung. She spent 18 days in hospital, and for the first 48 hours was continually shackled to an officer, with another officer in attendance. When they wished to leave the room for a break, she was shackled to the bed. Her chains were removed only when a female officer took the trouble to visit her and declared the chaining unnecessary. The woman survived but will have to take anti-coagulant medication for the rest of her life.

The distress caused by such inhumane treatment cannot, to say the least, have improved sick prisoners' chances of recovery. These high profile cases are often quite properly targeted by the press, but little is reported about day-to-day health problems in prisons. This chapter is about the distress of imprisonment and its effect on the physical and mental health of imprisoned women.

Another woman I interviewed showed me a letter she had just had published in the prison newspaper *Inside Time*. She wrote that she had been in prison for twelve months:

> . . . and in all this time I have come across nothing that saddens or disturbs me more than witnessing the great degree of emotional suffering that women prisoners, especially those with young children, have to endure. As a result of this, I have had to watch many previously normal and reasonable women suffer behavioural problems which include hurting themselves—tragically sometimes fatally—or hurting other women or prison staff. They also seem to suffer from various stress-related illnesses. Does nobody really care about this tragic problem—apart from the medical staff who seem forced to prescribe endless anti-depressants, tranquillisers and sleeping tablets?

The first thing you notice when you go on to the wings of women's prisons is how unhealthy most of the women look. The unnatural pallor of their skin and their dark-rimmed eyes seem like evidence of poor diet, lack of fresh air and lack of exercise. (Holloway women reported spending just three-quarters of an hour outside daily, in the early morning, so they had little access to sunshine). Many are overweight— also the result, they say, of stodgy food and sedentary occupations. The minority of prisoners who are middle-aged or older find prison life particularly wretched. There are those like the woman described above who have been prescribed HRT for menopausal problems. They report missing their medication for several days—with potentially damaging side-effects—because nurses have made mistakes. Others suffer from bladder problems and find it humiliating to have to wash underwear in front of other much younger women in dormitories, where the noise and lack of privacy can prevent them sleeping and damage their health still further.

While people are in prison, their health care is the responsibility not of the National Health Service but of the Health Care Service for Prisoners. Prisoners' NHS medical records do not automatically follow them into prison, unless a prison doctor requests that they be sent.

HM Inspectorate of Prisons voiced its concern about the standards of provision of health care for prisoners in a discussion paper, *Patient or Prisoner?* published in 1996.[3] The inspectors asserted that in prisons 'the overall service provided does not match up to National Health Standards, or satisfy the provisions of the Patients' Charter, and concluded that 'the National Health Service should assume responsibility for the delivery of all health care, by the introduction of a purchaser/provider relationship that acknowledges the full and peculiar needs of the Prison Service.' The chief inspector asked the blunt and obvious question: 'NHS standards apply before and after custodial sentences, so why not during?'

Prison reform groups welcomed the Inspectorate paper. The charity Women in Prison has for years called for the Health Care Service for Prisoners to be dismantled, for all prison health centres to be contracted out to the NHS and for all imprisoned women to have access to NHS services (including the use of community psychiatric nurses) just like any other member of the community. INQUEST, the organization which monitors deaths in custody, agreed with the Inspectorate's recommendations, saying that the prison health care service was 'too closely linked with punitive aspects of the regime'.[4]

When the Inspectorate paper was published, the then acting director of prison health care, Dr Mike Longfield, responded, saying he welcomed the opening of the discussion, but the Prison Service already contracted a range of health care provision from the NHS as well as from independent and private providers. He emphasised however that recent increases in the numbers of prisoners could place severe burdens on the NHS, and there were many other difficulties in NHS provision of a service that would have to meet the statutory requirements of the Prisons Act 1952.[5]

Only one reference to the specific needs of women prisoners was made in that Inspectorate paper: 'The health care needs of women, especially those who are pregnant, are not adequately catered for in prison.' However, in their major thematic report on women's prisons published the following year[1] the inspectors devoted a whole chapter to health care, emphasising throughout the different health needs of women prisoners, and recommending the appointment of a head of women's health.

The Inspectors recognise that the treatment of the health problems of women prisoners, especially on those with children, will have a wide-ranging impact far beyond the prison walls. A few months before the publication of the Inspectorate's first document, Yvonne Wilmott, director of nursing at HM Prison Service Directorate of Health Care, had written:[6]

> Women in prison require health care services tailored to their needs. There is great scope for health promotion and illness prevention as well as care and treatment. The impact of successful intervention can go much further than the woman herself into her family and society.

The Prison Service's approach to women prisoners' health was graphically illustrated at a conference in October 1997[7] when Carole Rigby, a project worker with WISH [Women in Secure Hospitals], showed delegates a chart supplied to Holloway to be used in medical officers' reports on new prisoners. It showed a back and a front view of a *male* body! There is now a groundswell of professional opinion calling for a clearly differentiated policy for the health care of imprisoned women, based on consultation with the women themselves.

Yvonne Wilmott endorses these views: 'Research has demonstrated a mismatch between how women perceive their needs and how prisons perceive and respond to them.' There is, she says, a 'general failure to recognize women's needs in prison. Although in some respects, women and men in prison face similar health problems, for example substance abuse, mental illness and communicable diseases, there is a significant difference in the nature of the problems in the gender groups. Women are likely to have additional and different needs with respect not only to maternity care and gynaecological health but also psychological health and a greater incidence of past or recent abuse whether physical, emotional or sexual in nature'. Wilmott also acknowledges imprisoned women's 'histories of severe social and relationship issues' and their lack of 'choice or control over significant events in their lives.'[6]

The inspectors' initial paper[3] did single out for urgent attention the treatment of prisoners suffering from mental health problems: 'There is particularly urgent need for increased provision for the care of those with mental health problems, who make up a larger proportion of the prison population than they would of any other group in the community'. The inspectors recognised that 'prison can exacerbate mental health problems, which has a long term impact on the individual concerned and the community into which he or she may be released.' Sir David Ramsbotham has since said he is particularly concerned about prisoners with very serious personality disorders who are diverted from prisons to special hospitals like Rampton and Broadmoor—only to be said to be untreatable and returned to prison: 'If they're not treatable in a special hospital, then they're certainly not treatable in prison'.[8]

Women in Prison has long demanded the decategorisation of prisons and police cells as places where mentally disordered women can be held, on the grounds that the Mental Health Act 1983 (section 136) requires that such people be held in a place of safety for assessment. As WIP's Director, Chris Tchaikovsky puts it: 'It should not be possible to categorise anybody as criminally insane: the term is an oxymoron.'

The Penal Affairs Consortium, in its January 1998 paper *An Unsuitable Place for Treatment,*[9] says that 'prison is the worst possible place for someone with a mental disorder'. It quotes a 1992 Home Office research study[10] which looked at a group of 952 remand prisoners with psychiatric problems. Of the group, 254 were Holloway women, and 85 per cent of these were referred by prison doctors to outside psychiatrists. The report's authors concluded:

As a method of obtaining psychiatric help for mentally disordered offenders, the custodial remand has nothing to commend it: it is inhumane, expensive and ineffective. It exposes mentally disordered people to conditions and regimes which are cruelly harsh and inappropriate. It brings into prison thousands of defendants who do not need to be there and for whom penal disposals are never contemplated.

These views are backed by Home Office guidance: Circular 66/90[11] says that 'it is government policy that, wherever possible, mentally disordered persons should receive care and treatment from the health and social services'. Further guidelines issued in 1995[12] say mentally disordered people should be cared for or treated 'as far as possible, in the community rather than institutional settings.' I spoke to women with severe mental problems who felt they were not getting the treatment they needed. Of the twelve women in the sample who said they had been diagnosed as suffering from some form of mental illness, (nine per cent of the 130 who gave me this information), three-quarters (nine) had been sexually abused in childhood. One-third of them (four) were arsonists, a crime commonly linked with sexual abuse; five had been convicted of murder or manslaughter; one of affray, one of criminal damage and one of a sexual offence. Nine mutilated themselves—though there were many other self-harming women in the sample who had never been diagnosed as mentally ill and certainly did not regard themselves as ill in that way. They frequently described self-harm as a coping mechanism. The general perception among staff I interviewed was that more and more mentally ill women were ending up in prison. Officers repeatedly told me of women who were 'poor souls' who 'should not be in prison at all'—it 'wasn't the right place for them' and they 'are only here because the mental hospitals are all closing down'. 'Care in the community is an underfunded nonsense', said one officer, 'and we're the only places that'll take these women in'. As another put it, 'we are a dumping ground for society's inadequates'.

The mental health of imprisoned women has been a cause of concern in ways that have never applied to male prisoners. Nineteenth century reformers[13] feared for the mental state of women kept in solitary confinement. Since the end of the nineteenth century, the history of women's incarceration has been wracked by the ongoing debate about whether criminal women are bad or mad, with the pendulum of penal reform swinging from one opinion to the other over the centuries. The 'bad' lobby regarded criminal women much more harshly than criminal men, because they were felt to have fallen so far from the natural feminine state of grace that they were virtually beyond reform. The 'mad' lobby, coinciding with the growth of the then new medical science of psychiatry, was of the view that women who committed criminal offences could be excused for falling from that state of grace because their minds were deranged.

Early twentieth-century jail administrators complained of the difficulties of dealing with 'feeble-minded' women who were 'not amenable to prison discipline'. Going round the women's prisons I frequently heard the word 'inadequates' used as a modern equivalent to describe people who are not insane but who 'lack coping skills'. In 1907, Aylesbury Convict Prison for Women was the first British jail to segregate such women in a separate wing called 'D Hall', the first antecedent of units like Holloway's notorious C1, the wing for mentally disturbed prisoners.

Feminist criminologists have always objected strongly to this 'medicalisation of deviance' on the grounds that it has been applied to women far more widely than to men. They have equally challenged the practice of 'defining women criminals by their biology'—in other words, using 'hormonal' factors like pre-menstrual tension, postnatal depression and menopause as explanations for offending which should rightly be explained by social and often economic factors.

Feminist objections also focus on dubious 'cures' for women's deviance: to gain their parole, imprisoned women have been expected to conform to stereotypes of feminine passivity and docility prescribed by a patriarchal society. Those unable or unwilling to do so are given the highly suspect assistance of tranquillizing medication, not always with their own consent. Most feared are the special hospitals—Ashworth, Broadmoor and Rampton—where women (if they are thought to be 'treatable' and remain there) are no longer prisoners subject to a fixed sentence imposed by the courts, but become patients subject to mental health legislation. There have been allegations that until they conform to prescribed standards of womanhood these women will never be released.

The 'medicalisation' theory reached its apotheosis in the rebuilding of Holloway prison over the 15 year period from 1970 to 1985, as evoked by Paul Rock in *Reconstructing a Women's Prison*.[14] Professor Rock sums up the prevailing attitude of the late 1960s and early 1970s in a quote from an official letter written in 1972: 'There is a growing recognition that *most women in custody* need some form of medical, psychiatric or other remedial treatment.'[my italics]

Now at the end of the twentieth century, the Prison Service at least acknowledges the concerns of feminist criminologists, recognising that there are usually social, economic, educational and relational causes implicated in the illnesses of imprisoned women. As Yvonne Wilmott wrote:[6] 'Surveys and research have consistently shown high levels of psychopathology in the female prison population. This is compounded by histories of significant social and educational deprivation. A presentation in custody that appears clinical may have its roots in relationship issues. If the latter are not identified then symptomatic clinical intervention alone is unlikely to be totally successful.'

In his 1997 review[1] the chief inspector points out that without appropriate intervention, women 'will return to the high risk behaviour and health-adverse situations from which they came'. Like women in any community, imprisoned women may at some point need treatment and advice for any number of conditions relating to their physical and mental health. Because of the stress/distress of their situation and, in many but not all cases, of their background, they may be in greater need of medical help and advice than members of the community outside prison. Home Office statistics show that the incidence of women prisoners reporting sick each day is twice the rate of men prisoners, one tenth of whom report sick. An unpublished PhD thesis[15] compared the health problems of imprisoned women with those of women covered by an ordinary general practice and found that the women prisoners were at a disadvantage, especially considering that 71 per cent of the sample were aged 35 or younger.

How far is the Health Care Service for Prisoners able, as it now operates, to respond to the problems which make life so difficult for imprisoned women? The Inspectorate's review[16] recommends that part of the reception process should be medical screening by specially trained doctors, preferably female. As earlier chapters have shown, women coming into prison are often in shock and may be incapable of giving adequate medical information, especially as the reception period is so rushed. There is often an appalling lack of information coming into prison about women from GPs or other sources. Far from a careful assessment of their healthcare needs, women reported cursory checks, and there were some instances of real neglect. Probation officers in one prison told me of their concern about a young deaf woman with little speech, who had that day been strip-searched on reception without anyone being able to explain to her what was going on. When she became hysterical she was put on her own in a cell 'to calm down'. The next day she managed to get on to the roof of the prison aviary and stage a protest and it was only after this pathetic and desperate act that another prisoner was brought along who was able to sign to her. If such an obvious special need was neglected, what hope is there for other women with less visible problems?

In terms of *physical* health care, prison medical staff should at least listen to the women and consider what they say they need to improve their physical wellbeing. There may be a need for measures to alleviate the symptoms of malnutrition, poor dental care, drug misuse, physical and sexual abuse and so on. Much of this may not be 'treatment' in the medical sense of the word, but provision, for instance, of decent food and vitamin and mineral supplements if necessary.

In terms of *mental* welfare it is equally important to listen to what the women have to say. Dr Norman Hindson, senior medical officer of the Health Care Advisory Office at Prison Service Headquarters, says:

There is diagnostic confusion: women who are "difficult" are getting a mental illness diagnosis when they are not mentally ill — though there may be psychological damage. These are women in distress, and we have to get to the point of listening to the women, hearing about their lifestyles, about serial experiences when they had never had a choice. Officers need to know the poverty of these women's circumstances — the lack of employment, or if they were employed, it was often in the sex industry. They have no reliable educational background and at school nobody ever listened to them. Listening is not just about being there. You need a whole different dynamic: if an officer can't empathise, he or she will never engage with the prisoner. I remember once saying to a woman: "You will be here with us for about

247

nine months and we would like to offer you confidential sessions, with psychologists and so on, so we can go through certain things with you." This woman listened then she said, not rudely or anything, "That's fine, Dr Hindson, but say we do these sessions: if you *listened* to me, would you be able to *hear* what I'm saying to you?" Apart from listening and empathising, we should be giving women some choice in closed institutions.

The Inspectorate's discussion paper *Patient or Prisoner*[3] noted the lack of medical qualifications in prison health care staff. In its survey of 126 prisons, it found that 71 per cent of health care officers and health care governors were without nursing registration. The Inspectors recommended that 'Nurses should have a set of recognised qualifications with a single recognised uniform'.

The Inspectors also noted that 'Most doctors are not psychiatrically qualified, and have received no recognised training in assessment and treatment of mentally disordered offenders or addicts. Nursing staff require far more expertise in the handling of the mentally ill, depressed and suicidal patient'.

Concern about the quality of in-house prison doctors is not new. As early as 1922 Mary Gordon,[17] the first woman to hold the post of Inspector of Prisons, expressed her concern about the ethics of doctors working for the Prison Service. Outside prison, she said, '. . . the usual doctor-patient relationship is based on mutual respect and the absolute freedom of the patient to begin and end the consultation.' But in prison, the doctor was part of a punitive official regime and the prisoner had no right to confidentiality and secrecy. Doctors, she felt, colluded with the prison regime, deciding if women were fit to work or to be sent into solitary confinement. A much criticized function of prison doctors at that time was the force-feeding of suffragettes, (who were themselves early victims of the 'medicalisation of deviance', regarded by many contemporary commentators as mentally deranged for behaving in a manner that betrayed their class and sex).

Mary Gordon's successors have also complained of the lack of confidentiality. The inspectors' Annual Report[18] in 1993-94 complained of rushed surgeries conducted without privacy because health care workers were often present.

Working as a doctor or nurse in a prison health care centre is very different from working in the community and the health care staff I interviewed frequently reported great difficulty in adjusting from civilian life. They found themselves forced to collude with practices long outdated in the community. They reported being confused by having to reconcile conflicting policies—such as the war on illegal drugs and the heavy prescription of psychotropic drugs (discussed later in this chapter). They expressed distaste at (and sometimes had refused to participate in) their role in Mandatory Drugs Testing (MDT) and intrusive mouth searches to make sure women were not hoarding medication. Health care officers trained initially as disciplinary officers sometimes expressed irritation at the 'naivety' of nursing staff about security matters. One said 'I have to train them that inmates are prisoners first and patients second and that keys do matter'. Healthcare staff working in Scottish prisons say this problem does not arise as nursing staff have no disciplinary function there.

Prison work requires training in awareness of the special issues involved, but an education coordinator told me how she frequently had to deal with the effects of insensitivity:

> A nurse would take a woman out of a class, tell her she had tested HIV positive, then send her back to class where—not surprisingly—she would start smashing things up. Or they'd send her to the hospital wing where she might be left alone and everyone else was also depressed. Yes, counselling was available but nobody was organized enough to be able to set it up in advance so it would be there *before* they told woman she was HIV positive. All it would take would be a bit of coordination and planning and thinking ahead to get the counselling in place.

A nurse in an open prison said: When I first came into the Prison Service I thought prisoners were horrible people—I didn't really know what to feel about them. I felt people should be punished. I was a single mother and I needed the job. But now I have changed completely. I think the whole concept of women in prison should be dealt with differently.' Another nurse said 'I used to be hospital-based and I find it hard that women can't phone their relatives immediately if they are ill. You have to lock up all the drugs behind bars and dole them out from behind a counter. That means you lose intimacy with the client who is after all a person. Health care standards in prison are designed for males. I feel prison doctors should be community GPs right across the board—because they are in touch.' Indeed, one of the greatest problems for prison-based nurses is the blurring of the boundaries between care and control.

The Inspectorate[3] commented on the isolation of prison health care staff: 'The constant flow of new ideas, training and development within the National Health Service passes them by.' They recommended opportunities for professional development: 'This can only be achieved if medical and nursing staff in prisons belong to the mainstream providers of health care.'

Many of the women prisoners in my sample spoke of the need for female doctors, gynaecologists and nurses in women's prisons, where so many prisoners have been victims of past sexual abuse. Several women said they would prefer to suffer in silence than go to a male doctor whom they would have to see on their own. A life-sentenced prisoner who suffered terrible abuse as a child said 'In here there's no way of seeing a female doctor. I did ask the doctor and he said "Any woman doctor would be intimidated: they'd be petrified to come in here and see you lot, you'd give them too much grief!" I went and complained to the governor and he said "We've been with that general practice for years"'. Another lifer remembered that until a few years ago the doctor visiting her prison was a male Army doctor who turned up to conduct internal examinations on the women wearing his military uniform.

In one prison, the women told me, 'We never go to the doctor here if we can help it. He runs what he calls his "special clinic" for smears and so on and all the girls say "Don't go to him—he touches you up!" Many other women expressed similar suspicion and fear of male doctors, whom they frequently saw without a nurse or female member of staff being present. Nurses in hospital wings shared the prisoners' concerns: 'We should have a woman doctor but we can't get them because female doctors are not interested in prison work.'

The Inspectors' paper[3] acknowledged the reasons for the unpopularity of prison work: 'Because doctors working in prisons belong to an independent medical service they are isolated from their peers in the National Health Service and suffer comparatively low status'.

According to a recently retired education coordinator this is a common attitude in the medical profession:

> The prison where I worked had surgery every morning with a male doctor —and many of those women had been abused by men. The health care in our prison was diabolical. The medical officers were terrible. It is not exactly a career booster to work in a prison so you can imagine the kind of doctors who do. Even my own GP, whom I consider quite a reasonable bloke, said to me "You could get a good job in any private school round here. Why do you work with those awful women?"

Most of the evidence I collected during my research in women's prisons pointed to a poorer quality of service than that provided in the National Health Service. A frequent problem was the lack of consistency between prisons: women with specific medical conditions said they were unable to continue with the medication they were on when they entered prison. One woman said she was diabetic and was not getting her implants. I interviewed women whose vital medication for potentially life-threatening conditions had been removed on entry into prison, with weeks of delay before they could be resumed. The same thing happened again when they were transferred to another prison. Staff at a prison which later closed told me: 'When the women came into prison all their medicines and drugs were taken away from them. One woman came in with a supply of Tamoxifen[19] which she had been prescribed for breast cancer. But it was taken away and it took her four weeks to get any more. Don't know what happened to it—probably given to somebody else.' The former senior medical officer of a different women's prison agreed:

> One of the real problems of the prison healthcare system is its lack of consistency: if you were a diabetic patient you would be given insulin if you lived in London—then if you went a few miles up the M4 to stay with your boyfriend in Bristol you would get insulin in a hospital there. Why not have the same consistency with medication throughout the prison service? The Department of Health is trying to get drugs treatment programmes the same throughout the country—so if you have a heroin problem you'd get the same treatment at a unit in St Mary's as you would in Reading or Bristol. You can't tell individual doctors what to do, but you should have protocols so that treatments are the same whether a woman is in Durham or Holloway.

Many women's complaints concerned gynaecological problems—one area where women prisoners' needs are plainly very different from men's. In the community, all women now have access to preventive medicine: they can attend NHS well-woman clinics. The Inspectorate's 1997 review[20] recommends that such clinics should be set up in every prison. There *are* currently some examples of good practice. In one prison the GUM clinic [Genito-Urinary Medicine] in the hospital wing has a new facility for colonoscopies[21] which means that pre-cancerous cells can be detected and removed. Early sexual activity is connected with cancer and the nurses have found women in their early twenties with abnormal cells. But as one of the nurses said 'The male managers of this prison can't understand why we need a well-woman clinic. The whole prison hierarchy is male-dominated. But women do need to come and talk about gynaecological problems, about the menopause'. A Foston Hall prisoner complained of symptoms for months before being diagnosed as having cervical cancer and needing a hysterectomy.

In one prison the senior charge nurse on the hospital wing said there was always a high percentage—probably 35 per cent—of women with pelvic problems resulting from their lifestyles: 'Prostitution, abuse, not having proper care. Many have chronic pelvic inflammatory disease. Many have never had cervical smears and we pick up cervical cancer and give them laser treatment. This is lifesaving work'. Dr Sylvia Casale emphasizes[7] the importance of health education: 'We should be looking at the health of young women in prison. Since the UK has the highest number of pregnant teenagers under 16 in the whole of Europe—12,500 in 1995—surely prison should be an opportunity to educate them?' The Inspectors' review[22] lamented that not all women's prisons conduct cervical cytology despite the number of women at high risk. They set a deadline of July 1998 for the implementation of early detection programmes for breast and cervical cancers.

This is indeed good and admirable theory, but what happens in practice? Vicky (see *Chapters 5* and *6*) is 17 and in an open prison:

> See that nurse over there? I went to her for a smear. I've had two kids, one when I was nearly 14, the other when I was nearly 15, and my doctor told me that because of that I've got to have a smear every year because of the risk of cervical cancer. I went to that nurse for a smear but she told me there was no need because it was 'all in the mind'. They don't look after you properly here.

Alison (see *Chapter 2*) is nearly three times Vicky's age:

> I've got fibroids and the doctor here gave me some stuff for it but it did nothing and I'd stood outside the health centre queuing for it for hours. I have terrible period pains and bleeding which wakes me up in the night. If you call the officers and it's a male officer it's embarrassing for me to tell him I've got period pains. So usually I just stick it out. Luckily I'll be out in a couple of months and I've got an appointment to see a gynaecologist then.

Other areas of health that depend upon preventive treatment are often neglected. For instance women commonly reported problems with access to dentists, an issue identified by Inspectorate reports[23] over the years. Holloway women noticed that the dentist did not change his surgical gloves between patients. A Durham prisoner said that H wing women delay visits to the dental surgery because it is situated in the main prison, and they fear the verbal abuse they get from male prisoners as they queue for treatment. In any case, she said, there are no preventive six-monthly checks like those common in the community, and women have to wait until there is an emergency. A young Risley woman said:

> I broke the bridge at the front of my mouth. There's a dentist on the men's side but the women can only go over once a week and you could wait a month for an appointment. I waited and waited. I had no teeth in the front

of my mouth and I felt terrible. I kept holding my hand over my mouth all the time. My family would have paid for me to go to my own dentist who's only in the next town but the prison wouldn't let me go. The prison dentist wanted me to have false teeth but there's no way — I'm only 32. In the end I got a temporary bridge and I'm praying it'll last till I get out.

Other women complained of waiting up to a year to see chiropodists and opticians. In Durham the optician, like the dentist, sees women in the main men's prison.

Women with serious period pains complained of longing just to be able to lie in a hot bath, which was rarely allowed, and of being unable to get painkillers during the night. Migraine sufferers said they especially feared an onslaught at night: in the community outside prison, migraine is three times as common in women as men, and can be triggered by three sets of factors, all of which are present in prison: the factors can be stress-related, food-related or sensory-related (such as bright light and loud noise).[24] One woman said she waited most of the night —six hours—before anyone came to give her a painkiller. As she lay awake she heard another woman crying and banging her head on her cell wall for hours, and nobody came to her either.

Health care officers told a different story: they spoke of a nurse being on 24-hour call, and in open prisons I heard that the local GP came in to run a daily morning surgery. But many women said that officers refused to take them to the health care centre at night however ill they felt, and that nurses were reluctant to come to them. Nor is access to a local GP always as easy as prisons may claim. An extreme case was reported to me by a male prison officer who happened to be on duty one night at a prison recently converted from a male establishment:

There was just me and another male officer — this was before we had the nurses. [The prison has since employed ten nurses]. It was about two o'clock in the morning and one of the prisoners was in agony. She said she had a bad period and blood was gushing out of her. The other officer and I were at a loss. I rang the local GP three times but he wouldn't come out. So I asked the girl if she could possibly be having a miscarriage. She didn't think she was pregnant but supposed she could be. When we told the doctor he said "Oh God, you'd better call an ambulance!" and then he did finally come out. By this time there was blood all over the cell. We put a 999 call out for the ambulance and we had to send a male officer to hospital with the woman. She could have died.

This chapter began with women being shackled while giving birth. From 1990 to 1995 there were 269 babies born to women who were in prison, and during the same period there were an estimated 2,205 pregnant women in prison.[25] The Inspectorate discussion paper[3] stated its concern for the health care of pregnant women, a concern voiced in the same year by a Department of Health team inspecting mother and baby units.[26] The Health inspectors expressed their alarm at Holloway's D0 [D zero] wing where pregnant women had to put up with 'cockroaches, broken windows, inappropriate mattresses and floors which broken plumbing had made slippery and a safety hazard'. They condemned Holloway's 'old fashioned medical approach to pregnancy', though they accepted that pregnant women chose to stay on D0 [D zero] wing as a refuge from the drug-induced violence in the rest of the prison.

The same team recommended that 'services for pregnant women should be purchased from the National Health Service'. In most prisons pregnant women do now have access to a community midwife who comes into the prison for checkups at the usual regular intervals and a bed is booked for the birth in a hospital close to the prison. The Inspectorate review[27] said there was an urgent need for a comprehensive NHS maternity service for pregnant women. It praised the care of pregnant women at HMP Styal, where since February 1996 a team of local community midwives has been linked to the prison to provide the total ante-natal, delivery and post-natal care of pregnant prisoners. The midwives run a 24 hour telephone hotline for the women and 85 per cent of women are delivered in the local hospital by a midwife known to them. The midwives are trained in child protection and in addressing the problems facing women on release as they return to deprived inner-city areas. Styal women said their hospital check-up visits had been handled sensitively and they were never embarrassed by having to wear handcuffs in the hospital. The MBU manager said it took eleven months to set up protocols to reconcile the very different cultures of prison and hospital.[7] In May 1997 the Howard League carried out its own survey of the care of pregnant prisoners. It concluded that there was urgent need for reform and indeed demanded an end to the imprisoning of pregnant women.

Although between ten and twelve per cent of pregnancies reach full term while the mothers are in prison, babies are rarely actually born in prison. According to official statistics only three have been born (in Styal and Holloway) since 1983 and though prison hospitals do have emergency delivery equipment, nurses told me they do their best to avoid having to use it. One nurse described a touching conspiracy between prison and hospital nurses:

> We have had babies born here before the ambulance arrived, but we would not cut the cord and would get the mother and baby to the hospital. Then

they cut the cord and it could then be said that the child was born in the hospital. It's not good for a baby to have "prison" written down as the place of birth on the birth certificate.

Women return to the prison within 24 hours and arrangements will have been made either for them to go with the baby to a prison mother and baby unit or to 'hand out' the child to relatives or social services (see *Chapter 3*).

Many women wish to continue with contraception while they are in prison and most prisons arrange for them to remain on the same birth control pill, though again, provision is variable. In one closed prison the nurses said they had to prescribe the pill surreptitiously through local community midwives because the senior medical officer disapproved: 'Dr X won't give the pill because he's a Muslim'. Women are commonly prescribed the three monthly contraceptive injection of Depo-Provera.[28] It is also available to women outside, though it is usually only used in the community for women thought incapable of remembering to take contraceptive pills regularly. There are also said to be problems of weight gain, initial breakthrough bleeding, swollen ankles and breast tenderness.

Not all pregnant women want their babies, and they should plainly be offered the same opportunities for a termination available to any woman in the community. However, a worrying trend seemed to be emerging, according to staff I interviewed at one closed prison. A senior female officer was discussing with the prison probation officer her concern about a very young Irish traveller woman who had come into the prison the previous weekend and was seen by a Roman Catholic nun. She was pregnant and seemed quite happy to have the child:

> Then Sister X [the nun] came in on Monday, very upset, and told me the girl had had a termination. Sister found her crying in her room all on her own. She'd had no counselling before or after the termination. Now this girl may not have wanted the baby, but if she only came in on Saturday and was sent straight off to the clinic, she'd had no time to decide properly.

Later the officer expanded on her concerns:

> I've had my suspicions that this is happening. The girls come in, all shocked, and at the Reception Board the male officers will say to them, "You won't get to an open prison as long as you're pregnant". The pregnant girls are offered this incentive of open prison, they are too shocked to refuse, then the next day they find they've been booked into a local hospital and they've had the termination before they know it. In this prison we've got a load of men channelling young vulnerable women towards hurried terminations. We should not be using expediency as an argument, just to

255

get girls out of here into open prisons where there's more room. In fact, if the girl has only found out she's pregnant since coming into prison, there's always the possibility I could get her out on bail by pleading "change of circumstances". I did this with one woman and she went back to the community and decided not to have the termination after all.

The probation officer later told me she shared the officer's suspicions:

They get channelled very strongly towards termination—that is certainly the rumour we've heard. Termination is looked on as a routine op. I think termination should be available as it is on the outside, with plenty of counselling before and after. I have seen women months and even years after abortions and they are still suffering.

If there is any truth in these allegations it would of course be an appalling breach of these women's human right to choose, while in a calm frame of mind, whether or not to have their babies—and it would be yet another illustration of what happens when expediency takes precedence over humanity in a closed institution set apart from the mainstream of community health care.

It is appropriate in a chapter on health care to consider the subject of nutrition,[29] and indeed the Inspectorate review includes food in the heading of its healthcare chapter.[30] Jokes about 'porridge' are prison stalwarts, but there are more serious issues. A study of 150 young male prisoners at Aylesbury young offenders' institution found that aggression is linked to poor nutrition. There was a dramatic decline in disciplinary incidents among those given essential nutrients.[31]

Food in women's prisons is the subject of constant complaint, especially in shared-site establishments where all the food is prepared in kitchens in the main male prison and taken in heated trolleys to the women's side, where it may have to stand for some time, becoming cold and losing its nutritional value. The women also fear contamination by male prisoners: one of the most powerful prison rumours is that food has been spat in or urinated on. Whether this is myth or truth, the quality of the food is certainly variable. One woman in a shared-site prison said:

They bring the food over in the trolleys in them big yellow thermos boxes but it gets cold. All the food is semi-cold unless you can persuade them to reheat it in the microwaves. But then it isn't always hot right through and that's dangerous. So we don't eat it. We just live on cheese butties.

HM Inspectorate particularly criticised food at Risley and Winchester where the majority of prisoners are male. Women's dietary needs are very different from men's. The work they are offered is far more likely to be sedentary and there is generally less opportunity for sport or other exercise. Women are far more likely to be on some form of prescribed medication, which often produces weight gain as an unwanted side effect.They complain of being served mountains of tasteless stodge, and there are few imprisoned women who do not have a problem maintaining their correct weight, which does little for those who already have low self-esteem. It seems appropriate that with wry irony, women prisoners refer to the Prison Service's equal opportunities policy as 'pie and chips'—a typical man's diet![32] Those women with babies and small children in prison mother and baby units are at a disadvantage too because there is no inbuilt budget for children's food. Pregnant women and breastfeeding mothers are given no special diet.

In one open prison the male civilian kitchen staff were uncompromisingly honest about the quality of the raw materials they bought in, revealing an astonishing disregard for the prisoners: 'The vegetables come from the prison farms and gardens and let's say they don't exactly go in for the same sort of quality control you get in supermarkets! As for the frozen goods we tend to get supermarket ends of lines—goods they are trying to move on when they get in new labels. But then these women would normally be eating junk food anyway. If you ask them what they eat at home, most of them say burgers, chips, pasties and pies. They've got a takeaway mentality. In any case, what can they expect—I only get £1.38 a day for each prisoner to supply food for three meals. How do we do it?' He gave a sideways wink at his fellow-worker: 'We get very good prices, don't we?' A woman in this prison had begun her sentence working in the kitchens:

> The prison has a terrible attitude to food. They buy in meat that's off and the kitchen girls who see it before it's cooked try to warn the other women not to eat it. But then the next day they'll serve it up again in pies and curries, so it's better to be a veggie. Even that's dodgy: they've got a bucket they use for washing the floor and I've seen them wash the cabbage leaves in it. Even if they get in good vegetables they reduce them to a pulp so there's no nutrition left in them. When the kitchen men shout "Seconds!" and all the young girls rush up for more, they delight in telling them to sit down and wait till last.

Women in Prison has repeatedly demanded the lifting of Crown immunity from prison establishments. Although environmental health officers can inspect prisons, they apparently have no power to prosecute the Prison Service as they might a hotel, because of this immunity. For instance, Islington Health Authority had no power to make Holloway deal with the cockroaches and filth which the prisons inspectors found there in 1995. In-cell sanitation to replace 'slopping-out' was welcomed as a great breakthrough, but as a WIP spokeswoman said: 'It means that women often have to eat in their cells next to a lavatory: at home you wouldn't be allowed to install a toilet in a room where you eat.'

Women with special dietary needs were treated insensitively in that same open prison by the male kitchen workers: 'We get some anorexics in here', said one of the men. 'They have to eat their food in front of the officers and if they start missing food we have to report them. The ones on special diets, we put their prison number by their meal and call out the number and they come and get the food.'

Although vegetarian and vegan menus are supposed to be on offer, they are rarely balanced. Special menus are in any case ludicrously inflexible. Women in different prisons commonly reported being banned from taking servings of rice unless they had opted to be on a special 'rice diet'. Some opt to become vegans for the extra nutrition they hope this diet may offer: in Holloway vegans receive a 'special vegan pack': a small bag of muesli, a bag of nuts, three oatmeal biscuits and a spoonful of marmite and peanut butter, unceremoniously smeared into polystyrene cups.

Vitamin and mineral preparations are routinely taken by millions of people outside prison and until recently women could have proprietary brands purchased by relatives and handed into the prison. They used to be accepted as long as the seals were unbroken. But increasingly strict anti-drugs security has brought an end to this practice. They may be on sale in the canteen but are expensive on meagre prison wages. Even medically prescribed supplements may be delayed, or at worst banned altogether: a woman in her early thirties, about to be released from an open prison, told me:

> I am anaemic and my sister brought my iron pills to the first prison for me. I have had to take them since the age of seven. I wasn't allowed the pills but the prison doctor agreed to order them for me. I had left that prison and was in this one for two months before I got the iron pills again. I haven't had a period since I came into prison. I think it must be the shock as well.

More than anything, of course, women fear serious illness. Prison medical staff claim that women have as much access to health care as they would on the outside. In one open prison I was told: 'If a woman is very ill we would ring the local doctor. All the doctors in the local practice live within half a mile of the village and will come out if something is severe.'

But in practice, as the miscarriage incident described earlier in this chapter showed, care may well fall short of this ideal. One lifer reported severe neglect when her jaw was fractured in an attack by another prisoner and she was unable to eat solid food for a month. Another woman in her mid-fifties suffered dreadful pain from a hernia while held in a closed prison, and was ill for twelve weeks, unable to eat properly and eventually vomiting after every meal so that she lost two stones in weight. She also fainted frequently. She claims that for weeks the only treatment she was given was Paracetamol. An appointment was finally arranged for her at a nearby hospital and the woman was told she would be going to the hospital in three weeks' time. A few days before the appointment she was told it had been cancelled. The reason given was funding.

The Inspectorate has in the past acknowledged that when specialist help like this is required 'the problems with charging for services had been solved by giving the hospital the home address of the prisoner so that the bill could be sent to the "home" health authority'.[33] But in this case the woman was told that the delay was caused because funding had not yet been received by the local hospital from the hospital in her home area. In any case, she was told, the appointment would have had to be cancelled for two other reasons: 'because you knew about it in advance' and because there would not be enough officers on duty that day to provide an escort. By this time the woman was in such pain that the prison took the unusual step of allowing her to sleep in another prisoner's room at night. Several weeks later she had a four-hour hernia operation. These accounts beg the question whether very sick women— who even in health have posed no threat to the community—should be in prison at all.

Women constantly complained about prison health care. May is 51 and serving two and a half years for fraud. She was jailed and sent to a closed prison while undergoing chemotherapy treatment for breast cancer. 'I had had radical lumpectomy four months before going into prison and I was told I was the first lady to be sent to prison while fighting breast cancer'. Another woman with an ulcer said she was not getting the correct medication: officers told her it would be too expensive. Her reaction was one shared by many prisoners: 'All the money goes on the tranquilliser drugs to keep the women quiet, that's why!'

Indeed, many women said they had refused to seek medical help for fear of being given tranquillisers or psychotropic drugs. One ex-prisoner decided herbal curatives were safer:

I used to pray I never got ill. Once I did and I was shitting blood. So I managed to get a garden job and picked myself some chickweed, which is a wonderful curative. At my next prison I got a bad chest. I couldn't get outside the building but from my cell window I spotted some red clover herbs at the side of the prison yard and got one of the yard girls[34] to pick it for me. It's wonderful for catarrh.

The inadequacy of the physical facilities in many prison health care centres was noted in the Inspectorate review.[35] One of the problems facing prison hospital units is that they have traditionally been treated as dumping grounds for people with a variety of problems not necessarily connected with either physical or mental illness. I found it confusing when I first interviewed prisoners to meet women located on the hospital wing who appeared to have no medical problems at all, only to discover that they were rule 43[36] women, confined in the hospital because they were at risk from other women, for instance if their offences involved abuse of children. One nurse told me:

> The hospital wing in women's prisons is usually a VPU [vulnerable prisoner unit] as well as a hospital and I think this is wrong because women who have hurt or killed children can be in great danger even here. Some women are here on an 1861: this is a form filled in to say why the woman is here and it will list the supporting disciplinary reasons. So our numbers can go very high.

As well as the rule 43 women, prison health care centres now have to cope with increasing numbers of women withdrawing from drugs, and mentally ill women with drug-induced or other psychoses. A senior nurse in one prison hospital wing described the layout:

> On the top floor we have 20 beds in a dormitory wing but there's also a separate room for some women who just can't bear being with others. The "upstairs girls", as we call them, are usually drugs withdrawals who need a bit of tender loving care. Or they can be women who killed under a lot of stress. Or they can be rule 43 women. Then downstairs we have the women with mental impairment. They're only in prison because there are no beds left in the mental hospitals and in my view they shouldn't be here. We've got a cell called CC [cellular confinement] which is a special cell for women who are very violent and might injure themselves. They're so deranged at the time it's the only place for them. This is a completely empty room except for a mattress and they wear a strip dress. Nobody wants to put people in there, though it was the norm years ago.

Hospital wings are also used in some women's prisons to provide 'time out'—a short period when women at risk can have some respite from the stress of normal location. One of the lifers I interviewed in

Nightingale, the hospital wing of HMP Bullwood Hall, was Josie O'Dwyer: 'I'm here because I need a bit of space,' she told me. 'I get too involved with the others and I need to be on my own. Sometimes I can't stand the pain of others—you take on their misery too. I opened up an artery in my foot because I hit rock bottom. At least in here the nurses do try and listen to you.' The pain ultimately proved too great for Josie to bear: a few months later she had taken her own life.

The fear of illness was universal and palpable among the women in my sample. They feared physical pain because they suspected there would be little relief, and they feared mental pain because among the most powerful and enduring myths of women's prisons is that of mad women in the hospital wing—the equivalent of the Victorian 'madwoman in the attic'. Wherever I went women whispered stories of the terrors of the 'specials'—secure psychiatric hospitals like Broadmoor: 'We had a teenager in here—she was just mucking around in a train and pulled the communication cord. When they came to arrest her she freaked and she was carted off to a special hospital—she'll probably be there for years'.

Earlier chapters have explored the mythology that has grown up around women's prisons, fed by tales of violence and predatory lesbianism by staff and inmates. But at the heart of the myth is a different terror—the fear of unknown and unseen things in the deep heart of the prison. Perhaps it is the 'Mrs Rochester/madwoman in the attic'[37] syndrome, that still strikes fear in to the heart of the outsider: the same fear does not exist about men's prisons.

The key word is 'unknown'. Prisons are places necessary to hold people who have offended seriously against the criminal law and the need for strict security is undisputed. But at the end of the twentieth century, when the old mental hospitals have been emptied and mental illness is discussed openly, why are there still these secret places, and why do we feel that unspeakable things still happen there? The former deputy governor of a women's prison feels such secrecy is quite unnecessary:

It is about the exercise of power. Abuse of power can apply equally in any institution, whether it is a prison, an old people's home or a children's home. Visitors can be shown round a prison but they won't be shown a protected room or the seg, so there is the perception that all sorts of things are going on in there. Of course I wouldn't parade a woman in a protected room in front of visitors, but there is no reason why people shouldn't be shown the room and told the reason why people sometimes have to be detained in what is virtually a padded cell for their own protection. I don't see why prisons can't show these rooms and explain why they are needed and the strict rules that govern their use.

No secret place strikes such fear into the heart as Holloway's C1, the prison's psychiatric unit. Paul Rock[14] has described how between 1970 and 1985 the old Victorian Holloway prison was gradually demolished and replaced by a new 'therapeutic' prison. During the long period of reconstruction, the pendulum of penal theory (called by one commentator the 'Yo-Yo theory') swung in the opposite direction, away from an acceptance that women criminals were mentally unstable and in need of therapy, and back to traditional views of containment and punishment. The roots of Holloway's recent problems, leading to the 1995 walk-out by HM Inspectors, seem to lie in this basic conflict. The building designed as a hospital has been condemned by staff as impossible to manage as a closed prison.

When Colin Allen (now Deputy Chief Inspector of Prisons) took over the job of Governor of the 'new' Holloway in February 1985, he inherited a system where the balance was weighted in favour of the needs of the institution. Women on normal location were locked in most of the time, and the terrible stories whispered about C1 had made it so notorious that the home secretary was being asked questions about it in Parliament. The new governor set out to shift the balance back towards the needs of prisoners, instituting a far more open regime, with women out of their cells for longer periods, and the new senior medical officer, Dr Norman Hindson, embarked on a transformation of C1.

The punitive atmosphere was replaced by a more relaxed one where the emphasis was on caring; the women were consulted about their feelings, and given access to outside agencies like the Samaritans and Mind. The methods used in C1 appeared to achieve some degree of success. In 1986 the incidents of self-harm had reached epidemic proportions: three years later the number of incidents had been cut to one seventh of the previous level.

Nearly twelve years on, the pendulum seems to be swinging back again. At a seminar in London in September 1997[88] Chris Tchaikovsky, Director of Women in Prison, deplored the fact that the most seriously mentally ill women in C1 are put at the end of the L-shaped wing 'because frankly the officers and the other women are frightened of them. So they are put down at the end and forgotten and they stay there for ages.' At another conference a few weeks later[7] Carole Rigby of WISH gave an even more graphic account. As a weekly visitor to the C1 women she was able to give delegates up-to-date information and they sat in shocked silence at her words:

C1 is a national scandal. Women with a wide variety of mental illnesses, from depression upwards, are in a 25 bed ward. Some of the women are very isolated and in acute distress. The women articulate their distress — the self-harm, the mutilation, are appalling. There is group cutting and the cutting of one woman by another for payment. Some learn the technique at Holloway. Recently a woman ripped all the sutures out of her arm in front of me. Some inflict bites and prick at their skin.

Carole, a trained nurse, was critical of the staffing of C1:

C1 is jointly staffed by nursing staff and prison officers. This does not mix. The present nursing staff feel undervalued and cheapened. They give out too much medicine and have become cynical and bored, with no illusions about their job. It's not easy to get another job if you have "C1" on your CV, and there is also the overriding prison culture. I have heard nurses say things like "She's suicidal that one — she's pathetic. I feel like showing her how to tie the bloody knot!" The prison officers show more care than the nurses. There are some outstanding officers who are committed to their work on C1 but there are very few of them. They need training to equip them to deal with disturbed women. There are male officers on C1 who have no experience of women. They can't deal with damaged women. This is a slur on our society.

Women in Prison has called for assessment centres for people with mental problems and drug problems. Indeed, this new element, the enormous influx into prisons of women addicted to drugs, discussed in *Chapter 9*, has confused the issue of health care even further. It is not surprising that women with, or withdrawing from, a drugs habit are put on psychiatric wings because drug-induced psychosis can replicate so closely the psychoses caused by mental illness.

In *Chapter 9* I quoted extensively from a 1996 report[39] by the Advisory Council on the Misuse of Drugs. The working party that produced the report recommended abandoning the use of major tranquillisers or neuroleptic medication in the treatment of drug withdrawal states. They said they had found evidence of these major tranquillisers, of the kind used mainly to treat serious mental illness, being prescribed in a *few* prisons for treatment of drug withdrawal [my italics]. The report then commented: 'We are aware that there are relatively high levels of prescribing *minor* tranquillisers in women's prisons' [my italics]. The working party concluded: 'While in many circumstances prescribing such drugs will be an appropriate response, we are concerned that a lack of monitoring of these drugs once they have been dispensed can result in their diversion to the illicit prison market. We recommend that their use should be limited in extent and duration because of the dangers of dependency'.

It would appear from my own research that this document

underestimates the extent of drug-prescribing, certainly in women's prisons. The Inspectorate's review[40] acknowledges that 'the high level of prescribing in some establishments for women is a cause of concern'.

The gross over-prescription of strong anti-psychotic drugs as a form of control was exposed in the 1994 scandal involving Ashworth high security special hospital when nurses, concerned about the level of medication prescribed, kept a record which they showed to an outside pharmacist. The levels were up to five times the recommended doses and had been prescribed for women with personality disorders rather than any form of psychosis. Side effects include blurred vision, continuous drowsiness, slow reactions, lethargy and shaking like the symptoms of Parkinson's disease: such high levels can also cause sudden death.

During the months I spent speaking to women in twelve different prisons all over the country, I heard repeatedly of high levels of medication which they had been prescribed. Those who would dismiss the women's claims as exaggerated should remember they were made independently of one another, by women whose daily lives are empty enough for them to pay great attention to detail. Many have used drugs before coming into prison and are well versed in exact measures. Though they often quoted dosages in 'mls' (millilitres)—fairly meaningless unless the strength of the syrup is known—independent doctors to whom I quoted the figures estimated that most were by any standards extremely high doses, and would only be prescribed in the community in extreme cases. Some doses, described by one doctor I consulted as 'enormous', would actually be regarded as overdose levels.

One of the drugs implicated in this control by medication was Chlorpromazine, and this, alongside others, was repeatedly mentioned in interviews I carried out. It is a generic anti-psychotic drug more commonly known by the brand name Largactil. Many of the women I spoke to showed symptoms typical of these side effects and the kind of lethargy seen in women's prisons was quite unlike anything I had seen in any of the six men's prisons I visited during earlier research. Many of the women had poor skin and were pale-faced, dark-eyed and drowsy, often rubbing their eyes to keep awake. Their unsteady shuffling walk is so commonly seen that the term 'Largactil shuffle' or, even more cruelly, 'muppet shuffle'—have become part of the prison lexicon. Another commonly used anti-psychotic drug is Melleril. Side effects can be abnormal jerky movements, dizziness and muscles stiffness and these can become irreversible if such drugs are used over time. High doses over a long period can also damage the retina of the eyes.

In the workroom of one open prison I sat round a table where four women were completing repetitive packing jobs. 'They dole out

Largactil here all the time', said a bright teenager. 'We had a friend they did that to, didn't we?' The other women, one in her forties, two in their early twenties, nodded vigorous agreement: 'She didn't want to take any medication—she was just a bit depressed. But they gave her 100ml of Largactil to start with then they put it up to 250 ml and she started turning into a cabbage. It did her head in. They said she was "unsettled" but she was just upset after her boyfriend said he wasn't coming to see her no more.' The older woman joined in: 'When they first gave her those drugs she was fighting within herself against it and she started doing strange things, like turning cartwheels. Then she set fire to her bed. They haven't got the facilities in this prison to deal with things like that so they just drug you into a zombie. And because women regard doctors as figures of authority they don't like to argue with them and they accept the drugs they give them.'

Later in the same prison a woman who was being released the following day told the same story:

There is lots of Largactil prescribed in this prison. It is routinely given to women who can't get their heads round their sentence. They give them anti-depressants as well and they get addicted to them. They give them double doses and some girls use them to boost up the illegal drugs they are taking.

Many women expressed concern about such drugs being prescribed for young offenders, which, shockingly, seems to be a fairly regular practice. A 40-year-old lifer in a closed prison told me:

In here they dish out Melleril and Largactil not simply as medication but to control people and I don't agree with giving it to young offenders. I don't like to see 16-year-olds going round with the faces of 40-year-olds, with their speech slurred. It's not right.

Marie, another lifer in the same prison, is in her early thirties:

I was on C1 in Holloway at the start of my sentence and they dope you up. They give you Largactil and it makes you sleep and makes you like a zombie. Largactil is used a lot in here and what I don't agree with at all is that it's used on a lot of youngsters. They are just 17 years old. I used to kick off a lot at that age and they do as well and the prison just wants to keep you quiet.

I was on Largactil for about seven months in Holloway. When I got here I had a row with the male nurse and he threatened to stop my medication. I decided I didn't want him holding that over me so I decided to stop it. You can't get off it straight away but I cut it down over a couple of months.

I spoke to this nurse and asked him about the prison's policy on the use of drugs like Largactil:

We have three visiting psychiatrists here and the doctors won't prescribe major tranquillisers unless the psychiatrists tell them to. Years ago I think these drugs were given for control but now they tend to be given to women with longstanding addiction to heroin. I would conclude that in the past we have over-medicalised women in prison and that medication should not be given to keep women quiet but for therapeutic reasons. After all, these are legal medical treatments and they would get them on the outside.

I went back to Marie and told her the rule about the involvement of psychiatrists to approve the prescription of Largactil:

That's a load of crap. You are just put on it as I was in Holloway and in here. They automatically put you on Largactil, specially if you're cutting up [self-mutilating] like I was.

Even women serving shorter sentences are given Largactil when all they seek is counselling. Lorraine knew she would only be serving just over a year in prison for a minor drugs offence, but she was very depressed at the thought of her four young children left behind at home:

I asked for help but the doctor just put me on Largactil. It had a terrible effect on me. I was like a zombie and I couldn't speak properly. When my boyfriend came to see me he honestly thought I was drunk because my speech was all slurred. After the visit I couldn't remember anything I'd said.

In another prison a woman heroin addict whose baby was taken away to be adopted was desperate for help:

I was prescribed a drug to calm me down. I knew it was Largactil which makes you like a zombie. Prison doctors just scribble a prescription and hand it over to you without looking at you. There's no asking what your problem is. Women line up at the medical office and the doctors scribbles "50ml Largactil" without checking who the woman is or if that's the right medicine for her. I kept going back to the doctor to try and get some help or different medicine but he kept giving me more and more of the same stuff and in the end I had enough pills stashed away to kill myself ten times over. I never took any of them.

A 24-year-old woman in the same prison said 'I can't sleep at night so they gave me 25mg of Promazine.[41] They give 100 mls of Promazine to 17-year-olds, which is really bad. When I was 17 that would have done my head in. You're supposed to see a psychiatrist before you get that but they don't bother with that in here.

The most frequently mentioned sleeping drug was Chloral hydrate, one of the oldest treatments for insomnia still in use today. Sheena, a wing cleaner on the induction wing of a closed prison, said:

They put me on Chloral before the trial. I think it's a tranquilliser to keep me calm and I've got to stay on it. I don't really want to be on anything: I did try one night taking nothing but I felt really ill the next day and I was told you can't just give it up like that. I used to get moody and kick off a lot but the drugs do stop me doing that. Now as well as the Chloral I'm taking 50 mls of Anafranil[42] and 10 mls of Triperidol.[43] [An outside doctor told me these are all big doses].

Valium, said one prisoner, is 'dished out like Smarties. I had a bad back and they gave me Valium, the same dose three times a day. I was like a zombie. Drugs controls are very lax—they will just hand out 75 mls of Valium, 50 mls of Chloral—what a cocktail!'

Staff in some of the prisons agreed. On senior medical officer said, 'I think Valium should be banned full stop. Coming off it is horrific. One girl came in here taking 60mg a day whereas you would expect 20mg to 30mg maximum. Valium was the drug of the sixties—Temazepam[44] is its nineties equivalent. We had one girl still withdrawing from Valium after six weeks.'

Other nursing staff confirmed the scourge of Valium addiction. 'The Valium was terrible when I first got there. The doctors here wouldn't give the women what they said they needed and they were all going mad, saying they couldn't do without it. It was the same with their other addiction, Temazepam. You can't reduce those drugs instantly, you have to do it gradually.'

But according to several prison SMOs, the prisons, as in so many other areas, are merely picking up the pieces of practices in the community outside:

We have lots of women in their forties who are totally addicted to Valium. We can only reduce the doses very slowly maybe by just 1mg a week or fortnight. If they can't come off anti-depressants we give them Prozac which is non-addictive. People have terrible panic attacks coming off these drugs and it's very difficult, specially for women in their forties and fifties. We had one woman in her late forties addicted to Temazepam and we managed to get her off it. She wrote to us after leaving prison and thanked us, though she certainly didn't thank us at the time! But I don't see why women shouldn't continue on a drug like Lithium[45] which is given for conditions like manic depression. It can be a great help in controlling mood swings.

In a prison recently converted to take female prisoners after years as a male establishment, the male health care officer reported: 'When we started taking females our drugs budget trebled. Women suffer more from anxiety and they will turn to a chemical solution. 'In another closed prison a nurse summed up the difficulties of his work:

Many of the women in here suffer from situational depression which I would regard as quite natural. That's what you'd expect if a woman has had to leave her home and her children. I'd also judge that 80 per cent of the women who come in here have some sort of psychological if not psychiatric problem arising from their life before they came into prison. If a woman is psychotic that's easy: if she says "I think I'm the Queen" then we can deal with it. But the average women's prison will have a lot of sexually abused women, women coming from broken homes, victims of domestic violence, lots who cut up, women with eating disorders, women with sexually transmitted diseases and so on. No wonder they have psychological problems.

Some of these problems may be exacerbated by the insensitivity of healthcare staff inadequately trained to understand and meet women's needs. In *Chapter 4* I described how Ellen's eldest son, a man in his twenties, was diagnosed as having Hodgkin's disease:

The night I found out about this over the phone, I asked one of the nurses what it was because I knew nothing about it. The nurse said "It's cancer and there's no cure — so you might as well get used to the idea and face up to the fact that your son's going to die!" Then I got locked in my cell and I seriously contemplated stringing myself up — I remember working out how to do it.

Chapter 12 looks at those women who are desperate enough to harm themselves and in some instances take or attempt to take their own lives.

Endnotes

1. *Women in Prison: A Review*, HM Inspectorate, 1997: 5.23.
2. *Daily Mirror*, 19 December 1996: quoted in Prison Reform Trust briefing paper *Chain Reaction:*

The Shackling of Prisoners, July 1997.

3. *Patient or Prisoner? A New Strategy for Health Care in Prisons*, Home Office, 1996.

4. As reported in *The Guardian*, October 1996.

5. His response was quoted at the end of the Inspectorate paper, see Note 2, above.

6. Yvonne Wilmott, Director of Nursing, HM Prison Service Directorate of Health Care, quoted in training pack produced by the Trust for the Study of Adolescence, *Understanding and Working with Young Women in Custody*, Lyon J and Coleman J, TSA, 1996.

7. Presentation at conference 'Imprisoning Women: Recognising Difference', 23 October 1997, HMP Styal.

8. Interviewed on *Breakfast with Frost*, BBC 1, 8 March 1998.

9. *An Unsuitable Place for Treatment: Diverting Mentally Disordered Offenders from Custody*, Penal Affairs Consortium, January 1998.

10. Home Office Research Bulletin, No. 32, 1992.

11. Home Office Circular 66/90, *Provision for Mentally Disturbed Offenders.*

12. Home Office and Department of Health: *Mentally Disordered Offenders: Inter-Agency Working*, 1995.

13. See *The Oxford History of the Prison: Chapter 11, 'Wayward Sisters'*, Lucia Zedner, Oxford University Press, 1995.

14. *Reconstructing a Women's Prison: The Holloway Redevelopment Project 1968-88*, Paul Rock, Oxford University Press, 1996.

15. Smith, C, *Women, Health and Imprisonment*, Bangor, 1995.

16. See Note 1, above: 6.23.

17. See *The Imprisonment of Women*, Dobash R, Dobash R and Gutteridge S, Basil Blackwell, 1986.

18. *Annual Report of HM Chief Inspector of Prisons, 1993-4, Chapter 5.*

19. A generic anti-cancer drug.

20. See Note 1, above: 9.15.

21. Examination of the inside of the colon by means of a long flexible fibre optic viewing instrument called a colonosope.

22. See Note 1, above: 9.31.

23. See *Annual Report of HM Chief Inspector of Prisons, 1993-4*, 5.33.

24. British Medical Association: *Complete Family Health Encyclopaedia*, 1990.

25. See Note 1, above: 9.34. In the USA, one in every 16 women entering prison is pregnant.

26. See *Inspection of Facilities for Mothers and Babies in Prison: Third Multi-Disciplinary Inspection by the Department of Health*, November 1996.

27. See Note 1, above: 9.34.

28. Brand name for medroxy-progesterone, used as a contraceptive by three monthly injections.

29. See *Chapter 10* for the special dietary needs of ethnic minority and foreign national prisoners.

30. See Note 1, above: 9.01.

31. Reported in *The Sunday Times*, 4 January 1998,by Lois Rogers, Medical Correspondent. This was a trial led by Bernard Gesch of Surrey University and backed by the Home Office.

32. I am indebted to Chris Tchaikovsky of Women in Prison who told me of this expression.

33. *Annual Report of HM Chief Inspector of Prisons, 1993-94*, 5.13.

34. Yard cleaners, also called 'yardies'. Comes from the Jamaican expression where 'yard' means 'home'.

35. See Note 1, above: 9.18.

36. Rule 43 enables a prisoner to be removed from association with others, usually for the maintenance of the Good Order and Discipline (GOAD). But some prisoners elect to go on rule 43 at their own request if they feel they are at risk from others, usually due to the nature of their offence, e.g. child molesting.

37. In Charlotte Bronte's *Jane Eyre*, Mr Rochester kept his mad wife in the attic of the house where Jane was employed as a governess.

38. *Rethinking Imprisonment*, Seminar organized by the Institute for the Study and Treatment of

Delinquency (ISTD), King's College, London, 25 September 1997.

39. *Drug Misusers and the Prison System*, HMSO, 1996.
40. See Note 1, above: 9.22, 9.25
41. An antipsychotic drug used as a sedative. Possible side effects are abnormal movements of the face and limbs, drowsiness, lethargy, dry mouth, constipation, blurred vision. Long term treatment may cause the symptoms of Parkinson's disease.
42. Brand name for Clomipramine, an anti-depressant drug used as a long term treatment for depression. Side effects are dry mouth, blurred vision, constipation. If an overdose is taken, can cause dangerously abnormal heart rhythms and coma.
43. Brand name anti-psychotic drug: same side effects as Melleril.
44. A benzodiazepine drug, used in the short term treatment of insomnia, or an anti depressant, but abused by addicts as 'tems' and sold at raves in the 'chill out room'.
45. A generic drug used to treat manic-depressive illness.

CHAPTER TWELVE

Slashers and Swingers

I met Sarah in the hospital wing of a women's remand prison. She was there for stabbing a policeman. Her house, which she had saved up to buy for years, was about to be repossessed. She was so upset she began going round smashing the windows. When a policeman intervened she attacked him with a garden knife. At the start of my interview with Sarah I noticed that her forearms were a mass of small scars and asked her if the window glass had caused the damage. She looked puzzled. 'Oh no', she said, 'that's where I cut up'.

When I first began researching the experiences of prisoners, I was, like most lay people, quite unaware of the practice of 'cutting up', used by those who have been damaged to bring relief to their suffering. Sarah was 33 and her description of her life so far—her impoverished and abused childhood, the rape at 19 by a trusted relative—gave clues about her condition.

The phenomenon officially known as DSH—deliberate self-harm—was first brought to the attention of the wider public in 1995 when millions of television viewers heard the late Princess Diana admit in a *Panorama* interview, 'I hurt my arms and legs'. This was a revelation to many people, and those who knew of the practice but dismissed it as the behaviour of a disadvantaged underclass were forced to admit that this is a serious disorder which crosses social boundaries. Diana explained that she cut herself in response to 'so much pain inside that you try to hurt yourself on the outside. I didn't like myself. I was ashamed because I couldn't cope with the pressures.'

What was once a secret illness has since been analysed and explored in various newspaper articles and television programmes. Though official figures for such a condition cannot be exact, it is believed that three times more women than men deliberately harm themselves.

Most of the self-harming women I interviewed in all the prisons I visited, suffered from terribly low self-esteem, though there was no way of knowing how far this was partly a result of being in custody. There is some evidence that mutilation becomes part of the culture in certain prisons. Why is it that it is said by Kate Donegan, governor of Cornton Vale, to be almost non-existent in that prison, where suicides have been rife, yet commonplace at Holloway? The 'copycat' or 'contagion' theory of self-harm as hysterical behaviour by a group of women seems to diminish and trivialise their pain. An explanation may be that women

271

who experience similar kinds of distress may choose to respond to it in similar ways. My self-harming interviewees said they disliked most aspects of their own personalities and their own bodies and could not see why others could find anything to love in them either.

Many of the prisoners complained of putting on weight as a side effect of prescribed drugs and saw no place for themselves in a world where skeletal supermodels reign supreme. Joy Pollock-Byrne in her study of American women's prisons[1] quotes prison officers she interviewed as saying that self-mutilating women were 'always zero in their own eyes.' Pollock-Byrne concludes that the reason for such women's sense of failure is that they see themselves only in terms of how well they can play the parts defined for them by others—the roles of wife, lover, mother or daughter. Men on the other hand largely rate their own success in terms of their work.

Self-mutilation has always been familiar to those working in closed institutions like mental hospitals and prisons. In nineteenth century prisons, women who mutilated themselves were accused of 'wanton destruction of health' and of resorting to this 'troublesome behaviour' to secure a move to an infirmary where they would be allowed association with other women. Those who persisted[2] were confined in special cells in straitjackets and other physical restraints like ankle straps. There was never any suggestion that self-harm could be a logical response to what had happened in these women's lives, and was likely to continue and worsen in prison because of the uncaring nature of most prison regimes.

Of the 130 women I interviewed who gave this information, 19 per cent (25 women) had a history of harming themselves and all of them were still harming themselves in prison. The proportion is similar to that in a 1995 report commissioned by the Home Office, called *Managing the Needs of Female Prisoners*[3] where nearly a quarter of the women reported harming themselves before coming into prison. Experts estimate that the condition afflicts as many as one in ten women in the community.[4]

The prison psychologists I spoke to acknowledged that there is now known to be a clear link between childhood sexual abuse and self-mutilation, though this is not true of Cornton Vale where 80 per cent of prisoners are victims of abuse, but only a very small number harm themselves. In the Home Office sample, all the women who harmed themselves had suffered previous sexual or physical abuse. A 1995 study[5] by Lois Arnold of 76 self-harming women at the Bristol Crisis Service for Women found that 49 per cent had suffered childhood sexual abuse, and 22 per cent had been raped or otherwise sexually abused as adults. In my sample 76 per cent (19) of the women who harmed themselves had suffered childhood sexual abuse and 32 per cent (8 women) had suffered sexual abuse (in all but one case, rape) as adults.

HM Inspectorate's review of conditions in women's prisons[6] recognises self-harm as a response to pain and recommends that women who harm themselves should be listened to and given help. Helen Liebling, who left her job as principal clinical psychologist at Ashworth Hospital because of her concerns about the treatment of women patients, found that self-harming women she worked with said they wanted to be provided with a regular listener whom they could trust. More than two-thirds said they wanted to talk to other women who self-harm. They wanted to be involved in planning their own future, and they wanted help in expressing their feelings.

But in today's prisons the way such women are dealt with is still not informed by any real understanding. Technically, self-mutilation is still a punishable offence and (as the stories quoted in *Chapter 5* confirm) it is this punitive approach that leads to women who harm themselves being routinely sent 'down the block' in some prisons. Even in more enlightened prisons where women are 'stitched up' and allowed to return to normal location on the wings, they are regarded, as Pat Carlen[7] has put it, as 'an inconvenience for the officers'. Dr Alison Liebling of the Cambridge Institute of Criminology[8] has written: 'Few studies seek to understand deliberate self-harm as a response to and expression of pain, which may occur well within the boundaries of "normal mental health."'

In all the prisons I visited there would invariably be staff who dismissed women who 'cut up' as 'attention-seeking', ignoring the fact that the women are almost invariably alone when they harm themselves, and will for many years have kept their activities secret. In any case, as one education co-ordinator put it, 'If these are the lengths people have to go to get attention in prison, we're in a pretty sorry state.'

Even more shocking was the callous use of jocular terms—two of which are used in the title of this chapter: 'We've got another slasher coming in today', I heard a male officer say. Other cruel words routinely used were 'swinger' (a woman who attempts suicide by hanging), 'slicer' (a woman who cuts herself), 'scratcher' (a woman who uses needles or pins to damage her skin, usually her face) and 'scourer' or 'green-padder' (a woman who injures her face with a metal kitchen scouring pad).

Lois Arnold[5] found that in her sample, much distress was caused by the 'negative or dismissive attitudes of staff, whether this was expressed in terms of condemnation, disinterest or failure to provide any help.' The Inspectors' review[9] recognises that dealing with self-harming people is stressful for prison staff, who will require special training. The attitudes indicated by the harsh expressions I quote above would not fairly represent the views of all the disciplinary staff in my sample. Some had thought seriously about the women's motives: 'I look at these women, what they have done to their faces, and I think "What a poor opinion you must have of yourself to do such things to your own body."' One middle-aged woman imprisoned for stalking and repeatedly exposing her body to a man who obsessed her was the object of many officers' pity. They said she should certainly not be in prison. She rarely emerged from her cell and would, they said, starve if they did not bring food to her. A few months after I spoke to the woman, the governor of her prison told me she had just dreadfully mutilated her own breasts.

Such women can however be vilified both by staff and by other prisoners equally ignorant of the nature of their problem. Pat Carlen[7] has pointed out that this revulsion can be fostered by the officers. Women who had spent time in prison hospital wings emerged to speak with horror of what they had seen: 'I saw terrible things in the hospital wing that I couldn't even talk to anyone about. One woman slit her throat. She didn't die—she didn't even feel it.'

Bernadette was nearing the end of a six month sentence for a first offence of benefit fraud (see *Chapter 3*). She was still terribly bitter about being separated from her four small children and felt nothing but impatient contempt for self-mutilating women whom she regarded as foolish, immature, self-indulgent or mad. She interpreted their behaviour as a pointless attention-seeking-device which had no chance of influencing the hard-hearted screws:

> Another thing that's terrible in here is the cutting up. They're forever doing that. I'd never abuse my body like that. The other day I was on the phone and there was this girl behind me in the queue yelling for something. She couldn't get what she wanted so she started yelling more, then when she still couldn't get it she went off to her cell to cut up. I said to her "Why are you doing this to your own body? The screws don't care. They couldn't give a shit what happens to you!"

One of my most disquieting interviews was with Tracey, a tiny androgynous woman from Leicester. She had completed the questionnaire I had sent out during my first research project. On a question asking about her leisure activities she had written: 'GETIN IN TO TRUBLE'. Tracey is 32 but looks about 14, sitting cross-legged on a chair in her dungarees. All the visible parts of her body below her chin are entirely covered in tattoos. On her neck are two swallows and on her left shoulder a brilliantly coloured tiger's head. She has the high-pitched voice of a child of five or six and grins and chuckles constantly. She was very happy to be interviewed and gave rapid staccato answers to my questions then sat back giggling and waiting for the next question. She is serving a sentence of life imprisonment for arson. Since she was born she has been inside one institution after another—children's homes, secure units, prisons and Rampton special hospital: 'I went to borstal first for theft and burglary. I stayed there till I were 18 then they let me out and the day I got out I smashed a window so I could get back in again.'

Her head, shaven almost to the scalp, was terribly disfigured at the front by self-inflicted wounds, some beginning to turn septic. Her left eye was almost closed by a huge purple bruise, which she said she had also done herself. Tracey was well aware of her condition and her need for psychiatric help:

> The judges, they say "This woman has a history of mental instability. She must have therapy". But they don't give you any. It's all talk. I'm always cutting up, I'm always over the hospital wing or down the block on punishment. I do things like punching people, stuff like that. Why? Don't know — I just do. I'm only happy when I'm in prison. I'm all right now because I've got life. I set fire to this DIY shop in Leicester. The fire only got to the door mat but it was enough to put me inside and now I can get settled. Can I go now? It's tea-time.

Even the most seriously lacerated women often said that they had received no help at all. On the contrary many said they had been punished for being a nuisance, their wounds stitched by the prison doctor, sometimes without anaesthetic. Often they were left isolated for days in the segregation unit. It seems incomprehensible and scandalous in nineties Britain that women so badly in need of help should be sent to the block which in any prison is the primary symbol of punishment. This approach is reminiscent of long outdated attitudes regarding self-mutilation as 'wanton' and 'troublesome'. The Inspectors condemn the practice of isolating self-harming women as 'a simplistic response. Nobody engages in self-harm capriciously and the response needs to support the individual through that pain as well as dealing with the injury'.[10] They recommend support from a professional counselling service like the Bourne Trust working with remand prisoners at Holloway.

Rae is a pale plump woman in her late twenties, with the old scars of extensive laceration criss-crossing both forearms. She has spent nearly two years in her current closed prison, where the hospital wing has been removed and no nurses are now employed in the women's wing:

> There's no health care here. There's no hospital wing for women at all. I
> used to cut up, right. When I came in here my head wasn't right so I used to
> cut up. But they never gave me any treatment. They just put me down the
> block and left me there in a paper dress. I still used to cut up and I was in a
> real state. I smeared blood all over the place. They just told me I'd have to
> stay there till I stopped. But I was ill—I had real paranoia. I needed help.

Another prisoner in the same prison told an almost identical story:

> There's no proper medical care here. I was in shock in my first stage[11] and I
> tried to commit suicide. There was a hospital wing in my first prison and
> they stitched me up there and sent me back on the wing. There was no
> support for me there but at least there was a hospital wing. They give us a
> lot of medication in here. I reckon 35 out of the 40 women here are on
> medication. We used to have nurses on call on this wing 24 hours a day and
> you could go to them but now we have nothing.

A third prisoner said that at least the nurses had provided some access
to medical care at night: 'And one of them had psychiatric nursing
training: she was excellent. But now they've got rid of them all'.

I put these complaints to the governor. Why were there no nurses
on the wing? He said they had been under-utilised and had become
'part of the tea-break culture'. Why was no counselling given? The
governor said he didn't agree with the women having counsellors
'raking over endlessly what goes on inside their heads. One week they
will have one problem, the next week another.'

Sam is 21 and in a different closed prison. Like Tracey she has
covered much of her body with tattoos—lurid pictures and names all
over her forearms. A second glance reveals that they are heavily
underscored with razor scars, some of them still gaping wounds. Sam's
face is pleasant and open, but with a palpable vulnerability. Both her
parents were only 16 when she was born and she was brought up by
her grandmother and bullied at school. She is gay and has had difficulty
coming to terms with her sexuality. She became addicted to glue-
sniffing at the age of 13. She is serving three years and nine months for
slitting her ex-girlfriend's throat. Luckily the attack was not fatal:

> I started cutting up when I was 15. When I first did it wasn't painful—I felt
> so bad inside anyway. The pain inside was a lot worse than the pain of
> cutting myself. It was all to do with coping with being gay and I overdosed
> as well because of that. I made two real suicide attempts: the first time I cut

my wrist and I really wanted to end my life. I didn't care about anything and I felt everyone had rejected me. Then as I sat and watched myself bleed I realised I didn't really want to die. It was the same when I ODd [overdosed]. I went into a coma and when I was lying in the hospital coming out of it I saw my family all round me and I realised again that I didn't want to die.

So now I cut up if anything upsets me. I feel much better afterwards. It's like it relieves the pain, it lets it all out. Like in here—if I have an argument with my girlfriend she'll just blank me out and I can't stand that. I'd rather fight her and get it over with. But if she just ignores me, that's when I go and cut up.

I get out of here in six months and I need to see a psychiatrist before I go because when I get confused and I can't sort my life out, I just go back on the glue. I used to talk to a counsellor here and the first few times she was all right, she used to give me solutions to my problems. But then she seemed to lose interest. She just wanted me to get up and go. She couldn't give me any reason for the things I do to other people.

Like so many self-harming women, Sam was punished rather than helped:

They put me on the block for four or five weeks because they said I had a depressive illness and I'd attempted suicide. I'd smashed my room up— that was to do with my girlfriend. Now they've put me on Melleril.[12] I'm on 50 mls three times a day. I'm also on Prothiaden.[13] They give you medication to give themselves a quiet life. Melleril makes you feel real slow so you can't be bothered to do anything. They should talk to you instead. I know I need help and I've asked to see a psychiatrist a lot of times but nothing happens.

One education coordinator had spoken at length to prisoners:

The women who cut up told me it was a great sense of release, of letting everything out. It is often triggered by a flashback of sexual or physical abuse when they got into prison and there was nobody there to talk to. But I don't think many of them started cutting up for the first time in prison, nor was it any kind of "hysterical woman" craze, as some prison officers like to pretend. Most had done it for years—you could see by the age of the scars, and it was an established pattern. They usually had a lot of heavy scarring. I remember one woman officer telling a prisoner she was an attention-seeker. She told me afterwards: "She loves cutting up so she can get into the hospital wing." I thought how desperate that woman must be to go that far. The Home Office produced a policy document on self-abuse but it was in my view only produced because of fear of suicide and the bad

277

publicity it brings.

Asked what would have helped them most, all the women I interviewed said they needed someone *to listen* to them. All denied that self-mutilation is a simple cry for help. They recognised it as addictive behaviour but saw it also as an enormous release of stress, a coping mechanism which for some was the only thing that prevented them taking their own lives. Other women prisoners are sensitive to the needs of such damaged people and feel powerless to help. One said she used to work in the healthcare centre of a closed prison: 'I would see women lining up one after another with slashed arms and the nurses would just stick tape over them and send them away. There was no counselling, nothing for them at all.'

In one prison I sat with the governor who had to break the bad news of a parole 'knockback' to a prisoner: Vanessa had been refused parole and instead of leaving the prison in June as she had hoped, she would have to stay till the following February. She was a vulnerable prisoner, held on rule 43 in the hospital wing because of the nature of her offence: she had set fire to her house with her own two small children in it. Fortunately they were rescued but Vanessa was still at grave risk from other prisoners. The governor tried to prepare the woman for the disappointment, but when she heard the news, Vanessa burst into tears and rushed out of the wing office. 'She'll ligature tonight, no doubt about it', said the governor. 'I've told the other girls to see if she goes into the toilet', said the health care officer. 'They tie their shoelaces or something round their necks very tightly', he explained. 'Vanessa does it for attention but she does it so well it can be dangerous'.

The officer's comment, like the comments of so many others, again shows a lack of understanding of why women take such actions. Ligaturing, like cutting up, is described in medical terms as a form of parasuicide usually committed in circumstances that make rescue possible. Parasuicide in the general population is three times more common in women than in men and is most common in the 15 to 30 age group. It has to be taken seriously because statistics show that 20 per cent to 30 per cent of people who attempt suicide try again within a year and 10 per cent eventually succeed.[14]

Changes in the prison environment are not necessarily the answer. The former deputy governor of a women's prison said: 'There is no such thing as a ligature-free cell. If you prevent one method of ligaturing there are dozens of other possibilities left. You don't need height—you could tie your throat to a table leg and pull the string and you'd be gone. We have had women ligaturing using the door handle, and clothing or bedding will always supply the ligature'.

278

Prison Service statistics for 1994 to 95 show that over the previous two years the number of incidents recorded as self-injury increased by 48 per cent. These figures show that on average *every day* there were no fewer than 13 incidents of self-harm or suicide attempts. The Inspectorate's review noted that approximately a quarter of women prisoners reported a history of self-harm or suicide. In fact their own survey found an even higher figure of 40 per cent—more that one in three.[15] Self-injury and suicide in prison are commonly linked together, with self-harming incidents being regarded as attempted suicides. In fact, as the above accounts show, self-mutilation can be the very safety valve that *prevents* suicide. The links are inevitably made because self-injury can sometimes be so severe it results in death. A former education officer said 'There was a lot of self-mutilation when I started working at a women's prison in 1988. Women who cut up are not supposed to be suicide risks but the point is that they get so near the main artery in the wrist that there is an added risk, although self-mutilation and suicide are not supposed to be related.'

At a Cambridge conference on deaths in custody in April 1994, Michael Jennings, a forensic psychologist working at Styal prison, co-presented a paper on women prisoners at risk of suicide and identified as vulnerability indicators the following factors: worries about children, difficulties of maintaining links with family and fears of losing accommodation (which might lead to loss of custody of children).[16] A report published in April 1997 by the Prison Reform Trust[17] emphasised the multiple causes of suicide, including anxiety and depression, stress from being bullied and triggers such as a missed visit or a change of location. The same report warned that many suicides of women in custody may not have been recorded as such, because 'suicidal intent is not expected and other explanations are sought'.[18]

Another reason for self-mutilation, identified by Sylvia Casale[19] is a feeling of helplessness and powerlessness which afflicts many women in the community but which is inevitably exacerbated inside prison. In *Chapters 3* and *4* women described their grief and frustration at being cut off from their children. Andy[20] said that separation from her ten-year-old daughter Stacey had led her to self-harm and thoughts of suicide. The little girl had begun to emulate her mother and harm herself too.

Other women described the same feelings being triggered on certain days that had special significance in their lives. This phenomenon is common enough for staff to have coined the phrase 'anniversary syndrome' to describe it (see *Chapter 2*). A woman who had killed her abusive partner described the support given to her by the prison probation officer on such an occasion: 'I was so upset on the date

279

of John's birthday and I kept crying and crying and saying "It was his birthday" over and over again'.

Lois Arnold[5] identified a number of 'situational triggers' that made women vulnerable to suicide attempts. They included prison-induced stresses such as the reception and transfer periods, disciplinary problems, review boards, being told the sentence length, and parole refusals. Other triggers were peer pressure caused by threats and debts, and outside problems such as bad news from home or broken relationships. This is why the inspectors say it is essential that every prison has access to expert bereavement counselling.[21]

Jackie described an event which triggered a suicide attempt. She is 29 and on her second sentence for arson, an offence commonly linked to childhood abuse which Jackie had herself suffered. She regularly 'cut up' but had not attempted suicide before:

> After I was raped when I was 16 I started cutting up and I still do it a lot. I feel it helps me relax. In here they send you to the hospital wing to get stitched up and they do numb you so it doesn't hurt, then they bring you back to the wing. I tried to take my life the other day because a close friend of mine died in another prison. The funeral was up north and I went in a taxi with two women officers — they weren't in uniform and they took the handcuffs off when we got to the funeral. I came straight back here at the end of the service and a week later I tried to hang myself. An officer found me in time but I'm sorry that she did.

The women and prison officers with whom I maintained contact following my periods of research would sometimes telephone me to record their distress at the suicide of another prisoner. Throughout 1996 and 1997 these deaths became more frequent, and for a few days after each telephone call I would search the national newspapers for any mention of the tragedy. None of them attracted any attention. Was it because their perceived mental illness or drug addiction had made them into non-newsworthy items—'non-persons'?

One exception to this lack of media attention was a story that appeared on Sunday 8 September 1996 in *The Observer* about five suicides in the previous 15 months at Cornton Vale women's prison. All the women were under 27 and all were on remand for petty offences. This finally led to the appointment of a new senior management team. On the same page, that day in September, the newspaper also reported an unannounced inspection by the chief inspector of prisons of Risley women's prison. Sir David Ramsbotham condemned long hours of lockdown, over-worked and exhausted staff, and even an infestation of fleas. The report included a mention of a prisoner, on remand for drugs offences, who had hanged herself two weeks earlier. A few days later a member of Risley's staff told me:

> The day *The Observer* printed that story it was dreadful here. We had four attempted suicides and one was so bad the woman had to be taken to hospital. The second one almost died and they only just cut her down in time. The third one swallowed all her medication and another one swallowed glass. It was only by chance the staff happened to look in. The reason for that flea infestation was because the women were locked in their cells for five days from a Thursday to the next Tuesday because there weren't enough of us to guard them. There were only six staff to guard 150 women and the women couldn't get out of their cells for a shower. The staff were all so depressed that weekend. Nobody is speaking up for these prisoners. What is being done to the women's service is immoral.

The Inspectorate's review the following year[6] quoted studies showing that the rate of suicide in custody is as high for women prisoners as for men, though outside prison, fewer women than men take their own lives. (Though a Samaritans' study of 7,000 young people between 1991 and 1997 found that one in five girls had *attempted* suicide before the age of 25, compared with 8 per cent of boys).

The suicide of a prisoner is the ultimate failure for the Prison Service. Suicides are increasing in the community, especially among young people, and the prison population, being much younger than the population outside, is likely to be more at risk. But incarceration must in itself heighten the risks both of suicide and self-harm, and prisoners are six times more likely to commit suicide than people outside prison. Though the Home Office keeps figures of deaths in custody, with separate figures for suicide, there is no analysis of how many suicides are linked to drug misuse. From the cases described in *Chapter 9*, a causal link either directly with drugs or indirectly with drug-related intimidation may exist.

In *Chapter 2* I quoted prisoners' descriptions of the reception period when they had felt like harming themselves. Prisoners at risk of self-harm and suicide are sent to prison with a form known as POL 1 (Police Exceptional Risk). Women who are accused of committing murder or manslaughter in a domestic situation are automatically given such a form. In a remand centre, women can be received from the courts just hours after allegedly committing such an offence and should automatically be held in the hospital wing under close supervision. Despite these provisions a high risk remand prisoner, Claire Bosley, committed suicide in Holloway on 26 November 1995, the day after she was alleged to have killed her husband. Reportedly, she was left alone without supervision in a pre-search holding room and choked herself to death with toilet paper. It is said that her body lay undiscovered for an hour and a half on the toilet floor. One of the receiving officers was a member of the prison suicide awareness training team and Claire had come with a POL 1, having three times tried by the same method to take her life in police custody. The police had also telephoned the prison warning that Claire was distressed and that a psychiatrist had recommended sending her straight to the prison hospital wing.[22]

In 1992 the Service set up the Suicide Awareness Unit in response to a thematic review by HM Inspectorate on suicide and self-harm, though as already discussed the two are not necessarily linked. The function of the unit is to achieve a cultural change in prison staff so that all are aware of the risks of suicide. In the past there has been heavy reliance on medical staff to diagnose and resolve the problem. The role of unified grades—all disciplinary staff from basic grade officers to governing governors—was simply to refer the woman to the prison doctor for assessment to see if she should go to the health care centre for psychiatric intervention.

The unit's strategy is quite different: it is a multi-disciplinary approach with different members of staff focusing on the individual prisoner and her problems. Training is given at the Prison Service College at Newbold Revell where in-service courses are held, and trained officers are then spread among establishments where they train other staff and also prisoners volunteering to act as Samaritan-trained listeners[23] (known in Holloway as 'befrienders'), the peer counselling scheme referred to in earlier chapters, which many women said they found helpful. This scheme was commended by the inspectors[24] who said listeners should be linked to the reception process to give support to suicidal women. The unit also claims to be more proactive in its dealings with prisoners' support groups and sends information to the Howard League for Penal Reform and to INQUEST, the body that concerns itself with deaths in custody.

I described earlier the limited success of measures to lessen the risk of suicide by making changes to a prison's physical environment. But at present many prisons base their suicide prevention strategy on just such measures. In several prisons staff said they were removing protuberances from which prisoners might hang themselves and installing closed circuit television cameras in cells. At one open prison the works manager explained how he and his team had just installed special outward opening doors to prevent a suicidal woman barricading herself in her cell. Staff can remove a small plate and the door will swing outward. An official at the Suicide Awareness Unit was unimpressed:

I really don't know what an open prison is doing, thinking about barricades. I would be wanting to know why they have got that sort of problem there. They of all people should be looking at encouraging people to know each other so well that prisoners feel supported. CCTV could be regarded as an invasion of privacy and such continual observation could heighten, rather than lessen, the risk of suicide. Anyway it's a very expensive form of observation.

Our strategy must be to show that it is not desirable to isolate and supervise people. We must let people see that there is another way out rather than suicide. We must make staff observant and aware of the vulnerability factors. The point about suicide risk is that it is not a static state, so you have to be aware of these factors when they arise.

Kate Donegan, who was appointed governor of Cornton Vale in the wake of the suicides, agrees: 'We used to have remand prisoners being observed every 15 minutes, and this led to high anxiety levels. We consulted the Royal College of Psychiatrists who said we should not observe so much. Now we try to be more interactive.'[25]

In view of all the work done by the unit in training staff in this kind of awareness, why did 1997 establish an all-time record for self-inflicted deaths in custody, with 70 suicides in British jails? Stephen Shaw, Director of the Prison Reform Trust, said in March 1998,[26] 'There is one death in prison every five days. There are more hangings now than in the days of capital punishment.' The previous year there were 64 suicides, nearly half of them by people with a known previous psychiatric history. Four of that year's fatalities were in Cornton Vale where in the year 1995-96 there had been six suicides and six incidents classed as attempted suicides.

Deborah Coles, Director of INQUEST, said 'There should be no more serious issue for the Prison Service than the untimely death of a prisoner in its care. With no provision for full public enquiries into these deaths, it is shocking that the Prisons Ombudsman is precluded from looking into complaints from the families.'[27] At present, deaths in custody can only be investigated through the internal prisons investigation system, not open to the families of the deceased. But in October 1997 Sir Peter Woodhead, the Prisons Ombudsman, asked the prisons minister for the right to investigate these deaths.[28] An Appeal Court decision in November 1997[29] clarified the situation regarding liability for suicides in detention and provided prisoners and their dependants with the possibility of legal redress. In the past, judges have been reluctant to recognise any liability on the part of the Prison Service when prisoners have taken their own lives.

The only group that seems under-represented in these raised suicide figures are foreign national women drug couriers. Workers at

Hibiscus, the charity that helps foreign national prisoners,[30] think the reasons for this are cultural: 'It is not in the culture of these women to take their own lives. They live in such poverty at home, and have such a poor quality of life, but it is their culture to survive and something has got to be very wrong indeed for them to consider suicide: their culture is all about surviving.'

After the Cornton Vale disasters, Clive Fairweather, the Scottish Chief Inspector of Prisons, joined the growing number of experts demanding more research into the lifestyle and family background of women coming into prison. Kate Donegan acknowledged in a radio interview[31] the need for a careful induction process, especially for remand prisoners, and for consistency of treatment. She said she had tried to 'ventilate' the prison by bringing in outside agencies like the Samaritans. In the same programme the criminologist Dr Alison Liebling said society should be looking critically at the current women's prison population, asking why women accused of non-violent crimes should be remanded into custody, and considering how many should be given custodial sentences.

Yet almost a year later, in December 1997, another woman hanged herself in Cornton Vale. Her name was Sandra Brown and she was a drug addict. Her solicitor, interviewed on a Radio Five Live *Special Assignment* programme,[32] questioned the policy of using jail to punish women who are often more dangerous to themselves than to anyone else:

> Women offenders are very much different from the average male offender in this respect. There are very few women offenders who are simply bad. Many are in one way or another seriously ill, either suffering from depression or from the consequences of their addiction. They are separated from their families and from their source of narcotics.

Sandra Brown's suicide led the home affairs minister for Scotland to commission a joint study, by the Scottish Chief Inspectors of Prisons and of Social Services, to look at community disposals and the use of custody for women: 'We've got to make sure that prisoners get the best care and rehabilitation. But we've also got to try and prevent women who are damaged coming into prison in the first place'.[32]

On 19 December 1997, a statement from Sir David Ramsbotham made headlines when he expressed his deep concern at the continuing rise in prison suicides. He said that the number of prisoners who had taken their own lives in 1997 was an all-time high, and that this figure included increasing numbers of women and young offenders.

Richard Tilt accepts that 70 suicides are 70 too many, but

emphasises that Britain has the lowest prison suicide rate of any Western European country and that the Prison Service does have a strategy for suicide prevention[26]. Sir David announced an Inspectorate review early in 1998. He said said he doubted whether the Prison Service's suicide prevention measures were being properly implemented, and called for area managers to take personal responsibility.

Meanwhile, what help can be given to women as desperate as those described in this chapter, and to others who may soon reach the same levels of despair? In *Chapter 13* I look at some of the therapeutic initiatives on offer in women's prisons.

Endnotes

1. *Women, Prison and Crime*, Joycelyn M Pollock-Byrne, University of Houston-Downtown, Brooks Cole, California, 1990.

2. See *The Imprisonment of Women*, Dobash R, Dobash R and Gutteridge S, Basil Blackwell, 1986.

3. Morris A, Wilkinson, C, Tisi, A, Woodrow, J, Rockley, A, Home Office, 1995.

4. Dr Brian Lask, consultant psychiatrist, who runs the young persons unit at Huntercombe Manor Hospital, Berkshire, which specialises in DSH quoted this figure in an interview in the *Mail on Sunday*, 10 December 1995.

5. Quoted by Debs Kelland, Department of Psychology, HMP Holloway, in her paper 'Working in a Custodial Setting with Young Women who Self-Injure', included in the training pack *Understanding and Working with Young Women in Custody*, Trust for the Study of Adolescence, 1996.

6. *Women in Prison: A Review*: 7.27, HM Inspectorate, 1997.

7. *Criminal Women*, Ed. Carlen, P, Polity Press, 1985.

8. *Suicides in Prison*, Alison Liebling, Routledge, 1992.

9. See Note 6, above: 7.29.

10. See Note 6, above: 7.30.

11. Life-sentenced prisoners are moved from prison to prison through the four stages of their sentences.

12. An anti-psychotic drug: side effects can be abnormal jerky movements, dizziness and muscle stiffness. High doses over a long period can damage the retina of the eyes.

13. A brand name anti-depressant drug.

14. Figures from *Complete Family Health Encyclopaedia*, British Medical Association, 1990.

15. See Note 6, above: Executive Summary, 26.

16. See *Chapters 3* and *4*.

17. *The Rising Toll of Prison Suicide*, Prison Reform Trust, April 1997.

18. The Prison Reform Trust report quotes research by Dr Enda Dooley (1990) which estimated that of all consciously self-inflicted deaths between 1982 and 1987, 7.8 per cent were 'probable suicides' committed by women, though of all prison suicides in England and Wales between 1972 and 1987, only 1.7 per cent were officially recorded as suicides. Dr Dooley also found that mental disorder was among the reasons for suicide in 22 per cent of cases, that over a third of those who took their own lives had a previous history of psychiatric contact, and that 23 per cent had received some form of psychotropic medication in the month before death. A later Home Office study in 16 prisons (1993) found that 47 per cent had a previous psychiatric history. See also, generally, *Deaths of Offenders: The Hidden Side of Justice*, Alison Liebling (Ed.), Waterside Press/ISTD, 1998.

19. *Women Inside*, Sylvia Casale, Civil Liberties Trust, 1989.

20. See *Chapter 4*.

21. See Note 6, above, 7.35.

22. Claire's case was extensively reported at the time in the media. Details here are taken from a case study quoted in Prison Reform Trust leaflet *Is Your Vision of Life Positive? or Negative?*, July 1997.

23. See *Chapter 8*.

24. See Note 6, above, Executive Summary, 27.

25. Presentation at conference at HMP Styal, 23 October 1997, 'Imprisoning Women: Recognising Difference'.

26. In interview on *Breakfast with Frost*, 8 March 1998.

27. 'Wall of Silence Surrounds Prison Deaths', Heather Mills, *Observer*, 21 September 1997.

28. As reported on the *Today* programme, BBC Radio Four, 8 October 1997.

29. See *Suicides in Detention and the Duty of Care*, Steve Foster, principal lecturer in law, Coventry University, *New Law Journal*, 6 February 1998. The case quoted was *Reeves v. Commissioner of Police of the Metropolis*, 20 November 1997.

30. See *Chapter 10*.

31. Interviews, 12 January 1997 on BBC Radio Four's *World at One*.

32. Interviews from *Special Assignment*, broadcast on Radio Five Live on 21 December 1997. The report of the joint study was published on 13 May 1998 and was welcomed by the Scottish Office as 'a watershed' in the approach to women's offending. See *Epilogue*, p.381.

CHAPTER THIRTEEN

The Dreaded 'TOB'

At a London seminar in May 1996[1] Chris Tchaikovsky, Director of Women in Prison, said:

> People are always talking to me about the dreaded "TOB"—tackling offending behaviour. It's a very good thing to try and limit the damage that prison does. But if people think they are "doing good" to women in prison they are wrong, because people will always go back to the same problems. What we have is well-meaning people "doing unto" other people, instead of sorting out their welfare problems.

At the same seminar Professor Pat Carlen, co-founder with Chris Tchaikovsky of WIP, said:

> Going round the women's prisons I keep meeting people who are worried about prisoners and their problems and I say "Do you really think you can help them in here?" I think there are a lot of people supposed to be helping, but all they are doing is paddling in misery.

From any review of the literature about women's prisons, it is clear that the roots of feminist scepticism about work within them may also lie in the fear of compounding traditional stereotypical views of women fallen from a state of grace and in need of reform—views that informed Victorian penal theory.[2] The suspicion endures that captive women will only be seen to have 'come to terms with their offending' once they have complied with codes of conduct defined by a patriarchal society, and become 'good' wives, mothers and daughters.

These doubts have equally raised concern about therapeutic programmes for women in prison: are the attempts of therapists to search for the roots of women's offending, and to 're-educate' them, just another way of controlling the minds of captive women as completely as locks, bolts and bars control their bodies?

HM Inspectorate acknowledge in their review of women's prisons[3] that 'custody is not the best setting for therapeutic work' and that to embark on the process of trying to address women's emotional needs can be like 'opening Pandora's box'. They complain that existing programmes tend to be delivered in isolation, and recommend instead that the whole prison regime should be directed towards tackling offending behaviour, with constant evaluation of effectiveness. Most important, they say, every woman must be regarded as an individual whose particular life experiences have contributed to her offence.

Whatever the views of radical feminist commentators, most professionals working within prisons see, or are required to see, 'tackling offending behaviour' as part of their job. There is no female equivalent of Grendon Underwood, the therapeutic prison for men which—according to the statistics[4]—can reduce recidivism. An attempt a few years ago to set up a female unit at Grendon was strongly opposed by women's groups and by female prisoners (often abused themselves), who objected to the idea of being held on the same site as male sex offenders. Many feel that women should certainly have this kind of unit, but based in a women's prison. Meanwhile a wide variety of staff in female establishments may be involved in some form of therapeutic work—from prison-based psychologists, probation officers and chaplains to visiting counsellors and therapists. Most prisoners at some point will be required to prove that they have indeed addressed their offending behaviour, most significantly for the purposes of parole reviews. So it is important to consider some of the issues involved.

First, can the kind of therapeutic work needed to help people address the reasons behind their offending behaviour possibly co-exist with punitive regimes? Second, if this work is to be undertaken in prisons, who should be doing it? Third, is offending behaviour best tackled in group sessions, and if so, should prisoners be grouped according to the offence they have committed?—or is individual counselling more likely to be successful? Fourth, what methods are used during TOB sessions, and how is effectiveness monitored?

These questions all pre-suppose that prisoners, and the professionals working with them, accept that an offence has been committed. Apart from those prisoners who maintain their innocence, there are many who will rationalise actions which, although they constitute criminal offences, can (the perpetrators argue) be justified by the circumstances in which they occurred.

At the end of *Chapter 12*[5] I quoted the views of Dr Alison Liebling that far too many women are sent to prison, and that the idea of tackling the offending behaviour of women driven to crime by the exigencies of their social circumstances is pointless: it would be more humane—and in the end more cost-effective—to tackle the social circumstances. In the Inspectorate's review of women's prisons, Sir David Ramsbotham chose to use the phrase 'women who become prisoners' as a deliberate recognition of the previous life experiences of women in prison.

Many of the women in my sample had certainly come into prison from circumstances of abject poverty, and were burdened with crushing debts. They were victims of long-term unemployment afflicting the whole family—often the result of past privations and present economic factors far beyond their control. In *Chapter 1*[6] I quoted Home Office statistics which show that three quarters of imprisoned women have been remanded into custody for non-violent property crimes. My sample shows a similar proportion of women in this category.

One prison counsellor was troubled by the thought of TOB for such women: 'It's not so easy to think what you should do about all the women imprisoned for TV licence fine default, specially as they are usually on very short sentences.[7] But maybe we can deal with it by giving advice on debt, how to organize your money—a lot of the offences are about not being able to cope in that way.' She made a clear distinction between TOB and therapy:

> What I do is therapy—and therapy is not tackling offending behaviour: the offence is peripheral to my work. But if therapy is effective then there will be less offending as a result. For instance a woman might say she's a shoplifter, she is addicted to shoplifting, she loves it, she loves the adrenalin and so on. But she might also say she wants to give up the addiction because she's fed up with being in prison, she misses her kids or her dog. Then I can say "Let's look at this, let's deal with it." And I will roll up my sleeves.

Prison probation officers—often asked to undertake 'the dreaded TOB'—shared this counsellor's misgivings. The senior probation officer in one open prison said angrily:

> I have fought long and hard against "doing TOB". I get so annoyed with all these management theories about offending behaviour. If a woman has lost her house she can't possibly hope to go straight. The new rules on housing benefit[8] have caused *chronic* problems. I monitored the first three months of the new regulations and found that in this prison alone 15 women and 33 children became homeless as a result. This is outrageous. You can't talk about not shoplifting when women have nowhere to live. There are a lot of poor women in prison, very poor women. I feel there's a vindictive attitude, especially towards women.

A probation officer in a remand prison agreed:

> It's all too easy to patronise people with things like "money management". Personally I think it's impossible for anyone to manage on £49 a week: I can't see the point of telling people how to manage on the low levels of income support some of them receive. They will just pay the first urgent bill that comes along then will be left with nothing for food and the other bills.

However I do think we can help women with what I call "coping with the system" — how to use the DSS rules, how to get the best out of various services. There is an awful complacency around that people do know how to access these services — but they don't.

Perhaps the best research is to ask the prisoners, to listen to their replies and to respect their judgment: it was moving to hear Vicky, a 17-year-old girl with two small children (see *Chapters 5, 6* and *11*), expressing her simple needs:

> I would like these things in prison: to learn how to budget for money, for instance if you only have £50 a week, how can you make do on it? You need help with making a list for food, toiletries, how to learn to pay all the essential bills first. Otherwise when you go out with that £50 you'll just blow it if you don't learn to do it when you're in here. The other thing I'd like would be for self-harm and abuse courses to be put on to teach people to have confidence in themselves and ask why they behave like they do. There should be more group work to tell people how they can stop and what alternatives there are. Like how if you feel like cutting up you can go for a run, kick a ball.

In the absence of any of this kind of help at her open prison, Vicky had had to resort to self-help.

> In a way it's done me good, coming into prison. Behind my door[9] I've done a lot of thinking. I've had time to think about life. I wrote down all the things I don't like about my life on one side of a piece of paper, and all the things I do like on the other — sort of "For and Against". I want to be able to throw away the things I don't like.

Prison officers felt that male prisoners would usually accept their crimes and do their time, but women were much more likely to argue that they should not be in prison at all. Certainly staff find the most difficult prisoners to work with are those who rationalise their behaviour, claiming that their offence is a 'victimless crime'.

One woman, jailed for credit card fraud, explained how she had begun 'doing cards' to make ends meet. Her story illustrates the problems likely to be faced as a result of the 'Welfare to Work' schemes planned by the Labour government, unless jobs for single parents are accompanied by subsidised, high-quality childcare provision:

> After I had my son when I was 21 I went back to work but I had to pay £75 a week for the childminder, I had to buy the nappies and food and everything, and I was only earning £130 a week. But once I started doing

290

cards it was so easy I ended up getting greedy. I had two children by then and I wanted the best of everything for them. If only I'd stopped before I got caught.

This woman said she regarded her offence as a victimless crime, because the insurance companies always compensated the card-owners.

Probation officers at different prisons all seemed to deal with this 'rationalising of crime' in similar ways: 'We have a debate and de-rationalise the crime. We do it by role play—which works very well with young offenders—and assign different roles to prisoners. One would be the insurance company rep and so on. The women are very good at keeping to their roles and this is how we try to show the ripple effect of crime.'

Another probation officer said she tries to shows that crime makes victims of everyone: 'Their crime means that there are whole council estates where people can't get insurance. Because of their shoplifting, prices go up and people can't afford to buy so much.' The logic of this approach does of course depend on the chance of detection: I interviewed women who had carried on shoplifting or doing cards for many years without getting caught, and who knew of dozens of others still continuing undetected. They could not see why they should not get a piece of the action, and indeed, if prices rose higher, this was seen as an even greater incentive to shoplift the goods they needed and wanted.

A senior probation officer at an open prison says that rationalising of crime is an idea she often has to address:

There does not appear to be an immediate victim to a crime like credit card fraud. So it's our job to look at who really are the victims. We say "If you take a whole rail of clothes from Marks & Spencer, what do you think the store assistant feels, how does she feel making the statement."

We look at the women's own families and ask them how they think their children feel, now that their mum's in prison. We try and tell them that it's selfish to offend, that their kids are missing a lot by not seeing them. This may seem like emotional blackmail but I think it's justifiable if it goes some way to prevent further offending. We get them to write down the pluses and minuses: we say "OK, you gained short-term, maybe you got some nice clothes for your kids. But on the minus side you are now in here for two or three years and you have no control over your life. Was it worth it?" Then we will start being positive. We say "How can you get your life together from now on?"

The desperate circumstances of poor foreign national drugs 'mules' were discussed in *Chapter 10*. But young European couriers, according

291

to probation officers, are often unwilling to accept that drugs importation is a crime at all. 'They say that addicts choose to take drugs and all they are doing is providing a service, just like a wine merchant. They are often not involved in drugs themselves and do not regard themselves as criminals.' This prison runs one-day workshops to explain the effects of specific drugs to those who import them as well as to users. They recently had a 'cocaine day' run by a London group that deals with cocaine addiction for women.

HM Inspectorate, reporting in 1997 on courses available at Holloway Prison,[10] complained that 'the system for identifying the needs of individuals was unsophisticated. We found some evidence that the targeting of women was not good'. The importance of targeting women for relevant courses was stressed by a woman recently released from prison: 'Because of the delays in the criminal justice system, a lot of women have long ago left the problems that caused their crime. My offence [fraud] occurred during a vacuum in my life when I was dysfunctional. I was a victim of domestic violence and once I had managed to leave the problems receded. So the course they wanted to put me on was utterly inappropriate.'

The only form of TOB that Women in Prison supports is cognitive analytical therapy, which attempts to change people's behaviour by getting them to think about the likely results of their actions. One experienced counsellor who works with women remand prisoners agrees:

> I don't see it as my job to deal with offences, because these women have a history of people supposed to be dealing with their offending behaviour and yet the recidivism still goes on. I want them to learn to take responsibility for their actions. If this happened there would not be so many offences committed in the first place. This is really what cognitive therapy means—making people realise the likely consequences of their behaviour and making them take on the responsibility for what they do. Perhaps I could help a woman say no to things she doesn't want, for instance to say no to a man who is abusing her, or to say "no" to taking drugs, or to say "no" to carrying a packet of drugs on a plane. All we can do is to give women choices. A good image is jumping over a cliff. A woman may think there are only two choices: to jump over the cliff or not to jump over it. I would try to show her there might be a path down that cliff.

The Prison Service has introduced a cognitive skills programme into some of its establishments, including two women's prisons— Holloway, where it has been running for two years, and Cookham Wood, where it started more recently. The programme, called

Reasoning and Rehabilitation (R and R), has been used on a large scale in Canada. It focuses on appropriate criminogenic needs and is multimodal—that is it recognises that offenders may have a wide variety of problems. Psychologists running the programme in Britain have so far targeted longer term prisoners—usually lifers, drugs offenders and violent offenders in groups of about eight prisoners—and are in the process of evaluating the programme in terms of reconviction rates.

Alice, a lifer nearing the end of her sentence, says R and R is the best course she has ever been on and thinks it should be on offer in every prison. It differs radically from the usual TOB course in that the prisoner's offence is never mentioned:

> Some of us are murderers, some are shoplifters or kiters [passers of forged cheques] — it doesn't matter. Today's session, for instance, was about failure — and the best thing is that we learn that though something we have attempted may have failed to happen, we are not ourselves failures. We learn to find another way to reach our goals, or how to move on to a different goal.

Perhaps the aim of cognitive therapy is best summed up in the words of Melvyn Rose, former head of the therapeutic community Peper Harow, near Guildford (sadly now closed) which rescued so many damaged and damaging youngsters: 'What we are about is turning thoughtless acts into actless thoughts'.

Many of the offences of the women in my sample had certainly been the result of impulsive behaviour. So many of the drugs couriers I spoke to, for example, had made a sudden decision to get on a plane at short notice. They may have been women (like the foreign national prisoners described in *Chapter 10*) made desperate by poverty and debt. Or they may have been young girls excited by the prospect of a free holiday, of fast, easy money, or even—as one said—'just for a laugh'. A psychologist who often works with these women said 'They do it for a lot of reasons and it is rarely finance alone. It is often to escape from a humdrum daily life. I think the buzz and excitement, the opportunity of a trip to Jamaica, is often underestimated.' In her play *Yard Gal* Rebecca Prichard, a writer in residence at Bullwood Hall, brilliantly recreates the lives of girls in a Hackney posse (gang), with their indiscriminate use of drink and drugs in pursuit of 'the buzz'. The impact of prison on these girls is very great because it has rarely occurred to them to think of the consequences of getting caught. Several of my interviewees were all too aware that impulsive behaviour can also become addictive behaviour: they too described their crimes in terms of an addiction which they did for the excitement, the buzz, the adrenalin. This is the kind of behaviour one prison psychologist tries to tackle with many of her prisoner clients:

> We look at the short term and long term consequences of impulsive behaviour. So many people will say "I have no control over what I do or over what people do to me." I thought it was very telling when one woman said to me recently "My temper keeps losing itself" — as if it was nothing to do with her! We need to teach people responsibility, how to identify the warning signs. I try and get them to look at patterns, to analyse, to think for themselves, to think what to do about it if it happens again. You have to be realistic and move in very small steps.

The Prison Service may eventually decide to implement its own cognitive skills programme throughout all its establishments, including all the women's prisons. Until then, TOB courses will continue to be delivered in various ways by a variety of staff—though most professionals said they try to use cognitive therapy in their work with the women, for instance by using 'spider-web' diagrams to show the ripple effect of different crimes.

Of all the prison-based professionals I interviewed, probation officers and psychologists, often working in partnership, were most likely to be concerned with TOB, though as the Inspectorate review noted[11] only three women's prisons have at least one full-time psychologist. The inspectors recommended that every women's prison should appoint an in-house psychology team.

Holloway still maintains eight probation officers but as one of them said 'We feel very lucky because our services have to be bought in by the governor and we are expensive. Luckily he feels we are important'. Holloway's probation team is divided up among the wings, where separate groups are run. For instance those working with women on C1, the psychiatric wing, run a young offenders' group called 'Chill and Chat' to give young women techniques to deal with trauma and to cope[12] in prison. Other prison probation teams are less fortunate than Holloway's, and probation officers commonly made comments such as:

> We are cutting back so much and there are so many pressures of work. I have already been pulled off a lot of the group work I was doing here and I am likely to be sent back outside very soon which means there will be no prison-based probation officer here. I feel I can do some good in this prison because there is time for counselling, which there is no time for outside. I believe in probation as it was when I trained. There is no social work element left in probation now except in prison and that is getting less and less.

294

In a House of Lords debate on cuts in the probation service (16 July 1997), Baroness Masham of Ilton spoke of her distress at discovering, in an enquiry into the holding of girls in prison, that there was only one probation officer for every 100 women prisoners. Because of overcrowding, she said, prison officers had no time to operate the personal officer scheme and deal with housing and childcare problems, so this work fell to probation officers, leaving them little time to offer any form of rehabilitative courses.

All the prison probation officers I interviewed were insistent that offending behaviour cannot be tackled in isolation but must be firmly rooted in the offender's social circumstances. As one explained:

> I see our role as helping women start to think about the problems in their lives which led to offending behaviour. We don't live in a reality-free environment and I think we have to give women strategies to try to resolve their problems when they get out. When I first came to work in a prison I thought my work would be just about practical matters. But now I would be concerned if probation officers only offered practical help. You can feed in endless resources but you need to get in underneath people's offending behaviour, look at the range of options and give them choices. Their choices may be very limited but you hope to show them that there *are* choices.

During the period of my research, most probation teams were still managing to run a number of groups, and the accounts in this chapter give a flavour of what was on offer. One probation team in a closed prison has started a group called 'Women in Relationships':

> In fact this is really assertiveness. We look at how society sees women. We begin by looking up the words "masculine" and "feminine" in *Roget's Thesaurus* and find that the section for "masculine" includes words like "bold" and "daring", while for "feminine" there are words like "amenable" and "pliable". Then we consider words for men and women. For instance there is no real female equivalent of the word "stud", and words for women are often the same as for animals and children, like "chick" or "babe". We teach the women to be assertive rather than aggressive, and how to stand back and avoid confrontation.

Joy, 26, robbed a bank with a toy gun for money to feed her crack habit and was given a six year sentence: 'I'm doing therapy with the probation officers in here. It's assertiveness training and it's about how to tell people [to say] no. I thought I was assertive anyway. I'm kinda straight. But this stuff has helped me temperwise if someone insults me'.

Probation officers I interviewed were divided about whether such groups were best run as 'mixed-offence' or 'single-offence' groups. The second method targets women according to their offence, with separate sessions for life-sentenced prisoners, violent offenders, property offenders and so on.

Some prisons were already implementing the Inspectorate's demands for monitoring and evaluation.[13] One of the psychologists evaluating the work being carried out in an open prison (by a joint team from the probation and psychology departments) felt that mixed-offence groups were better for women: 'Male prisoners tend to present with one problem but women present with a whole range of things which are harder to separate out. Disclosure of sexual abuse is more likely to happen in a group situation than in a one-to-one session as women feel more comfortable in disclosing to other women in a safe environment'. As a senior probation officer at the same prison explained:

> Women are very good at throwing out lifelines to each other. They are more supportive to each other than men in a group. Research shows that it is more effective to target different offences in one group. The reasons why women offend might be very similar, with a common source, for instance childhood abuse. But the way people react in their offending might be very different. The women challenge each other on why they behaved the way they did. Men are often quite anxious and will not let down their defences and talk about their offence. It requires a lot of courage to do that. The women however are very open about their offence and also very supportive. We find we have good group cohesiveness and of course we insist on confidentiality within the group, which works very well.

There were other gender differences too: 'I find men will jump through the hoops necessary to get them through parole reviews, but they don't want to change their lives. Women do. Women will already be several steps ahead of the men because they will have thought about their lives, read articles in woman's magazines'.

There are some women whose offence makes group work inappropriate for them. Some are schedule one offenders—women who have committed offences against children. There is only one vulnerable prisoners' unit in the women's estate, at HMP Styal, so unlike male sex offenders, these women either have to remain on normal location, where they are often in grave danger from other women, or be put on rule 43 and remain apart, sometimes in the prison health care centre. They are advised for their own safety to lie about their offence and can only receive counselling one-to-one. One of the Holloway probation officers pulls no punches: 'Schedule one offenders are integrated with the other women in this prison and our duty is to start from the beginning to monitor the woman and try to work with her on her offence. The woman has to know what being a schedule one offender means. It means no children's visits on a Sunday, no control over her own children.'

One probation officer felt that by having the time to form a relationship she had helped a young woman who had killed a 14-month-old baby though initially the woman had staunchly denied the offence:

Then one day she suddenly admitted to me that she had killed the child and told me all the details. She was treating a 14-month-old as if it was a 14-year-old and so if the child made a mess she would yell at it as if it was a teenager. We both left the room in shock at this revelation but after that we were able to do some useful work together looking at the nature of parenting.

Because schedule one offenders are advised never to disclose their offence, probation officers say that it is especially difficult for them to help them challenge their offending behaviour:

We can't collude with them in hiding it and at the same time help them to face up to it and challenge it. They also lack a stable environment, because they are often sent from prison to prison when the other women find out about them. So they don't get the input they need from people like us. Though we do individual work with sex offenders and lifers, it's not easy for the sex offenders to come and see us. In this small prison everyone knows if a woman is a lifer or not, and if they see a non-lifer coming to see us it doesn't take much to work it out—so a lot of the sex offenders won't come.

It can also be very hard for them to show their feelings. We did some training here with our senior prison officers to teach them to work with sex offenders and we said to them at the start of the session: "Turn to your neighbour and explain your latest sexual fantasy." Of course they said they certainly would *not* do that! Then we said, "Well, think about what it feels like to be asked to do that even when you are 'normal'". If that fantasy is abnormal and involves, for instance, children, it would be far harder.

A *Panorama* investigation on BBC television in October 1997 shocked viewers with victims' graphic accounts of sexual abuse of children by women. These hitherto unheard-of crimes are becoming more familiar to probation officers:

We are certainly getting more of this category of women coming into prisons now, though I think it's just because victims are now more prepared to talk about abuse. Normally a man is involved as well and the woman will at first deny she did anything. So we will work on what he did and how he did it and she will begin to understand the context in which all this was going on and it will be a healing opportunity to her.

Most staff felt strongly that therapeutic work in women's prisons should be gender-specific. Rosemary King, head of psychology at Holloway, stresses the importance of anger management: 'There are much higher anger levels among women prisoners than among men. Other psychological needs have been noticed recently: learning difficulties, eating disorders, coping with HIV and hepatitis, gender identity problems and addicted women's distress at separation from their children.'[14] Many women's offences are directly linked to male violence in the home, and as another psychologist said:

For so many women it is the first time they have been removed from violence for years, and prison for them will seem like a haven at the beginning. It will be the first time they can have some time off for themselves. And if we can keep people here a little longer we can do something. In the longer term we may see a very gradual change in a woman, when she has had time and space to stand back and evaluate what has gone on in her life, the dangerous things that she has got sucked into. All we can do is facilitate change, be with them through the tangled mess of their lives. We can help them look at who they were before they came into prison, who they are now, who they would like to be.

One prison brings in workers from a local Women's Aid Federation to provide a forum for women to talk about their feelings. The probation officer running the group warned:

We have to be careful not to end up simply as a men-bashing group, but usually the women themselves sort that out. If the younger women blame the men entirely the older ones will say "Hang on a minute!" and we find they will take more advice from each other than they will from us. In fact I find the women very caring for one another within the group. Female prisoners are much more emotional than men and they'll show their feelings and the other women will help them.

The reasons behind an offence may of course reach far into a woman's past and some offending, such as arson and criminal damage, has been linked with continuing anger about childhood abuse. As a probation officer put it: 'It's no good looking at shoplifting in isolation. You have

298

to look at the drugs habit that caused the shoplifting, and the sexual or physical abuse that may have led to the drug or alcohol abuse.'

These prisoners are often the self-mutilating and suicidal women described in *Chapter 12*. They are certainly victims, but can they be helped—and *should* they be helped—to escape from 'the victim mode'? Rosemary King says, 'We don't perceive women as victims but as survivors'.[14]

The director of a women's support group, herself an ex-prisoner, is concerned that counselling can be self-defeating by trapping women in the victim mode:

> I have spent a lot of time talking to women who suffered sexual abuse and I tell them I am not a counsellor. I think you can argue, can talking really help? There is a simmering saucepan of human misery and it will all explode. There comes a point when you have to say to people "Stop making excuses: I know all the reasons why you are here in prison and I know it's all true. You are here for the same reasons I was here—and far, far worse. But while you are still blaming all this, while you are still using it as an excuse, you can't grow, you can't develop, you can't move on". We do not want a feeding feast on the agony. So—counselling can be a problem, because you have to get on with the future.
>
> Women *love* being counselled. They think it's great. But what is happening to them is that they are being problematised. Of course they have suffered educational, material and emotional privation but some counsellor digging around in the past may not be very helpful. I think a lot of these women prisoners are "people-pleasing". They love to tell counsellors—they love to tell you or me—that "you are the only person I have ever told this to". Rubbish! They'll tell anybody! They'll *give* you their lives! This stuff is roted. Their lives become a mosaic of "stuff" and this over-exposure of what has happened to them in the past doesn't help them—it just means they are out of touch with what is going on round them.
>
> We have got to get women away from feeling self-destructive because if you feel like that you don't mind who else you hurt either. But if you feel good, you can *do* good.

One therapist from an outside organization works with many such women:

> I absolutely agree that women should not remain in the victim mode. If a woman comes to me as a victim and tells me she was abused from the age of three to the age of 16 I will then be able to say "Right, you were abused, and of course you were a victim. But now let's see how we can use this to generate energy to change your life". It's a creative progression and I tell

people how to come out of all that shit in the past, to stop it corroding their future too. I would want to say that the abuse is something that can be worked *with*, not as an excuse for illegitimate behaviour, or for being ineffective in your life.

What seems most important is that prisons should be able to offer positive help to those women who ask for it. As one counsellor said:

There is a lot of negativity in prison. It is easy to be negative, for instance about some of the drugs programmes. But it's important to keep something going to support women with problems of drugs, sex abuse and so on. So at least there is *something* going on for them. Otherwise what are you supposed to do with people in prison—just let them sit round on their backsides all day saying they are victims? There must be some positive input, even if it may not always work.

The inspectors regretted that prison officers were not always involved in managing programmes and they found few staff who had received training for counselling abused women. They recommended training officers in such issues because, they said, some of the best therapeutic work in women's prisons 'depends on the awareness and skills of individual staff and the rapport achieved with individual prisoners'.[15]

Although most groups were run by joint teams from probation and psychology departments, in several of the prisons I visited, a Prison Service initiative called Shared Working in Prisons (SWIP) is put into practice. SWIP was set up to facilitate the running of multi-disciplinary groups, where probation officers, psychologists and prison officers work together. But in other prisons I was told that the clash of two opposing cultures—the punitive and the therapeutic—make this scheme unworkable. This problem begs many questions about the success of a suggested merger between the prison and probation services.

One probation officer thought such clashes were regrettable: 'Some of the officers are positive, keen and enthusiastic, and they are not allowed to use their training.' But many prisoners said that a group with an officer present would not help them: they could never speak freely about their offence because they could never trust the officers not to use information against them in compiling reports which might affect their parole. In the view of one experienced professional therapist (from an outside agency):

There is no doubt about it—officers are the enemy. They are not just *perceived* as the enemy by prisoners, they *are* the enemy, because they are the ones locking them up and stopping their freedom. The personal officer[16] is just a prison officer by another name who can lock a woman up, stop her visits, send her to the seg.[17] Can we really expect an officer to say, "I can do all this to you—now tell me all about yourself."? Would *you* tell them anything? I sure as hell would not—because they have so much power over you.

A spokeswoman for Women in Prison is convinced that former prisoners could be most effective in helping women still in prison: 'Women need ex-prisoners going into prisons to show that they have come out on the other side. They need a lot of inducements and no bullshit. I would have lots of groups with ex-prisoners. They must be drug-free and crime-free and they must have come out on the other side to show that it can be done.'

Dr Mary Eaton, writing in the journal *Criminal Justice Matters*,[18] praised an anti-addiction programme called the Personal Empowerment Programme (PEP) which was run at Holloway in the early nineties by trained women who were ex-addicts and ex-prisoners: 'Previous programmes for addicts have been officer-led, which raises basic questions about the role of disciplinary agents in a process which should increase the autonomy of prisoners by challenging their dependency.'

Increasingly harsh security measures have in recent times made it difficult for ex-prisoners to be accepted as workers in therapeutic programmes. When HMP Coldingley allowed an ex-prisoner (a convicted drug dealer) to counsel addicted prisoners the Prison Officers' Association told the media that its members were furious. The charity Rehabilitation of Addicted Prisoners Trust (RAPT) had used the man in their three month programme which relies partly on ex-prisoners as peer counsellors, and the *Mail on Sunday*[19] ran a story headed 'Drug Dealer gets keys to Prison'. But the charity has persevered and now works at Downview and Pentonville as well as Coldingley—though not yet in any women's prisons.

The value of former prisoners returning to work in prisons in this type of capacity seems undisputable: everyone fighting an addiction needs living examples of people who have had the same problems and overcome them, who understand and who cannot be hoodwinked. They know too that their advice is based on experience not simply on theory. Commercial organizations like Weight Watchers and self-help groups such as Alcoholics Anonymous and Narcotics Anonymous are well aware that this method works.

There are other imaginative and valuable initiatives like Prison Dialogue, whereby experienced facilitators set up and run voluntary, agenda-free conversation groups in prisons, involving prisoners, prison officers, probation officers, chaplains, members of Boards of Visitors. In

July 1997 Jimmy Robinson, one of the freed 'Bridgewater Four', returned to just such a group in HMP Whitemoor. He was able to give the group the benefit of the philosophy he had developed over the years in prison ('I zigged when I should have zagged') and to listen to their views non-judgementally.[20]

It seems unlikely in the current still punitive political climate that many ex-prisoners will be permitted to undertake this kind of work. An alternative is to bring into the prisons workers from other outside agencies. Although prisons remain in some respects very secret places, one healthy sign is the number of outside agencies now being co-opted to take on 'the dreaded TOB'. Kate Donegan, in her desire to 'ventilate' Cornton Vale, has brought in no fewer than ten voluntary organizations including bereavement counsellors and marriage guidance advisers.[14]

One absolute essential is to keep these outside professionals entirely distinct from the process of parole, unless specifically asked by their prisoner-clients to write a report on their behalf. The difference between external independent counsellors and all the other prison-based professionals is that the latter all have the burden of reporting on a prisoner, and that report affects, most significantly, the prisoner's date of release. Only complete outsiders can be without this burden.

Although the Prison Service claims to be committed to TOB I found it shocking to discover that in fact some of the most damaged women are not getting any help at all. As the stories in the last two chapters illustrate, it is still standard practice in some prisons to confine those who harm themselves in the segregation block, or at best to stitch up their wounds and return them to the wing. And as described in *Chapters 11* and *12*, there is also, still, heavy use of psychotropic drugs in some women's prisons.

In one closed prison, male senior managers spoke proudly of a new pilot group set up to deal with a small number of such women, all serving long sentences, who do not 'fit in with' the rest:

There are about five or six women who don't fit in anywhere and they have a high rate of self-harm incidents. They don't fit into the activities group, they can't clean the wings, they are disruptive and potential suicides and they cause a lot of hospital watches. They are the sort of women who would not be in prison if the mental hospitals hadn't been closed down. But we've got to deal with them somehow. So we set up a group called the Pilot Project Group—a multi-disciplinary group which gives them ten hours a week. There is input from the education staff, the chaplains, probation and so on.

This seemed hopeful, though the next comment was rather worrying:

302

'One of the things we teach them is personal grooming. They have two sessions—four hours a week on that. Now they can do their own hair and nails. We also do sugarcraft—cake decorating'. The group meets five days a week. The day I was invited to join in, it was run by a woman assistant chaplain, a member of the multi-disciplinary team, in a small cramped room just off the chapel. Four women (the other two were off sick) came in reluctantly and slumped down on easy chairs, sullen and silent.

The chaplain, presumably with a view to tackling offending behaviour, began by challenging one of the women about her precipitate return from another prison: she had gone off for a three-week period for accumulated visits[21] but had been sent back in less than a week—for disciplinary reasons, the chaplain told me later.

'You know the reason you were sent back', said the chaplain, confrontationally. The woman immediately became aggressive: 'You don't know nothing about it, so why are you talking about it?' At this point another of the women decided to walk out of the room and the chaplain had to follow her.

As soon as she had gone, the women launched into their grievances. They were articulate and they were angry. The group, they said, was boring: 'There's nothing for us here, and we get no help', said one woman whose arms were covered with the scars of self-mutilation. 'For so long I've wanted people to help me. If we cut up we're sent to the block and left on our own. Four months ago there were eight of us who needed counselling about sex abuse and I found out there was a Christian group who would come in once a week. We put it to the governor and it's been on his desk two months now. Most women in here have been sexually abused. But all they do is give us medication. Most of us are on medication'.

Next day I asked the governor why women who harm themselves are put on the block. He said this was untrue: women no longer cut up, he claimed, since the pilot project group was started.

Two months later I went to Holloway to visit a woman who had been brought there from this prison for accumulated visits. I asked how the pilot group women were doing. She reported that they cut up more than ever, one of them slashing her throat in a terrible wound. The woman who had reacted so aggressively to the chaplain's remark had just attacked another prisoner with boiling water. 'So the group can't be doing much good, can it?' said the woman I was visiting.

Though any help is better than none, these were seriously disturbed women who could not be helped by a mishmash of uncoordinated initiatives by well-intentioned staff. The group seemed to me little more than an underfunded sin-bin lumping difficult cases together. The governor's assessment that these women should have been in a mental hospital seemed to be misguided. In my view, they were not 'mad women', though they were certainly seriously disturbed. They had all been abused as children and the abuse must have contributed to their problems. But their condition was certainly exacerbated by the boredom and frustration of their incarceration. They were reacting to their captivity like zoo animals that pace their cages, lurch their heads from side to side and gouge their own and others' bodies.

And yet there is so much they could have been offered. Never have there been so many groups, charities and agencies, prepared to go into prisons and offer the stimulation of education, drama, writing, art—all the activities that contribute to rehabilitation. As the American criminologist Joycelyn Pollock says,[22]

> Prison is not like the "real world" and the problems that one has in prison will not be the same as those the women will face on release. It may be the case that counseling in prison simply acts to reduce the negative effects of the prison environment. The fundamental problems the female offender will continue to struggle with when she leaves prison and returns to street life can be addressed, but it calls for extra effort by the female offender and the counseling professional to get past the prison world.

The whole issue of therapeutic work with women needs to be thought through more carefully, with courses tailored to meet their specific needs, run by people they can trust. Above all, any therapy needs to move women forward and equip them with strategies to face the future. Only then will they have any motivation to begin to 'tackle their offending behaviour'.

Endnotes

1. 'Women in Trouble with the Law', 28 May 1996, Criminal Justice Associates conference at Inner London Probation Service HQ.
2. See *The Oxford History of the Prison*, Chapter 11, 'Wayward Sisters', Lucia Zedner, Oxford University Press 1995; and *The Imprisonment of Women*, Dobash R, Dobash R and Gutteridge S, Basil Blackwell, 1986.
3. *Women in Prison: A Review*, HM Inspectorate: 11.14, 11.30.
4. *A Reconviction Study of HMP Grendon Therapeutic Community*, Peter Marshall, Home Office Research Series, No. 53.
5. See *Chapter 12*.
6. See *Chapter 1*.
7. Women are disproportionately convicted of this offence. In 1993, 63 per cent of those prosecuted for using a television set without a licence were women, and earlier research has shown that many of them were single parents. The average length of each female fine defaulter's sentence in 1994 was five days—a short period but one that will have had devastating repercussions on the woman's family and her future job prospects, let alone on her

own self-esteem and psychological health. In 1994, researchers at Leeds University estimated that the approximate total cost of detecting, prosecuting and imprisoning a single parent with two children for one week is about £2,130, 25 times the cost of the original TV licence (around £85). Yet as this book goes to press, each week two women are sent to Holloway for this 'crime', though soon after he became home secretary Jack Straw announced that he would end the jailing of TV licence fine defaulters.

8. *See Chapter 1.*

9. Prison slang for 'in my cell'.

10. *HMP Holloway: Report of an Unannounced Inspection by HM Chief Inspector of Prisons,* Home Office, 1997.

11. See Note 3, above: 11.26.

12. I often heard probation officers and prison officers saying women prisoners needed programmes because they 'lacked coping skills', a term which in itself can be regarded as patronising: many have 'coped' amazingly well outside prison in impossible circumstances. In the 1980s film *Scrubbers* about borstal girls, the main character, a woman whose baby is sent away for adoption, screams 'I don't want to cope — I want to be with my baby! It's a bloody insult to tell me to cope!'

13. See Note 3, above: 11.19.

14. Presentation at conference at HMP Styal 23 October 1997, 'Imprisoning Women: Recognising Difference'.

15. See Note 3, above: 11.29.

16. Each prisoner is allocated a personal officer who has a duty to look after that prisoner's interests and share work with the prison probation officer in relation to a sentence plan, and to put the prisoner forward for courses, education etc.

17. The segregation unit, or 'block' where prisoners who break prison rules are kept apart from others.

18. See *Criminal Justice Matters*, Vol. 14, Winter 1993/94.

19. *Mail on Sunday*, 15 September 1996.

20. 'Back to the Dialogue as a Visitor', Peter Garrett FRSA, coordinator of Prison Dialogue.

21. Prisoners held in prisons far away from family and friends can be allowed to amass their permitted visits: they will then be taken for a few weeks to a prison nearer home which is easier for visitors to reach.

22. *Counseling Women in Prison*, Joycelyn M Pollock, Sage, 1998.

CHAPTER FOURTEEN

Devils' Advocates?

Alice became a born-again Christian in prison. She also got married. She met her husband when, after she had served 13 years of a life sentence, her open prison allowed her out to work in a Christian Aid centre in a nearby town, cooking lunches for homeless people: 'He'd reached rock bottom with drink and drugs and he was living in a car.' The relationship blossomed and eventually Alice got Home Office permission to marry. The wedding, with Alice chained to an officer by a ten-foot shackling chain, was attended by many members of the local church congregation. Alice was taken straight back to prison but her new husband went to the reception the church had provided, then returned to a flat entirely fitted out by donations from church members.

Carol was a 30-year-old prostitute with two small children when she was arrested. She had been a heroin addict since she was 13:

> I only managed to give up drugs because of some Christian people who helped me. Before that I'd tried everything to get off drugs, all sorts of detoxes—and I've been in mental hospitals and everything. But it must have been the right moment for God because I gave up everything, just like that, without detox or anything.

In our increasingly secular and multi-cultural society, is there a role for ministers of religion in women's prisons? I came across other success stories like those of Carol and Alice: one Anglican chaplain told of a lifer who on her release hoped to become one of the first women priests. But of my sample of 150 prisoners, only a small minority—just 28 women (19 per cent) mentioned religion. Of these, 18 said they actively practised their faith: 12 were Christians (six born-again Christians), five were Buddhists and one was a Muslim. The Buddhists said their religion helped them personally, but complained that the Prison Service still did not recognise Buddhism as a religion.

HM Prison Service guidelines are ambiguous on what should be regarded as a religion. The Prison Service Chaplaincy publishes a *Directory and Guide on Religious Practices*, available to prison staff from the library, prison chaplain or race relations liaison officer. Its contents are summarised in a small pocket guide issued to all prison officers, called *Race Relations and Religion*,[1] a title suggesting that these two areas go hand in hand. The introduction to the booklet says it contains 'a brief summary of the major *religions* [my italics]. There follow seven sections—on Christianity, Buddhism, Hinduism, Islam, Judaism, Rastafarianism and Sikhism—with sub-headings like history, dress, diet, festivals and the work adherents can be expected to do in prison. But only five of the seven are then referred to as religions. Buddhism is said to be 'philosophy rather than religion', and, the booklet says, 'Rastafarianism is not officially recognised by the Prison Service as a separate religion'. However the guidelines state clearly that 'members of non-Christian religions' have the same right to practise their faith as Christians', and emphasise that provision must be made for them to do so.

Since the early nineteenth century, the Christian religion has been used to 'tackle the offending behaviour' (see, generally, *Chapter 13*) of incarcerated women. Elizabeth Fry and her Quaker ladies saw religion as a major tool of reform for the 'blaspheming, fighting, dram-drinking, half-naked women' she found in Newgate in 1813.[2] After the passing of Peel's Gaol Act in 1823 barring male warders from any access to female prisoners, the chaplains remained as the only men allowed into women's prisons, though the new legislation required them to be accompanied everywhere by female warders. All prison education was the responsibility of the prison chaplains[3] and the first governors were ministers of religion, combining disciplinary and pastoral roles. The Reverend Walter Clay, a renowned prison chaplain in those times, spoke of the problems of disciplining women: 'It is well known that women are far worse to manage and resist what is for their good far more vehemently than men.'[4]

Histories of women's prisons do however include records of the concern expressed by some prison chaplains. For instance the chaplain of Brixton Prison in the late nineteenth century (when it was a women's jail) pleaded for alcoholic and mentally ill women to be given treatment rather than punishment. His words could equally well apply to the drug addicts and mentally disordered offenders in today's prisons—though perhaps his motives sprang more from pragmatic concern about control than from humanity:

> It does seem important that women of this class should be treated in a special manner and in a special place, and that they should be placed under medical treatment, as their presence among other prisoners operates most injuriously upon those around them, and constitutes one of the chief difficulties in carrying out the discipline of this prison.[5]

It is hardly surprising that captive women regarded chaplains as agents of punishment rather than sources of compassion and support. Penal historians[4] describe how they persisted in barracking preachers in prison chapels, imitated and mocked their sermons and threw prayer books around.

A century later the role of prison chaplains is equally ambiguous. An incident one Sunday in May 1995, described in Sheila Bowler's diary when she was at Bullwood Hall, shows that little has changed:

> Church service a disaster yesterday. So noisy with many of the inmates not only talking, clapping and shouting but actually swearing when going to the altar for communion. The rumour is that they only come to chapel to pass their drugs, though there are always a lot of officers standing round the edge. It was a shame as the Methodist minister who led the service had brought his guitar along.

HMP Brixton, the South London men's prison, was a female jail for forty years between 1852 and 1892, and its magnificent chapel still stands as a monument to Victorian reforming religious zeal. Few of the chapels in today's women's prisons can boast the splendour of Brixton's soaring arches. The women's estate is an odd mixture of assorted establishments and the chapels are rarely purpose-built. Holloway's chapel is one of the few that is: it can seat 150 women in the main Church of England chapel, as well as those wishing to attend the smaller Roman Catholic chapel, added later and curtained off. Some chapels are very small: in one prison I visited just before Christmas, two chaplains were discussing the carol service: 'What about the Muslims? We can't fit them all in'. 'Don't worry about them', was the reply, 'they can do Ramadan.'[6]

Bullwood Hall's chapel is a converted classroom and the chaplain there was looking forward to installing some perspex 'stained glass' windows made by a prisoner 'to make it into a special room'. Drake Hall's chapel, though now quite pleasantly refurbished, is in a strange building like an aircraft hangar, which it has to share with the prison library. Styal's chapel, with its lofty beamed ceiling and lovely Victorian stained glass, also reflects its earlier incarnation (as a nineteenth-century orphanage). One of the few multi-faith chapels is Risley's, beautifully furnished and decorated. It has a special prayer room for non-Christian prisoners, with footwashing facilities and a shower for the performing of necessary ablutions. It is in the middle of the men's prison and because Risley is a category C training prison the men have some degree of freedom to come and see the chaplains, a freedom denied to the 150 women in Risley's female unit—though at least they have their own separate services in the chapel. In HMP Durham the 44 women on H wing are not allowed in the main prison chapel available to the 800 men—fortunately perhaps, the chaplain joked, because the roof leaked so much he had brought the chaplaincy's potted plants in to be watered.

In May 1996 the Archbishop of Canterbury, Dr George Carey, who was himself a part-time prison chaplain in Durham in the 1970s, was invited to give the annual lecture of the Prison Reform Trust. In a speech, entitled *Restoring Relationships*, he outlined the 'formidable triple challenge' facing the Prison Service: 'a sharply rising prison population; tight financial constraints including a 13 per cent cut in unit costs over the next three years and a greatly intensified focus on security which, interacting with the other two factors, could make it more difficult for the Prison Service to offer a constructive and humane prison regime.'

Dr Carey's personal interest in prisons continues. Sheila Bowler describes his visit to Holloway in late April 1997: 'We had a short service in the chapel with the governor and other dignitaries, but the Archbishop really wanted to talk to the women. He didn't dress up in his robes—he wore an ordinary suit. He brought his wife with him and they went to the wings people really should see—the psychiatric and medical wings and D0 [D zero]—the wing where pregnant women are.'

With such a degree of support from their leaders, what should be the role of the churches' foot-soldiers in the field—the prison chaplains? Standing order 7A of the Prison Rules states that 'the Prison Service respects the need for all prisoners to be free to practise their religion'. But like most other aspects of the Prison Service the chaplaincy provision is being cut, with the loss of many full-time posts. Increasingly, Anglican chaplains are assuming the same job-patterns as colleagues from other faiths, working primarily as parish priests and taking in the prison as part of the parish, just as they would a hospital or old people's home. Many prisoners I interviewed felt this was a change for the better: prisons should simply be part of the community in religious terms, with local ministers of all religions visiting regularly. The women thought this was the only hope of clergy having genuine independence and avoiding accusations of collusion with the prison authorities. This would be part of the process of 'opening up' the prisons to outside professionals, as with the provision of health care (see *Chapter 11*) and the probation service (see *Chapter 13*).

The present arrangements for the employment of prison chaplains are singular, to say the least. Every prison has the right to its official prison chaplain—whether full-time or part-time—who must be an ordained priest of the Church of England. Every prison also has a Roman Catholic chaplain, while the non-conformist faiths are represented by a Methodist minister. The Home Office has in addition a list of other religions whose ministers they will agree to fund.

Some prisons can call upon the services of a local Imam, who would be funded by the Prison Service. But to receive funding for an Imam or a Sikh minister, for instance, the prison must have some Muslim or Sikh prisoners in custody. Even within these Prison Service guidelines there are some strange anomalies. For instance, in April 1997 one women's prison had a Methodist minister who was paid for ten hours a week though there was only one Methodist prisoner; whilst the Pentecostal minister was paid to come in for only four hours a week, though Pentecostal prisoners formed the largest group, because of the popularity of this faith with the high percentage of black women held in that prison. In spite of the historical involvement of Quakers in prison reform, Quakers are never employed under the chaplaincy rules because there are rarely any Quaker prisoners. Many Quakers do help in prisons, but have to be brought in by Church of England chaplains under special arrangements like the Holloway Chaplaincy Visitors' Scheme.[7] Risley's chaplaincy team has to provide for a great variety of religious faiths: roughly two-thirds of the prisoners are registered as Anglican and one third Roman Catholic, but there is also a wide variety of other religions including thirty Muslim prisoners. Orthodox and Reformed Jewish rabbis visit regularly.

The Prison Service has not in the past provided any specific training for ministers of faiths other than Christian denominations. But in April 1997 the first ever multi-faith training day was held at the in-service Training College near Rugby. This pilot day was so successful that there are now plans to run it annually.

Until 1994 an important side-effect of the existing rules was that women were barred from holding a post as a senior prison chaplain, even in women's prisons. Now that women can be ordained as priests in the Church of England they are free to apply for this job, though some experienced women priests are still excluded because they are beyond the age ceiling of 50.

These anomalies have led to demands from groups like Women in Prison for the removal of state control from prison religion. In our increasingly multi-cultural society, some prison reformers now feel that prison chaplaincies should be disbanded, and ministers of religion from the local community should be invited into a prison by the governor to meet the spiritual needs of individual prisoners. One Church of England prison chaplain sympathised with these demands:

There has to be someone to facilitate the spiritual and pastoral needs of the prisoners but it need not necessarily be a Church of England minister. Prison management will of course say they are guided by the registrations of women's religions when they come into reception, and there are still more who will write down that they are C of E rather than anything else — though of course they may not ever have practised that religion. But the main point is that the need springs from the women themselves and that

310

this need should be met.

The organization of such provision would however be extremely complex, especially in a large remand prison like Holloway where nearly two-thirds of the prisoners stay in the prison only one month or less.

In five of the prisons I visited I was able to interview a sample of ten chaplains of different denominations: Church of England, Roman Catholic and Methodist, and equal numbers of men and women. I also interviewed one of the Roman Catholic nuns attached to an open prison.

Each of these five prisons runs a chaplaincy team, sharing duties and sometimes taking it in turns to provide chapel services. All my chaplaincy interviewees said that every woman newly-received into the prison should be seen by someone from the chaplaincy team soon after arrival, regardless of her faith or of whether she is religious at all. The chaplains usually offer individual counselling sessions by appointment. They will also try to visit women in the health care centre and the segregation unit. On Sundays they run a variety of chapel services, some of them inter-denominational. These are not always easy to fit in with their other parish duties. As one Methodist chaplain put it 'Every Sunday we have a half hour service and this is very inconveniently timed to fit in with the prison regime, not with the women or with us. We find there's a conflict with our own churches outside. The Anglican chaplains do three Sundays a month and I do the fourth. The Catholic service is every Saturday night.' Sometimes chaplains are asked by officers to see women who are going through particular trauma. They may be approached by a woman's personal officer or one of the nurses in the health care centre, and asked to support a woman going through a bad patch.

Most chaplains emphasised that their ministry was to the whole prison. Their duties were best summarised by a Methodist: 'We see ourselves as priests, conducting weddings, baptisms, funerals, but we also see ourselves as pastors who can be alongside officers as well as the women in times of stress. And we see ourselves as the prophetic voice, the voice of conscience of the prison.' Some duties were unexpected: 'I have been called to dedicate or bless a cell—I hesitate to use the word exorcise—because the women had a very strong sense of what had happened in there in the past'.

One Catholic priest at an open prison refuses to say mass in the prison chapel. He is a parish priest and feels that the women in the prison, as part of his parish, have the right to join other parishioners at the local Catholic church. For many years this arrangement worked well, with the women simply writing down their names on a list on a

311

Saturday evening, and then attending mass on the Sunday morning. But stricter security measures following escapes from the male prisons at Parkhurst and Whitemoor have meant a tightening of the rules on temporary release. The priest was angry: 'Now they can't come to mass at all until they are risk-assessed, and this process may take about four weeks. Even if they have been passed, they now have to apply on a Monday to attend mass the following Sunday. It's outrageous: going to church is treated as a privilege and it should not be.'

This priest has more than once clashed with the prison authorities. The week before my interview, two women had purchased cigarettes, Coca-cola and chocolate on the way back from mass. Someone in the village had reported them to the prison: 'The Governor called me in and wanted me to say who they were but I refused. I said to the Governor "I am a chaplain, not a custodian. It's your duty not mine to get to the bottom of this. Don't ask me to shop the girls." And I wouldn't betray them.'

I asked the priest whom he regarded as his boss: 'I am not employed by this prison. My boss is in fact the senior RC chaplain of the Prison Service—below the Almighty of course, who's the boss of us all!' I put the same question to the Church of England chaplains. They all said the Prison Service was their employer and paid their wages, and they were responsible to the number one governor—through their 'line manager' if they were assistant chaplains—but also to the diocesan bishop.

This anecdote reveals the potential conflict of interests that confronts many prison chaplains. The concept of the secrets of the confessional, of priests holding in their hearts the truth of many a murder mystery, has for years fed popular romantic imagination. But it is in reality a conflict that chaplains of all faiths have to face every day. Several chaplains also spoke of cases where they believed there had been a miscarriage of justice: 'It's our duty to listen to the women. We are supposed to help women come to terms with their crime, but if a woman continues to protest her innocence I would tell her to pursue her appeal because everyone should pursue what is right'.

How far, then, is it the duty of chaplains to represent the interests of their individual prisoner-parishioners? How can this be reconciled with their commitment to the interests of the whole prison and everybody in it—including prison officers and other staff who all fall within their ministry? All the chaplains I spoke to said they set definite boundaries in their conversations with women, making the guidelines clear at the outset of any consultation. The formula was almost identical in every case: if a prisoner reveals anything that threatens the security of the prison or is a threat to her own personal safety or that of the other prisoners, then it is the chaplain's duty to pass it on to another professional. As one Anglican chaplain put it: 'If I am told something in confidence, that remark will go no further unless the woman is planning an escape, or self- harm. In that case I'll try and say before she tells me, "Hang on a minute—for the sake of everyone else in the prison I'll have to repeat this if you tell me."' Some chaplains did however admit bending the rules for humane reasons—for instance letting prisoners use the chaplaincy office telephone for urgent phonecalls. One Anglican chaplain said:

> I was ordained fairly recently as one of the first women priests and so I have only just been allowed to hear confessions officially. Hearing a confession is quite different from just talking to a minister. It is a formal process which people must prepare for. I tell women to write down what they want to tell me and think about it. But there are boundaries and again I would make it clear that though I would not divulge anything I was told in that situation, I would still have to share with other professionals anything that could harm the woman herself, harm another prisoner, or threaten the security of the prison. The other distinction I would make is if a woman is ill and needs treating. If I think she is emotionally disturbed I would refer her to somebody who could help her. Some of my friends think I am out of order in this, but to me, if a woman is in desperation and distress, that means she is ill.

A Methodist chaplain in a different prison agreed: 'I try to talk to women and get them to think before they cut up.[8] There are all sorts of reasons why they cut up and one is the inability to express themselves and their pain—so they express themselves by expressing blood. I will also say to a woman "I don't want to know if you are taking drugs, but if you are, and want to give them up, I can put you in touch with the right agency."'

These are the daily problems chaplains have to face, but what of the greater ethical question: how can ministers of religion reconcile their calling with being in the service of increasingly punitive masters? Are they as much part of the penal establishment as their Victorian predecessors? Like the question posed in the last chapter about the difficulties of reconciling therapeutic and punitive regimes, it is one that does exercise the conscience of many priests and ministers.

Prison chaplains have a particular privilege endowed upon them by their calling—the right of access. Officially, prisoners do not lose their right to practise their religion even if they are segregated in the punishment block. Each day one of the chaplaincy team has the right to visit the segregation cells and the hospital:

We have the advantage of having keys and being able to go to any part of the prison. We have no obligation to be part of the structure. We can walk with authority into any place. We are on a par with senior management. (Methodist chaplain)

Chaplains are allowed to visit prisoners even when there is a general 'bang-up',[9] though they can only speak to them through the hatch in their cell doors. Several expressed their distaste for this 'hatch-culture' but they acknowledged that at least it gives them access to the women, though there can be no confidential consultation in these circumstances. In the segregation block, chaplains must sometimes bear witness to distressing events and inhumane events. How can they remain true to their vocations and yet keep silent about such matters?

One Anglican chaplain said

I see it as my function constantly to challenge the system. If the Governor respects you he will listen and he may ask for your advice. I see myself as a walking question mark. But I do have a problem in that I am in conflict with Michael Howard's whole idea that "prison works"'.

He pointed through the chaplaincy office window: 'Look at all this razor wire,[10] and there are security cameras and dogs everywhere. The Prison Service has spent £10 million on this prison but nearly all of it has been on security measures. They have all this obscene security and they are cutting regimes to pay for it'.

Chaplains can also give their prisoner-clients a public voice by speaking out through their union, the IPMS (Institute of Professional Managers and Specialists). Mike Dixon is a spokesman for Anglican prison chaplains. He used to be Anglican chaplain at Durham and minister and counsellor to the women on H wing, including Rosemary West. He was quoted in *The Observer* in December 1996[11] expressing his anger that the Prison Service was cutting the jobs of so many priests. He told me

As a member of the union I can go to the Prison Governors' Association and get my voice heard, which I would not be able to do as an individual. When I was still working at Durham I was asked to go on Radio Newcastle on a panel for a phone-in on law and order. The Governor was quite happy for me to speak on the radio as long as it was just in my capacity as a member of the union, rather than as the chaplain of HMP Durham.

However, one experienced criminologist I interviewed remains sceptical about the motives of prison chaplains. He believes that most are prepared to sacrifice the interests of the prisoners on the altar of their own religious freedom:

> Chaplains have a huge opportunity to influence prison culture but they have limited themselves to the delivery of religion to the inmates, when they could have ministered to the whole prison. This especially applies to Roman Catholic priests who don't intervene and won't do anything provocative against prison policy for fear of compromising their own religious freedom. They seem willing to subject themselves to the secular authority of the management providing they can retain their religious autonomy.

All of the chaplains I interviewed seemed able to compartmentalise their duties quite clearly into their formal religious observances and their personal counselling of individuals, to which most accorded equal importance. If any of them had inherited the harsh reforming zeal of their nineteenth century predecessors they were certainly not prepared to admit it: on the contrary, all were at pains to appear understanding, forgiving and, above all, non-judgmental.

A fitting symbol of current attitudes is perhaps the Holloway Easter celebrations: at the Maundy Thursday service two of the chaplains ceremonially wash the feet of women prisoners—while on Easter Monday 1997 Terry Waite came along to judge the Easter Bonnet competition!

None of the chaplains I interviewed saw it as part of a chaplain's job to undertake 'the dreaded TOB'—the task of tackling offending behaviour discussed in *Chapter 13*—though in fact all admitted that they did approach the issue, albeit indirectly:

> The crime is always at the back of my mind and sometimes I approach it in an oblique way. Offences are often caused by extreme stress or abuse and are often unpremeditated, sometimes when the women are under the influence of drugs or drink, or of another stronger person. If they had been rational free agents at the time they would not have committed the offence. But these women are not always amenable to my saying to them "Tell me why you did your crime". (Woman Anglican chaplain)

> Some of the women, the shoplifters for instance, see total justification in ripping off the big stores. I'm not here to be judgmental. I might say "How do you feel regarding your offence?" Some will brazen it out, say it's just taking from the rich. Others will feel dreadful shame. I speak very briefly to them about their offence and sometimes I will just say that we all make mistakes at times in our lives. (Roman Catholic chaplain)

My attitude is that these are women who have been judged by society and I am not standing in judgment on them again. I am here for their welfare — spiritual, emotional and psychological. (Woman Methodist chaplain)

I don't see tackling offending behaviour as part of my job — that's more for probation and other staff. I feel that a lot of these women didn't get a chance from the start. They are more sinned against than sinning, far more to be pitied than blamed. Many carry a terrible burden of abuse. (Roman Catholic chaplain)

How do we address offending behaviour? We show forgiveness and emphasise that we are open to everyone. We look not just at the past but at the future, build up self-esteem, see what could be, not what was. I don't judge what they are here for — I can't possibly know what they have had to put up with. We also have to think of the victims and when women realise the serious effect they have had on other people's lives they may want to atone for it. I would want to hear that from the prisoner herself. Once she says "Yes, I know that was wrong", then we could start asking "Well, how could you put it right? How can you avoid it happening again?" (Woman Anglican chaplain)

One priest uses the time-honoured method of the parables. He had had the sad task of assisting at the funeral of a prisoner who died in custody, allegedly of an accidental drug overdose. He had taken the woman's three cell-mates with him:

As the funeral cortege drove out of the prison all the paths were lined with girls paying their last respects. The woman was the mother of three young children and not long before she died she'd asked me to ring her mother to see if they were all right. Going round the prison after the funeral I told the women that the oldest lad's nickname was Tinfoil, referring to the foil used for drugs. I told them that in the hope it might get through to some of the smackheads in here who are mothers, bring them up short and make them realise this could be said about their own child.

Understanding and empathy are of course vital, but how far can the Church move these women forward, prepare them for release and help reduce the chance of reoffending? So much depends on establishing a genuine relationship of trust with the women, because most imprisoned women feel there are few people they can trust. Chaplains, like all prison-based professionals with the exception of independent external counsellors, have a duty to contribute to parole reports and other internal prison assessments. This puts them in a position of enormous power because what they write can affect a woman's security categorisation, the decision on what prison she is sent to next and most importantly, her date of release. One woman spoke bitterly of a negative report she felt the Anglican chaplain had written: 'I trusted him and he told a lot of lies about me'.

The chaplains, however, all rejected suggestions that they are seen by prisoners as an arm of the prison establishment. They maintained that they would always consult a woman's own minister for an input into prison reports if she were not of their own faith. None accepted that some women may find the same difficulty in trusting them as they do in trusting personal officers, other officers and probation staff.

A senior Anglican chaplain said he had to do F75 reports, the name for the periodic review reports on life-sentenced prisoners. He saw this as an opportunity for counselling: 'I have to comment on where they should be going next, what options and courses will be available to them and so on. As I talk about these matters I can drop in some discussion about what they did and why they did it—though of course many of the more serious offences were caused by a one-off set of circumstances.'

Several of the chaplains said they were simply there to comfort and befriend and one quoted a text from the gospel of St Matthew: 'I was in prison, and ye came unto me'[12] Several said they preferred to see themselves as 'comforters' rather than counsellors. As a Methodist chaplain put it: 'The problem with counselling in prison is that the word has been hijacked by the professionals. I would always say that I am a minister of the church and counselling comes under that bracket'.

'I invite the women to coffee and a friendly chat' said a Catholic priest. 'One girl told me "I'm not that bad. At least I only steal things—I don't beat people up." I try and say to them "How would you feel if that happened to your mum?" After two or three weeks, even if they have no religious background, I often find them coming to me and saying "My auntie's ill, will you say a prayer?" As chaplains we have no axe to grind, so very gradually trust is built up.'

The women chaplains stressed the importance of gender-specific counselling:

I find it helps to be a woman in a women's prison because there are so many issues of abuse. Women often come into the criminal justice system because of their background and frequently because of their partners. There is so much abuse—physical, mental, emotional and social—where assumptions have been made about a woman's role in the domestic family group without her agreeing to the agenda. So men can be regarded as a threat and women are not comfortable with them.

A male Anglican chaplain partly blamed the church for the high incidence of battered wives in situations of domestic violence:

A lot of women here have a history of abuse and very low self-esteem. The Church is part of the problem in that it insists they remain married at all costs even if they are beaten, especially if there are children. These women need strong female role models, positive images, and I don't think the church is offering these at the moment. One of my jobs is to offer choices to women and they find it difficult to make choices because for a lot of them their men have always made the choices.

A senior woman prison officer in a different prison was impatient when a new chaplaincy appointment replaced a woman with a man. 'I'm fed up at the way men are being brought in for these women. We used to have a nun who had a very good way with the women. But she has taken sick leave and instead they have sent us an oldish male deacon who goes round looking bewildered. There are so many nuns around I can't see why we couldn't have another of them!'

But in one open prison the Catholic priest is the only man in the chaplaincy team: the Anglican and Methodist chaplains are both ordained women. A Catholic nun, who used to teach in the South American missions, visits the women regularly:

I will go to anybody that asks for me and I might be able to help by just chatting. Though I'm a nun the majority will talk to me on equal terms, woman to woman. Their greatest cry is for their children: if only they could see them, what they are doing. This is a constant worry and they want to get back to them. This is usually true no matter what they have done. I think it's inhuman for them to have to leave a young family, often for a first offence and a mistake they have made. By locking women up for not paying their TV licences you have done great damage to the family and made it harder for the woman to get a job later. I think the children should be allowed to stay with their mothers here at least till the age of five when they start school. The woman talk to me as an outlet and at least I can direct them to someone else if it's something I can't deal with.

A Methodist woman chaplain admitted she sometimes found it difficult to establish a rapport with more serious offenders:

It's sometimes hard for me to come to terms with a horrendous crime a woman has committed. You can't sit and listen to it without a feeling of horror. But you have to be professional, receive it in the spirit of the confessional, and realise that it is good for the prisoner to face the full impact of what she has done. The major issue is the person herself and the

318

way she is working through the horror of what she has done. The horror is not the prime focus—the woman herself is the prime focus. How she responds to this working-through is important, but I also try to recognise and reflect back at her the nature of her crime. I don't want to lay on her any more guilt than she already has, so I would reflect back the crime in the most constructive way possible.

What about a woman's own religious beliefs—can they be reconciled with the most serious crimes? Can a strong faith help in rehabilitation? A woman Anglican assistant chaplain believed both were possible:

Part of my job is to comfort them through their sentence and some of them do get a lot of help from their faith. It is very difficult for those who have any religious faith to reconcile what they have done with what they believe. But we believe in Christian forgiveness. When they fully understand that, they are sometimes able to let go of their guilt. A lot of them cling to their guilt and feel they ought to be punished for what they have done. Many are grieving because they lost someone they loved, and they may also have lost contact with their families. Once they have reached a right understanding of the Christian faith it can strengthen them, but you can't push women to that. Moving on to a reconciliation between themselves and God is a real jump, and needs a maturity of faith because that is the nature of forgiveness.

What practical help can the chaplains offer? Some of the chaplains said they tried to interpret the prison system to women, explaining for example the sending out of visiting orders, helping visitors find accommodation if they have come a long way, escorting children from their carers at the prison gate to meet their mothers on children's visits. None had been asked to visit prisoners' families, but most said they were prepared to if such a request should be made. In some prisons where there are mother and baby units, chaplains arrange for local members of the Mothers' Union to come and take babies out to the park or the shops for a few hours so that they get more stimulation.

Chaplains see themselves as an important link between the women and the outside world. 'We are not social workers', said a woman Anglican chaplain, 'but we can direct women towards various agencies that can help them on release'. All chaplains have access to church networks that can help women while they are in prison and when they leave. There are many informal links: when a woman moves prisons and a chaplain may telephone his or her counterpart in the next prison and ask for continuing support. Sometimes a woman's own parish priest is able to come and visit her, and a Catholic woman may receive support from her local St Vincent de Paul Society on release.

In Risley, for instance, the Anglican chaplain runs 'Overcomers' groups to help people fight drugs and alcohol. There are separate sessions for male and female prisoners and the groups meet twice a week for 14 weeks. Seven women have joined the course and the chaplain feels it is working well. One of its strengths is the network of similar groups outside the prison, which means that women have a group to go to once they leave. 'We fix prisoners up with a prayer partner, who could be a Christian outside who is prepared to help someone. The network of supportive groups outside is very important so they can keep up the work and tie in with their local church.'

Prison chaplains have also been known to act as mediators between offenders and the victims of their crimes if they live locally. This kind of restorative justice is an increasingly popular concept for those working with young offenders, but it has to be handled with great sensitivity. One Methodist chaplain said she encourages women to write as if to their victims: they can then share the letter with one of the chaplains if they do not feel it is appropriate to send it.

Chaplains also bring into the prisons outside groups like the Prison Phoenix Trust, a meditation group. Mike Dixon said that when he was chaplain of Durham he felt it was part of his function to keep the isolated women on H wing in touch with the outside world: 'We ran a prayer group called the Julian group: a group of lay people came in every week to run meditation sessions. I also got in a lecturer from Durham University to run discussion groups. I brought a lot of students in too: I saw it as part of my function to make people especially young people, aware of what goes on in prison.' He was however aware that because of the high profile of some H wing prisoners, including Myra Hindley and Rosemary West, 'You have to be aware of goldfishing!'[13] What you need is a dialogue—people talking to the women. The prison visitor scheme[14] was very strong on H wing. We had 19 visitors going in to see the women once a week. Some were specialists, including a bereavement counsellor.'

Chaplains often act as the liaison officer for the prison visitors, the volunteers who can be such a valuable support. At an open prison I met a woman about to be released on appeal after serving six years of a life sentence 'The only visitor I've ever had is Sarah—she's a prison visitor. She comes and sits down and talks to me about my past and my future. We talk like friends and when she goes on holiday she sends me postcards to show me she's still thinking of me.'

Holloway also runs a special Chaplaincy Visitors' Scheme, started by a former head of inmate activities who felt that some prisoners had a special need for someone to talk to. As one of the chaplains put it: 'In prison everybody is always running about—there are so many people to see and people are always conscious of the clock. This man felt that the women, especially in the hospital units C1, D1 and H1, needed people to talk to them who had no statutory duties, no agenda. So we have at the moment seven volunteers called chaplaincy visitors who come in one day a week and go to the hospital units.' The Holloway chaplaincy volunteers come from a variety of backgrounds: one is from the Prison Fellowship, there is a Christian Scientist, someone from the Salvation Army and a Quaker minister. The chaplaincy visitors are mainly ministers of their religions but '. . . they are not coming in heavy-handed on religion'.

The chaplaincy visitors, like the chaplains, carry a set of keys and—also like the chaplains—are usually allowed to visit women in the segregation unit. One I met had spent 'a whirlwind of a day' comforting the friends of another prisoner who had just died of a drug overdose a few days after her release.

The problems facing official prison chaplains in an increasingly multi-cultural and secular society will not easily be resolved. Although many women regarded all chaplains as an irrelevance to the realities of prison life, others were grateful for the help they had received. As in all prison work, the quality of relationships is what counts. A Catholic chaplain told how he was recovering from a major operation when a lifer who had served 17 years got her parole:

Her husband and her entire family came to fetch her and they all left the prison at 7 a.m. Then they went to the nearest town for breakfast and waited for the shops to open. They bought as much fruit as all of them could carry and brought it to me at the chaplaincy. That's what I mean when I talk about befriending women in prison. They befriend us too.

Endnotes

1. Quoted in *Chapter 10*.
2. See *The Oxford History of the Prison, Chapter 1*, 'Wayward Sisters', Lucia Zedner, Oxford University Press, 1995.
3. Prison Reform Trust: *Education in Prisons: A National Survey*, Prison Reform Trust, 1995.
4. See *The Imprisonment of Women*, Dobash R, Dobash R and Gutteridge S, Basil Blackwell, 1986.
5. From an unpublished history of HMP Brixton compiled by serving male prisoners.
6. Obligatory fast for Muslims from dawn to dusk for one lunar month.
7. See later in this chapter; see also *Chapter 4* for an account of the work of chaplains as liaison officers for prison visitors.
8. Officially known as deliberate self-harm, as discussed in *Chapter 12*.
9. When all prisoners are locked in their cells.
10. The Prison Service insists that the wire used is not razor wire (which is an American product) but a wire of a different technical specification called 'S-wire'.
11. 'Cheap Deliverance for the Jailhouse Flock', *Observer*, 22 December 96.

12. Gospel according to St Matthew: XXV 35.
13. Some visitors are inclined to stare at prisoners, as if they were fish in a goldfish bowl.
14. See *Chapter 4*.

CHAPTER FIFTEEN

Rag Dolls and Muppet Shops

Notice at gate of women's prison

Liza, a life-sentence prisoner in Durham's H wing, has applied for legal aid to sue the Prison Service under equal opportunities legislation. As one of the 46 women held in the high security female block in the middle of Durham Prison, a local jail also holding more than 880 men, she complained to the Equal Opportunities Commission that the educational provision was far poorer for her and the other women than for the men. She also complained that while the men had access to full-time education, the women were limited to five sessions a week. She embarked on an A level law course:

> When I was arrested I knew nothing about the law—I had not even had a parking ticket. Prisons do try to put in many different obstacles to prevent you from study but I persevere. I could write a book about all the negativity and injustice. As I do not have the access to education here, I try to study in my room more and take the opportunity to read.

She was soon fired from her job in the H wing workshop: the works officer said she needed someone who could do the work properly and by this time Liza was felt to be spending too much time in the education department. She told me her workshop job was to press the red button on the back of a tumble-drier.

• • •

This chapter looks at education, work and training in women's prisons. The Further and Higher Education Act 1992 allowed for the contracting-out of prison education services. Amid enormous resentment, all prison education departments were put out to competitive tender, and by the end of August 1993 most of the new contracts were in place. New

College, Durham, won the contract to provide education for five prisons in the North East, including HMP Durham.

At Durham, the education department in the main men's prison is impressive, with a pleasant entrance foyer where men's art work of a very high standard is on display. I saw the large computer room with its twelve new Archimedes machines, the fair-sized and well-equipped cookery department, and plenty of classrooms and office space.

I was invited to stay for lunch with the staff, courtesy of the men's NVQ catering group. Part of their course is to cook and serve a three course meal. The food was excellent, served in the attractive surroundings of a large classroom converted for the day into a 'restaurant'. Tables were covered with peach-coloured tablecloths and each had a small ceramic vase with a matching peach-coloured rose. 'The women made the cloths and the vases', volunteered one of the staff. Another added rather nervously 'But you'd better not mention that when you see them. The thing is, they can't do NVQ catering themselves—there just aren't the facilities on H wing.'

After lunch I crossed the sloping rainswept tarmac patrolled by Alsatian dogs straining on their leashes and followed one of the teachers through a series of railings and a number of locked gates into H wing. The contrast between the provision for men and the provision for women could hardly be greater. Although H wing had been refurbished quite recently, there was only a small kitchen and one small classroom. On the day I visited there were just four women in the classroom and it looked crowded. The room opposite used to be a library but was being gutted and refurbished as an art room where an artist in residence would work with four or five women. The library had been moved to the top landing—'the Threes'—and when I saw it was still nothing more than two locked cupboards with not a book in sight. It was only opened once a week on Tuesday evenings, because the librarian spent the rest of her time in the men's prison: the books belong to the county library and no women were allowed access to them without the librarian being there.

The paucity of the educational facilities severely curtailed what the staff could offer. They had put in a bid to run an NVQ course in business administration but had to withdraw when the NVQ inspectors said they were not meeting the requirements—the women needed to be able to use a fax and deal with money. The education department did offer NVQ hairdressing ('in our apology for a salon') but even this was difficult because in such a closed community so much has to depend on simulations.

Each of the women was limited to a maximum of five sessions of education each week. If they wished to undertake an academic course such as an A level or an Open University degree (there is funding for only two OU courses) they had to study alone in their rooms. For the rest of their time 'out of cell' they had to do prison work—which in H wing was mainly cleaning—or attend the activities centre. Here they had a choice of four activities: sewing (mainly the soft toys ubiquitous in women's prison workshops); knitting (more soft toys, churned out on knitting machines), pottery (mainly ornaments) and 'laundry'—though this appeared to be little more than a series of large washing and drying machines in one corner of the room. The instructors said most of the women worked here full time, though a few did part-time education. They said they tried to offer a choice of activities according to a woman's preference and skills, but the women said that in reality newcomers were fitted in where there was a space, and many would remain on the same work for their whole time in the prison. The average time a woman stays on H wing is *four years*, with some remaining up to six years.

Sonya, like Liza, is serving a life sentence. She is the prisoner I described in *Chapter 8* spending the night in Holloway after losing her appeal. I met her when I visited the prison in November 1996 and she began writing to me in January 1997. By that time she had been in H wing nearly four years:

> I was put to work in the workshop [the activities centre]. It was soul-destroying. I am not interested in sewing so found it very difficult. The days were never-ending. I was in there for 12 months, then I was taken into a small computer department we had in there. It seemed like a breath of fresh air. The only work the two of us did was producing most of the paperwork for the wing. Hence it was not "profit-making" and therefore not viable and we lost it. I managed to get on a few classes and last year I passed an OU foundation course. I have done the second stage and am about to begin my third year OU. But I have to do most of it in my own time. My job on the wing is a cleaner. Nothing is done to encourage learning and if anyone has any inclination to better themselves, classes are limited to eight or ten women, so some wait far too long to get onto a class. Computers can only be used when a teacher is present and we only have *two half days* for these—*and* you can only be on one of those in computer classes.

I found it ironic that the male prisoners held at Durham, whose average total sentence is just three months, have access to a comparatively wide range of facilities and qualifications, while the women will spend at least four years in the prison and yet have such limited opportunities. Management however has an answer. A senior (male) manager told me:

It would be ridiculous to give employment training to women on such long sentences. The NVQ is seen as a preparation for release and courses like this would just be a wind-up for the women. They will eventually get all that when they go to a training prison for women for the second stage of their sentence—those prisons are geared up for that sort of work. We are a receiving prison. They have got to get their heads round their sentences and it is our function to get them to do that.

Another male officer used security as an excuse: 'The women do get education on H wing but they can't go to the main education department and their own education provision is not so extensive—we have Michael Howard's security measures to blame for that.'

The H wing women are certainly in a much higher security category than the men in the main prison. So a fairer comparison may be made with their male equivalents—the 420 life-sentenced prisoners, some of them, like some of the H wing women, 'natural lifers'[1]—at HMP Frankland, where education is also provided by New College.

Naturally, with ten times as many prisoners to educate, one would expect much higher staffing levels and more space: the education coordinator has 25 part-time staff as well as five full-time teachers and a full-time clerical assistant and there are seven classrooms and a library. But it is the range of courses on offer that is so much more impressive. Frankland is an industrial working prison specialising in wooden furniture, but the men can opt for full-time education and this is then regarded as the equivalent of a job of work. About a quarter of the men currently make this choice but they can also attend evening classes. The education department was looking at a job-share scheme so that it could extend its courses to far more men.

The men who opt for industrial work, unlike the women making soft toys and pottery ornaments, can get qualifications: they can do NVQs in painting, decorating and wood-machining and the higher GNVQ qualification is available in art and design. There are ten PCs and a computer workshop where there are a further half dozen PCs for computer-aided design. There is a small cookery department. The vulnerable prisoners have a special unit with three classrooms, art and design and a workshop with a woodmill and a polishing shop. The VPs can also have access to the computers and the cookery department one evening and one afternoon a week on their own.

Of course Frankland has its problems—for instance it proved impossible to offer NVQs in laundry and horticulture because the prison could not meet the requirements. Lack of funding led to a reduction in the number of Open University courses from 20 to 12, and there were 25 more men on the OU waiting list. But still the men in this dispersal prison are far better off than their female counterparts in H

326

wing. And nobody has suggested that for them NVQs are a 'preparation for release' that would be a 'wind-up'. Nor are they expected simply to fill in their time on mindless tasks while they 'get their heads round their sentences'.

At the opposite end of the educational spectrum from women like Liza and Sonya are women who are barely literate. In one of the few women's prisons with a particularly impressive education department, I was told by prisoners: 'The education here is excellent, but the women who need it most don't get it.' A senior officer in this prison agreed: 'A lot of women are not literate enough to take advantage of the computer provision. We don't have the remedial facilities to teach the ones who need it most. Unless you can read and write you can't have equal opportunities.'

The subject of education and training for women prisoners has, like so many other aspects of women's incarceration, been largely ignored. The Prison Reform Trust (PRT) published a study[2] of prison education which included a review of the existing literature. Its authors could find little in the literature on the subject of women's education, but quoted from the most recent policy statement they could discover, a 1973 document entitled *Education in Establishments for Women and Girls*. This could do little better than to refer to an even earlier Prison Service policy statement, issued in 1969, which stressed that education for women should be an 'aid to living' rather than a 'tool for a job'. There should, said the document, be an emphasis on courses with a domestic element, rather than on training for employment. The PRT points out that job opportunities for women are very different over a quarter of a century later, and concludes that 'it is to be regretted that no new policy statement on the education of women prisoners, which recognises the contribution of vocational skills, has been forthcoming from the Prison Service.' The emphasis on domesticity is not peculiar to UK women's jails: during the 1997 media coverage of Louise Woodward's trial and incarceration in the USA, reporters discovered that a report on Massachusetts prison regimes found that the only skills taught at Framingham prison in Boston, where Woodward was held, were flag-making, manicure and typing.

The inspectors noted in their review of women's prisons[3] that 36 per cent of the women they surveyed reported having had serious problems at school. The inspectors deplored the lack of coordination and co-operation between women's prisons on educational matters and felt this was yet another reason to appoint a director of women's prisons. They recommended regimes that are a mixture of daytime education classes, vocational training and industrial activities. They emphasised the importance of helping women to achieve a 'marketable skill' as an aid to preventing reoffending.

These aims would seem to fit in well with the Labour government's twin policies of Welfare to Work (with special reference to single mothers who may stand to lose their benefits if they refuse to seek employment) and Lifelong Learning whereby adults continue to improve their skills.

During my first research period in prisons,[4] primarily to explore the links between failure at school and later offending behaviour, I visited six men's and six women's prisons. I was also interested in finding out whether prison education departments were picking up the pieces where schools had failed.

I asked in the initial pre-interview questionnaire whether prisoners were continuing their education in custody. For those who said they were, I included two further questions:

- If you are continuing your education in custody, please give details of what you are studying: (please include vocational training, PE, construction industry training, NVQ etc)
- If you are continuing your education in custody, can you tell us how this has helped you/is helping you where perhaps school failed you?

The response, from 250 prisoners (138 men and 112 women) showed that 68 per cent had undertaken some form of education and/or training in custody. In the National Prison Survey, 47 per cent of all the prisoners questioned said that they attended education or training classes in prison, and nearly half of the remainder said they would like to do so.

The young offenders in my sample who were under school-leaving age were obliged to attend 15 hours of education a week, while the remand prisoners may not have been able to attend education classes at all, as there is no obligation on any prison to offer them education or training.

It has also to be recognised that although at my request prison staff undertook to distribute my questionnaires in four different areas of the prisons (the gym, the library, the education department and then at random anywhere in the prison) those who volunteered to fill in a 12 page questionnaire were more likely to be following an educational course, or at least interested in education. Nevertheless, I did receive replies from some seriously dyslexic prisoners who struggled to complete the form because they wanted their voices heard. Several illiterate prisoners, including two women, had asked other prisoners or officers to complete the form for them.

More men than women in my sample were involved in some form of education or training—79 per cent of the men compared with 53 per cent of the women. The women tended to give negative reasons for choosing to go on courses. Common comments were: 'It passes the time'; 'It's relaxing'; 'It keeps me occupied'; 'It keeps me going and makes the time go faster.' Men on the other hand were more likely to see education and training as a chance to enhance their future career prospects: 'I'm doing education to further my career, or to change it'; 'Prison education is helping me to gain a new vocation'; 'I may be able to use my qualifications to find employment on release'; 'Computers have helped me with job applications'.

Twice as many men as women took Adult Basic Education. Three times as many men as women took English examinations. Eight times as many men as women were studying a foreign language to examination level. Twice as many men as women had begun or applied to begin an Open University degree course (this could not be accounted for by sentence length, which was fairly similar in the men and women in my sample). However, proportionately twice as many women as men studied art and craft, pottery and calligraphy. The percentage of women taking part in groups for aromatherapy, yoga and reflexology was six times higher than the percentage of men. The therapeutic value of such courses is undeniable, but unless they offer some form of accreditation they are unlikely to enhance a released prisoner's job prospects.`

Forty per cent of the women said they were on some sort of course, but the courses they listed were very limited in the range of choices they offered. At first it seemed encouraging that the largest group of women mentioned computer skills. But their qualifying remarks and the follow-up interviews revealed that 'computers' often meant very basic office skills, and only a few women had been given enough hands-on experience or tuition in keyboard skills or programming to enable them to seek employment on release. Most of the other courses were, depressingly, stereotypically 'feminine': including needlework, soft furnishing and dressmaking; health and hygiene, beauty and fashion. More useful were catering; business administration and hairdressing. Two-thirds of the women had either taken no courses at all, or had mentioned a mixture of courses, most of which could be classed as 'leisure' or 'relaxation' rather than work or training. Only a very few of these led to any formal qualifications.

The six men's prisons in the sample offered a much wider choice of education and training courses. Twenty-nine per cent of men were taking computer courses: some of the computer departments I visited had state of the art hardware and software and men were producing high-quality work; eleven per cent were doing business studies; the other 60 per cent were being trained in a very wide range of practical and vocational skills. Among the courses they mentioned were: building construction; industrial cleaning; electrical wiring; technical shopkeeping; forklift truck-driving; carpentry and joinery; bricklaying; welding; electronics; road transport qualifications; agriculture; horticulture; bespoke tailoring; cookery; library qualifications; marketing; technical drawing and the ABTA certificate for travel agents.

During my second research period I noted several positive developments. The first was the publication in February 1997 of a *Directory of Education and Training Provision in Women's Prisons*, produced by (ETAS) the Education and Training Advisory Service for prisons, with the help of prison education coordinators and heads of inmate activities. The directory should be updated on a quarterly basis.

The list shows the courses on offer in daytime, evening and weekend classes and the work and vocational training courses available. This is an important step forward because for the first time, as far as I am aware, all education staff (and, one hopes, prisoners) will be familiar with the courses on offer throughout the women's estate.

Although the educational and training courses and work available do not seem to have changed radically during my two research periods, there are a few other welcome trends, such as the increase in availability of business studies course and the introduction of new and interesting options like psychology and media studies. Most encouraging is the increase in accreditation of so many courses.

There are other interesting developments. One of those I discovered when I contacted ETAS in summer 1997 in preparation for a seminar on possible links between dyslexia and offending. ETAS has set up a pilot project at a male young offenders institution[5] to offer diagnostic screening and follow-up treatment to dyslexic prisoners. It is hoped that the project will be extended to all prisons and that diagnosis and treatment of specific learning disabilities like dyslexia will be available to all incoming male and female prisoners.

Another is a proposal for a project by the Suzy Lamplugh Trust, working with NACRO and the London Action Trust, to look at dyslexia and offending from the crime prevention angle.

• • •

Historically female prisoners have always been subjected to mindless and laborious tasks.[6] The Dutch Spinhuis, built in 1645 in Amsterdam as the first prison in the world designed specifically for women, was taken as the model for the employment of captive women as spinners, weavers and seamstresses. Throughout the centuries, while men were sent outside the prison and employed on public works such as building and stone-breaking, women remained inside engaged in soul-destroying repetitive tasks. Their labour was also essential for the upkeep of the largely male prison population. It took 200 years longer for Brixton Prison to be converted into Britain's first exclusively female jail, and almost immediately the treadwheel, a vast drum with slatted steps on which male prisoners had been made to grind corn, was replaced by a new laundry to take in washing from the men's prisons.

It could be argued that, given the very limited employment options open to nineteenth century women, the domestic tasks they learned in prison were better targeted at enhancing their prospects of supporting themselves on release than the training given to women prisoners at the end of the twentieth century.

In the mid-nineteenth century, released women prisoners faced such stigma that employment was virtually impossible, and attempts to address the problem were made with the setting up of state-run refuges. It was felt that employers would be more likely to accept women from a refuge than a prison. The Fulham refuge took a few of the less troublesome women and tried to provide them with skills like household cleaning, cooking and laundering, and most of all a 'good character' [reference] which would make them marketable as domestic servants.

During my first research period[4] I was visiting prisons at a time when education departments were still in turmoil and some staff were anxious and demoralised because of the job insecurity created by imminent privatisation.[7] This coincided with the devolving of budgets to individual prisons. From 1 April 1993, prison governors became holders of their own purse-strings, able to parcel out funds for education and training as they saw fit.

However at the beginning of that period the recommendations of the Woolf Report[8] were still able to engender a feeling of optimism that, given the resources and the will, education and training could make a real contribution to rehabilitation and the reduction of recidivism. Judge Tumim's innovative ideas[9] about 'real work for real wages' led to exciting initiatives involving commercial enterprises like Reed Secretarial Services (Holloway) and the fashion group Red or Dead (Full Sutton). Though there were mistakes, failures and even disasters, there was still a feeling that things were happening in the prisons and anything was possible.

When I embarked on my second period[10] of research three years after the start of the first project, I had no reason to revisit any men's prisons, but I was able to revisit the education departments of two of the women's prisons from the earlier project: I will call them Prison A and Prison B.

When I first visited Prison A I had been impressed by the entrepreneurial energy of the education coordinator who was working hard to attract industrial and business sponsorship for Open University degrees and other courses. I was also able to see at first hand one of the most daring, controversial and, as it turned out, short-lived experiments in modern prison education. Prison A is a shared-site prison with male and female prisoners in separate wings. At that time the education department set out to reflect the ethnic and gender mix of the providing college. This meant that the department was coeducational, and it also included VPs,[9] many of them sex offenders on normal location in the classrooms with other prisoners. All the men and women I interviewed at the time said they liked the arrangement because it felt 'more normal'. One woman said 'I found the education all a bit artificial over there on the women's block. There's a much better atmosphere over here with the men. They're no trouble at all.'

The education staff at that time made comments of their own: 'Having the women in the education department has a calming effect on the men: it makes everything seem normal.' Though they added the caveat: 'We have to be very careful who we take, because some of the women only want to come over to pass their drugs'.

Three years later, everything had changed. Again I interviewed the teachers. The mixed department had been, they said, 'a distraction' and now there was once again separate education for men and women. At the beginning of the experimental period, the women had been carefully selected, but as time went on things became more lax and real problems had arisen. 'One woman found she was in the same room as a man who was in prison for raping her when she was on drugs.' The teachers felt that both men and women were put in an invidious position, under great pressure to carry drugs and letters between the male and female prisons.

The three teachers I interviewed this time (all female) put the blame very much on the women:

The men found it distracting that the women used to dress up provocatively. Some of these men are in prison for a very long time and it's just not fair on them.

The women were doing the rounds, cadging cigarettes off the men. They knew some of these blokes from outside and it put us in a very difficult position.

332

Personally I think the women ruined the system for themselves. They picked silly young women and I could do nothing about it. They had total disregard for me. I remember one of the women grabbed one of the men by his private parts! If he'd done that to her there would have been assault charges and goodness knows what!

If you are a nice bright girl you have to be extremely careful. You are in a difficult position. It was hopeless — they were all ogling the blokes and that created a lot of bad feeling. There was jealousy over here too, among the women who were not chosen. Yes, it was all very difficult.

The concept of mixed-sex classes in prison is undoubtedly problematic, especially when a high percentage of male sex offenders is involved, and when it affords yet another opportunity for the passing of drugs. But what concerned me about these interviews was the way most of the blame was directed at the women. The mention of provocative clothes cast the women once again in the role of temptresses arousing uncontrollable male lusts, and the teachers' words were reminiscent of the views of female staff on the 'proper' way for women officers to dress—for the same reasons.[10]

One of the teachers did register concern about the underlying purpose of the coeducational experiment:

The governor thought it was more civilising for the men to have the women in there. It's true they did get more resources over there on the men's side. There's a fabulous hairdressing salon there — but mind you, the women never learnt any hairdressing skills — they were just the models!

I was unable to compare the experimental coeducational period with the education currently on offer to the women in Prison A, because for the entire period of my three-day visit the women were hardly allowed to attend any classes at all. There were severe shortages of disciplinary staff to act as escorts round the prison and to supervise the classes. The teachers were despondent:

There are so many problems with the officers — there have been problems since Fresh Start.[12] We have a lot of officers off sick or on bed watches. The women are locked up a lot. Classes are cut day in, day out. Out of eight sessions we have four cut today. Thursday morning all the classes were suddenly cancelled.

I have to go to other areas of the prison if classes are closed down here in the education department. I'm doing the run-around. I try and see girls on the hoof. Sometimes we might be allowed wing classes if they are on unlock.

333

I've found it impossible for them to do the WordPower exams—there isn't enough constant contact time.

The women are very keen on arts and crafts—very enthusiastic. But of course we can't do a thing with them if we can't get them into the craft rooms. If there's a problem with officer supervision, education is always the first to go.

We have now got to the stage where the girls are saying "What's the point?" If they are stuck with only one lesson a week they just don't want to know. So we have no students at all at the moment.

On the way from the education block to the main wing, I spoke to another teacher, a bright and obviously very committed young man. He seemed popular with the women waiting in the lunch queue who were angry at losing yet another morning's classes. The teacher was just as angry and disillusioned:

I'm looking for a transfer to another prison and if it's no better than here, I'll leave the Prison Service altogether. We can't teach the women because they're banged up the whole time because of staff shortages and the work to rule. We can't even get them over to our department, much less teach them anything. It's an explosive situation and if we don't divert these women, give them something to do, it will get worse.

When in 1996 the Conservative government imposed on the Prison Service a 13.5 per cent cut in unit costs to be implemented over the next three years, it was inevitable that this would have an adverse effect on prison education. Some prisons have tried to become as entrepreneurial as schools in seeking funding and sponsorships. At Prison A British Nuclear Fuels funded an Open University degree course. More recently a classroom in the same prison was refurbished with money provided by a TV company in return for using the premises as a film location, with some of the prisoners and officers used as extras.

· · ·

When during the first research period I visited Prison B, the new education coordinator had only just been appointed and admitted there was 'much scope for improvement'. She knew there was a lot to do but 'being realistic it is going to take quite a while to get it right'. One of the prisoners said at that time that courses were rarely completed: 'Only one or two a year if you're lucky, due to frequent absences of staff. In hairdressing the staff have one week off in four'. Another agreed:

334

Organization is poor and many girls are allowed to play up in class and some do nothing in education. There is a shortage of places so they should get rid of the girls who just muck around in class. The Office Skills course is very well run, but in DTP [desktop publishing] there are not enough machines and those we do have are not the sort you'd find in any place of work outside.

Three years later, the department seems much better organized. Three-quarters of the courses are now accredited and the education coordinator hopes for full accreditation soon. Women wanting full-time education are allowed this in place of work. If they need help in maths and English alone they are allowed off work for this. There are now extra courses in First Aid, Childcare and Hygiene. The full-time secretarial skills course is run as a workplace: there is a dedicated room with 10 PCs and a photocopier and the women work towards an NVQ qualification. Although most of the work is simulation, if real work opportunities arise, such as memos and photocopying for the staff, then the women do this work. Last year they did all the organization for the Christmas meal. The department also runs a modular programme with mixed activities and creative work, IT and practical skills like dressmaking, personal development, childcare and social studies. Six of the women do Adult Basic Education. Three do Open University courses: one is in the third year of an OU psychology degree, the second is in her second year of a degree in social sciences and the third is just starting a technology degree.

Throughout the whole of August the department runs a summer school with a range of activities, mainly creative—though it was at summer school that they introduced psychology 'and it has just carried on.' Initiatives like this can provide stimulating links with life outside by bringing in artists and writers from the community.

At Prison B the education staff have also been working hard to build up more positive relationships with disciplinary staff and hope to avoid the universal complaint that if there are officer shortages, 'education classes are always the first to go.' The education coordinator described how barriers had been broken down:

It's much better now though there are still a few problems. We're not affected by lockups in the day, though staff shortages do affect our delivery of evening classes almost every week. It's all about personal relationships and we try to be approachable and to socialise with the officers. We went to their Christmas party last week and they are coming to ours. It used to be very much "them and us" but now we are all beginning to talk to each other. We need their support—we can't do it without them. Some still have the old attitudes—that it's wrong for prisoners to get all those computers and so on—and there is not always goodwill from some of the older

335

officers. But there have been major changes in the three years since I got here.

But are these changes anything more than organizational changes, when what is needed is a radically changed approach to the education of imprisoned women?

Prison officers are fond of saying that prisons are merely a reflection of life outside prison. Prison life, they will say, reflects the violence, the drug-taking, the amorality of nineties society. In *Chapter 5* I described how nearly two-thirds of the disciplinary staff I interviewed said women were become more aggressive and violent, and some blamed it on 'women's liberation'. Yet imprisoned women have remained largely untouched by feminist movements. They are the least liberated of all women, especially in terms of their education and job prospects. The *NPS*[14] found that nearly half of all prisoners left school before the age of 16, and 52 per cent of all prisoners under the age of 21 had no qualifications, compared with 23 per cent in the general population. The Basic Skills Agency[15] found that a sample of prisoners were more than twice as likely as the general population to produce test results below foundation level education as defined by the agency. My own research[16] found that prisoners were seven times more likely than the average member of the public to have left school without a single academic qualification.

Prison education departments have a unique chance to offer prisoners the true liberation of economic freedom that education brings—-as well as all its cultural and social benefits. So why do women's prisons persist in offering the kind of leisure activities favoured by middle-aged 'ladies who lunch'? In Prison B's education department there were 36 women in full-time education, of whom 23 were young offenders under 21.

Prison B's education coordinator is a highly organized professional woman and she is well aware of feminist allegations about stereotypical 'women's courses':

> Well, cookery is only stereotyped if you let it be. The approach depends on the staff running it and if they want to challenge perceptions then they can. But I do take your point—dressmaking, cookery, even IT—you could look at typing and say "women's subjects again". We have tried other things like interior paint effects, house decoration.

Prison B's education coordinator is right when she says that 'women's subjects' are what you make of them. There is nothing stereotypically male or female about catering or fashion design for instance, or, interior design or hairdressing.

What *is* stereotypical is the attitude that women can afford the luxury of these skills as a hobby, while for men they must lead to qualifications for employment. Women are just as likely to need to be—and want to be—breadwinners as men—(as the Labour government's Welfare to Work initiative seems to suggest by targeting single mothers). It is patronising not to provide them with the professional qualifications they deserve.

In one open prison the education coordinator could now proudly say that every course she offers is accredited:

> My philosophy is to give people a training they can use, give them options so they can be more independent on release. There are lots of reasons why a woman may be motivated to pursue her education: she won't want to go back to an abusive relationship for instance. And some women *can't* go back to what they were doing before, because of the nature of their offence. I would see my job as 100 per cent commitment to the cause of preparing women for release and trying to prevent reoffending. Here we are geared to giving them skills that will make them employable. I have done a lot to raise the profile of training to give it status congruent with the status it would have outside.

Another education coordinator said 'I did offer DIY as an industrial course but the women weren't interested. Only two or three took it up and they complained the whole time. If you are student-driven and you listen to what they women want, this is what happens.' Three of the education coordinators I interviewed pleaded demand and take-up of courses as the reason for the limitations on what they had on offer.

At one of the open prisons the education department offers four main programmes: business administration; food preparation and cooking; hairdressing; and fashion design. The coordinator was annoyed at any suggestion of stereotyping:

> I get very angry when people criticise us and say all this reinforces "women's occupations" and that we should be doing car mechanics. We have a small budget and we have to do what will benefit the vast majority of the women. We *do* ask them what they want. In 1994 we did a questionnaire and asked them what they would find useful. We also took independent advice: back in 1990 we contacted the local Training and Enterprise Council and asked what were the most marketable skills for women. The answer was office skills, followed by food preparation and cooking because the catering industry always need people.

The inspectors' own survey[17] found that women identified 'getting a job' as being the most important factor in helping them to avoid reoffending. The inspectors concluded: 'It follows that helping women to gain a marketable skill can be the most important practical aid in preventing reoffending'.

When I interviewed women about prison education, work and training, I found they had a very clear idea indeed of what they wanted. The vast majority suggested useful, practical courses that would provide potential for employment on release. These were definitely not gender-specific. The women suggested building, bricklaying, plumbing and house-maintenance, catering, woodwork and metalwork: 'Things that could help you earn your living when you come out.' More than anything they wanted proper qualifications that would stand up outside. They recommended PE qualifications: 'Some of us are not academically inclined, but you can get fantastic jobs these days with the fashion for fitness—if you have the right certificates. My ambition is to be somebody's personal trainer!' HM Inspectors applauded the growth of PE coaching certification for women,[18] though they found that scheduled PE evening classes were often cancelled to allow PE staff to cover disciplinary staff shifts.

Hairdressing was popular with the women as long as it led to professional marketable skills: 'You can rent a chair in a salon, or you can set up your own business and take your baby around with you to clients.' They had no objection to pottery and sewing as relaxation, and indeed, many prisoners—male and female—have changed their lives through the discovery of a creative talent. But many women were pragmatic: 'Who does that sort of thing for a living? It's just a hobby.' 'I made a lot of furry animals, and I went to one class for making necklaces, but it was just threading beads. I did that at primary school!' As one woman jailed for credit card fraud graphically explained: 'I can now run up a pair of curtains, but what's the use of that for earning a living? Nobody round where I live can afford curtains! And people who can afford them buy them ready-made. It's time the Prison Service caught up with reality.' The Inspectors recognised that 'there is scope for more construction, industry and vocational training courses offering training in manual skills[19].

Word-processing was much in demand: women recognized that with good keyboard and desktop publishing skills they could command high rates of pay from city temping agencies. When I put this to the male governor of an open prison his reply was kindly but patronising:

Computer skills are available here—though I sometimes wonder if we are not falsely raising the expectations of women. We give them these skills and say "Now you know how to do this you can go out and get an office job." Then this woman, who may live on the fourteenth floor of a tower block with all the windows boarded up, and is beaten up by her husband, may go home full of inspiration about what she can do, and the husband will say to her "You're not going out to work, woman! Where's my tea?"

Second to the demand for practical accredited courses came requests for links with the 'real' world outside. This was why initiatives like the cheese-making enterprise at East Sutton Park, and Reed Restart, the secretarial agency scheme at Holloway, were so welcome when they began. Women said it made all the difference to be able to go to 'work' each morning in a properly equipped factory or office, where the work was real rather than simulated and not, like most prison work, merely for the upkeep of the establishment. There was also the opportunity to enhance the meagre prison wages with more realistic payment:

> With Reed I was earning wages and contributing towards my keep in prison, plus I have hopes of future employment on leaving prison. For me Reed was a godsend, the one break I've been looking for. It's an incentive for that smooth integration back into society that is so elusive.

But, a woman with more recent experience said things had now changed: 'Most Reed work in Holloway now is nothing better than packaging mailshots—very boring, repetitive work'. Staff said that because initiatives like these, often more highly paid, are available only to a very small number of women, they cause divisive envy. However HM Inspectors welcomed the development of private contracts because they offer chances of enhanced wages to women without access to private cash[20]. Since the Inspectorate review, there have been some other encouraging initiatives, like the £250,000 telesales centre set up at HMP Styal, partly funded by the European Union. Ten carefully vetted prisoners do telephone research, take bookings and sell products. They can gain NVQ qualifications for teleworking.

Many women commented that prisoners approaching the end of their sentences should be allowed to work or attend college in the community. These possibilities have been severely curtailed by new security restrictions following the Learmont and Woodcock reports,[21] though open prisons like Askham Grange and Drake Hall do run pre-release hostels for this purpose.

The women's comments show that they have a clear and realistic perception of what they need to equip them for life on release. The need for vocational skills training has been recognised for many years. As long ago as 1989 a NACRO report *Education and Training for Offenders* said prisons should be improving job chances, teaching particular skills and providing qualifications. The 1995 Prison Reform Trust survey[2] of prison education quoted above highlighted the need also to 'familiarise prisoners with the changing world of work'. Yet of the 41 education departments in the PRT survey (four of them in women's prisons) only seven said this was one of their aims.

What most annoyed the women about the education and training on offer? A major complaint was the lack of continuity. Men's prisons can more easily be grouped into clusters for the purposes of educational continuity, but women's prisons are much further apart. The women expressed frustration at the fragmentary nature of prison education and training, mainly caused by the instability of prison life—the shipping out from one prison to another—though women are less likely to be moved because there are fewer women's prisons. However, teachers said that 'people can get very upset when they are moved, then they also discover that they can't continue with courses they've started.' One woman had paid for a business administration course out of her own money, only to find herself moved to another prison just before the final examinations. The new prison did not run the course.

Mandatory 'sentence planning' was introduced progressively following the Criminal Justice Act 1991, though the Inspectorate survey[22] revealed that the majority of women prisoners 'had not experienced sentence planning at all'. All prisoners serving a sentence of 12 months or more, and all young offenders, are now supposed to have a sentence plan, which includes education, training and if necessary treatment for drug and alcohol abuse. The plan should be reviewed periodically throughout the sentence and should be continued from one prison to the next. At least with the advent of new technological communications, the transfer of prisoners' records should have improved.

Several education coordinators complained about the constraints imposed upon them by the new core curriculum, and HM Inspectorate felt that it was inadequate to meet prisoners' needs. Prisons are now obliged to offer literacy, numeracy, information technology and social skills courses. Some education coordinators deplored the official Home Office assessment tests devised by the Basic Skills Agency to be given to all incoming prisoners. One said 'It is an insult to graduates and upsetting to illiterate women. There are other ways of finding out this information.' Prison special needs tutors voiced similar concerns to teachers in main stream education: 'So many people need intensive help with literacy and numeracy and there just isn't enough time or staffing'. Even worse, the lecturers' union NATFHE said in September 1997[23] that it feared some prison governors were using the national curriculum as an excuse to pare down courses to the bare minimum, using education as a soft target, and in some cases cutting 80 per cent of their programmes.

The inspectors stressed the importance of *all* prison staff working together to encourage women to set and achieve educational targets.[24] But according to the prisoners I interviewed, the most common reason for discontinuity was the cancellations of classes because of staff shortages, officers working to rule and increasing amounts of bang-up: 'You look at your timetable and it looks OK. But when it comes to the day, you'll find a lot of the classes are missing. They just don't have the staff.' One prison I visited had an excellent education department but the impressive art department was deserted. 'No officers to supervise', said the tutor wearily, 'Art's always the first to go—very frustrating for the women—and for us!' There was just one student in the hairdressing salon: the tutor employed to run the class was furious. The officers had without notice chosen class time for canteen and the women, desperate for supplies, had rushed off.

Several women said they could not see why prisoners could not be trained as tutors: 'There are some very talented people in prison and they should be allowed to teach others, specially in things like foreign languages and computers. It would occupy their time and be valuable to everyone.' The Inspectorate also regretted that 'too little use is made of the talents of other prisoners as teachers and organizers'.[25]

Another major complaint was the lack of input for women to help plan their own education and training:

> Education officers need to adopt an induction programme like they have in some of the men's prisons. Then the women can feel free to choose the sort of courses and training they feel interested in doing, not what the education officer decides is good for them. Why can't courses be tailormade for each individual? After all the numbers are not all that great.

One lifer embarked on an Open University degree course when she first arrived at Holloway. But when she arrived at her next prison and asked the education officer for application forms for the next stage of the degree, permission was refused: '*You*—doing a degree? You *couldn't*—just listen to the way you speak!' The woman persisted and when she finally achieved success the same education officer boasted of the support he had given her. Another woman on an OU course had been a model prisoner, spending all her spare time studying. She was told by prison staff that all her reports were so good that she was very likely to get her parole: 'I was shocked when I got a knockback for another year. My parole was refused: the report said I seemed to be more interested in bettering myself and improving my career prospects than in addressing my offending behaviour. A lot of the officers resent you trying to educate yourself'.

Many women reported a continuing conflict between work and education, with the operational requirements of the prison given priority. Women said they were often told by officers 'This is a working prison' and their access to educational courses was limited: 'They want you working in the gardens or kitchens more than in education. But I think you should be able to do education if you're motivated.' They also complained about pay differentials, with education at the bottom of the pay ladder. In the Prison Reform Trust survey[2] 58 per cent of the 94 education coordinators said education was paid at a lower rate than prison work or training, with the average wage just £5.85 per week at that time.

Women prisoners also objected to the unfair distribution of facilities, and those on rule 43 particularly complained of poor access even to the limited facilities that existed. Many women complained that Holloway, despite its troubles, has far better education and training facilities than other women's prisons which were regarded as cultural backwaters with little on offer. They specially praised Holloway's art department and computers—though with increasing overcrowding and more locking in cells these were often inaccessible. A woman currently imprisoned in Holloway said several classes had had to be axed because of shortage of funds. Many women said they particularly missed Holloway's evening classes. At Brockhill, for instance, they paid tribute to the high standards of daytime education classes, but complained 'there's nothing to do in the evenings here, or at weekends: nothing creative—no drama, no DIY, no shows, no competitions—nothing!'. The Inspectorate report found no examples of educational activities taking place at weekends.[26]

A woman in her fifties, serving the first stage of a long sentence in Holloway said:

> The education department here is good and it does provide a variety of things to do, but it doesn't cater for mature students. Most people like me are often computer-literate and can use a word-processor, yet there is no opportunity to do advanced computer courses. There is a good art class, and a dressmaking class, but very little to stimulate mature people. I understand that the gardening officer tries to instruct inmates on garden machinery/plants etc, and instruction is given in the tailor's shop on different aspects of machinery. I also think those who work in the kitchen get some form of instruction, but apart from that there doesn't seem to be much else. Not much for 500 inmates!

There is no obligation for education or training to be offered to remand prisoners, unless they are juveniles. One education coordinator admitted bluntly: 'I have to worry about convicted women serving long sentences and I don't want their classes disrupted by remand women popping in and out. If however this were to become an entirely remand prison, I'd work out a modular system and offer free-standing short modules'.

Unfortunately prisons like Holloway, Risley and Brockhill have to hold a mixture of remand and convicted prisoners—though at the time of writing there are changes in the pipeline which will radically change both Risley and Brockhill: women are scheduled to be removed from Risley altogether, and Brockhill is to become a remand centre. It is not easy for a prison like Holloway, with such a rapid turnover and such a high percentage of remand prisoners, to supply meaningful courses. For more than 60 per cent of Holloway prisoners, the average length of stay is 28 days.[27] Though on the outside a woman might gain real benefit from, e.g., an intensive one-month computer or foreign language course, it is quite unrealistic to hope that newly-imprisoned women, who are often in shock and worried about family, debt, accommodation and so on, are going to have the motivation to knuckle down to the keyboard or the phrasebook. The best practice for short-stay prisoners may be to make sure they are made aware of access courses to further and higher education and to link them with agencies, charities and support groups outside prison who can give advice, education and training for those who want it. This particularly applies to women with a drug or alcohol problem (see *Chapter 9*).

There are some exciting projects for prisoners and former prisoners: the Clean Break Theatre Company was founded in 1979 by two Askham Grange women and was recently awarded £1 million of Arts Council funding (lottery money) to train women in prison and ex-prisoners in theatre skills. CAST, the Creative and Supportive Trust, runs skills development courses and provides education, training and careers advice.

Officially there are no women's resettlement prisons such as the male establishment Latchmere House which have as their primary purpose the preparation of prisoners for reintegration into the community on release. The women's open prisons are the nearest equivalent in the female estate, so it is worth considering how far the work, education and training they offer fulfils this function.

During my second research period, I visited a women's open prison which I will call Prison C. How far were the work, training and educational opportunities at this prison equipping the women for an independent life outside?

In Prison C the women have a week's induction period when the possibilities are explained to them. They can state their preferences and will then be allocated by the Labour Board. If there are enough places available (and young offenders and women with special educational needs take priority) they can opt for full time education. Or they can work in the laundry, the kitchen, on works and maintenance, in the gardens, or in one of the two workshops.

The Works Officer is responsible for the day to day maintenance of Prison C the carpentry and the 'locks, bolts and bars', the painting and decorating. But, as he says, 'I have another role which I see as just as important, and that's to let the girls gain knowledge. I think it gives the girls an opportunity to learn new skills and they can make good use of them to do their own decorating at home.'

One of the 'girls', Lucy, aged 31 and with two children aged nine and five, said she enjoyed painting walls and found it therapeutic. She had in the past been a heroin addict but had now been off drugs for some years. She had learned to shoplift to fund her drug habit but afterwards she carried on shoplifting 'just to get by. I'm from Liverpool and there are no jobs if you don't have any qualifications.' Lucy is unlikely when she leaves prison to have enough money to decorate her own home as the works officer suggests. In fact, she does not have a home to go to. Perhaps an NVQ in painting and decorating might have helped her at the job centre which she may be obliged to attend under the Welfare to Work scheme.

In the smaller of Prison C's two workshops 20 of the prison's 280 prisoners were packing chiffon scarves for a chain store. They had to be pushed through a gilt scarf ring, put on a small plastic hanger and price-tagged. Mrs Thompson (not her real name), is the officer in charge of the workshop. She said they were getting some good new contracts in:

> The women like doing this because it's more feminine work. At first the firm approached Littlehey [a male prison] but the work wasn't suitable for the men with their rough hands. We also assemble brooch packs and put the butterfly clips on earrings. The girls love doing this as they can do the work without concentrating, and this means they can chat. They discuss politics and so on. It's all part of tackling their offending behaviour.

The women I spoke to in the workshop were not discussing politics—in fact they were discussing the iniquities of giving high doses of Largactil[28] to young offenders:[29] they referred to this workshop as the 'muppet shop' and described the work as boring and repetitive. According to Mrs Thompson these are mostly 'the inadequates'—a term bandied about by officers with startling frequency:

> They are a mixed bunch but I mostly get those who are physically and mentally infirm—'Labour Three' unfitted for work[30] The work we do in

344

here could prepare them for homeworking on their release. These days a lot of firms employ people at home and women like these often prefer to do that so they can look after their children. Unfortunately no qualification is available for this kind of work.

In other words, this workshop is preparing 'the inadequates' for slave labour—fodder for homeworker employers notorious for long hours, low wages and a disregard of employee rights. Mrs Thompson said she had been working at this same prison since 1975:

> The old female governor in those days felt that women were unfit to work at all. To start with we only had 14 women here as it was meant to be a short term prison. There was nothing for them to do and I wanted to start a knitting circle. When it was realised the women would be staying longer we started up the big workshop next door and we used to do re-work on textiles. This meant that the women were re-doing work that the men prisoners hadn't done properly. We were re-cycling men's underpants, would you believe it!

In one corner of the workroom next to a pile of the inevitable prison rag dolls stood a spinning wheel—the prison used to graze its own sheep and the women would spin the wool for knitting into garments. This antique seemed to stand as a fitting symbol of the Prison Service's outdated attitudes to women's education, work and training—attitudes that decreed that until just a year or two ago Cornton Vale women were employed sewing shrouds.

As I reached the larger workshop the women had just finished work for the day. Mrs Machin (another pseudonym), unlike Mrs Thompson, is a civilian training instructor: before she began work at the prison 17 years ago she was an instructor in a textiles firm. Here the women make heavy duty industrial workwear such as the fluorescent jackets worn by motorway workers. The garments are ordered on contract by outside suppliers and made by the women on industrial sewing machines which most take about two weeks to master. If they cannot manage it they will be set to work as checkers, pressers, packers or unit cleaners. If enough orders do not come in, the workshop goes back to producing its standby—the green workwear jackets worn by male prisoners. The women also learn to cut patterns and make tracksuits and sweatshirts which they can buy themselves at cost price, and which are sold to long sentence prisoners on reception into prison, using a clothing grant which they repay out of weekly wages. To start with the workshop wages are low, even by prison standards, at £4.70 a week, but if the women prove to be good machinists they can progress in a few weeks to £9.88 which is the highest rate in the prison.

Although the work of the machinists is more skilled, it is still repetitive. But at least women serving three months or longer can aim for an NVQ qualification in the Manufacture and Production of Textiles Level Two—the highest level in the industrial section. Mrs Machin says the qualification would certainly enhance the women's job prospects—as long as on release they live in an area with factories where this sort of machining work is available. She also has to limit the number of NVQs because each one costs £140.

Prison C has a fair-sized laundry which takes in washing not just for the prison's own women but for three or four male prisons as well. The laundry instructor Mr Peters (not his real name) has worked there for 20 years. He could run the laundry with ten women but has been told he must employ 20. He feels aggrieved that laundry wages, which used to be top of the list, have slipped down the pecking order to £7.50. He is given a budget by the governor and has to allocate wages from it: 'I think it's unfair because in many ways the laundry is the hardest job in the prison'. Three years ago he began running NVQs Levels One and Two which, like the Textiles NVQ, cost about £140 each. But now the money has run out and the women will have to wait until the beginning of the next financial year to embark on any more NVQ qualifications.

However, the Prison Service appears to have given men's fashion priority over women's qualifications; until recently the laundry women's duties included the complicated process of stone-washing all the blue denim jeans ordered for male prisoners: 'We have always stone-washed the jeans for the men's prisons—this is what they asked for in the Prison Service stores because it was the fashion. But now we're going to stop doing it because it is not cost-effective.'

Mr Peters thought the NVQ qualification had helped the women get jobs on release: one is now employed in the laundry of a hospital, another in an old people's home—which Mr Peters said was a growth industry. However he agreed that the men's prisons offered far more choices of work and training:

> It would be good to bring in courses for painting and decorating. In the men's prisons I've worked in, they could learn to make shoes and slippers, do car maintenance, bricklaying. I have no problem with the women learning all these things. I'd like to give these opportunities to everyone. In fact I've got a woman working in the laundry who used to run her own business as a plumber on the outside.

The civilian gardens manager had refused to run an NVQ: 'I don't like the NVQ!' he said impatiently. 'There's too much paperwork and I can't get through it and spend any time with the women. The gardens are split into seven areas and we have teams of two or three women who are responsible for everything in that area. We grow our own bedding plants and supply some to two other prisons. There's just too much to do to bother with NVQs'.

In Prison C's education department were two large murals which had won a Koestler award.[31] Women prisoners were given basic instructions on paint mixing and asked to paint a mural on the subject of work. Interestingly, neither mural portrayed women doing stereotypical women's work. The first showed a building site run entirely by women in dungarees engaged in heavy construction work. The other painting was a cosmopolitan marketplace showing both men and women in traditional clothes from many different cultures, buying and selling fruit, vegetables and flowers.

Prison C's Labour Board decides which women are chosen to attend education classes. Not all women want to come, because the wages are even lower than for the laundry—£5.20 a week at first, rising to £6.00 'if they are no trouble after a week.' From the women who are sent to them, the education staff try to screen out those in need of basic education by asking them to fill in a form about themselves. They will then spend the first six weeks on a programme loosely described as 'lifeskills'. The department has devised a six to eight week course called LAY, an acronym for Look After Yourself. The education coordinator described the course:

> We have craft but we do practical things like how to change a zip, which is cheaper than buying new jeans, "One Hundred Things to Do with Half a Pound of Mince", which is cheaper than bought lasagne and so on. For very short sentence prisoners we have one-week short courses, such as good housekeeping, cooking for a family, cleaning skills, budgeting, ironing—a lot of these girls don't know how to iron—they don't bother ironing. Not *my* favourite job, I might add. They can also spend a whole afternoon on something that interests them, like aromatherapy, or they can get books from the library and do a project on something like grooming horses.

The course sounded rather like a wartime Home Service broadcast on how to 'Make, Do and Mend', or how to 'Dig for Victory'. To be fair, the department does offer a range of other courses, but a glance through the courses information booklet shows the same stereotypical courses once again: hairdressing, beauty care, dressmaking and so on. The evening classes included flower arranging, soft toys, T-shirt design, knitting, pottery, drawing and painting, light crafts and good grooming.

More inspiring was an access course called NOW (New Opportunities for Women) which women in other prisons had mentioned. Sessions on this eight week course include women's studies, creative writing, English literature, assertiveness training, women's health and IT skills. The course is based on a programme used in women's prisons in Washington DC and New York in the 1970s, called WOW (Wider Opportunities for Women), which promoted non-traditional careers in such areas as carpentry, welding and electrical work and placed women in construction jobs which were far more lucrative than traditional 'women's work'. Most of the women I interviewed thought NOW was an improvement on the mince and its 100 variations!

Rebekah, a graduate who works in the gardens of the same open prison (see *Chapter 4*), was scathing when I asked for her comments on education, work and training:

> Pathetic! Look at the courses they put on — good housekeeping, cookery, that sort of thing. Though that new group called NOW doesn't sound too bad — a bit of psychology and stuff. Women are second class citizens outside, and it's the same again here in prison. You get work like that stuff in the workshop — dull and repetitive. No wonder women regress in prison. I am amazed how appreciative the other women are of my qualifications. They say "Oh, you've got a degree!" They really admire education and wish they could get some.

Anita (see *Chapter 8*) feels prison education staff can be judgmental: 'One of the cookery teachers asked a young girl what she fed her kids on and the girl said "McDonalds". The teacher said "That's no food to give a child!!" which I thought was very cruel considering that girl's away from her kids and now the teacher's made her feel bad about how she looks after her own children'.

Anita herself is looking forward to going out to the job club in a nearby town the following week. She has six months left to serve of her sentence—three years for a major social security deception—and wants to get a job when she is released, though she is now 40 and has never held a regular job. 'The job club knows all about me and they're going to give me extra help to get a job. One girl from here got a job in a old people's home. I'd like to look after the disabled, though I wouldn't mind working in a hotel or a kitchen.' Prison C has a resettlement unit and from here risk-assessed women can go out to work. Even with the new rules on temporary release they are still able to do some community work with the disabled or work on other local projects.

Women in closed prisons are not so fortunate. Bullwood Hall, for instance, used to run a working farm, and until 1993 they grazed herds of cattle from other prisons, and kept a small herd of goats. Women used to work on the farm and staff felt it helped to rehabilitate them. Now the fields lie fallow and the women are not even allowed to work on the gardens. Because the works department is outside the prison's inner gate, prisoners cannot come to the workshops where officers used to give them carpentry lessons.

In another prison, where almost all the sentenced prisoners are involved in educational courses, I asked the education coordinator what difference she thought prison education could make: 'I accept that most of the women we see have massive personal problems. But a lot of those might diminish if they are given educational opportunities. I really think education can have an *astonishing* effect'.

I asked Chris Tchaikovsky, Director of Women in Prison and herself a former prisoner, what she would include in the ideal education and training package:

I would give a screening test to every prisoner and I would offer basic literacy — the three Rs — for women who need it. If they have no basic education they have no chance. You must be able to read, write and speak well. I have seen the frustration of women who couldn't read and kept it hidden because of the shame of it, because of put-downs by officers who love to see women prisoners as poor, sorry and ignorant. There should be proper wages for attending education, and incentives linked to parole and temporary release. They will need a lot of inducements and no bullshit.

I would put in women's studies — books written by strong women. They don't have to be feminist books. Women need the backing of teachers and they need ex-prisoners coming back into prison to show they have come out on the other side.

I have travelled the world and been to every capital city and I drank all the good wine and ate all the good food but I couldn't taste any of it. It was education that opened all the doors to me. The straight life is the sweet life, the good life. Nobody is telling the women that.

Some would go further. Lord Woolf still emphasises the importance of education seven years after his ground-breaking report. Indeed he goes further: 'I would support prisoners being able to earn remission by educational achievements'.[32]

Just before this book went to press in March 1998 I received a moving letter from a young woman prisoner at Foston Hall. It shows the redemptive potential of education:

It is early evening at the moment and I'm sitting in Education longing for 8.30 lock-in time. No, I haven't gone completely insane. Today my Open University course materials arrived and I just can't wait to start working through them. I had a visit this afternoon so it wasn't until 4 p.m. that I got back to Education to collect the materials. I managed to glance through everything briefly before evening education classes, and I'm so elated and excited about starting that I haven't stopped smiling since. The materials look absolutely great—books, books and more books, videos, CDs—I feel truly in my element. I now realise I'm following the right path and gaining a greater understanding in following my talents and potential. Now I look forward to the future.

Yet the following month the *Times Educational Supplement* reported[33] that 'education is close to being axed completely in some prisons. Hundreds of hours are being slashed from prison timetables by governors forced to save money in the face of funding cuts. The *TES* published a leading article[34] pointing out the irony of the cuts: 'Just when the government is emphasising lifelong learning for all'. 'Surely', the leader ended, 'ministers could justify spending a bit of a money on a system which would send offenders back into society better-educated—and better people—than they were when they left it?'

Endnotes

1. Prisoner who has been told by the Home Secretary that he or she will never be released.
2. *Education in Prisons: A National Survey*, Nick Flynn and David Price, Prison Reform Trust, 1995.
3. *Women in Prison: A Thematic Review*, HM Inspectorate, 1997.
4. From 1992-95, I was researching for my book *Criminal Classes: Offenders at School*, Waterside Press, 1995.
5. The pilot project took place at HM YOI Onley: the provider of education there was Northampton College. It is to be hoped that when education contracts for prisons go out for tender again in 1998, the requirement to screen, diagnose and provide suitable solutions for dyslexic prisoners will be part of the specification.
6. See *Oxford History of the Prison, Chapter 11*, 'Wayward Sisters', Lucia Zedner, Oxford University Press, 1995; and *The Imprisonment of Women*, Dobash R, Dobash R, and Gutteridge S, Basil Blackwell, 1986.
7. The Further and Higher Education Act 1992 allows education services in prisons to be contracted out. Before this, prison education was delivered by local education authorities. The contracts went out to competitive tender and by the end of August 1993 most had been awarded. The contracts are due for renewal in 1998.
8. *Report of an Enquiry into Prison Disturbances*, Cmnd. 1456, HMSO, 1991.
9. See *Doing Time or Using Time*, Cmnd. 2128, report of a review by HM Chief Inspector of Prisons, 1993; see also *Doing Constructive Time*, S. Tumim, *Sunday Times*, 1 January 1994.
10. June 1996 to January 1997: research specifically in women's prisons for the purposes of the current study.
11. Vulnerable prisoners normally separated from others under rule 43.
12. See *Chapter 5*.
13. The name given to the 1987 restructuring of working practices following a dispute between the Home Office and the Prison Officers' Association.
14. *The National Prison Survey, 1991*, Tricia Dodd, Paul Hunter, HMSO, 1992.
15. *The Basic Skills of Young Adults*, Basic Skills Agency, March 1994.
16. The sample surveyed consisted of 250 prisoners: 138 men and 112 women.
17. See Note 3, above: 10.12.
18. See Note 3, above: 9.59.
19. See Note 3, above: 10.06.
20. See Note 3, above: 10.14.

21. The Woodcock Report was carried out by Sir John Woodcock following escapes from HMP Whitemoor in 1994. The Learmont Report was an enquiry carried out by General Sir John Learmont after an escape by three prisoners from HMP Parkhurst in 1994. He also reviewed implementation of recommendations in the Whitemoor Report.

22. See Note 3, above: 2.17.

23. 'Prison Study Confined to Essentials as Cuts Bite', *Times Educational Supplement*, 12 September 1997.

24. See Note 3, above: 10.10.

25. See Note 3, above: Executive Summary 61.

26. See Note 3, above: Executive Summary 60.

27. See *HM Prison Holloway: Basic Fact Pack for Visitors:* p. 6: 'Key Facts', July 1996.

28. Brand name for Chlorpromazine, a generic anti-psychotic drug, see *Chapter 11*, p. 19.

29. See *Chapter 11*, p.19.

30. Labour 1, 2 and 3 are classifications of levels of work that prisoners are felt to be capable of. Labour 3 is the lightest work. A prisoner is 'fitted' or 'unfitted' for each of these categories by the Labour Board, officers given this assessment duty when prisoners are received into prison.

31. The Koestler Awards are cash prizes awarded annually to prisoners who produce good work in the arts.

32. Quoted in 'Can We Eliminate Evil?', Joel Parkes, *The Times*, 16 December 1997.

33. 'Cuts Will Sentence More to Ignorance', *Times Educational Supplement,* 10 April 1998.

34. 'Prisoners of Middle England', leading article, see Note 33, above.

CHAPTER SIXTEEN

Gate Fever and Liberty Clothes

The first time I went out of the gate it was unbelievable. I was afraid to cross the road at first. I nearly ran back into the prison. The cars were going so fast! It's a 40 minute walk to the village and it was a lovely April day. It was the freedom — to see cows and sheep — I had to go and touch a tree to believe it was real.

That first day I went into the Co-op in the village. I wanted some cigarettes but I was so frightened I kept standing back letting everybody else go in front of me in the queue. I bought the cigarettes in the end but by then I was sweating and I had to go out of the shop though I meant to buy some biscuits for my break.

Then seeing a real church, and seeing little children around after so many years. I never got any visits when I was in prison. So I never went to the visits room and never saw other women's children.

The speaker is Doreen, describing how she had just been allowed out of an open prison to do shopping and cleaning for a local convent. She is in her mid-fifties and had served six years of a life sentence before the Court of Appeal ruled her conviction unsafe and unsound and she was finally released.

This chapter is about getting out and staying out of prison. 'Gate fever' is prison slang for the mixed feelings of excitement, hope and terror that afflict those about to be released. 'liberty clothing' is the quaint phrase still used in the Prison Service to refer to the clothing grant that may be given to prisoners as they leave. But in the metaphorical sense, what protective suits of clothes can be given to women to help them adjust to life on the outside, and to lessen the chances of their returning to prison? HM Inspectors found that 70 per cent of women prisoners felt that prison had a negative effect on them: not only were they more angry and depressed than before but they were also more criminally sophisticated. When asked what would help them not to reoffend, they identified employment, stable relationships, accommodation and proper help and support.[1]

I interviewed Doreen one Thursday afternoon in late August, shortly after the Appeal Court ruling quashed her conviction. That very morning she had heard she would be released the following Monday.

They said I wouldn't get out till the end of September. Then this morning I was getting ready for work and an officer asked me to go to the wing office. I thought—that's odd—something's wrong. He said "You'd better sit down. I'm pleased to tell you you've got your parole and you'll be leaving on Monday!" I was shaking—I didn't know whether to laugh or cry. In a way I was sad, leaving all my friends in here. There's nothing out there for me really.

For the whole of her six years in four different prisons, including Durham's top security H wing, this slight grey-haired woman had no visitors at all except for a prison visitor who befriended her in her last prison. Now she was going to a hostel not far off. 'The prison is setting me up in there. With my NVQ Level Three in hairdressing and the work I've done in counselling abused women, I should be able to manage somehow.' Her voice trailed away, her face suddenly crumpled into anxiety. For six years she had longed for this moment, and now, four days ahead, it was upon her.

The Inspectors' review[1] emphasises that every part of a prison regime should be regarded as pre-release training. Prison Service officials and staff often use the word 'throughcare'. It is defined in the latest *Prisoners' Information Book*[2] as:

> The assistance given to prisoners and their families by the prison, probation services and voluntary agencies. It includes training, education, work experience and preparation for release. It should help prisoners to fit back into society, get a job and a home, and cope with life without re-offending.

Fine words. But earlier chapters have shown the threadbare reality of so many of these worthy aims. For a start, this aim takes no account of the power of the institution to undermine every single aim in this list. Doreen's account of her first excursion shows graphically the institutionalising effect of prison.

Sheila Bowler, whose conviction for murder was quashed, like Doreen's, by the Court of Appeal, tape-recorded her feelings a few days after her release in July 1997 after four years in prison:

> The first night at home I couldn't sleep so I got up and crept into the kitchen and ate some cake. I felt really wicked walking through a door that was unlocked in the middle of the night. I think I'm still slightly manic, running round doing things, because subconsciously I keep thinking I've got to get things done *right now*, before we get locked in again. I'm still programmed for the times we were allowed out of cell. I just thought to myself "It's raining, so they won't let us out on exercise today." Last night I heard a van door slam outside on the street and it made me jump a mile because it sounded like a prison van door. Then there's little things, like I

can't believe I can ring directory enquiries—you're not allowed to do that in prison. Just as I was saying that I nearly stopped myself, because in Holloway they monitor every single phone conversation. I suppose I must still be a bit paranoid.

The subtle process of institutionalisation begins the minute the gates shut behind a new prisoner. In earlier chapters I have attempted to recreate the insidious processes whereby institutions—by design or default—rob prisoners of their identity and individuality. The use of numbers instead of names, the loss of all previous status and niche in society, however humble. The demeaning questions, the degrading strip-searches. The collective stereotypical classifying of every woman as a manipulative and devious criminal. The petty rules, the infantilising, the dehumanising.

Then there is the effect of peer pressure: the desperation to demonstrate conformity to the 'nick culture' to survive; or the rare courage to set yourself apart and run the risk of what one counsellor called 'deserts of loneliness'. The winning or losing of long-fought battles against drugs or self-harm, the admission of defeat when the 'no-grassing' rule becomes too hard to resist.

Then there is the gradual withdrawing from the outside world into the world of the institution. Relatives and close friends of prisoners often report the distress of long-awaited visits where a mother, sister or girlfriend will seem more interested in what is going on at the next table than what is happening at home. It is difficult for families to accept how quickly human defence mechanisms move into gear, creating new societal structures wherever people find themselves. Imprisoned women may also lose their 'outside' values, forsake their better judgment and succumb to peer pressure and intimidation, especially where drugs are involved.

Institutionalisation is not necessarily a long-term process. One remand prisoner had been in prison just a few months when she said: 'When you're in a place like Holloway, the outside doesn't exist for you'. Once the initial period of captivity has dissipated the fear of the unknown, some women begin to cling to the newly familiar surroundings, and commonly speak with dread of moving to another prison. Others, especially those serving long sentences, may take the opposite view, always hoping with each new move that the next prison will offer better facilities, better courses, less intrusive security, easier access for visitors.

One of the first pointers to the effects of the institution is the use of language. Whatever their social background and command of language, women who had been in prison just a few weeks seemed quickly to have assimilated the language of the jail. By tapping into and using with some fluency the language of power—the official prison jargon used by their jailers—they could re-establish some of their lost identity and status. But to achieve a sense of belonging in the peer group, prisoners need also to master the *argot* of other prisoners. The problem lies in keeping these newly acquired language registers separate from the world outside the jail and difficulties arise when the new world of the prison collides with the old world the prisoner has left behind. She has constantly to juggle the two worlds of 'inside' and 'outside'. A chance mention in a telephone call of 'crutching'[3] or a 'piss test'[4] may send the family back at home into paroxysms of terror.

All the women's prisons I visited were characterised by a pervasive lethargy far less prevalent in men's prisons. Some of the reasons for this have been explored in earlier chapters. They include depressing, sometimes sordid, surroundings (on one prison corridor I remember seeing a used sanitary towel in the litter lying around); the boredom of mindless repetitive 'muppet-shop' work, and uninspiring courses. Many women made dismissive comments: 'A lot of what you do here is just filling time'. Then there is the paranoia created by the mass of petty rules, especially in open prisons, which stamp out any flickers of creativity: 'I'm always on tenterhooks in here [an open prison] in case I do something wrong and lose my parole'. Finally there is the 'numbing out' by the misuse of drugs and acceptance of the creeping control of prescribed medication. Women would commonly use expressions like 'the downing atmosphere' and talked of 'sleeping the time away'. 'It's so boring in here—I don't even know my EDR[5] so there's nothing to look forward to'. 'It's the same faces, day in, day out'. It is small wonder that prison offers so little hope to women wanting to give up a drug habit. Powerful and attractive incentives are needed to make an addict forsake the pleasurable (and numbing) effects of drugs, and there are few genuine incentives in most women's prisons.

Women already low in self-esteem soon feel any remaining self-confidence seeping away after they have been in prison a short time. Depression, self-disgust and a fatalistic acceptance of failure are common: a 19-year-old girl wrote: 'Maybe I was always meant to lose. Some days I just don't eat. I've lost the fight for living really.' Another woman, aged just 22, said 'What about the future? I don't plan ahead, me. I know I'm always bound to mess up. I've always messed everything up.' A woman recently released from prison after serving a sentence for killing her boyfriend said: 'I killed a person so I'd failed. I'd become everything that society hates.'

Prisoners told of the pain caused by well-meaning but patronising volunteers whose lack of understanding and empathy was sometimes quite breathtaking. One woman about to leave prison applied for a

355

clothing grant:

> I'm eligible but it takes a long time to come through. I'd put on a lot of weight in prison and bras for my size cost about £25. I mentioned my problem to one of the Board of Visitors, a grey-haired lady, very posh. She asked if I'd be offended if she offered me some clothes from a friend of hers — a large lady like myself. The officers said "You'll be all right there — she's a very rich woman".

> When the clothes came into the prison I got quite excited. They were in these smart Harrods bags and I went to Reception to open them in front of the officers. I was so upset and ashamed! There were some old dresses covered in dog hair and old knickers rotten with piss stains. They stank so much we had to throw them straight in the bin. The officers wondered if she'd sent in the wrong bags, all the old clothes she meant to throw away. But I think she really believed she was doing a convict a favour. I was angry as well as upset. I thought, "What do you take me for"?

Women spoke of disempowerment as 'loss of control over your life'. Mothers gave graphic descriptions of their frustration at being unable to help when things are going wrong at home. Those in open prisons said they felt even worse because of the temptation of the open gate with their children a train journey away on the other side.[6] The temptation was too much for some women and they tried to break loose from the institution. The disempowering force of the jail however stayed with most absconders and they did not get far. One mother of four young children was sent to an open prison after two weeks in Holloway: 'I absconded straight away. I only got as far as the prison gates but I wouldn't come back in. I just said I was staying out there. I got ten days added to my sentence for standing outside in the freezing cold for three hours.'

Candida also absconded. She was a heroin addict withdrawing on Methadone[7] when her baby daughter was born, also withdrawing (see *Chapters 2* and *5*). The child had to be left behind in the hospital and given detoxification treatment.

> I was allowed out from the open prison for a day just before Christmas. On the way back I was so depressed I went to Brighton instead and walked up and down the seafront, trying to sort things out in my mind. But in the end it was no good. I just handed in my pass and they brought me back to prison.

Officers commonly spoke dismissively of 'chaotic lives and

dysfunctional families' but some of the women I interviewed had in fact managed families and businesses efficiently and energetically. These were sometimes the women hardest hit by prison, the red tape and the agonizingly slow bureaucratic processes. One of the few professional women criminals I met, a forger who had organized a team of male subordinates to plant counterfeit notes, was constantly irritated: 'I like to get on with things—to get things done. That's why it drives me mad in here because nothing ever gets done and things just go on for weeks. I can't be bothered with most things in here. I just stay in my room.'

Chapter 11 described the effect of distress on women's physical and mental health. The fear of becoming physically ill in prison is rooted more in common sense than in paranoia: women have seen plenty of others suffering from inadequate treatment and lack of care. The fear of becoming mentally ill is even more pervasive. Women commonly described conditions like claustrophobia from long hours of bang-up behind 'doors with no handles'; or the fear of eating in the company of others. Madness is difficult to distinguish from the debilitating depression that engulfs most imprisoned women at some point in their sentence. Fear of madness is exacerbated by the certain knowledge that depression and self-harm will only rarely be treated with any empathy or tender loving care. The 'treatments' these women had witnessed were confinement in strip cells and the liquid cosh of the psychotropic drug. They had seen enough 'zombies'—some of them teenage girls—to know that this is the stuff not of nightmares but of prison reality. The unspoken dread in many women's minds is of kicking off once too often and ending up locked forever in institutions regarded with ultimate horror: the special hospitals.

For some women, of course, the institutionalising process began many years before they entered the criminal justice process, and though they may seem the best-adjusted to prison life, these are the saddest people of all. Nearly one third of the women in my sample had spent all or part of their childhood in care.[8] For many of these women, prison was a refuge—just another institution like the others they had known. These were the women who never mentioned their parole dates. Jodie, 24 and serving her latest sentence for criminal damage, was abandoned by her mother at an early age. She admits she smashed windows to be readmitted to prison:

This is my home really. What better place to get attention than prison? You're never going to be alone twenty four seven.[9] I love prison because I get attention all the time. Where else would I get all my food, my light, my heat, my medical care? And some of the screws are OK. I expect I'll always be back in here off and on.

Mandy, a young offender aged 17 held in a closed prison, loved being there. It was an improvement on her last children's home: 'It's great in here. There's a full YO course and I'm doing exams in equi-studies—it's all to do with horses. They've got everything in here and I love having a laugh with the girls and the officers—only a couple of them are bastards.'

Tracey's story was told in *Chapter 12*. Like all her siblings, she has been in care since she was a baby, transferring from children's home to a series of secure units from the age of 11, to borstal at the age of 16, then to prison when she was 18. She is now 32 and has spent most of the intervening 14 years in a series of prisons, including Rampton, the secure special hospital: 'I liked borstal—you could have a good laugh in there. I get on quite well with the Leicester police. As soon as I'm let out I get back on the Special Brew, do a bit of puff, smash another window then they bring me back in here again. I'm only happy when I'm in prison.'

With the exception of already-institutionalised women like Tracey and those life-sentenced prisoners recently given long tariffs, almost all the women I interviewed mentioned the word 'parole'—their release date—several times as we spoke. They all referred to it warmly in personal, possessive terms—'my parole date'—a light shining at the end of a dark tunnel. There was time to be done, a sentence to get your head round, review board hurdles to negotiate, and sometimes loss of remission and additional days added. But at the end of it all the parole date would be there ahead.

At one closed prison I interviewed the civilian parole clerk whose task it is to give women their parole decisions:

> When the decision comes I have to let them know and they do say they like me to tell them personally, whether it's good or bad news. Some of them are very vulnerable at this time and if I have a bad result to tell them I make sure the hospital and the officers know. But it's lovely to be able to tell them they've got their parole and I often get hugs and kisses.

But are those with a 'good result' any less vulnerable than those condemned to remain even longer in prison? What have their prisons done to prepare them for the moment when the gates close—with the woman on the outside. The National Association for the Care and Resettlement of Offenders (NACRO), focuses—as its name suggests—on throughcare and aftercare. NACRO's policy committee on resettlement in its report says: 'Resettlement should be the main aim of everything that is done in women's prisons'.[10] The report calls for sentence planning to be extended to cover all convicted prisoners, however short the sentence.[11] It also stresses that the sentence plan should be extended to cover the first few months after release: 'No woman should walk out of the prison gates without a plan of action for her life outside that offers a real prospect of a productive and law-abiding life in the community.'

At present, only prisoners given a sentence of more than a year are supervised after release by a probation officer, unless they are young offenders, in which case they are usually given a three month period of supervision. But the majority of women are unlikely to get any support: they are either remand prisoners, most of whom do not then receive a custodial sentence; or they are serving sentences of less than a year. There has until now been a system of voluntary supervision where a prisoner's outside probation officer should write and offer support after release. But in many areas such offers are having to be withdrawn because of caseload pressure. For prisoners like Doreen and Sheila Bowler, released on appeal, there is no provision at all—though such releases, by their nature often sudden and unexpected, can be the most traumatic of all.

Dorothy, a grandmother with an alcohol problem was jailed for hitting a policeman. She already has a plan of action:

> When I get out I'll be going on the social. I'll be stuck at home and it won't pay me to work or I'll lose my benefits. So I want to set up a little pottery business—I learned how to do pottery in here. Now that'll cost £1,000 minimum and as an ex-con you can't get a bank loan, can you? So unless NACRO start giving loans for ex-prisoners, I'll just have to go and shoplift for that £1,000, won't I?

Former home secretary Michael Howard may famously have proclaimed that 'Prison works', but I met many women like Dorothy—and many men in my earlier research—who could not guarantee that they would stay crime-free for long. The public may indeed have been protected from their crimes while the offender was in prison, though only very few imprisoned women present any public danger. But by coming into prison they had lost so much that there was little hope of regaining their former status by legitimate means.

Women who may have committed a one-off debt-related offence will not only return to an even worse financial situation: many will return to it with an anger and bitterness that make reoffending far more likely. Their stake in society has gone, they are already stigmatised, prison is no longer an unknown terror, they may have acquired a network of criminal friends—and they have nothing else left to lose. As one woman said 'I've lost everything—my house, my car, everything.

To get it back I'll just have to resort to a dodgy mortgage, won't I!' It was a statement not a question.

The Penal Affairs Consortium, in a paper entitled *Reducing Offending* published in May 1997, recognised these problems:

> Far too many prisoners are released with only the clothes they stand up in and a small discharge grant to support them in a community in which they have no stake. Because of their criminal record, they are excluded from mainstream society and all too easily drift back into crime. It is therefore unsurprising that 53 per cent of all prisoners, 75 per cent of young offenders and 89 per cent of juveniles leaving custody are reconvicted within two years.

So many women in my sample spoke of major worries about debts, spiralling ever higher while they were 'away', of loss of furniture and other possessions through theft or the bailiffs, and most terrifying of all, loss of their homes.

Several women mentioned their very real fears of a 'gate arrest'[12] for other offences. One woman with a further eight months still to serve was already in a panic: 'I could get a gate arrest. They can arrest you when you're leaving prison, for rent arrears, and I still owe all my council tax as well'. This woman had already been in prison almost a year, yet little seemed to have been done to allay her fears. Nobody had suggested any sensible strategy to consider how the debts could be met.

Bernadette[13] was going home to her four small children in two days' time:

> I'm going home on Friday. I'm glad to be going home but I don't know what I'm going to do. I've got bills up to my eyeballs, the electric's been cut off. I've got to get the kids back to school—they've not gone to school since I've been in prison. They give you £40 to go out with. How'll I do my shopping with that? The little one's still in nappies and you know what they cost. You get £100 to live on, or £60 if you're working. It took me years to get my home together. We were sleeping on the floor for yonks.

NACRO's 1992 large scale resettlement survey found that nearly half the sample were at risk of being homeless on release. Jessie is 40 and throughout the interview she wept with fear for the future, especially about the impending loss of her home:

> After a year you have to give up your flat and I don't know what to do because now I've done ten months. All my furniture's in that flat and when it's a year they chuck all your furniture out. About a month ago they said

they'd put my furniture in a store but still nothing's happened. Now I've got to fill in all these forms and give up the tenancy. The officers here say don't worry — but I do worry. At my age, to have to give everything up. All my things were in that flat, all my kids' photos of when they were small. There's my cooker, my music centre. It's not like a young girl losing things. At my age I'll never get those things again. They don't care about that though. they'll try and sell it to take off the money from your rent arrears.

Since I interviewed Jessie the rules have become even harsher. New regulations on housing benefit for tenants in rented accommodation have greatly increased the risk of homelessness on release[14] and Jessie would have lost her home long ago.

The Penal Affairs Consortium estimates, in the paper quoted above, that up to 4,000 additional prisoners could be released homeless each year because of this change in the benefit rules. Prison-based probation officers described the repercussions on imprisoned women and their dependent children as 'incalculable' and 'horrendous'. 'Women have nowhere to go and the children have to go into foster care'. 'The implications are huge for women prisoners deserted by their partners.' At best there may be bed and breakfast accommodation, at worst the children will have to stay in care. Whether or not they have dependent children, homeless women are particularly vulnerable. Yet the shock of coming into prison, especially for the majority of women who do not expect a custodial sentence, often has such a numbing effect that initially they are rendered incapable of taking any preparatory measures. The shock is exacerbated by worries about losing their homes: as one probation officer said 'Until people have a roof over their heads they can't think'. Often the primary need is for practical help, and this has to begin as soon as women come into prison if problems are not to mount up and overwhelm them, demolishing any chance of success on release.

This duty often falls to prison probation officers, though as *Chapter 13* showed, their numbers are being savagely cut. Those I interviewed repeatedly voiced their anger at being asked to 'tackle offending behaviour' in such circumstances. Wherever possible they try to challenge the enervating influence of the prison by enabling women to sort out problems for themselves.

In one prison the senior probation officer had produced a Housing Pack with information, advice and even specimen letters to help women think about their post-release accommodation arrangements long before the date arrives. The page starkly headed 'NO FIXED ABODE' warns:

If you are going to be homeless on release from prison it is up to you to do something about it at the earliest possible moment. You are no doubt aware of the difficulty of finding accommodation and may well have experienced problems yourself. However the best time to start is now.

The rest of the page is filled with lists of local authority housing departments, housing associations, voluntary organizations, Citizens' Advice Bureaux (They have a list of bed and breakfast addresses), NACRO and the area Homeless Welfare Officer.

The Penal Affairs Consortium suggests that selected prison officers should be trained to advise prisoners on housing and employment issues. Several probation officers certainly felt that more help was needed:

> We could do more to help women cope with the system. We should be telling them how to get the best out of the DSS and probation services. There is an awful complacency around in the services — that women do know how to access them. But they don't.

> I would like a fully resourced and staffed unit in every prison which would teach women basic stuff — how to approach the right people for help, how to fill in the right forms, how to deal with any crisis situation.

NACRO's Women Prisoners' Resource Centre has expanded to most of the women's prisons, and now runs advice surgeries to help women get financial support for their basic needs on release. But a probation officer in an open prison was pessimistic: 'NACRO comes once a fortnight, but the major difficulty is the lack of affordable public housing. Council houses have been sold and they haven't been replaced by new building. So where are these women to find homes?' HM Inspectors stressed the urgency of helping newly imprisoned women contact their local authority about housing. They recommended that the Prison Service should ask local authorities to provide liaison personnel to help prison staff deal with these matters.[15]

Probation staff in one closed prison told me of the recent release of a woman in her forties after seven years in jail. The probation officer had found her a warden-supervised flat of her own:

> She had never been on any pre-release courses. We sent her to an open prison but she did a runner and came back and knocked on our gates. After all these years in prison she had 20 prison bags of belongings. The officers here felt so sorry for her they took her and her stuff in a prison van on a three hour journey to her new flat, helped her settle in and didn't get back to the prison till nearly midnight. The next day I spent 45 minutes on the phone to her at the Home Office's expense.

This seemed a good example of SWIP—shared working in prison—but a prisoner who knew the released woman well was not optimistic about her chances of survival: 'She'd been inside seven years. She was institutionalised. It wasn't right to put her all on her own in a flat—even if it did have a warden. She'll be back inside in no time.'

While older women and those with families spoke of their distress about the loss of possessions and the severing of family ties, younger prisoners spoke just as passionately of their anger at the sheer waste of months or years in prison, which could perhaps have equipped them for future independence, for escape from abusive relationships or from the sex industry.

One woman had spent her schooldays seeking help for her dyslexia which had remained undiagnosed until she reached prison. But now that her problems were understood she was even angrier that the prison could offer no help: 'This is a second chance and I want to see something come out of it. I know what I want out of my life and I don't want to be a loser. But if they don't do nothing for me, I tell you, I'm gonna go right out on a bank scam again.'

Suzi is a highly intelligent woman in her mid-twenties. She is almost entirely self-educated: as a child she travelled round India with her mother, who contracted hepatitis. They returned to England and Suzi's mother committed suicide when she was 14. She survived alone by working as a fruit-picker, a night-cleaner and a stripper in London night clubs. 'Then the big one came along—the chance to make a lot of money and set myself up. I thought if I could get a car I could set up a minicab business and be independent of everybody'. The 'big one' was a large haul of drugs which Suzi tried to import from India. She was caught and given seven years, reduced to five on appeal: 'The judge recommended that every provision should be made for my education as he was sure the lack of it contributed highly to why I'd got into trouble. He was impressed at how far I'd come already in Holloway by the time my appeal came up.' Suzi made such progress with the prison music teacher that he recommended she should try for a place at a London music college. A friend outside offered her work in his studio on release once she had some qualifications.

But then she was moved to another prison. Though arrangements were made for her to take a similar course in a nearby college, the governor refused to let her go for interview. The course would have started in the September before Suzi was to be released the following January. She was given no reason for the refusal, but assumed that as a drugs smuggler she was considered too high a risk. Suzi was bitter and angry:

The course would have continued after my release, giving me a purpose and chance to put my life on a non-destructive track. I thought prison would give me an opportunity to do something with my life. I had the idealistic notion that that's what prison is all about—an opportunity, a chance. I pleaded guilty, I admitted that what I had done was serious. I said I'd like my time in prison to be a chance to get education and career opportunities. I am very bitter that I was not allowed to use my time in prison constructively.

Since I interviewed Suzi, opportunities for prisoners to attend college have been decimated by new security rules post-Woodcock and Learmont.[16] In November 1994 the then Home Secretary announced that there would be a 40 per cent reduction in the number of prisoners released on home leave and temporary release. In April 1995 the new system came into effect, and prisoners are now far less likely to obtain release on any kind of temporary basis. The implications of the cuts in home leave on family ties were discussed in *Chapters 3* and *4*.

But the changes had important implications for resettlement too. Although the new rules recognise the importance of reintegration into the community and this is reflected in the term 'resettlement licence', the restrictions are much greater. The stated purpose is 'to seek accommodation or work on release.' Resettlement licences are not available at all to prisoners serving twelve months or less. Those serving between one and four years have to serve at least one third of their sentences before becoming eligible. If they are serving four years or more they must have served at least half their sentence.

Another new form of temporary release is the 'facility licence'. This is the form most likely to affect opportunities to work in the community. To be eligible, a prisoner must have served at least a quarter of her sentence, and no category A or category B prisoner is eligible.

Staff at all levels in all the prisons I visited were unanimous in their condemnation of the new rules. One Holloway officer said 'This has desolated us.' Those working in open prisons felt particularly strongly:

> We are all about rehabilitation, about de-institutionalising people, being a bridge between a closed and an open society. That is why what has happened over temporary release is so annoying because it now means that the outside world will be so much more of a culture shock.

HM Inspectors recommended in their review[17] that the criteria for eligibility for temporary release should be reviewed in the way they apply to women prisoners.

At one closed prison I was allowed to observe a risk assessment board, chaired by a male governor five and attended by a principal officer (male), a senior officer (male) and a female probation officer. The principal officer had told me in advance: 'As you'll see, this entire exercise is all about risk—*that's* what we've got to look at'.

In preparation for the board I was shown how prisoners' data is fed into a Home Office computer programme which will then produce a printout headed *Risk Prediction for Sentence Planning*. The data entered includes the prisoner's age when first convicted, and details of all previous convictions in various offence categories. The printout supplies a risk prediction of the likelihood of a prisoner with this background being reconvicted or re-imprisoned. The programme emphasises that this is only one aspect of the risk assessment process and can be no substitute for personal judgment.

With these predictions and the rest of the files in front of them, the board discussed nine women seeking temporary release. Women's behaviour in prison was also discussed: the first application was refused because the woman had failed two mandatory drug tests. She would have to re-sit the board a month later. The second woman had asked for resettlement leave to coincide with her husband's release from another prison. The leave was allowed but at an earlier date: 'We must look at our own rules and regulations, not at fitting in with her husband. She'll still get another two leaves before release'. On the other hand, the third woman, who wanted her leave to begin the following day, had her application allowed, despite the PO's protests that the paperwork would be difficult to process in time. 'Her child is being taken on holiday to Italy', said the governor, 'and this is her last chance to see it before that. We must put the child first—it's important she builds up a relationship with the child.' The fourth woman was refused leave because 'she threatens her parents and demands money from them. They're petrified of her—they don't want her anywhere near them and they won't give her any money'. The PO explained to me that prisoners going on resettlement leave can no longer claim any money as they used to be able to: 'It's assumed—often wrongly—that they have family who can keep them while they're outside'.

The rest of the prisoners were given leave or 'knocked back' in a manner that seemed to me rather casual—though it has to be remembered that these were experienced officers who have dealt with such processes day in, day out for years. A large plate of hot buttered toast had been ordered and was brought in by a timid woman orderly. As the board munched its collective way through its deliberations, I could not help thinking of the women waiting anxiously on the wings for results that would mean so much.

In the 1993 NACRO report *Women Leaving Prison* Sir John Cassels, Chair of NACRO's policy committee on resettlement, said that the absence of a proper resettlement strategy for women prisoners was 'expensive in economic and social terms.' He pointed out that over one-third of women are reconvicted within two years of their release.

One of the open prisons I visited runs the nearest female approximation to the male resettlement prisons. This is a pre-release hostel where women live and go out to work in the local community, though the numbers it can cater for are of course very small. To qualify, a woman must be serving a sentence of 18 months or longer, and she will spend between three and nine months in the hostel. The hostel is staffed 24 hours a day because some of the women work on night shifts and have to report in and out. The woman officer with responsibility for the hostel explained how the system works:

> We deliberately don't help women find a job at first. They have to sign on at the job centre in the local town and they are obliged to tell the staff that they are prisoners. They are given four weeks to sort themselves out a job. If they fail to get work in that time we will put them in touch with our own contacts. For instance we have good links with a hotel where a lot of our women work. If they don't like the job they can try again but within four weeks we would expect them to have found work they can stick at. They can earn between £120 and £170 a week after deductions, which gives them an income to help them save for their release. They have to put £16 towards these savings, which can add up to quite a lot by the time they leave. They have to pay the prison £25 a week for their keep. In the hostel the women can cook their own food, though a hostel orderly prepares the evening meal for the women who go out to work during the day.

The prison probation team helps select candidates for the hostel. The senior probation officer praised the scheme:

> We think the hostel is excellent because it is direct empirical experience for these women: they are paying rent, working, saving money for the future. We also have Employment Focus where outside experts come in and train the women on how to conduct themselves at an interview, how to write a CV, how to improve their phone techniques.

One of the hostel women was reaching the end of the 12 years of a life sentence she had served and worked at a local animal refuge: 'It took me seven months to get the job and I did so well they wanted me to take more hours on. I get out in two years and I'd like to work with animals.'

Savita (see *Chapter 8*), who has now been out of prison for just over a year, was sceptical of the efficacy of this prison's pre-release courses:

There is no real preparation for release. They should let you out very gradually, a few hours at a time, before you go into the hostel, because if things go wrong, as they invariably do, all hell breaks loose. To be honest I think the hostel is used as an excuse for the prison to get rid of women they regard as undesirable. If a troublesome woman is put in the hostel and absconds she will not be sent back there, but will go off to closed conditions, so the prison will get rid of her. The hostel is cynically used as a control mechanism. There is lots of information available to help people leaving prison but it is not disseminated by the prison itself. If only they would just give you the information on what agencies to approach for help, ready for when you are released. I know I did wrong [fraud] and I have to take responsibility for what I did. But the prison doesn't help you to move on and that's why so many women keep returning.

Like Suzi, Savita is bitter about the treatment she received:

At no given time did anyone sit down, look at my background and say, "Let's see what we can do to make you more employable when you get back into the community". Because I already had a first degree I could have applied to university when I was in prison to do a master's course. I rang one university from the prison and they said this would be possible, but nobody in the prison gave me any support. I did manage to get on a computer course but I have now been out of prison a year and I have still not received my certificate.

I also contacted Joan (see *Chapters 3* and *8*) a hostel woman who had been released a few months after Savita, to see how effective the hostel preparation had been for her. When I phoned her at home she told me:

I went on the Employment Focus course about a week and a half before I went out. The course was good and I came out with my CV and everything. They went through all the jobs you could and couldn't do if you'd been in prison and it sounded great because they reckoned there were only three or four jobs you couldn't do. They were trying to get you back into work, trying to tell you your rights and all that. But since then nobody's given me any help. I've been out five months now and I've been left to do the best I can. So I've been working in a packhouse packing fruit and veg. Nobody's contacted me from the prison at all. They forget about you once you leave.

Joan felt abandoned after her release. The Penal Affairs Consortium paper quoted above stresses the importance of post-release supervision, likely to be further reduced under the Crime (Sentences) Act 1997. The paper complains of the patchiness of resettlement provision.

It also cites a large scale resettlement survey carried out by NACRO in 1992 which showed that 89 per cent of prisoners were likely to face unemployment on release. In future, prisoners will find it even harder to find work because of the provisions for 'criminal conviction certificates' contained in the Police Act 1997. These introduce a new policy whereby employers can require applicants for any job to obtain a certificate listing 'unspent' convictions, regardless of their relevance to the job.[18] PAC recommends that ex-offenders should become part of employers' equal opportunities policy, and that their convictions should be ignored unless they are relevant to the post in question.

Employment and accommodation worries aside, leaving prison means facing up to family and communities once more. Months or years may have passed, family weddings and funerals may have been missed. Shame had led some women to conceal the fact of their imprisonment from friends and family and leaving prison would mean having to face everyone again. One woman I interviewed after her release said her mother had lied about her imprisonment:

> She wrote to everybody and she bloody well told everyone that I'd died! She was so ashamed of what I had done [manslaughter] that she couldn't accept the social stigma. That's the irony of being a middle-class prisoner. You are rejected by the other prisoners and also by your family who can't stand the scandal. My son was nine and he had to have bereavement counselling at school because of what my mother wrote to the headmistress!

Foreign national women can suffer badly in their own communities when they return home after a long sentence in a British prison for drug couriering. A probation officer described the fears of one African prisoner

> One lady has got her parole date and is going home to the Gambia. But she's been telling me how scared she is of the terrible ablutions she will have to undergo when she gets back. She will have to bathe in the river and go through all sorts of rites, and there will be certain doorways she won't be able to go through because of the shame she has brought on her community. Members of her family may shun her.

Workers at Hibiscus, the charity whose workers support foreign national women, said this practice was particularly common in West Africa. 'We have to try to educate the families. We go and see them in their villages and beg them to be sympathetic and to continue to support these women, to understand that they are often the victims of a kind of blackmail.'

Most women, in Britain or abroad, seek out their families on release. But there is always the danger that some women, even if they have gained strength in prison, will return to an abusive partner—because of lack of money, loneliness, custody of the children, power relationship control. However strong the help in prison everything conspires to draw a woman back.

One of my most distressing interviews was with Donna, a 19-year-old woman with the looks of a model. As I passed the doorway of the TV room in an open prison she came out and volunteered to speak. She was to be released in a few days' time.'I'm quite scared about going out next Friday. The probation officer wants to find me a place in a refuge for the homeless. I've changed a lot since I came in here.'

Donna showed me a small torn photograph of her three-year-old son, Daniel, a beautiful little boy with a mop of blonde hair.

> I'm not seeing Daniel while I'm in here. I've been here a year and I'm supposed to see my son once a month but my boyfriend said "He's not seeing you in here". This is the only photo he's let me have. My boyfriend's mum's looking after Daniel. But things have changed between us. I'm a much stronger person now. My boyfriend got me on to crack but I got off it all on my own. When I first came into prison I'd had enough.

Donna's life so far has been a nightmare. She and her five siblings were all abused as children and put into separate care homes and she has lost touch with her whole family. Her boyfriend, whom she met when she was 15, forced her onto the streets to feed his crack habit:

> I wasn't a prostitute but I was rolling men for money. My boyfriend sent me to get the kerb crawlers in and I'd take some of my clothes off and get the money then I'd tell them my boyfriend was coming and I'd see them round the back later. I had Daniel when I was 16 and after I had the baby I used to beg my boyfriend not to make me go out again but he's five years older than me and quite dominant. But I've changed a lot in here.

She said she planned to go and collect her son and take him to a refuge:

> While I'm in here I think I've got to leave my boyfriend. Then he'll come on a visit and he'll give me that smile and I think, he really does love me. Then when he's gone I think, "No", if he loved me he wouldn't let me suffer in here. He sent me out on the streets and he never writes me a single letter. I

369

just hope I can do it, that I can be strong enough to leave him.

Donna was one of many women for whom prison, with all its faults, at least offered a temporary respite from abuse and violence.

The women spoke of plans and dreams for the future, of setting up home alone with their children, of starting up businesses. But so often their plans were interlaced with doubts and the overriding fear that loneliness and poverty would drive them back to relationships they knew they should leave. Donna knew she was going to need a great deal of support to enable her to rebuild her life. She was in touch with POW—Prostitutes Outreach Workers, an organization that supports workers in the sex industry—who had promised to help her.

NACRO recommends that prisons establish links with outside agencies whose workers can support women while they remain in prison, and continue that support in the community when they leave. The Penal Affairs Consortium endorses this view, suggesting that, for this very reason, 'regime activities should involve outside agencies to the maximum extent possible'. *Chapter 14* described how chaplains can link women into church groups and other charities and many religious organizations have the advantage of a national network. But because women are often held far from home, it is harder for them to retain such links on release.

This chapter began with Doreen and the news about her release. What actually happens on that last day when a woman leaves prison? First of all it has to be a week day: prisons do not release at weekends or on Bank Holidays. Had Doreen's release day fallen on a Saturday or Sunday she would have left the Friday before.

Most people recall the old myth of leaving prison with 'a suit of clothes and £50'. In fact the reality is not so very different. A woman about to leave prison will have to go before the last of the ubiquitous prison boards, this time a Clothing Board, where she will be asked if her clothes still fit her, and if they are warm enough for the time of year. If not, the Prison Service is obliged to provide liberty clothing.

Prisoners who have served a sentence of more than three months can be considered for a community care clothing grant. But there is a stern caveat: 'If you reject clothes provided by the prison, the Benefits Agency will reject any claim you make after release for clothes'. Women who have lost all their furniture and other possessions may apply to the Benefits Agency, where Social Fund Officers will usually decide to award them a loan rather than a grant, repayable by deducting between £2 and £10 a week from income support. The amount of the grant is discretionary but the average sum is about £250, meant to cover expenses such as household equipment, connection of electricity and removal costs.

When I telephoned Joan at home I asked whether she had this kind of help. She said she had not:

> You're supposed to get a clothing grant but with me they turned all that down. As long as you've still got the pair of shoes and the coat you came in with, you don't get a thing. To be honest a lot of that stuff in the prisoners' manual is a load of bull.

All prisoners are given a travel warrant to take them to their home or to whatever address within the British Isles they choose. If a woman is sick she can make the (improbable) decision to remain in prison till she is cured. If she has no-one to take her to her destination, she has the right to be accompanied by a plain-clothed prison officer. Joan was driven home by car:

> I came out with a grant for £47 or so and nothing else at all. Out of that money I had to pay £5 petrol because a car from the prison took me home. If I could have got home by public transport they'd have given me a travel warrant. So that took the money down to £42 which had to last me five or six weeks—that's how long it took before I got any more money through.

Savita's benefits also took six weeks to start again:

> I had a partner waiting for me outside. If it had not been for him I would have been entirely alone. I applied for a crisis loan from the benefits agency, but I didn't find out I could do that till I came out of prison. Nobody there tells you anything.

The mythical £50 has failed to keep pace with inflation: a woman will usually be paid the standard discharge grant of £47.70 if she is over 25, or £36.15 if she is aged under 24.[19] The grant, roughly equivalent to one week's benefit, is supposed to cover living expenses until the woman receives her income support payment from the DSS *two weeks* after release or, as in Joan's and Savita's cases, far longer. In America the grant is similar: released women are given $100, though women leaving prison nurseries with their child are also given diapers, bottles, food and clothing for the baby. In a recent Policy Studies Institute study[20] of a sample of released prisoners, all the ex-prisoners interviewed had spent their discharge grant in a week or less, on food, clothes, travel and telephone calls which were necessary to help them resettle into the community. Although the prisoners could have applied for income support *three months before their release*, none of the PSI sample had done so.

371

An ex-prisoner who runs out of money before the two weeks are up —
as seems very likely—can apply as Savita did for a crisis loan from the
Social Fund at the DSS. But repayments will be automatically taken
from benefit. Six weeks before leaving prison, he or she could also apply
for a discretionary community care grant, designed to help people move
or stay out of institutional or residential care. But in the PSI study
quoted above, none of the ex-prisoners had made such an application.
The Penal Affairs Consortium suggests that the Benefits Agency should
go into prisons and let prisoners know that they can make advance
claims of this kind so that the money is immediately available on
release.

There are several even harsher exceptions to some already harsh
rules: if a girl is under 16 she will get no grant—it is assumed (often
wrongly) that she will return to the family home. Now that 16 to 17 year
olds are no longer eligible for income support, they will not get a
discharge grant either, unless they can manage to prove 'a real need to
look for, secure and pay for accommodation before being released.'[21]
Women imprisoned for less than 15 days, or those in prison for fine
default get no discharge grant either. Two-thirds of sentences for TV
licence fine defaults are given to women.

The amount of the grant may also vary slightly depending on
whether a woman has a home to go to, or whether she is likely to be
homeless—still referred to in the antiquated language of the law as
'being of no fixed abode'. Any prisoner unable to find accommodation
may be given a higher grant.

Housing benefit is the only benefit a prisoner can claim while
remaining in prison. Anyone serving a sentence for longer than 21 days
may not claim anything else, including a state pension, though a
woman's family can continue to claim some benefits such as the lone
parent premium.

Women prisoners reaching the end of their sentences were much
more likely than the men I interviewed in an earlier research project to
regard the time spent in prison as entirely wasted time. They had got
through it but had little positive to show for those months or years.
Most were very anxious about their approaching release and it seemed
predictable that many would shortly be back inside. Erving Goffman,
from whose work[22] I have quoted in other chapters, summed up the
situation of people leaving institutions like prisons: 'Release is likely to
come just when the inmate has finally learned the ropes on the inside
and won privileges. Release means moving from the top of a very small
world to the bottom of a very large one.'

Joycelyn M Pollock[23] stressed the need for women prisoners to have
programmes:

that teach self-sufficiency, responsible behavior, and improve interpersonal relationships. Unfortunately, prison is a poor place to acquire these skills. The nature of prison retards self-control and responsibility; basic decisions about when to eat, where to work, whether to work, and when to get up are usurped by prison authority. [The] control and arbitrary enforcement of countless rules reproduces the powerlessness and unpredicability that [women have] experienced in their lives outside prison.

Pollock concludes: 'Most women in prison need help but it is extremely doubtful whether prison is the help they need. If we must incarcerate, then at least let's try to make sure that they exit prison at least no worse than when they went in'.

On her last day in prison, that Monday in late August 1996, Doreen would have been offered one final breakfast. Then at 8.45 a.m. she would walk out of the prison clad—if she was lucky—in her liberty clothes, her purse bulging with her travel warrant and her £47.70. She would step alone into her future.

Endnotes

1. *Women in Prison: A Review*, HM Inspectorate, 1997: 2.18, 2.19.
2. *The Prisoners' Information Book 1996*, jointly published by the Prison Reform Trust and HM Prison Service.
3. Secreting of drugs or contraband goods in the vagina.
4. Mandatory drug test using urine specimen.
5. Earliest Date of Release.
6. See *Chapter 3*.
7. A synthetic narcotic opiate used to treat opiate dependence, especially heroin.
8. *The National Prison Survey 1991*, HMSO, 1992, found that over a third (38 per cent) of all prisoners under the age of 21 had been taken into care before the age of 16, compared with just 3 per cent of the general population.
9. 24 hours a day, 7 days a week: in other words the whole time.
10. *Opening the Door: Women Leaving Prison*, NACRO, 1993.
11. Sentence planning officially covers only prisoners given sentences of 12 months or more, and all young offenders.
12. When a prisoner has completed his or her sentence but is rearrested immediately on leaving the prison and charged with other offences or detained as liable for deportation.
13. See *Chapter 3* and *Chapter 12*.
14. See *Chapter 13* and *Chapter 1*.
15. See Note 1, above: Executive Summary: 43.
16. Enquiries by Sir John Woodcock into the Whitemoor escapes and by General Sir John Learmont into the Parkhurst escapes, all in 1994.
17. See Note 1, above: 8.33.
18. Under the Rehabilitation of Offenders Act 1974 convictions which lead to a jail sentence of 30 months or more can never become 'spent', while sentences of between six and 30 months become spent after 10 years.
19. These are the figures at time of writing: Summer 1997.
20. *Financial Difficulties on Release from Prison*, Ann Hagell, Tim Newburn and Karen Rowlingson,

Policy Studies Institute, 1995.

21. See *Prisoners' Information Book*, 1996, Prison Reform Trust/HM Prison Service.
22. *Asylums*, Penguin, 1961.
23. *Counseling Women in Prison*, Sage, 1998.

EPILOGUE

What of the Future?

The nineties have seen enormous and rapid changes in women's prisons. During the period of my research, four prisons were re-designated to take women: HMPs Eastwood Park in Gloucestershire, Brockhill in Worcestershire, Highpoint in Suffolk and Foston Hall in Derbyshire. Staff at Risley women's unit have been told that they have to take 170 women until the summer of 1998, though the unit's certified normal accommodation is just 150. That unit will then be closed and the women moved to Styal—though staff privately express fears that new accommodation there will not be ready in time, that there will be gross overcrowding, and that there will be increased bullying because of the diffuse nature of the Styal campus. (Styal is opening only 120 extra cells to accommodate the 170 women currently crammed into Risley—and no arrangements have so far been made to increase the size of the kitchens, the education department, the visits room or the mother and baby unit). The Howard League found that the young offender unit at HMP New Hall was operating at 203 per cent capacity, with 89 girls being held in a space designed for 44.

In March 1998 the Prison Service announced that a 450 place secure women's prison would be built on the site of a former male remand centre at Ashford, Middlesex, to relieve the pressure on Holloway (a quarter of all female prisoners come from London).

At the end of April 1998, the Prison Service announced that Low Newton, currently holding 253 young male offenders and 85 women, would become a prison for 245 women. Send prison, near Woking, would also be re-roled to take another 200 women. Prison Service officials commented that the changes were being made in view of the 21 per cent rise in female prisoners in the last twelve months, and are necessary to avoid holding women in police cells. Merseyside women sent to Styal, Low Newton, Send or elsewhere in the country, will be far from homes and families. Phone calls will cost more and visitors and professionals like lawyers, social workers and probation officers will have a much more difficult and expensive journey.

Perhaps some of the Merseyside women will end up there—hundreds of miles from home. Or they might be sent to Peterborough. Though there has, at the time of writing, been no official announcement, the Prison Reform Trust reports[1] that the Prison Service has plans to build a new prison at there to take 360 women and 480 men, despite local opposition. The PRT claims that:

375

. . . as far as prisons are concerned, the [government's] policy seems little more than cross your fingers and hope for the best. Yet as all the recent reports from HM Chief Inspector of Prisons have shown, conditions and regimes are deteriorating in gaols up and down the country. It is the pace of deterioration which is most worrying.

Even more alarming was the Prison Service's announcement, on 24 April 1998, that a further 80 places for women were to be created in Durham's F wing, adjacent to H wing, where conditions are already unsatisfactory. This means that 126 women will be held in the midst of an 800-strong male prison. In total, an extra 1,000 places are to be provided for women prisoners by early 1999—the biggest expansion of women's jails since World War II. It is clear that the Prison Service expects the rapid increase in female custodial sentences to continue.

• • •

It is now accepted by many professionals that at least part of the prison overcrowding problem could be solved by diverting women into non-custodial options. The funding implications are also considerable: a prison place for a woman costs £512 a week—£26,624 a year—compared with £420 a week for a male prisoner. A probation order costs £2,270 a year and a community service order costs £1,700 a year.[2]

But of course such a solution is not nearly as easy as it sounds. First, there would be the task of persuading sentencers and the general public of the effectiveness of community alternatives. As a senior Holloway governor told me, 'I could release nearly all of the 500 women in this prison tomorrow, and there would not be a crime wave in London. But the problem is convincing politicians, the public and the media of that.' Indeed, Mike Sheldrick, Holloway's governor, endorsed these views publicly on a TV programme in March 1998:[3] 'You have to be more discriminating about who ends up in prison and whether there are opportunities for more community-based outlets'. David Roddan, general secretary of the Prison Officers' Association, said on the same programme: 'We have said for a long time that many females in prison should not be there'.

Second, sentencers would need to know that appropriate community alternatives for women were readily available. They would have to be properly resourced to meet women's particular needs in terms of the work on offer—though magistrates' apparent reluctance to sentence women to community service involving manual labour is not always shared by the women themselves. Careful thought would need to be given to safe hostel accommodation for women (many of whom

376

are likely to have been physically and sexually abused) and sometimes for their children too. Childcare and transport would have to be provided to enable mothers of young children to fulfil the demands of the court order. In *Chapter 3* I described a woman sent to a Kent bail hostel, the only woman among more than 20 male sex offenders. The nearest place in an all-female hostel was 100 miles away from her family.

Third, funds will have to be made available to pay the costs of community service orders and combination orders. Yet at a time when there are signs that courts are becoming more willing to use these orders, the probation service with the duty of supervising them has been told it must cut its budget by 29 per cent over the next five years.

Many imprisoned mothers I interviewed said they would prefer to be tagged if it meant they could stay with their children—though electronic tagging, even with new sophisticated technology, is not the panacea that many believe. There is potential for dangerous tension, even for child abuse, when people are confined to their homes with small children for long periods. And sentencers are likely to react more harshly to those already 'given a chance' those who breach a tagging order. As Dick Whitfield, chief probation officer for Kent warns,[4] tagging can either become a cost-effective answer to crime prevention, or it could be an 'electronic trip-wire' into custody because offenders who may originally have been tagged for non-custodial offences may end up in prison for breaching the order, further increasing the prison population.

Only a groundswell of public revulsion against the conditions in women's prisons will produce the political will, and with it the necessary funding, to push through such radical changes. In the meantime pragmatic decisions about the women's prison estate are made 'on the hoof' in response to panics about overcrowding. As one experienced criminologist said:

I'm afraid I have become rather cynical. People have said "We'd better do something about the women because so many more are coming into prison". But then other people will say "We can't do much because we haven't got the money". So they think of setting up women's units near male prisons and calling them "annexes". The word "annexe" says it all really — the women's service is regarded as an annexe, the little sister of the men's service. There has never been a big academic study of the options for custody for women to suit their particular needs.

Sir David Ramsbotham's thematic report on women's prisons,[5] quoted extensively throughout this book, is the first major attempt in recent

377

years to draw all the strands together and make some sense of what can only be termed a chaotic situation in the women's estate.

The inspectors' report is lengthy and detailed, but it makes four main recommendations:

First, that wherever possible women should be diverted from custody (as in the Holloway remand pilot scheme) and reintegrated into the community.

Second, the report recommends that the women's prison system should be managed separately, headed by a single director who would be responsible to the Prisons Board and accountable for everything in the women's estate, including centrally managed allocations and resourcing and properly organized coordination to minimise local variations when women are moved between prisons.

Third, the inspectors recommend an urgent and thorough analysis of the needs of women prisoners, which would inform a national strategy to provide suitable regimes to meet those needs.

Fourth, they point out the disastrous effects of a current management structure that is largely geographical, resulting—because there are only 16 prisons that take women—in inevitable dislocation of women from their homes, families and communities. The other major problem with this system is the unnecessarily high level of physical security under which most imprisoned women are held. The inspectors recommend three linked solutions:

- Women requiring varying levels of security should be held in multi-purpose, graduated-security establishments.
- Women serving short sentences or on short remands should be held in new units—small urban 'transitional prisons'—to enable them to retain family ties more easily. Allocations, say the inspectors, should take account of women's individual needs such as health, work and training, access to counselling and proximity to home and children.
- Those few women who if they escaped would pose a serious danger to the public should be held in one of two secure units, one in the North of England, one in the South.

The inspectors emphasise throughout that they are not seeking any favours for women prisoners. But they also stress that giving women prisoners opportunities that are equal to men's does not mean treating them in the same way. Everything I have written in this book points to the need for different—though not special—treatment.

• • •

There are some signs of hope for the future. All prisoners may benefit from the government's planned adoption of the European Convention for the Protection of Human Rights and Fundamental Freedoms. There may be successful challenges from prisoners under Article 3: 'No one shall be subjected to torture or to inhuman or degrading treatment or punishment'. Surely—properly applied— this will rule out practices like the shackling of sick and pregnant women and many of the other scenarios described in this book.

In Sir David Ramsbotham and his deputy Colin Allen, women prisoners are finding powerful advocates who are refusing to compromise until radical changes are made. They have not been afraid to 'name and shame' prisons, like Brockhill, in need of 'special managerial attention' and to demand the appointment of a director in charge of the female prison estate. Above all they have raised the profile of women in prison so that they can no longer be dismissed as an insignificant minority.

Other organizations are now embracing the women's cause. In February 1998 the Prison Reform Trust announced that it had launched a major inquiry into women's imprisonment. The Wedderburn Committee, commissioned by the PRT to report by mid-1999, includes distinguished experts in the law, penology and mental health. It set out to cover all aspects of women's imprisonment ranging from the prosecution policies of the Crown Prosecution Service to the treatment of women in custody and after release. Professor Dorothy Wedderburn said as the committee was launched:

> Fundamental issues of policy and practice are raised by the imprisonment of women. In the light of the nature of the offences which women commit, just how many women do we need to imprison? How can a Prison Service dominated by the needs of male prisoners best meet those of a small female minority? What sort of prisons do we need—if, that is, we need any? In recent years, the whole issue of women behind bars has become more controversial. My Committee will be trying to map out a better way of responding to female criminality in the new Millennium.

In January 1998 a new Directorate of Regimes was created at Prison Service Headquarters. The directorate is divided into groups as follows: Regime Services (looking at offending behaviour, education, work and training); Prisoner Administration (risk assessment and the law relating to prisoners, including the incorporation of the European Convention on Human Rights into UK law); Chaplaincy; Lifers and Adult Males; Young Offenders and Juveniles (looking especially at the implications of the ruling which made it illegal to hold young offenders in adult prisons); Catering; and—finally—the Women's Policy Group.

On 20 April 1998 Linda Jones was appointed head of the Women's Group, seconded from her ten-year-long post as chief probation officer for Leicestershire. Her Probation Service background may be significant, in view of the government's decision to consider the merging of the Prison Service and Probation Service into a single 'Department of Corrections' (see *Chapter 2*), and the fact that Joyce Quin is Minister for both services. Linda Jones has already declared her interest in working closely with the Probation Service to help prepare prisoners for release and to support them in the community afterwards.

Certainly many commentators welcomed the fact that the new appointee does not come steeped in Prison Service culture. Her first public speech in post[6] was greeted with enthusiasm as she outlined positive initiatives she hoped to implement as soon as possible. These included:

- reviewing the security categorisation of women to see whether some are held in conditions of greater security than needed
- chairing a working group to look at the way forward for female juveniles
- looking at providing regimes appropriate for women (a governors' conference was held in March to look at 'purposeful activity', and £1 million of additional funding has been made available for the creation of two 'model regimes' at Holloway and Styal)
- drawing up regimes standards
- training staff to work with women
- accrediting offending behaviour programmes based on newly commissioned research
- forming a working group of representatives from all 16 prisons to look at courses that will meet women's special needs
- integrating health services into a 'holistic service for women', to include a revision of the policy on pregnant women in prison and on prescribed medication levels
- looking at the best ways of managing 'difficult and disruptive' women
- considering resettlement plans
- continuing work with NACRO to train Prison Link officers who will help women find accommodation before release, and to train prisoners in this work;
- piloting Welfare to Work at HMP New Hall to increase job skills and employability of prisoners in the 18 to 24 age range; and

- surveying women's work experience and intentions.

Linda Jones denies that this is merely a 'wish list': she ended this first speech by expressing her determination 'to work closely with establishments to develop regimes for women which work in practice'.

On 13 May 1998, just as I was completing this book, a remarkable report[7] was published in response to the tragic suicides at Cornton Vale, Scotland's only women's prison. Jointly produced by the Social Work Services and Prisons Inspectorate for Scotland, it considered the profile of Scottish women offenders and concluded that it was often very different from that of men. Indeed, almost all women could be safely punished in the community. The Scottish Office minister for home affairs, Henry McLeish, gave an immediate and positive response:

> This is a watershed report. We will use the findings and recommendations as the basis for a new, full integrated approach to dealing with women's offending. The report sets the context for action up to and beyond the millemmium.

In her moving book[8] about imprisonment around the world, Vivien Stern, secretary-general of Penal Reform International, shows that in every country 'there is a prison system for men, and women are everywhere tacked on in an awkward afterthought'. Could Britain be the first to radically change this approach? Until then women prisoners will, as Vivien Stern says, remain 'the prisoners in the shadows'—the invisible women.

Endnotes

1. Reported in *Prison Report*, 2 December 1997.
2. Figures quoted by the Earl of Mar in a debate in the House of Lords on cuts in the probation service, 16 July 1997 (He also recalled Lord Jenkins, when Home Secretary, saying that 42,000 was an intolerable figure for the prison population).
3. BBC2 *Newsnight*, 24 March 1998.
4. *Tackling the Tag*, Waterside Press, 1997.
5. *Women in Prison: A Review*, HM Inspectorate, 1997.
6. At a conference at Liverpool Hope University, 23 April 1998, on the theme of 'Positive Directions for Women in Secure Environments'.
7. *Women Offenders: A Safer Way*, Social Work Services/Prisons Inspectorate for Scotland, 13 May 1998. This was the report of the study referred to in *Chapter 12*: see Note 32.
8. *A Sin Against the Future: Imprisonment in the World*, Penguin, 1998.

Appendix 1: Prison Visits and Interviews

The following prisons were visited:

Remand prisons

HMP Risley female wing
HMP Holloway
HMP Pucklechurch (now closed for women)

Closed prisons

HMP Cookham Wood
HMP Bullwood Hall
HMP Durham (H Wing)
HMP Styal
HMP Brockhill
HMP Foston Hall

Open prisons

HMP Askham Grange
HMP Drake Hall
HMP East Sutton Park

Interviews were conducted as follows:

Staff

I interviewed a total of 112 prison staff as follows:

60 disciplinary staff; 9 civilian staff; 9 healthcare staff; 2 psychologists; 10 prison probation officers; 12 education staff; 10 chaplains; also a number of visiting staff (counsellors, voluntary workers, prison visitors, members of Boards of Visitors); a number of Home Office and Prison Service officials; and a range of academics/criminologists, members of prisoners' support groups etc.

Interviews with women prisoners

I interviewed a total of 150 women (48 in the first project; 102 in the second).

Bibliography

Adelberg E and Currie C (Eds.), *Too Few to Count: Canadian Women in Conflict with the Law*, Press Gang, Vancouver, 1987

Adler, F, *Sisters in Crime*, McGraw Hill, New York, 1975

Adler, F, 'The Rise of the Female Crook' in *Psychology Today*, 1975:9

Advisory Council on the Misuse of Drugs, *Drug Misusers and the Prison System: An Integrated Approach (Part II)*, HMSO, 1996

Allen, C, 'Speech to the Bourne Trust', 1996

Babies in Prison, *Annual Newsletter*, 1996

Basic Skills Agency, *The Basic Skills of Young Adults*, 1994

Bennett, T, *Drug Testing Arrestees*, Home Office Research Study No. 70, 1998

Blud, L, 'Cognitive Skills Programmes in Prisons' in *What Works with Young Prisoners?* Hayman, S (Ed.), Institute for the Study and Treatment of Delinquency (ISTD), Report of a conference, November 1995

Box, S, *Recession, Crime and Punishment*, Macmillan, 1987

British Medical Association, *Complete Family Health Encyclopaedia*, 1990

Burnett, R and Farrell, G, 'Reported and Unreported Racial Incidents in Prisons', Oxford University Centre for Criminological Research, Occasional Paper No. 14, 1994

Caddle D and Crisp, D, *Imprisoned Women and Mothers*, Home Office Research Study No. 162, 1996

Campbell, A, 'Media Myth-Making' in *Criminal Justice Matters*, Spring 1995:19

Carlen, P, *Women's Imprisonment: A Study in Social Control*, Routledge and Keegan Paul, 1983

Carlen, P (Ed.), *Criminal Women*, Polity Press, 1985

Carlen, P, *Women, Crime and Poverty*, Open University Press, 1988

Carpenter, M, *Our Convicts*, Longman, 1864

Casale, S, *Women Inside*, Civil Liberties Trust, 1989

Chesney-Lynd, M, *The Female Offender: Girls, Women and Crime*, Sage Publications, 1997

Chigwada-Bailey, Ruth, *Black Women's Experiences of Criminal Justice*, Waterside Press, 1997

Cole, D, 'The Case of Claire Bosley: Another Suicide Statistic' in *Prison Report*, Prison Reform Trust, Summer 1996

Coleman J and Lyon, J, *Understanding and Working with Young Women in Custody*, Trust for the Study of Adolescence/HM Prison Service, 1996

Colin, J and Morris, R, *Interpreters and the Legal Process*, Waterside Press, 1996

Department of Health, *Inspection of Facilities for Mothers and Babies in Prison*, November 1996

Devlin, A, *Criminal Classes: Offenders at School*, Waterside Press, 1995

Devlin, A, *Prison Patter*, Waterside Press, 1996

Dobash R, Dobash R and Gutteridge S, *The Imprisonment of Women*, Basil Blackwell, 1986

Dodd, T and Hunter, P, *A Report to the Home Office of a Study of Prisoners in England and Wales* (The National Prison Survey, 1991), OPCS/HMSO, 1992: see Walmsley, R, below, for *Main Findings*

Dowling, C G, 'Women Behind Bars', USA *Life* magazine, October 1997

Eaton, M, *Justice for Women? Family, Court and Social Control*, Open University Press, 1986

Eaton, M, 'Women in Custody' in *Criminal Justice Matters*, Winter 1993/4: 14

Edmonds, M, 'A Better Service for Women', in *Advanced Probation Studies*, Somerset Probation Service, 1994

Edwards, S, *Women on Trial*, Manchester University Press, 1984

Faulkner, D, *Darkness and Light: Justice, Crime and Management for Today*, Howard League, 1996

Female Prisons Welfare Project/Hibiscus, *Annual Report 1995-1996*

Foucault, M, *Discipline and Punish: The Birth of the Prison*, Penguin, 1979

Fraser, J, *Drug Use in Prison*, 1994 (Unpublished: available from Psychology Department HMP Holloway)

Gelsthorpe, L, *Sexism and the Female Offender*, Cambridge Studies in Criminology, Gower 1987

Goffman, E, *Asylums*, Penguin, 1961

Hagell, A, Newburn, T and Rowlingson, K, *Financial Difficulties on Release from Prison*, Policy Studies Institute (PSI), 1995

Halow (London), *Annual Report 1995-1996*

Hayman, S, *Community Prisons for Women*, Prison Reform Trust, 1996

Hayman, S (Ed), *Imprisoning Women*, Institute for the Study and Treatment of Adolescence (ISTD), 1997

Hebblethwaite, M, 'One Day in Holloway' in *The Tablet*, 9 March 1996

Hebblethwaite, M, 'Befriender from Abroad' in *The Tablet*, 23 March 1996

Hebblethwaite, M, 'In a Man's World' in *The Tablet*, 30 March 1996

Heidensohn, F, *Women and Crime*, Macmillan, 1985 (9th edition 1996)

Heidensohn, F, 'Did the World Move? A Brief Overview of 25 Years of Feminist Criminology' in *Criminal Justice Matters*, Spring 1995: 19

Hewitt, B, Nelson, M and Velez, E, 'Mothers Behind Bars' in *People Weekly* (USA), 11 November 1996

HM Chief Inspector of Prisons, *Women Offenders and Probation Service Provision*, 1991

HM Chief Inspector of Prisons, *Doing Time or Using Time*, CMD 2128: Home Office, 1993

HM Chief Inspector of Prisons, *HM Prison Bullwood Hall: Report of HM Inspector of Prisons*, Home Office, 1992

HM Chief Inspector of Prisons, *HM Prison Brockhill: Report by HM Chief Inspector of Prisons*, Home Office, 1994

HM Chief Inspector of Prisons, *Patient or Prisoner? A new Strategy for Health Care in Prisons*, Home Office, 1996

HM Chief Inspector of Prisons, *HM Prison Durham: Report of a Full Inspection By HM Chief Inspector of Prisons*, Home Office, 1996

HM Chief Inspector of Prisons, *The Female Prison at HM Prison Risley. Report of an Unannounced Short Inspection*, Home Office, 1996

HM Chief Inspector of Prisons, *HM Prison Holloway. Report of an Unannounced Inspection By HM Chief Inspector of Prisons*, Home Office, 1997

HM Chief Inspector of Prisons, *Women in Prison: A Review*, Home Office, 1997

HM Chief Inspector of Prisons, *Young Prisoners*, Home Office, November 1997

HM Chief Inspector of Prisons, *HM Remand Centre, Low Newton – Female Wing. Report of An Unannounced Short Inspection*, Home Office, 1997

HM Inspectorate of Probation: *Report on Women Offenders and Probation Service Provision*, July 1991

HM Prison Service, *Race Relations and Religion: A Pocket Guide for Prison Staff*

HM Prison Service, *Caring for the Suicidal in Custody*, 1994

HM Prison Service Briefing Paper No. 97, 8 August 1996

HM Prison Service Briefing Paper No. 101, 23 October 1996

HM Prison Service Briefing Paper 103, 14 November 1996

HM Prison Service, *Regimes for Women*, 1995

HM Prison Service, *Mother and Baby Units*, 1996

HM Prison Service, *Welcome to the Prison Service*, 1993

HMP Holloway, *Basic Fact Pack for Visitors*, July 1996

Home Office Prison Department, *Handbook for Prison Visitors*, 1987

Home Office, *Prison Statistics, England and Wales, 1994*, published 1996

Howard League for Penal Reform, *Families Matter*, 1993

Howard League for Penal Reform, *Women in Prison*, Fact Sheet No. 7

Howard League for Penal Reform, *Imprisonment for Debt*, Fact Sheet No. 13

Howard League for Penal Reform, *Young Adults (Aged 17 to 20 years)*, Fact Sheet No. 15

Howard League for Penal Reform, *The Use of Imprisonment for Girls*, Fact Sheet No. 16

Howard League for Penal Reform, *Suicide and Self Injury in Prison*, Fact Sheet No. 19

Howard League for Penal Reform, *Gender*, Fact Sheet No. 28

Howard League for Penal Reform, *Prison Mother and Baby Units*, 1995

Howard League for Penal Reform, *The Voice of A Child: The Impact on Children of their Mothers' Imprisonment*, 1993

Howard League for Penal Reform, *Foreign Nationals in Prison*, Fact Sheet No. 22

Howard League for Penal Reform, *Lost Inside: The Imprisonment of Teenage Girls*, October 1997

Jeevanjee, A, *Immigration Laws: Are they fair to Black Britons?*, 1994

Hume, Cardinal Basil, 'Lighting the Way' in *The Tablet*, 30 March 1996

Kelland, D, 'Working In a Custodial Setting with Young Women who Self-Harm' in *Understanding and Working with Young Women in Custody*, Coleman, J, 1996 (above)

Kennedy, H, *Eve Was Framed*, Chatto and Windus, 1992; Vintage, 1993

Learmont, General Sir John, *Report Into HMP Parkhurst Escapes*, 1994

Leech, M, *The Prisoners' Handbook*, Pluto, 1997 (The Prisons Handbook, Waterside Press, 1998: now published annually)

Liebling, A, (Ed.), *Deaths in Custody. Caring for People at Risk*, Whiting and Birch, 1996

Liebling, A, *Suicides in Prison*, Routledge, 1992

Lloyd, A, *Doubly Deviant, Doubly Damned*, Penguin, 1995

MacInnes, E, 'Light behind Bars' in *The Tablet*, 17 August 1996

Maden, A, Swinton, M and Gunn, J, *A Survey of Pre-arrest Drug Use in Sentenced Prisoners* in *British Journal of Addiction*, 1992: 87

Maden, A, Swinton, M and Gunn, J, 'Women in Prison and Use of Illicit Drugs Before Arrest' in *British Medical Journal*, 301, 1990

Maden, A, Taylor, C, and Gunn, J, *Mental Disorder in Remand Prisoners*, Home Office, 1995

Measham, F, 'Equality in Ecstasy? Young Women and Drugs' in *Criminal Justice Matters*, 19, Spring 1995

Miller, Susan L (ed.) *Crime Control and Women*, Sage 1998

Morris, A and Wilkinson, C, (Eds.) '*Women and the Penal System*'. Papers presented to the 19th Cropwood Conference, University of Cambridge Institute of Criminology, 1988

Morris, A, *Women, Crime and Criminal Justice*, Basil Blackwell, 1987

Morris A, and Gelsthorpe, L, 'Not Paying for Crime: Issues in Crime Enforcement' in *Criminal Law Review* 839, 1990

Morris A *et al*, *Managing the Needs of Female Prisoners*, Home Office, 1995

NACRO, *A Fresh Start for Women Prisoners: The Implications of the Woolf Report for Women*, 1991

NACRO, *Women and Criminal Justice: Some Facts and Figures*, Briefing Paper No. 91, August 1992

NACRO, *Opening the Door: Women Leaving Prison*, 1993

NACRO, *Community Prisons*, 1994

NACRO, *Women in Prison*, Briefing Paper 33: September 1995

NACRO, *Women Prisoners: Towards a New Millennium*, 1996

NACRO, '10 Key Messages About Crime', *NACRO Annual Report 1995/1996*

NACRO, *Women and Criminal Justice*, Briefing Paper No. 91

Nadel, Jennifer: *Sara Thornton*, Gollancz, 1993

NAPO (National Association of Probation Officers), *Women and Crime*, 1997

Padel, U and Stevenson, P, *Insiders: Women's Experience of Prison*, Virago, 1988

Penal Affairs Consortium, *The Reduction of Home Leave and Temporary Release Opportunities*, 1995

Penal Affairs Consortium, *The Imprisonment of Fine Defaulters*, 1995

Penal Affairs Consortium, *The Imprisonment of Women: Some Facts and Figures*, 1996

Penal Affairs Consortium, *Housing Benefit and Prisoners*, 1996

Penal Affairs Consortium, *Drugs on the Inside*, 1996

Penal Affairs Consortium, *Race and Criminal Justice*, 1996

Penal Affairs Consortium, *Prisons – Some Current Developments*, 1996

Penal Affairs Consortium, *Crime, Drugs and Criminal Justice*, 1997

Penal Affairs Consortium, *17 Year Olds and the Youth Court*, 1997

Penal Affairs Consortium, *Reducing Offending*, 1997

Penal Affairs Consortium, *The Crime (Sentences) Bill*, 1997

Penal Affairs Consortium, *An Unsuitable Place for Treatment: Diverting mentally Disordered Offenders from Custody*, 1998

Pollock-Byrne, J M, *Women, Prison and Crime*, Brooks-Cole, California, 1990

Pollock-Byrne, J M, *Counseling Women in Prison*, Sage, 1998

Prison Reform Trust, *The Future of the Prison Education Service*, 1993

Prison Reform Trust, *Education in Prisons: A National Survey*, 1995

Prison Reform Trust, *The Prison Population: Britain, the Rest of Europe and the World*, 1996

Prison Reform Trust/HM Prison Service, *The Prisoners' Information Book*, 1996 (now published annually)

Prison Reform Trust, *Chain Reaction: The Shackling of Prisoners*, 1997

Prison Reform Trust, 'Adults Only' in *Prison Report*, No. 40, Autumn 1997

Prison Reform Trust, *The Rising Toll of Prison Suicide*, 1997

Prisoners' Advice Service, *Annual Report 1994-1995*

Rock, P, *Reconstructing a Women's Prison: The Holloway Redevelopment Project*, Oxford University Press, 1996

Smart, C, *Women, Crime and Criminology: A Feminist Critique*, Routledge, 1976

Smith, C, *Women, Health and Imprisonment*, Bangor, 1995

Stanko, E, 'Gender and Crime' in *Criminal Justice Matters*, Spring 1995: 19

Stern, Vivien, *A Sin Against the Future: Imprisonment in the World*, Penguin, 1998

Tchaikovsky, C, 'Enough Punishment' in *The Tablet*, 29 June 1996

Tchaikovsky, C, 'No Room of One's Own' in *Criminal Justice*, Volume 12, May 1994

Wall, D and Bradshaw, J, 'The Message of the Medium' in *New Law Journal*, 9 September 1994

Walmsley, R, Howard, E and White, S, *The National Prison Survey 1991: Main Findings*, Home Office Research Study No. 128, HMSO, 1992 (see also Dodd, T above)

West, Tessa, *Prisons of Promise*, Waterside Press, 1997

Whitfield, Dick, *Tackling the Tag*, Waterside Press, 1997

Wilmott, Y, 'The Health of Women Prisoners' in *Understanding and Working with Young Women in Custody*, Coleman, J, 1996 (above)

Wincup, E, 'Gender and Imprisonment: Some Thoughts on "Mixed" Prisons' in *Criminal Justice Matters*, No. 91, Spring 1995

Women in Prison, *Annual Report 1995*

Woodcock, Sir John, *Report into HMP Whitemoor Escapes*, 1994

Woolf and Tumim, *Report of An Enquiry into Prison Disturbances*, Cmd. 1456, HMSO, 1991

Worrall, A, *Offending Women*, Routledge, 1990

Worrall, A, *Troublesome Young Women* in *Criminal Justice Matters*, Spring 1995: 19

Zedner, L, 'Wayward Sisters' in *The Oxford History of the Prison*, Oxford University Press, 1995.

Index

A

B

387

O

O'Dwyer, Josie 122 261
Official Secrets Act x
Ohio State Penitentiary 94
older women prisoners 176-179
Ombudsman, Prisons 105 116 283
open prisons 21 50 56 103 107-110
    124 172 177-179 197 229 282-283
    337 343 355 366
Open University 325 326 329 335
    341
Operating Standards Manual 160
Operation Tornado 90
optician 253
overcrowding 33 52 376
overnight visits 49
Oxford Centre for Criminological
    Research 203

P

parasuicide 278
parenting classes 60
parole 278
parole reports/reviews 154-155 288
    302 317
Parkhurst, HMP 48
passports, confiscation of 229
pat down searches 83
Patient or Prisoner? 242 248
patriarchal assumptions 43
PE qualifications 338
Peel Gaol Act 1823 134 397
Peirce, Gareth 60
Penal Act 1839 171
Penal Affairs Consortium 244 360-
    361 367-368 370 372
Penal Reform International 381
Penal Servitude Act 1853 95
Pentecostal ministers 310
Pentonville, HMP 301
Peper Harow 293
period pains 252 253
Personal Empowerment
    Programme (PEP) 301
personal officers 128 301

personnel carriers (prison vans) 20
Peruvian drugs couriers 226 233
Peterborough 375
petty rules 107 111
phone calls 86-87 230-231
phone cards (prison) 86-87
pill, birth control 255
POL 1 281 28
Pollock-Byrne, Joycelyn 272 304
    372-373
Porridge 17 123 146
postnatal stress 93 95
pottery courses 338
poverty 288-289
prayer partners 320
pregnant prisoners 43 240 254
premenstrual tension (PMT) 54 95
pre-release
    hostels 366
    training 367
prescribed medication 263-268
Prevention of Crime Act 1871 56
Prichard, Rebecca 168 293
prison bent, see lesbian prisoners
prison caste system 166
Prison Dialogue 301
Prisoner: Cell Block H 17 157
Prison Fellowship 321
Prison Officers' Association (POA)
    209 376
prison officers
    black and ethnic minority 234-
    235
    early retirement 147
    language 122 123
    lesbian, 135, 141-142
    male in women's prisons 134-141
    147
    pay 149
    perception of women prisoners
    93
    promotion 149
    qualifications 149
    recruitment 149
    sexual misconduct 136 139
    sickness 101
    social background 123-124

Y

Z

Also by Angela Devlin

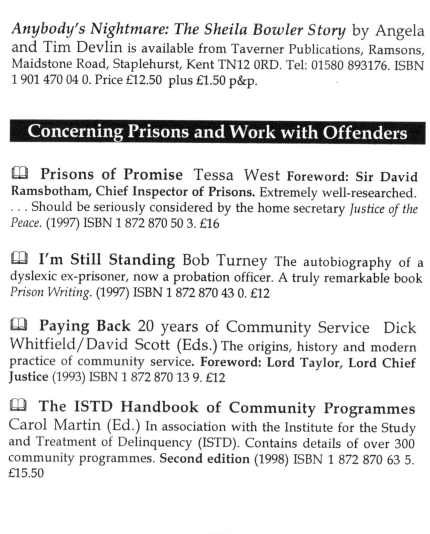

Criminal Classes Offenders at School Angela Devlin If you are in any doubt about the links between poor education, crime and recidivism, read it: Marcel Berlins *The Guardian.* (First reprint, 1997) ISBN 1 872 870 30. £16

Prison Patter Angela Devlin A dictionary of prison slang. Useful for the custody suite *Police Journal.* (1996) ISBN 1 872 870 41 4. £12

Anybody's Nightmare: The Sheila Bowler Story by Angela and Tim Devlin is available from Taverner Publications, Ramsons, Maidstone Road, Staplehurst, Kent TN12 0RD. Tel: 01580 893176. ISBN 1 901 470 04 0. Price £12.50 plus £1.50 p&p.

Concerning Prisons and Work with Offenders

Prisons of Promise Tessa West Foreword: Sir David Ramsbotham, Chief Inspector of Prisons. Extremely well-researched. . . . Should be seriously considered by the home secretary *Justice of the Peace.* (1997) ISBN 1 872 870 50 3. £16

I'm Still Standing Bob Turney The autobiography of a dyslexic ex-prisoner, now a probation officer. A truly remarkable book *Prison Writing.* (1997) ISBN 1 872 870 43 0. £12

Paying Back 20 years of Community Service Dick Whitfield/David Scott (Eds.) The origins, history and modern practice of community service. **Foreword: Lord Taylor, Lord Chief Justice** (1993) ISBN 1 872 870 13 9. £12

The ISTD Handbook of Community Programmes Carol Martin (Ed.) In association with the Institute for the Study and Treatment of Delinquency (ISTD). Contains details of over 300 community programmes. **Second edition** (1998) ISBN 1 872 870 63 5. £15.50

📖 **Black Women's Experiences of Criminal Justice** Ruth Chigwada-Bailey Highlights some major weaknesses in the system *The Manchester Justice*. Compelling . . . A must for decision-makers in the criminal justice process *The Law*. (1997) ISBN 1 872 870 54 6. £16

📖 **Tackling the Tag** The Electronic Monitoring of Offenders Dick Whitfield A wide-ranging first treatment of this topic. As featured in *The Independent*. A comprehensive and balanced guide *Prison Report*. Excellent *The Magistrate*. (1997) ISBN 1 872 870 53 8. £16

📖 **Deaths of Offenders** The Hidden Side of Justice Alison Liebling (Ed.) Examines deaths in police, prison and special hospital custody – including on remand and in court and police cells. Published on behalf of ISTD. (1998) ISBN 1 872 870 61 9. £16

📖 **Punishments of Former Days** Ernest Pettifer A good read *The Magistrate*. (1992) ISBN 1 872 870 05 8. £9.50

📖 **Interpreters and the Legal Process** Joan Colin and Ruth Morris Weighty and immensely readable *Law Society Gazette*. An extremely practical guide *The Law*. A scholarly work with everyday practical messages for all professionals *Wig and Gavel*. (1996) ISBN 1 872 870 28 7. £12

Forthcoming titles

📖 **Introduction to Prisons** Nick Flynn *et al* A new addition to this popular series. **Foreword: Lord Hurd.** In association with the Prison Reform Trust. (Summer 1998 onwards) ISBN 1 872 870 37 6. £12

📖 **Murderers and Life Imprisonment** Eric Cullen and Tim Newell ISBN 1 872 870 56. £20 Further details to be announced.

📖 **Geese Theatre Handbook: Working With Offenders and Youth at Risk** Drama therapy for offenders – including exercises and instructions for group work. (Scheduled for late 1998/early 1999) ISBN 1 872 870 67 8. £16

Waterside Press is pleased to announce that from 1998 onwards it is to publish:

The Prisons Handbook

Mark Leech

The definitive guide to penal establishments in England and Wales

The Prisons Handbook will be published annually in November

600 pages (approx)

Price £37.50

1998 Edition ISBN 1 872 870 72 4

WATERSIDE PRESS
DOMUM ROAD • WINCHESTER • SO23 9NN

☎ **Tel or fax 01962 855567 or by E-mail to**
INTERNET:106025.1020@compuserve.com

Direct mail prices are quoted for all publications mentioned on pp. 398-399.

Cheques should be made payable to 'Waterside Press'.

Organizations can be invoiced for two or more books.

Please add £1.50 per book p&p. *The Prisons Handbook*: £2.50 p&p.
(UK only: postage abroad charged at cost).

Please give details if the delivery address differs from the ordering address.

We accept: VISA, MASTERCARD and similar charge cards. When using a card to place an order by telephone or by post, please quote: the name on the card, delivery address and postcode, the address and postcode of the cardholder if different to the delivery address, the full number on the card and its expiry date.